BEEN WHERE? DONE WHAT?

Roland Watson

Craftsman Press
Bangkok, Thailand

First edition - June 1996. Printed in Thailand.

ISBN: 974-89676-9-7

Disclaimer

Life is inherently dangerous. Indeed, you can die at any moment, and the Grim Reaper is going to get you someday, anyway. In this book I advocate living life to its fullest, which means exposing yourself to some of its riskiest activities and environments. While I have provided advice for these situations, you are, effectively, always on your own. (Good luck!) Therefore, and although I have tried to make the material presented as useful and as accurate as possible, I accept no responsibility for any loss, injury or inconvenience sustained by any person using this book.

Author's notes and acknowledgments

Please alert me to any errors or inconsistencies, and feel free to suggest any changes or additions to the advice presented, by writing care of the following address:

P.O. Box 263
Gradyville, PA 19039
USA

I am also interested in meeting anyone familiar with book distribution!

My regards, and great thanks, to the artists and other sources quoted. Thanks also to Jeff Bergman for his assistance in arranging publication of the book. Rear cover photo: Felix Helfesreider.

For my international readers, please excuse the small sections of text written for Yanks. Who knows, you might find them interesting as well. Mucho thanks to all my travel partners, for their friendship, advice and stories. P.S., I told you guys I would write this book! Lastly, to all travelers: *bon voyage*, *in bocca al lupo* and happy trails. See you on the road!

To my parents - thanks for bringing me into the world, and for being there when I needed you.

TABLE OF CONTENTS

"*Roam if you want to. Roam around the world.*"

- The B-52s

1. BE A WORLD TRAVELER!

Maybe you remember the TV ad - for some soft drink. A bunch of gnarly dudes hanging out:

Kayaked the Amazon? *Been there, done that.*
Paraglided off Everest? *Oh yeah.*

It sounded cool, but it was a farce. The joke was, nobody had been *there* and done *that.*

Oh yeah?

This book is for world travelers, for people who dream of going to as many places, and experiencing as much of life, as possible. I am a world traveler. It is my life. But I, and other circumnavigators like me, are still a rare breed. This will not last! Our numbers are sure to increase as more people become aware of the opportunities that are now available.

But maybe not. I mean, you might ask, why travel? Why not just stay at home?

Good question.

When I began to write this book, I had been outside the U.S. for most of the prior decade. I was also out of touch with American culture, and did not think I would have to work that hard to sell the world. After all, its attractions, to me, seemed obvious:

- If you want to experience the wonders of the globe, both ancient and modern, you have to be a world traveler. Television, including PBS and Discovery channels, is not a substitute. Even the U.S., which is a great country, still contains only a small portion of what the planet has to offer.
- If you want to understand the world, really understand it - its people, cultures, politics, whatever, you have to be a world traveler. (This is a truism.)
- If you want your life to make a difference, you should be a world traveler. Perhaps a single vote does not count for much anymore, but every traveler has an impact. Your presence in foreign countries, making friends with the locals, helps further mutual understanding. You become an international goodwill ambassador.

- If you want to develop as an individual, to explore your identity and decide on a course for your life, you should definitely be a world traveler. Taking a long trip allows you to develop the objectivity that you need to think clearly about yourself, your background and your options for the future.
- If you want to lose weight, or work on similar personal issues, being a world traveler is for you. Everyone who does a world trip loses at least a few pounds, especially people who spend time in India! (If you are already quite fit, travel is an excellent way to apply it.)
- If you want to test a loving relationship prior to making a commitment, you should travel around the world together. If you enjoy yourselves this should cement your relationship for life. If not, if there are problems, then at least you have learned about them.
- If you want to make money, you should be a world traveler. America has a mature economy and the business opportunities here are limited. This is not the case with many other countries, where economic development is rapid and still in its early stages. Besides, business trips to Rio de Janeiro or Jakarta are much more glamorous than an overnight stay in Cleveland.
- Finally, if the U.S. is just not right for you, if you do not feel comfortable here, you should be a world traveler. There is a place on earth, at least one, where you will be content, with your type of people, climate and opportunities, a place where you can be truly happy.

These are only a few reasons to be a world traveler. There are in fact at least five billion of them. What's yours?

Maybe this isn't enough; perhaps you are not yet persuaded. Let me try another approach. Being a world traveler is also simply an excellent way to treat yourself well. This is your life, the only one you will get, so live it up! Many people find that their day-to-day lives do not keep them fully satisfied. A boring existence, and vicarious living through a few media heros, do not match their twentieth- (or 21st) century expectations. If this is your situation you should rebel against it. Consider this: people in the U.S. take an average of two weeks vacation a year. If you travel non-stop for one year, this is equivalent to twenty-six years of vacations. How old are you now? How old will you be in twenty-six years? Are you willing to wait that long for personal fulfillment?

Since returning home I have learned that many Americans are unaware of these benefits, and also ignorant of the ease and minimal cost and risk with which the planet can be toured. For example, whenever I talk to people about world travel, they always say: "*But how can you afford it?*" The total expenses for a long trip are a substantial sum, but they are not that great for a budget traveler to lesser developed regions. A good comparison is with university charges. A world trip should cost less than a year at a good school. You should ask yourself which is more beneficial: a year in classrooms, or a year in the university of life? Which is the better teacher?

I believe the greater barrier is psychological, the difficulty of breaking with what we have been taught from childhood: "*There are foreigners out there. They're not like us. They won't treat you well. It's dangerous. You'll be killed!*"

It is normal to feel insecure when you begin a long journey. Your safe and familiar world is left behind (it is hard to leave your friends), and most of what lies ahead is unknown. It is also a significant challenge to strike out on your own and break with the social conformity of accepted lifestyles and career paths. Most of us have been indoctrinated to believe tnat our careers will suffer if we take an extended leave. The implication is that we will become unemployable. In the U.S. today we are expected to get on the treadmill at kindergarten age and stay on until retirement, with no time off for good behavior. Under this system your chosen career should follow graduate school, which should follow a year or two of relevant work experience, which should follow college, continuing on and on all the way back to birth. The pathway to the American Dream has been replaced by something remarkably similar to a computer program, or even a prison cell.

Arthur Miller once said, as a commentary on the madness of Willy Loman, his protagonist in *Death of a Salesman*, that he broke "*that law which, we believe, defines us as men...that a failure in society and business has* ***no right to live.***" Unfortunately, under the U.S. model of corporate success not everyone can succeed. Most don't. This is why so many young people are unhappy, why bands like *Nirvana* and *Green Day* sell so many records. We are faced with an impossible task.

In today's America you are continually exposed to, assaulted by the images of, a small group of fantastically successful people, who are unbelievably attractive, talented and popular, and who make millions of dollars, or even tens of millions, *every year*. And maybe you're not so attractive, or talented, or popular. You'll probably never be a millionaire. So what should you do? Kill yourself?

Being a world traveler is a way out of the American success trap, perhaps the only way. It enables you to discover a different measure of success, which is of how much you live and experience. Madonna goes on a world tour. So can you.

Many people are so conditioned by society's emphasis on ambition and performance that they cannot leave it behind. How about you? How conditioned are you? Are you a conformist? On the other hand, would you like to have an extraordinary life? Would you like to see the world? Would you *really* like to? If so, then making this psychological break is your first step, the *essential* first step.

World travelers are a diverse lot, but we all share one attribute: everyone has taken at least one extended trip across the planet, quite often an actual circumnavigation. Because of this we have all experienced the greatest benefit that travel offers, which is in fact the ultimate goal of many, many people. We have all known the supreme joy of *complete freedom*. When you are on the road, with the end of your journey in the far distant future, you really can go anywhere and do anything. You have total flexibility: to do what you want, to stay somewhere a long time or leave after an hour, to change your plans at a moment's notice, again and again and again. You answer to no one but yourself.

And it is not only action; you also have complete freedom of *thought*. You do not need to think about your job all the time. More importantly, you are divorced from the influences that shape your attitudes and opinions. For once in your life you can become a *freethinker*.

This is why world travelers in effect form a separate culture. When you have found a life that grants you this much freedom, your former life, including such characteristics as the country you are from, becomes less important. You no longer define yourself as a Yank or a Swede or an Aussie. Instead, you are a *traveler*.

As all this suggests, world travel is an absolute blast. It is one of the most satisfying activities that life has to offer, on par with raising a family or achieving your highest career goals.

You only have to get up and go. For instance, I met two Americans in Kathmandu, Nepal, which is probably the Mecca of world travelers. (Thank you Bob Seger.) Marty and Kevin were refugees from Silicon Valley. They had had enough of computer screens and decided to take a serious break; two old friends sharing a common dream. They were traveling for about a year, and also had a poetic start to their journey. The day he left his job, Marty burned his suit and mailed the ashes to Kevin. His message was clear: "*The time has come. Let's get out of here, have some fun and see the world!*"

Haven't we all had days when we've wanted to do this?

A year is a standard trip for a world traveler, but if you can't spare or afford this much time, go anyway, for as long as you can. Hit the road, see the world and get a life, an original one, your very own. Go for it!

Book objectives

This book's main objective is to encourage you, and many other people (your friends?), to become world travelers. However, an even deeper objective is to get you to think of the planet not only as your playground, but also as your home, any location on which you can establish a career and raise a family. Nowadays, if you have intelligence and drive - and a passport, you can go anywhere - live anywhere, and do anything. Nations, as in: "I am from this nation, and therefore must stay there," have become obsolete and irrelevant. The world is open. What you make of it is up to you.

My objective, though, is not just to expand your horizons. It is also to help you understand the cultures and environments that you explore. The world has dramatic problems, as anyone can see. Many of these problems are due to misunderstandings, and also to ignorance, since advancements that have been developed in some regions, such as ecological consciousness and thoughtful urban planning, have not been exported to others. If more people would travel in a sensitive and non-destructive manner, these misunderstandings should be reduced and the solutions to many of our problems should become more widely distributed.

Travel as a skill

Travel is often reckoned to be an art, and you can bring a great amount of personal style to an international trip. But travel is also a skill or, rather, a number of different skills, which enable you to deal with any possible situation in a foreign country. Frankly, many people (most?) are poorly skilled at international travel. They have difficulties getting along with the locals. They do not find nice hotels and restaurants.

They miss out on interesting activities. They pay too much. In the worst circumstances, they get sick or are robbed.

Skills, though, should not be confused with information. Expert travelers do not need guidebooks to tell them how to visit different countries. If they fly into new and completely unfamiliar environments, they know how to arrange good accommodations and enjoyable activities at reasonable prices. They also know how to avoid any dangers that might be present.

Travel skills are usually developed from experience; by learning from your mistakes. However, by reading this book you will quickly acquire these skills, make fewer mistakes, and increase your confidence in dealing with new situations.

The book is a presentation of many skills. (A great amount of information is also provided.) It gives advice that should be sufficient to take you anywhere, for any reason. In addition, there are major emphases on preventing risks and reducing expenses.

To impart a real life flavor, the advice is extensively illustrated with descriptions of actual travel situations. These have either occurred to me or people whom I have met, or they have been reported in the press. While there are stories about almost every type of situation, most involve travelers in lesser developed countries. This is because these environments present the greatest challenges. In other words, if you can deal with the problems in Asia, Africa or Latin America, you should easily manage the difficulties in the Caribbean or Western Europe. South and Southeast Asia, in particular, are referred to frequently, since they form a major part of the standard world traveler itinerary.

Author's background

So, how do I know so much about travel that I can offer advice to others? Well, I have been an overland traveler since childhood, although I really got going on my graduation from high school when a friend and I drove from Arizona up through the Rocky Mountains to Calgary, across western Canada, and down the coast from Vancouver to San Diego. (It was a major road trip!)

I come from a middle-class background - nothing far out of the ordinary. (I was the first person in my family to get a degree.) When I got out of college I spent the summer backpacking around Hawaii. My last stop was Kalalau Beach, which is at the end of an eleven mile trail along Kauai's Na Pali coast. It is stunning: you sleep on the beach under a huge cave and shower in a nearby waterfall. Jungle-covered cliffs tower above you. Nobody wears any clothes. (It was my first nude beach.)

I started law school after this, but only lasted a week! After Kalalau, torts and property law were too much. I became a ski bum instead, and moved to Telluride. I spent the next three years traveling around the U.S. (I have been in forty-three states), and ended up in Aspen. At this point it was time to settle down, so I started looking for a *real* job. I *expanded* my resume, and found one in New York. I had decided: I would give the corporate world ten years and see how far I could get.

Things worked out pretty well. I have lived abroad in Stockholm and London, where I got jobs with Citicorp, and also in Bangkok and Singapore. I have been to over sixty countries - so far - my goal is one hundred. (There are one hundred and ninety countries, give or take a few.) I have from reasonable to extensive knowledge of the following regions: the Caribbean; Scandinavia; Western Europe; the Eastern Mediterranean and East Africa; the entire basin of the Indian Ocean, including many of its islands; South and Southeast Asia; Australia and New Zealand; and the west coast of South America.

* * * * * * * * *

On the morning of January 26, 1991, one of the secretaries in Citicorp's London Mergers and Acquisitions Department made a quick circuit of the office, asking everyone to go to the conference room. Disgruntled, busy with the tasks at hand, we slowly gathered with the impatient question in everyone's mind, what now? The department head walked in and, in contrast to his normal upbeat self, announced with gravity that the New York head office, stung with losses in other businesses and scrambling to cut costs, had decided to shut us down. We were all, effective immediately, laid off! We were given one month notice to use office facilities to find new employment, and told that some amount of severance pay would be determined later.

Sound familiar?

Eleven years of slaving in offices had ended, and all the normal emotions of loss - shock, panic and denial - came rushing forth. Complicating the situation for me was the fact that my British visa depended on my continued employment with Citicorp. I could be deported!

This book is the culmination of my efforts to make something positive out of that predicament. After being laid off, I had a choice. I could take my savings and look for another job in the U.K., but my chances were slim because of the recession. I would deplete my bank account, and my psychology would be damaged from rejection in job interviews. On the other hand, I could return to the U.S. and suffer the impoverishment and rejection at home.

Some choice.

I decided to opt for a third alternative. My lifelong dream had been to travel around the world, through Asia and Australia, accomplishing a complete circuit of the planet. I realized that all the places I had visited, including living and working in Europe, were just preparation for this. I could turn a failure into an opportunity, buy some tickets, hit the road and realize my dream. (I also thought: enough is enough. I have done my ten years. To hell with the future. It's time to let go and follow my heart and not my mind for a change. It's time to take my chances and go for it.)

In April 1991, I flew from New York City to London on Kuwait Airlines, which had recently restarted operations after the Gulf War. It was a good deal. From there, it was up to Stockholm to say goodbye to friends, and then off to Asia for a journey along the classic overland route. I started in India, and continued to Nepal, India again, the Maldives, Sri Lanka, Thailand, Malaysia, Singapore, and Java and Bali, Indonesia. After Asia, I went to Western Australia for a 7,000 mile bus trip around the country, followed by a top-to-bottom tour of New Zealand. Almost one year after leaving the U.S., 344 days to be exact, I made it back. In all this time I was never robbed or seriously ill, and the trip was fantastic, the most enjoyable thing I have ever done.

You could do it too!

* * * * * * * * *

Subsequent to this trip I spent eighteen months in front of a computer writing the first draft of this book. After so much typing, though, my feet were extremely itchy. I decided to field test the advice with a second trip and left for another twelve months in November 1993, visiting England, Scotland, Sweden, Holland, India, Nepal, Bangladesh, Burma, Laos and Thailand. Anecdotes and adventures from this trip are also included. (Stories from the first are referred to as being from my *world trip*, since the second was not an actual circumnavigation). For example, under Special Permits in the Preparation chapter, I discuss my visit to Burma (Myanmar), where I persuaded SLORC, the military government, to let me visit Putao, which is the northernmost village in the country. It lies below Hkakabo Razi, Burma's highest peak, and between the borders of Arunachal Pradesh in India's Northeast Frontier Area and China's Yunnan Province. (Other than in central Africa, this is about as far off the map as it is possible to get.) This occurred only a few months after a cease-fire was signed with the Kachin Independence Army, a tribal resistance group, and I was the first traveler there in at least thirty years! I went to many remote hill tribe villages, by canoe, bicycle and on foot, and socialized with the locals and drank *Kachin psa* and *sapi*, their home brewed spirits and beer. Indeed, I was very well-received. Old men walked up to me and asked to shake my hand. Young couples dressed in their traditional costumes so I could take their photos. I also rode a logging elephant, and a school was let out so the children could see me, their first foreigner. It was incredible.

Subsequent to the second trip I worked on the book for another six months. I then went to New York to try to interest agents and publishers. Ha! What a joke! Were the big agencies or publishing houses interested in me? You must be kidding. No one would even look at the manuscript. Book publishing is a *business*. It's all about money now. Nobody is looking for the next great book. What they are looking for is some dirt from a celebrity that they can manipulate the public to buy. After all, you're nothing if you don't know the latest on O.J., or Kathie Lee, or Burt, or some other flavor of the moment. (I was also told: "*People in America don't travel.*")

Fortunately, America is a diverse place, and many people are interested in reading great books (and travel!). Also, as a world traveler, I don't take rejection lying down. I decided that after five years of work the book had merit and deserved to be published. I am certain it will stimulate, if not actively assist, all of its readers. So, I took another trip, back to Asia, to publish it myself. On the way I hit some old favorites and a few new spots, including Ireland, Northern Ireland, Rhodes (Greece), Cyprus, Israel, the Palestinian Autonomous Area and Egypt (the Sinai). I then headed for Thailand (via India and Nepal), which is one of my favorite countries and where I thought the printing would be inexpensive. What you are holding is the result. I hope you enjoy it.

2. BREAKING FREE

"*Are you experienced?*"

- Jimi Hendrix

Premises

The main premise of this book is that in order to find yourself, to develop a unique identity and make the most of life's opportunities, to find the opportunities that best fit with you, in other words, to be as happy as possible, you must rebel from the social forces that seek to control you. This rebellion will require you to take command of your psychology, your free will, and essentially to tell these social forces to go to hell: you are in control of your life and will make your own decisions; you are not a cog in a machine, or a *type*; you are an individual, you have a free will, and you will express it, live by it, no matter how much other people try to stop you.

Hence the title of this chapter, the significance of which is as follows: to escape from the pressure of social conformity requires a break, a courageous action, a violent action, in this case psychological; and to be free, because the quest for freedom, the freedom to be and do anything, is the core of the now almost dead American Dream.

Before I discuss this, though, there are a number of other basic points that I want to make. (They have in fact guided my life.)

- There is no universal knowledge.

As part of a system, in this case the universe, we can never step outside of it and perceive it as a whole. As such, there are no absolute answers to the most important questions about existence. The fundamental (and only) fact of life is that it is limited. Other than this, we cannot know anything for certain: nothing about gods, or saviors, or miracles, or afterlives, or our or the universe's purpose.

Many people, particularly the followers of different religions, have hard and fast views about these issues, but their positions require faith. There is no proof. Indeed, this uncertainty, and the disappointments that result from it, is the major challenge with which we have to live.

However, while such a state of affairs can easily be construed as restrictive and limiting, it is actually quite liberating. We are free to go out into the world and make of it, and ourselves, what we will.

Another interesting point is that what we know of the world we perceive through our senses, our eyes and ears. But this is a two-sided process. In order to fully understand these perceptions, we need to understand ourselves. Perhaps this is what Socrates meant when he said: "*Know Thyself.*" (Carl Jung put it another way: "*The individual is the only reality.*" *Man and His Symbols*, Carl G. Jung, Laurel, page 45)

- The distribution of human capability.

This book is dedicated to Jefferson's proposition that all men and women are created equal. While it would be hard to accept that this is true in today's world, what with the differences that exist from country to country and between different economic classes and other groups based on race, religion, sex, age and culture, it does hold, it will hold forever, for at least one characteristic: existential perception and intelligence. A student at Harvard may have ten times the education of a child in a rural Indian village, but both individuals are still essentially the same - they are humans. Regarding the most important aspects of life, what one has to deal with from day-to-day and, furthermore, how to understand and deal with life's conclusion, with death, there is no difference between them in their ability to observe and understand. Anyone, just through being alive, can grasp the deepest issues surrounding our existence (and take advantage of its greatest opportunities).

One of the consequences of this - there are many! - is that the distribution of human capability (the differences that exist between people in terms of what they can learn, and accomplish) is not as great as one might imagine. It is in fact quite narrow.

- Be a good person.

I have always had three basic goals in life, all of which fit together. The first is to be a good person, if only because it is easier and innately more satisfying. An excellent guide is the golden rule: do unto others as you would have them do unto you. But this begs the question, what about masochists?! Perhaps a more fundamental view is to try to live such that you *do not injure anyone*, in the broadest sense of the phrase. (*Anyone* includes other species. Also, I realize there are situations, particularly in romantic affairs, where this is impossible.)

- Experience as much of life as possible.

Secondly, our existence, the presence of the universe and us in it, is astonishing, a marvel. Life is a wondrous gift, and I have wanted to make the most of it, to experience as much of it, as possible.

This goal can be viewed in many different ways, but underneath these perspectives there is a constant. Past and future developments notwithstanding, there is a totality of human behavior and experience. I will, provided I survive, experience the different aspects of our existence from youth through old age. I can pursue different careers, and strive for success. I can raise a family, and experience what it is like to be a father. Of course, as a man, I can never have the experience of a woman. As an American, I can never have the experience of people born in other countries and cultures. I can, however, expose myself to, and try to understand, their experiences.

For me, a dominant aspect of trying to experience as much of life as possible is to pursue this goal literally, and this is how I became a world traveler. The planet is a fantastic place, and I want to visit as many of its environments and cultures as I can. This point is what this book is all about.

There is one other thing worth mentioning. If you try to experience everything that life has to offer, this will necessarily include some exposure to the bad, including both circumstances and people. Hopefully, you will avoid such things as prison, but you should expect accidents and injury (not to mention personal failure). They are the price that you pay for a life of exploration, what happens when the odds fall due, and against you. (Good luck!)

- Lastly, I always wanted to be the type of person who could talk to anyone, on their own terms, who could communicate without any barriers, cultural or otherwise, and in any circumstances, in other words, human to human. This objective actually has two beneficial effects. It obviously enables you to increase your exposure to, and enjoyment and understanding of, the full breadth of life experience, and, from the interpersonal skills that you develop, it better enables you to avoid the pitfalls.

In summary, world travel is about personal growth. By putting yourself in new situations you force yourself to learn and grow. However, after you have visited ten or twenty countries, new ones are not so intimidating. After dealing with all types of people in all types of circumstances, your confidence increases. You ultimately reach the stage where there is little with which you cannot deal.

At this point, something beautiful happens. With your confidence and ability, since you no longer have so much to worry about, you are free to enjoy, completely and with no inhibitions or guilt, your experiences and life.

You are now mature. You know who you are. (Your personal identity is well defined.) You are not confused about how to live your life. You know what career to pursue. Your relationships work better. Congratulations. You went for it, and have reaped the hard won results. Enjoy.

Generation X

The traditional American Dream is to have a good career, get married and raise a family, not to mention home ownership and two cars in the garage. These are all admirable goals, but look what has happened to them. You have to be a workaholic to have a prosperous career now, which means your marriage and family suffer. Divorces are endemic, and children, lacking time with their parents and the guidance that they need, grow up isolated, rudderless and unhappy. Virtually everyone is stressed out, if not miserable. It is a great state of affairs.

Another statement of the Dream, that anyone can grow up to be President (this is the idea that we have a classless society), is extinct. What is most important in America is not how hard you work, but *who you know*. And the latter is tied most closely to the circumstances of your birth: who your parents are and who they know. America is moving farther and farther away from being a meritocracy. Nowadays, if you want to make it to the top, you have to start there.

Young people understand this. They recognize that the American system has become a trap, a game in which there are few winners, and are frustrated because they cannot see a way out.

The turning point for me came when I realized that after a decade of effort, some seriously unorthodox career moves and extraordinarily good luck, I had made it to the top (investment banking), and I didn't like it! I worked all the time and had no social life (much less a wife). I was getting fat. My hairline was receding. I was losing my eyesight. This was too much! Nothing, not even a *great job*, was worth losing my health. It was too high a price to pay. Being a corporate slave, the voluntary slavery that so many people accept, had to end. There had to be a better way. I had to find something new.

To make the change I had to regain my independence. I also had to learn a lot of new things. I had to learn to live with less material goods. I had to learn to do without the satisfaction of buying things. Because other people buy things. Doesn't it feel good to buy things? God, I wish I could go buy some things right now. Let's go to the mall!

If you can accomplish this, if you can divorce yourself from this way of thinking, this culturally imposed way of thinking, you can cut your costs dramatically, and that really frees up your lifestyle opportunities. You do not have to work so much, because you don't need that much money.

Young people today are very prone to think of themselves as victims. They feel they are a loser generation, that they have been born into a world that sucks. Everything that is good has happened, and they are left with the refuse and excrement. Nothing can be done to make things better, and they are going to have to live through it.

Many of them are giving up and resorting to different types of escapes. What is rampant consumerism, if not an escape? More seriously, heroin addiction is exploding. Even worse, sharing needles is cool.

There is an alternative, though, through world travel and having a global lifestyle; rebellion not through some death wish escape, or even through a computer screen and virtual reality, but through exploring the planet and finding its, and your own, true reality. (This is a hell of a lot better anyway.)

World travelers

So, who becomes a world traveler? Who is able to make the break? What distinguishes such people in background, character type, whatever?

There are two ways to look at this. The first is that we are, in effect, all world travelers. Just by being born you have become one. It doesn't matter if you never leave your home town.

The other view is that to be a world traveler, you have to go places. Some would say you cannot call yourself one until you have completed a circumnavigation. Couch potatoes surf the TV. Computer buffs surf the Internet. World travelers surf the planet!

Western Europe, particularly the U.K., Scandinavia and Germany, is the source of the majority of current world travelers, both young and old. In such countries taking a break of a year or longer to explore the globe is an accepted cultural phenomenon. For example, doing a world tour prior to starting a career or university studies is almost expected of a young Swede or Brit. (The latter are called "*Gap Year*" travelers.) It is a right of passage.

The other major sources of world travelers are Australia and New Zealand. (It is a long ways from them to almost anywhere else.) You also meet a lot of Israelis in overland travel centers, since they often take lengthy breaks after completing their military service. There are fewer travelers from the southern European countries of France, Italy and Spain, and from the U.S. Indeed, one often meets more Canadians in foreign countries, particularly in British Commonwealth countries, than Americans.

As far as the rest of the world is concerned, poverty is pervasive and wealth is concentrated in the upper class. In all but a few countries only members of this class can afford to travel, and they usually go deluxe and for a limited period of time.

Most world travelers are in their twenties or thirties. Few people older than this seem to have been able to solve the puzzle of how to combine an obligation-filled life, with a career, family and debts, with world trips. However, this is likely to change. With the rise in independent lifestyles in many countries, there should be a great increase over time in the number of older world travelers.

Most travelers are men, but not by as large a proportion as you might imagine. For instance, there are many women from Australia and New Zealand who travel across Asia to the U.K. They usually find jobs in London after they arrive, work for a year or two, and then leave for additional travel - quite often to Africa. (Their mirror image are the Brits who travel to and find jobs Down Under.)

World travelers are almost all budget backpackers, but they come from all socio-economic groups. Most of the ones that I have met have actually been from lower and middle economic classes, and had to work for years to fund their trips. While this might seem surprising, it is not inconsistent with the idea (see below) that the rich are trapped by their money and fancy lives: "*Go to India? What an idea! And not stay in five star hotels, but rather two dollar a night guesthouses? You must be kidding. Heaven forbid!"*

I pity them.

There may also be a practical commonality in background. Many world travelers have had positive introductions to travel and foreign environments as children, either with their families or other groups. It is not surprising that a large number were raised in families that lived abroad. In such circumstances, children quickly learn how to deal with, and get comfortable in, new environments. For example, and while I did not get that many chances to travel when I was young (camporees, a bus trip to Florida, and a vacation to Jamaica), it always seemed to be the neatest thing I could do. I loved every trip I ever took.

- Psychological profile.

What type of person becomes a world traveler? Are you born one? Out of the womb? Is there a genetic predisposition?

Some people certainly do seem drawn to world travel. Perhaps it is the modern day equivalent of the call of the sea. I think one aspect of this is that we are dreamers. We recognize that the world, or at least what humans make of it, could be wonderful, much better than it is currently, but that for the moment this apparently lies outside our grasp. Still, the world is pretty great, and it is definitely worth a closer look. I mean, why not? You're going to die anyway. You might as well have some fun, some real fun, as much fun as it is possible to have, before you go.

Other characteristics are also common. World travelers are usually above average in intelligence, but not necessarily with advanced educations. We are also curious, courageous, adventurous, romantic and non-conformist. For the last, we do not readily accept what we are told. We want to see what is out there, and make up our own minds.

Another aspect is that most world travelers are resourceful and good at stress management. We can deal calmly and rationally with almost anything. We are also resilient when problems do occur. Indeed, I think we frequently push ourselves so far that we are injured, both physically and emotionally, to test our limits, both of what we can do, and of what we can recover from.

- Attitudes and philosophy.

World travelers also have a similarity in other types of attitudes. We refuse to limit ourselves, or to have boring lives. One way to look at this is to understand that almost everyone builds walls to protect themselves. People construct small, safe environments in which they can be comfortable and happy and keep the rest of the world at bay. This applies to all types of people, even the most wealthy and powerful. From Hollywood movie moguls, to the New York fashion community, to bankers and lawyers, to top corporate executives and the super rich, they all do it. They have their own little worlds, with their houses and clubs, and they feel pretty good about themselves because they can exclude the rest of us.

But they are actually no different. Like everyone else, they are afraid of the world. Rather than reach out and grab it for everything it is worth, they construct these barriers, they bring life down to their size.

Not world travelers. Over the course of our lives we want to do everything. If we cannot do something now, we will do it next year, or in ten. And we will! We keep our options open. We are generalists in an increasingly specialized world.

More deeply, most world travelers are philosophical, in the sense that we let our views on the philosophical issues of life guide our lives. Nowadays the world is dominated by commerce, and most people let it dictate their lives. Just witness the frequency with which people identify themselves with their jobs. But commerce is actually limiting. It is only one part of the world, frankly, a small part. But its power, as the economic engine behind development, has led to a vast overstatement of its importance. Life is incredible. Life is magic. A job is just a job.

World travelers also recognize that every second counts, that every moment of life is precious. Someone once said that the journey of a thousand steps begins with the first, but you do not want to accept the implication in this that it is the destination which is important. Every one of those steps is of equal importance, not just the final one which allows you to say: Been There, Done That. (I hate the shallowness of that phrase, the way it demeans the most impressive accomplishments.)

World travelers don't have an *attitude*, much less the right one. We are genuine. We are not phony, or posers. We don't brag about our accomplishments. We're not *in your face*. Appearance means nothing. Substance is what counts.

- Objectives.

World travelers want to find and experience the best that the planet has to offer, and this is not limited to the standard list of highlights. The earth is so diverse; there are so many interesting things out there which have never been reported, that are unknown.

There are in fact many ways to view this. You can travel to experience culture, or nature, or history, or war (the ones in progress), or art, or whatever. For instance, what is interesting and rewarding for me might be at the bottom of your list. But maybe not. I tend to focus on the nations that have the highest mountains, the densest rain forests, the most beautiful reefs, the cultures that have been least affected by development, the best cities for nightlife, and the prettiest girls!

Another point is that it is the small differences that exist around the world, the nuances in appearance, character and behavior, that regularly prove to be the most interesting. A large part of becoming an accomplished traveler is learning to appreciate this subtlety.

Finally, being a world traveler means more than just taking a long trip. We have a planetary-wide perspective on all issues, including where (and how) to live, work, raise families and play. We are the first true citizens of the global village.

Preparation

Getting to the point where you begin a world trip requires a tremendous amount of preparation, both practical and psychological. (I can lead you through all of the steps, but you will have to take them.) For the former, you will have to raise a large amount of money and make all of the necessary arrangements to suspend your life at home. For the latter, you will have to go from being the type of person who only dreams of doing a world trip (perhaps you are not yet at this stage), to someone who actually does it. This is a huge step. How many people have you met who talk about doing big things, but never accomplish them? It is only talk. Perhaps you are also such a person.

What you should realize is that to become a world traveler you will have to change, and we all know how hard that is. But before we consider change, let's return to the idea I mentioned earlier: social conformity and culturally imposed attitudes.

Form

"Now you do what they told you. Got you under control."

- Rage Against The Machine

This section has to do with the process of how we are influenced by other people. (It is the most important issue I will discuss.) It is applicable continually, in travel and in life in general, and it revolves around something that, for lack of a better word, I will call "*form*." (I owe a debt of gratitude to the great Polish author Witold Gombrowicz for these ideas.)

At its most basic level, form has to do with the differences between how we see ourselves and how others perceive us. To make the concept easier to understand, it might help to consider the process of how form is created and how it affects us.

- Everyone is a source of form, including your parents and other family members, and your friends, teachers, employers and representatives of other institutions. This is because they all perceive you, or anybody else, on the basis of the evidence that is available, which for the most part is tangible. In other words, you are what their senses reveal you to be. For me, personally, it would be white, male, an American, middle-aged, etc.

- Based on these initial impressions people tend to box you up, or stereotype you. This is form. They see you as something definite and respond to you from their own personal agendas, the natures of which depend on them and their relationships to you.

- Furthermore, they, consciously or subconsciously, want to influence you. They want to be right about you, to confirm you in your box. They want you to be what they want you to be: your parents want you to be a good student (not all form is negative), to enter a certain career, to marry a particular person; your friends want you to behave in a certain way; businesses want you to be a dutiful employee, or big shopper; etc.

- You, however, particularly as a child, are less clear about yourself. You may in no way be definite. You might be uncertain about many of the major areas of your life including, most importantly, your identity. (This is what is known as immaturity.) Because of this uncertainty you will tend to be susceptible to their influence.

- In many cases you will not be able to resist the pressure and persuasion. The sources of form will succeed in influencing you. (Form is power!) You will become what they want you to be. As a result, you will lose part of your individuality, uniqueness and free will.

It is essential to understand how subtle this process can be. For example, if someone asks you to do something, with which you do not really agree, but you do it anyway just to be nice, you have been formed. You are now the type of person who will do such a thing, when formerly you were not. In addition, finding your identity is particularly difficult now that there are so many people in the world, and because modern form, from television and advertising, is so powerful. It has made us uniform. (It has also had an unforeseen repercussion. When you do separate yourself from the masses, when you acquire a face, you will isolate yourself, and antagonize everyone else who remains under control. You will therefore want to find other original people to associate with, for friendship, and to give each other support.)

- Lastly, as a consequence of having been formed it is quite possible that you will be confused and unhappy. Because you do not have a clear self-view you may have difficulty finding a purpose in your life. Your relationships with other people might not work as well as they should.

Gombrowicz thought that form, the confusion caused by other people influencing us and our consequent difficulties in establishing unique identities and finding our free will, was the most powerful force on the planet, the underlying reason for most of humanity's troubles.

The only way to become a unique individual is to confront, and reduce the impact of, the sources of form in your life. One way you can begin to do this is to summarize the most important forms that have affected you (a world trip provides an excellent opportunity for this), particularly those from your early childhood, by considering how you relate to, including the reasons therefore:

- Your parents, siblings and relatives
- Your friends and lovers
- Schools, employers and other institutions
- The media
- Conventional lifestyle goals
- Yourself

Identity

I believe fighting form is the most important task an individual faces in life. It is pervasive, often very difficult to recognize, and exceedingly powerful. In some instances it is impossible to deflect. Indeed, our exposure to form begins in the earliest stages of our existence, as young children reacting to and learning from our parents. This is generally not a problem, but what about the children of abusive parents, or of bigots? It is well-documented that such children, when they become adults, regularly carry on these traits.

Form perpetuates itself.

As this suggests, it is important to recognize, and deal with, your own form - how you affect other people. You should always try to evaluate people as individuals. Fight your natural tendency to type, to make judgements and categorize. In addition, you should respect people for who they are, not because they fit some type that you deem warrants it, your definition of cool. "Cool" is just another word for form, another typing process. Finally, do not persuade people to think or act in a particular way because it conforms to your view of them. Practice self-effacement, and let them be themselves.

Another issue is the problem of *good* form. For instance, suppose you are at some crossroads in your life, and you have a heart-to-heart chat about it with a friend. He or she may suggest that you follow some course of action, and since they care about you, only want what is best for you, this will likely be well-considered and thought out. However, for all their care and concern it could still easily *not* be right for you. Only you can know what is right for you, and for that to happen you have to know who you are. You have to be clear about and confident in your *identity*.

Is identity ingrained, or is it created? Are you who you are born to be, based on your genetic makeup and parents' circumstances, or are you who you desire to be, who you make yourself become? I believe the answer is some of both, the proportions of which are up to you.

Who are you? To yourself, describe yourself: "*I am ...*" What would you say? To understand your identity you have to consider all of the characteristics of which it is composed, and this is not a simple task. To help you, what follows is an identity checklist. Read it through, ask yourself the questions, and be honest with your answers.

Identity checklist

- The basics.

  - What is your sex?
  - Race?
  - Religion?
  - Nationality?
  - Age?
  - Astrological sign?
  - Height?
  - Body type?
  - Hair length, style and color?
  - Eye strength and color?
  - Do you have any scars or birthmarks?
  - Other features, impediments or disabilities?
  - What is your dress style?
  - Do you wear jewelry?
  - Have tattoos?
  - Are you pierced?

- Background.

  - Who are your parents?
  - Are they alive? Married?
  - What are they like? What do they do?
  - Do you have brothers and sisters?
  - Older or younger?
  - Do you have a spouse?
  - Any children?
  - How are your family relationships? Good or bad? Close or not?
  - Have there been any traumatic events?
  - Any brushes with the law?
  - Where did you spend your childhood?
  - What is your class background?
  - Do you have the attitudes and opinions that are typically associated with this class?
  - How much money do you have? How many debts?

- What are your most important possessions?
- What schools did you attend? How good a student?
- Did you get along with your peers?
- What jobs have you had?
- Did you like them? Your bosses?
- What languages do you use?
- What do you do for fun?
- Any hobbies, sports and other activities?
- What types of music do you like?
- Where have you traveled?

- General self view.

- How do they feel about yourself, psychologically?
- Do you respect yourself?
- Do you like yourself?
- Are you happy?
- How much do you smile?
- How much do you laugh?
- What does your laugh sound like?
- Do you tell jokes, or sing, or dance?
- How do you feel about your body?
- Are you attractive? Ugly?
- Athletic? Clumsy?
- Are you well-adjusted?
- Repressed, or inhibited? About what?
- Are you down to earth or snobbish?
- Eccentric in any way?
- What are you addicted to?
- Are you self-destructive?
- How intelligent are you?
- Creative? Analytical? Curious?
- What are you curious about?
- Are you adventurous? Courageous? Resourceful?
- How adventurous? How courageous? How resourceful?
- Have you ever been heroic?
- Are you in control of your life?

- Emotions.

    - Are you emotional or cool-headed?
    - Worrisome and guilt-ridden or care-free?
    - How often are you bored?
    - How often are you frustrated?
    - By what?
    - How do you respond when things don't go your way?
    - Do you have good self-control?
    - What issues do you feel most strongly about?
    - How do you deal with controversy, stress and power conflicts?
    - What makes you laugh?
    - What makes you feel sad, vulnerable and frightened, and angry?
    - What do you hate?

- Relationships.

    - Are you an introvert or an extrovert?
    - Social, or a loner?
    - Are you independent?
    - A conformist or a rebel?
    - A leader or a follower?
    - Do you have a lot of friends?
    - What types of people are they? How diverse a group?
    - Why are they your friends?
    - Why are you their friend?
    - Are you a good listener?
    - Are you a good friend?
    - Do other people respect you?
    - Are you a force to be reckoned with? By whom?
    - Are you a good person?
    - Principled? Nice or mean?
    - Selfish, or bigoted?
    - Do you manipulate other people?
    - Do you keep your word?

- Romance.

  - How many lovers have you had?
  - Who were they?
  - Why them?
  - How long did the relationships last?
  - How much sex have you had?
  - What types of sex?
  - Are you good in bed?
  - How do you feel about love, relationships and marriage?
  - Are you romantic? Touching and intimate?
  - How often do you give small, uncalled for, presents?
  - How deeply do you bond?
  - What is your capacity for giving, and receiving, love?

- Goals and dreams.

  - What do you think of life, of the experience of being alive?
  - What is the most important thing in life?
  - What is the most important thing in your life?
  - What are your strongest motivations?
  - What moments do you live for?
  - What do you dream about?
  - Any recurrent nightmares?
  - Are you actively striving to achieve your unfulfilled goals?
  - What do you think of death?
  - Are you afraid of it?
  - Do you have any great regrets?
  - Do you believe in an after-life?

Okay. These are a lot of questions (I am sure you can think of others as well), but if you take the time to answer them, and not underestimating the difficulty of being objective about yourself, you should develop a better feel for who you are, in all of your complexity. But this is still not the entire picture: are you the sum of your characteristics, or is there something else in your identity as well, something that transcends them?

The answer is yes, and the extra factor is the certainty of self that you (hopefully) have and that you use when dealing with new and challenging situations, what tells you how to act. In each such situation you ask yourself how you should respond (this usually occurs subconsciously), and your transcendent identity gives you the answer: *This is how I should respond, because this is consistent with who I am.*

This is your core. It is a synthesis of all of your characteristics, a pulling together of all of the aspects of your nature to create a unique sense of self. Even more, this is where the most fundamental components of your identity, your ethics and morals, and your personal philosophy of life, assert themselves. It is hard to define them, but they are real, and when you are confronted with a situation that is an acid test of your character, they are what guide you.

People who do not know how to act in challenging circumstances have a confused sense of self and an inadequate personal philosophy. When they face such a test, they do not know who they are, and therefore how they should respond.

Personal change

Rejecting form, and consolidating your sense of having a unique identity, will help you make the changes that are necessary to increase your sense of purpose, and to find contentment and happiness. But even this is not enough. To change, you will also have to overcome your fear of the unknown. One practical way to do this is to learn to follow your impulses. The key here is to recognize that change is healthy. It is actually absolutely necessary to living a full life. You should shake yourself up periodically, reinvent yourself every few years. For example, if you do not keep getting promotions at your job, you should find another. We all need new challenges to keep growing, to prevent stagnation.

The nature of the change is not even that important. You do not necessarily need to move up, or follow some carefully charted course. The only thing that is important is that you change, and if you do not have any idea of how, then you should just follow an impulse. Don't agonize about where you are in your life and what you should do. Just act! Do something, anything. Keep moving. Wait for a strong impulse, any impulse, and follow it.

For instance, following an impulse is how I came to move to Sweden. To start, I took a vacation there. (This was also on an impulse. I had actually been planning to go on safari in East Africa, but at the last minute I got an invitation from a friend to go sailing in Scandinavia. I changed my plans.) During the trip I liked the country so much I decided to move there. I followed this second impulse, and it worked out.

But still, how do you take that step, the one over the precipice. The only guidance I can offer can be found in the following story. I was about ten years old at the time and at summer camp. One day we made an excursion to a nearby river, at a section where a cliff towered above. Everyone took turns jumping off the rocks into the river - there were a series of ledges leading up to twenty feet high, and then a gap to another ledge which was about forty feet above the water. I got comfortable with the smaller leaps, and then decided to go for the top. What the hell. Standing at the edge, it was a huge abyss. I had no idea if I would make it, if I would break my legs (I was really skinny), or even drown. But something clicked in my mind. I realized that whatever happened actually was not that important. In order to live I had to take that step.

Having reached that point, it was the easiest thing in the world to do. I walked forward, and rocketed down. I slammed into the water (my feet were bruised), but what exhilaration! It is amazing how exhilarating life can be, if you go for it. The feelings we can experience, they are unbelievable.

But you have to take that step.

Once you realize that, though, it's easy. We all have the courage. Walk to the edge sometime, and find yours.

To return to doing a world trip - your world trip, in order to become a traveler you will have to find the willpower to accomplish the transition from a sedentary life. You will have to overcome all of the hurdles in the way of being this new type of person.

To continue with psychology, there are two types of hurdles: internal and external. The internal variety includes overcoming your fears: the fear of the unknown, of the trip, and of doing something out of the ordinary. It may also take a lot of psychological effort to justify the expense, when you could use your hard-earned and saved money for some other purpose, such as to buy a car or to make a down payment on a house. Can you trade ten or twenty thousand dollars for the extraordinary experience of a year-long world trip, an experience that very possibly will change who you are and the course of your life? This is what you get for your money, but are you willing to make the investment?

It is also important to consider your basic approach to life. You should try to live in the present, and make plans for the future. You do not want to focus only on the moment, because you will never accomplish the possibilities of life that take years to organize. On the other hand, you do not want to live solely for the future, postponing present happiness for some distant end. An alternative is to try to think of, always be aware of, your life *as a whole*. Ideally, you want to put a structure in place, have an approach, that gives you the freedom to enjoy each passing day, while continuing down long and what may be difficult roads towards larger and more complex goals.

This is essential if you want to become a world traveler. It will likely take years to save for and plan, and if you do not keep the goal alive in the back of your mind you will forget it, or, more likely, end up positioning yourself such that it becomes impossible.

Another hurdle, of course, is general indecision, the habit people have of delaying important decisions until the opportunities that they represent are lost.

On the external side, you will have to deal with all of the people who will try to dissuade you from going. (Many people will encourage you!) Once again, this is the underlying issue of form and societal disapproval. You are embarking on a path that is non-conformist, and it is essential to realize that society has great systems of persuasion and control to prevent people from getting out of line.

To become a real non-conformist you will have to fight your desire to fit in, to belong, to be accepted. But this is extremely difficult: the contentment and happiness of most people are heavily dependent on having the social acceptance of others. In addition, rebellion is not about leaving one group of conformists for another, dressing or acting a certain way because some trend-setter tells you to or sets an example. True rebels are not just "*looking for a better conformity.*" (*The Little Drummer Girl*, John Le Carré, Pan Books, page 137)

One way to bridge the gap is to recognize that becoming a world traveler is an evolutionary process. People do not start out taking world trips (usually!), or getting jobs in foreign countries, or having any of the other variations on an international lifestyle. Instead, they begin with some sort of introduction to the world outside the U.S., hopefully a positive one so their fear is reduced and they learn to be comfortable in foreign environments. In my own case, after school I explored the U.S. Then, when I got a steady job, I started taking foreign vacations. This led to a desire to work abroad, which I supported with an MBA in finance and international business (at night school). Then came the Swedish trip, and the rest is history.

Practical issues

On the practical side, you will need to consider, and plan for, the consequences of your trip on your work and career (or education), your apartment and car (forget home ownership, at least until later in life - it's a ball and chain), your relationships (with family, lover and friends), and your general financial position.

You will probably need to think about these issues for a long time, and get prepared for and comfortable with all of the possible consequences.

These issues are considered in more detail in different parts of the text. Funding a trip, for example, warrants an entire chapter. However, it is also worth some preliminary consideration here. There are four ways to fund a world trip: someone might give you the money (have you received an inheritance, or severance payment, lately?); you can sell any substantial assets that you own; you can borrow the money; or you can save it. Whatever method suits your situation, the important thing to recognize is that it is never an impossibility - for anyone. You can put ten thousand dollars together. Hell, five thousand will get you to South Asia and keep you going there for at least a year. It might take some time, but you can do it.

If saving is your only option, go for it! Get a night job. Work your butt off. Don't spend money on *anything*: no new clothes, no CDs, no newspapers or magazines, minimal alcohol. Suffer whatever the consequences might be, but save every penny you get!

Conclusion

In an ideal world, the human population would be dramatically reduced. The earth would be turned into a park. All habitats, species and traditional cultures would be preserved. Over time all nations would become peaceful and developed. At that point they would become irrelevant. Everyone would be a world traveler. Form as an instrument of social control would be recognized and largely defeated. Individuals would take command of their free will, find their own unique identities, and be more content and happy. All of the dark sides of our nature notwithstanding, we would create a utopia.

Just listen to the lyrics of John Lennon's *Imagine* sometimes.

Things are changing fast, at a pace unlike any age in human history. It is possible.

World travelers are futurists. We see the world the way it should be, and the way it will hopefully someday become. We are trying to lead the way.

3. STYLE

In this book I will discuss every important issue that you will need to be aware of to plan, embark on and complete a world trip. Some of these issues are quite tangible, such as deciding on what gear to take. Others, though, are intangible and deal with psychological and cultural factors. One of the latter - it is also probably the best place to begin - is the issue of style, of what your overall approach to your trip should be.

Style is an imprecise word. Everyone uses it, but we are often unsure of exactly what it means. I used the phrases *accepted lifestyles* and *global lifestyle* earlier, but to what did they refer? Just what is a lifestyle?

Webster's defines a lifestyle as a "*typical way of life*," but that's not much help. At its most profound level, your lifestyle relates to - it *should* relate to - your goals for your life, which for most people revolve around a particular idea of success. For example, do you want to be successful career-wise, to earn a lot of money or to make a name for yourself in your chosen profession? Do you want to find the love of your life, and become a good parent? Do you want to be a moral individual and make a positive contribution to society? Do you want to find spiritual peace (or live to be one hundred)? Maybe you just want to be hip and cool! Whatever your goals are, your lifestyle is the basic structural approach that you use to accomplish them.

We choose different lifestyles because of what rewards us or makes us happy. However, the lifestyles of many people are tied to social influences, and this is generally unfortunate. Individuals who blindly follow their influences sacrifice their own identities and desires - they take on styles that are suggested or imposed by others. This is one dimension of style, the degree to which you follow a path of social nonconformity and rebellion. Nine-to-fivers are conformists. Rock-climbers and surfers are not. The former base their lifestyles on their occupation. Indeed, they are dominated by their jobs. They live to work. The latter, however, work to live. Any occupation is acceptable as long as it funds, and does not compete with or detract from, their pursuit of their chosen objectives and activities.

A few other important dimensions of style are your need for material comfort and goods, your personal selfishness versus your desire to help others, your need for safety or willingness to take risks, and your acceptance of sacrifices for personal development.

Being a world traveler is a style of life. Our goals are to understand ourselves, other people, the planet and existence. We are rebels. We require few material goods. We tend to be a bit selfish. We seek out the unknown and accept its danger. We are extremely motivated by personal and spiritual development.

(Perhaps the best advice I can give on personal development is to work on your *weaknesses*, whatever they might be. Don't worry about the things at which you are already good. Focus on what you can't do well, or at all.)

I think many world travelers also follow a specific philosophy, even if they are not aware of it. I call it the philosophy of "*No Regrets*," and it is certainly mine. What it means is that if I am in a situation where I have only a moment to live, and I know this, such as if I am on a plane which is about to crash, if I can think clearly, not succumb to the natural tendency to terror, I want my last thought to be: No Regrets! I lived life to the fullest that was possible for me. I went for it. I honestly tried to do everything of which I was capable, to push my limits as far as possible. I was courageous, and although I might have suffered a lot of hard knocks, I also had many, many moments of bliss and exaltation.

Travel style

Your approach to life is the most important factor affecting your world trip. However, there is another level of style, travel style, which revolves around practical concerns. There are many different ways to view this, but the traditional perspective is based on expense. We all know what high style is, although few of us have had the experience. Have you ever flown the Concord to Paris, and checked into the Ritz Hotel on Place Vendôme with ten Louis Vuitton cases? Have you ever been featured on *The Lifestyles of the Rich and Famous*? Ha! Neither have I. How about the opposite? Have you ever flown standby in a charter airline cattle car and stayed in a youth hostel dormitory? Probably not, although this may be more likely.

Another basic distinction is independent travel versus package tourism. People who take tours have signed contracts, in their minds if not on paper. The tour company will provide a specific variety of services, of a specific grade or quality, for a specific period of time. It will also provide a guide, who will make all of the arrangements. Virtually everything, twenty-four hours a day, is set. Tour participants do not even need to think - they are just along for the ride. These packages generally have high prices and limited flexibility to change itineraries. They also insulate the tourists from the residents and cultures of the countries that they visit. For instance, U.S. package tourists are often served Americanized versions of local foods. All in all, tours provide limited travel experiences. Many people abhor this, and choose instead to travel on their own. Such independent travelers usually want complete flexibility in their arrangements, and they often want to travel for as long as possible for as little money as possible. Rather than set a price in advance for every single service, they would prefer to get whatever they can for free. They live by the credo: why spend $50 a day, when you can get by on $10 and stay five times as long? Independent travelers also usually want to meet the locals, to make arrangements and bargain with them, and to understand and appreciate *their* lifestyles.

Put more broadly, your travel style is dependent on the degree to which you require guidance. This ranges from being part of a tour group, to having a private guide, to using a guidebook, to using only a map, to having no guidance at all. For the last, you just go wherever seems interesting and deal with whatever comes up. (This is actually another type of philosophy, and it is common among experienced world travelers.)

The most important considerations affecting your travel style are your budget and your trip objectives, including any specific activities that you would like to pursue. Other determinants are the amount of time that you have and your pace and flexibility. (The latter issues also depend on how much you have prearranged your trip, if only your airline tickets, and the interests of any people with whom you are traveling.) A few other stylistic concerns are how much cultural contact you would like to have, how adventurous you are, and even how much luggage you plan to take. Many of the characteristics of a travel style fit together, and it is also usual to adapt your style to the demands of different situations. One example of this is that you might increase your pace and expenditure, and limit your cultural contact, when traveling through a difficult environment. Then, when you find someplace wonderful, you can check into the cheapest available accommodation, make friends with the locals, and stay as long as you like.

I have purposefully avoided including fear as a determinant of a travel style. Many people have inappropriate fears about foreign travel, because they do not properly understand the risks. A major premise of this book is that travel risks can be understood and reduced, if not completely prevented, on almost any type of trip. Travel styles should only reflect realistic risks. They should not be dominated by unrealistic fears.

As a final general comment, style also refers to a quality that any individual can have. This means, of course, personal style, that *je ne sais quoi*. Actually, personal style is linked to your ability to be original, to overcome difficulties and accomplish the extraordinary, and to combine the simple and the elegant to create the sublime. Your personal style should mesh well with the stylistic choices that you make for your trip. For example, I heard of one traveler, a disabled man, who hitchhiked in his wheelchair all the way across Australia. He certainly had style, and he also proved the maxim that if you do have style, you can go anywhere and do anything.

One of the most important lessons of life is that once you have found your personal style, you should stick to it. Do not let other people change you. Stay true to yourself!

Budgets

If you are wealthy, you might think of heading for Europe or Africa with a retainer or two, or signing up for a round-the-world cruise. You should remember, though, that a tourist who stays only on a cruise ship or at four and five star hotels, the ubiquitous Hiltons and Hyatts, is not a real world traveler. You have to spend time with the locals, and experience their lives, to call yourself this.

Most travelers, of course, have limited funds, and need to plan well and be opportunistic to get the most for their money. Fortunately, even on a low budget many interesting destinations and activities are affordable. One way to get diversity out of a tight budget is to follow long stretches of low cost travel with brief, more expensive splurges. Similarly, you might want to splurge after a challenging experience. For instance, you could follow a mountain or jungle trek with a relaxing stay at a beach resort. Another option would be to enjoy a meal, with wine or champagne, at the best local restaurant. The amount of luggage that you take may also have style and expense ramifications. This is because it is difficult to be totally flexible, and follow a low budget, if you have a lot of gear. It is hard to avoid the tendency to take more convenient (and expensive) transportation and accommodation, and to use guides and porters more often.

Because of the need for economy, most world travelers limit their stays in expensive locations, including European cities, Japan, Hong Kong and Singapore. As another example, I did not meet any travelers in the Maldives, which is an island nation in the Indian Ocean, and where the bulk of the accommodation is at relatively expensive resorts. (This is unfortunate, since there are ways to stay there inexpensively.) On the other hand, there are many travelers in India, Nepal and other lesser developed countries. This is one reason why the Asian overland route is so popular. Not only is it a fascinating, beautiful and historic region, but it also has a large infrastructure of inexpensive accommodation and transportation to service budget-minded travelers.

Interests and activities

One of the best ways to make a world trip more rewarding is to pursue a variety of different travel themes. Everyone has a broad array of interests, and one of the great challenges of travel is to find a way to satisfy as many of them as possible. This is actually a direct planning issue as much as it is a style issue, although what really allows you to express your individuality is how you work out the connections between all of your competing interests and objectives.

During my world trip, some of my themes were mountain trekking, naturalist photography, scuba diving, the relationship of Buddhism to social systems, and traditional dances. To accomplish these disparate objectives was a major undertaking. I started my trip in Nepal, to complete the strenuous treks to Mt. Everest and other Himalayan peaks while I was still fresh and strong. After this, I alternated visits to wildlife parks and sanctuaries, for my photography, with stays at scuba diving areas and resorts. The former were also generally much less expensive than the latter. In addition, I spent substantial amounts of time in Nepal, Sri Lanka and Thailand, which have ancient Buddhist traditions, and was able to observe how the religion influences and permeates their societies. Lastly, I found many opportunities along the way to go to cultural performances, including Kathakali dances in southern India, Thai dances, Javanese dances and Balinese dances.

There is also a stylistic connection with other types of trip objectives - goals which are more esoteric or fundamental than the interests and activities just mentioned. For example, after years of working in offices my deepest travel goals revolved around better understanding the world and myself and, frankly, finding my humanity again and enjoying my life more. I also wanted to meet people from other cultures and all walks of life, to find a romantic partner, and to talk less, be more relaxed and laugh and smile more. Finally, I wanted to get more in touch with my feelings - to be more honest with myself. With most of these I think I succeeded, but certainly not by taking package tours and staying in five star hotels.

When you consider your style and plan your trip, what you should be trying to do is assemble the components of a *great journey*, one that will be uniquely suited to you.

Adventure and exploration

Many world travelers are particularly interested in adventurous activities and exploring remote regions. There even tends to be a bit of snobbery in the group, based on how long you have been away and how far off the beaten track you have gone. And it is definitely still possible to be an explorer. Perhaps you cannot be the first person to sail around the world, or to climb Mt. Everest, or to trek to the South Pole, but you can repeat these exploits. There are also many ways in which you can be an original explorer. The world is 24,900 miles around at the equator and has a surface area of almost two hundred million square miles. It is simple to map out many long trips that link remote regions and countries in ways that have never been accomplished. Such journeys will probably not be easy to complete, of course, but that is the attraction of exploration: to find a new route and to surmount all of the obstacles along the way.

Indeed, global exploration, like dangerous sports, regularly involves putting yourself in situations which exceed your competence, where your only hope is that your discipline, drive and sheer will to survive will see you through, will take you to the next level.

Travelers who live their lives as explorers join an illustrious tradition. They follow in the footsteps of ancient traders, envoys, warriors and adventurers, who traversed and then went beyond the limits of their known worlds. Although it is unlikely that the general public will ever recognize your name, if you pursue this type of travel style you can consider yourself a compatriot of Alexander and Marco Polo, of Pythagoras, the first person to realize that the earth is a sphere (world travel is also a state of mind), and Magellan, the first actual circumnavigator.

Timing, pace and flexibility

You should try to get away for as long as possible, and it is important to be realistic about what you can accomplish. (Once you start you will think a year is a short trip!) You should allow yourself plenty of time to relax - this may be the only time in your life where you can do it, so enjoy - instead of following a schedule where you must continually rush around. For instance, the standard American tourist routine of visiting a handful of European countries in one or two weeks is ridiculous (particularly in the eyes of the locals). The only thing this type of travel allows is a small amount of sightseeing. Exploring the world can be an incredibly rich experience; there is no need to limit yourself to the appetizer when a full gourmet meal is available.

When you begin your trip you should take some time to work into a rhythm and find an appropriate pace. You have a natural pace, and so do the environments that you visit. Your goal is to find a comfortable compromise between the two. A good pace will enable you to complete a reasonable amount of activities with a minimum amount of stress. It will also keep you fresh and healthy and aware of your surroundings, including both its joys and dangers. You should also periodically change your pace. One way to do this is to take relaxation days, and not only when it is raining or you are ill. You should take a day off whenever you want to, to rest, to catch up on your journal or postcards, or even just to watch foreign television.

From another perspective, the issue of pace has applicability to your entire life. You should ask yourself the question: are you living at a pace that is comfortable, keeps you happy, and through which you regularly achieve major goals; or are you overly stressed, miserable, and taking on too much to accomplish anything?

You should generally allow at least a month for each country that you intend to visit. (You may want to plan two or more months for some.) This should satisfy your interest in smaller nations, and provide a good introduction to larger and more diverse ones. It is also a good idea to stop periodically, for from a few days to a few weeks. You should look for a beautiful and relaxed environment, and then settle down and *do nothing*; just sit around and watch time pass by.

(A common joke among world travelers is: "*I hate this!*" You usually say it someplace like a tropical beach bar, while sipping a cold beer and watching another fabulous sunset.)

Regardless of the length of your trip, it is essential to retain the flexibility to change your plans. You should be able to stay at any location for a longer period of time, leave early if you get bored, or even completely change your itinerary. (You might want to do the last if you meet someone with whom it would be great to travel, such as a romantic partner or another person who has more interesting plans.) Flexibility is limited by rigid arrangements - for world travelers this is usually restricted to plane tickets which cannot be changed, at least not without a substantial charge. You should avoid having these at all times. (Your amount of independence is also a function of the interests of your travel partners, and of your psychology - by what you are willing or able to deal with.)

Other reflections on travel styles

A few other points on style are as follows:

- If you find someplace that you really like, you should stop and become a temporary resident. One way to do this is to move in with friends. For example, during my world trip I spent a month in Bangkok with an American friend and a month in Singapore with an English friend. Staying with friends is one of the most enjoyable ways to travel. You feel like you are living in the country, rather than just visiting it. This style of travel will usually lead to far more cultural contact, and it should reduce your costs to a minimum. However, you should not be a mooch, so remember to contribute your portion of shared expenses, such as for gasoline, if you drive places in your friend's car, and bar and restaurant bills. It is also a nice idea to give your host a present, or else have a party, when you leave.
- If you find a dream location, but are not in a position to move there, you should revisit it on future trips in later years, even if to other people it is a once-in-a-lifetime destination. You will get a tremendous feeling of accomplishment from doing this. For instance, why should you go to Tahiti just once, since if you plan it right you can go there many times? You could even be like Paul Gauguin, and take some canvasses, paints and a palette! I have a German friend who visits the Seychelles (in the Indian Ocean) every year, even though they are probably 5,000 miles from his home. The Seychelles are among the most beautiful and relaxed islands on earth, so it is easy to understand his attraction. My personal favorites for repeat destinations include Alta, Utah (the best powder skiing), Chamonix, France (the best mountain town), Nepal (the most photogenic place I have ever been), the Maldives (the best scuba diving?), Stockholm (the most beautiful women?), Paris (the *joie de vivre*), and New York (the best nightlife).
- Another, more unusual style is to travel long distances following the most unlikely routes, to expose yourself to great environmental contrasts and shocks. An example of such a world trip might be from your home to Zaire, to Athens, to Calcutta, to Bali, to Tokyo, to north Alaska, to New York, and then back home. (Warning: this can take a lot of cash!)

- Lastly, and as the above section on exploration suggested, you might want to visit somewhere that is completely out of the ordinary. You can still find places that are totally untouched by western influences such as newspapers and telephones, and with no other western travelers around either. It is a real education to see how people in these places live, and how they make do without the things that we take for granted, including clothes in some cases! (Please remember, though, that some of these cultures may not want to be visited, which is their right.) Taking these types of trips may even lead you to adopt the most fundamental travel style, which is to visit the farthest corners of the earth, on your own, with a minimum amount of gear, and on an extremely low budget. This will test the limits of your independence, self-confidence and courage, and, ultimately, of your humanity.

As an aside, you know you are off the beaten track when:

- You cannot buy a t-shirt, or a postcard.
- There are no touts.
- You cannot buy a bottle of water, or a Coke.
- You always pay the same prices as the locals.
- You are surrounded by dozens of people wherever you go.
- There are no maps.
- There are no radio stations.
- The locals have never seen a foreigner in the area.
- The locals have never seen a foreigner in their lives.

4. PLANNING YOUR ITINERARY

Planning a world trip can be a long and complicated process. Fortunately, it should also be enjoyable, because of your anticipation of the trip. You should typically start planning a few months ahead of your departure, to have plenty of time to research your destinations. In addition, you may need to apply for a passport (four to six weeks by mail), and you will have to arrange any visas and vaccinations that are required.

Every traveler will also have unique planning requirements, based on individual needs and styles. For example, some people like to organize everything, while others take it as it comes.

You should begin by making a preliminary itinerary listing the locations you would like to visit and the activities you would like to pursue. You should then take this and schedule it on a calendar. For instance, the beginning of my world trip itinerary was as follows:

Date	Activity	Duration
4/23/91	Fly London to New Delhi	1 day
	Visit Agra and the Taj Mahal	2 days
4/26	Fly New Delhi to Kathmandu	1 day
	Nepal options:	
	Annapurna Sanctuary trek	9-12 days
	Jomson trek	12-16 days
	Annapurna Circuit trek	19-21 days
	Mt. Everest trek	26-30 days
	Raft Trisuli River	3 days
	Raft Sun Kosi River	8-11 days
	Visit Royal Chitwan N.P.	3-5 days
5/26	Fly Kathmandu to New Delhi	1 day

I stuck to the itinerary during my first stop in India, but deviated from it in Nepal. I had intended a one month visit, but I liked the country so much I stayed over ten weeks. I did the Annapurna Circuit and Mt. Everest treks (the latter took less time than anticipated because I flew in), and visited Chitwan for two weeks to ride elephants and look for rhinoceros and tigers. I did not go rafting because the rivers were low at the time - it was the end of the dry season.

It is important to consider carefully your transportation requirements for days when you will be on the move. Will inexpensive transport be available, and will the amount of time between connections be sufficient if you experience delays? It is better to schedule a later departure than try to meet a tight timetable. One of the classic examples of poor travel planning occurs on the trek to Mt. Everest. Many people arrange to fly to Kathmandu from the mountain airport at Luckla after finishing the trek. Some of these people also schedule flights out of Nepal for shortly after they expect to arrive in Kathmandu. What they do not realize is that the airport at Luckla is often closed for up to a week or more because of bad weather, and that the only other option is a week-long walk to the nearest roadhead. Many, many trekkers have been stuck there and missed flights, and at such times the stress level in the village can be extraordinary. (Another trap that travelers regularly fall prey to is to be stuck on remote islands, perhaps for weeks, while waiting for the next boat or ferry.)

Where to go

For your itinerary you should list any countries or other locations that you have always dreamed of visiting, regardless of where they are. At this point you should not limit yourself in any way; if you want to go to Antarctica put it on the list! Then, as your list grows, a number of things will likely become evident. First, you may notice that many of your greatest interests lie within the same region(s) of the globe. Second, you will probably list too many places; it will be impossible to visit them all in the time or with the funds that you have available. Finally, after prioritizing your interests and deciding on your main objectives, it will become clear if you need to make a complete circuit of the globe (this may well be one of your goals) or that an out and back trip is sufficient.

Another perspective on the issue of where to go is that you should not let the availability of inexpensive tickets to some destinations deter you from traveling to the places that you would really like to visit. Some world travelers become aware of cheap round-the-world airfares, and then force their itineraries to conform to these routings. It is better to decide on your preferred destinations, and then approach the issue of how to get to them.

Most people would like to travel to beautiful locations, where there are many interesting activities, and which can be visited inexpensively. This last point is particularly important. Why should you pay $100 to do something in one place, if you can do it for $25 somewhere else? Using a little ingenuity in deciding where to go will save you a lot of money, and it will also help you avoid hordes of tourists. For example, many travelers to China visit the Great Wall, but usually at only a few specific locations. If you go to one of these spots on a nice day, you may be part of a crowd of thousands of people. However, if you rent a car, or a car and driver, you can easily reach deserted sections of the wall. You can then walk on top of it for hours, and be completely on your own.

You should also recognize, if you are a circumnavigator, that it can be psychologically difficult to retrace your steps, since backtracking will take you farther away from your ultimate goal. You should avoid planning an itinerary that includes reversing your direction, or repeat visits to a location, unless there is a clear or unavoidable reason for doing so.

You can of course traverse the globe in any direction, but most people find that east to west or west to east routings, with detours north and south, work best. On such a trip the basic regional options, assuming you start in the U.S. and head east across the Atlantic, are as follows:

1. Europe

- Scandinavia (Norway, Denmark, Sweden, Finland), continuing into Russia and the other former states of the USSR, perhaps all the way across to the Pacific via the Siberian Express. (There may be complicated visa issues after Finland.)
- Scandinavia, around the Baltic states, to Northern Europe. (I hope to do this soon. I'll go to Stockholm, ferry to Helsinki, train into Russia to St. Petersburg, and continue down the coast to Estonia, Latvia and Lithuania.)
- Around Northern Europe (Holland, Germany, Switzerland) and then across Central and Eastern Europe to Istanbul, perhaps via the Orient Express. (The latter would make a great extension of the preceding trip. You could continue across Poland to Prague, and then train through Vienna, Budapest and Bucharest to get to the Black Sea.)
- Southern Europe, along the north shore of the Mediterranean (Portugal, Spain, France, Italy, Greece), to the Middle East.

2. Middle East

- Due to the Turkish occupation of the northern half of Cyprus, there are two distinct itinerary options for the states bordering the eastern Mediterranean. The first is to proceed from Turkey to Syria to Jordan, and then to Israel and Egypt. (You have to visit Syria before Israel.) The other option, which I did on my current trip, is the ferry from Greece to Cyprus to Israel.
- Much of the rest of the Middle East, at the present time, is either off limits or very dicey (Lebanon, Saudi Arabia and the Gulf states, Iraq, Iran, Afghanistan).

3. Africa

- A full top-to-bottom African journey, starting in Morocco and heading across the Sahara to West Africa, or in Egypt through Sudan to East Africa, takes many months and is generally a trip unto itself. Indeed, both are among the most challenging itineraries on the planet. You will pass through sixteen countries if you follow the west coast from Senegal to Zaire, and at least a couple of these will likely be embroiled in civil conflicts. The entire region is also tropical, with few roads and many dangerous endemic diseases.

4. Asia

- The classic overland Asian route begins in Turkey and continues to Iran, Afghanistan (during times of peace), Pakistan, India and Nepal.
- The Indian option takes you down the subcontinent to Sri Lanka and, perhaps, the Maldives. (This is also a trip unto itself.)
- The direct route continues with a flight from Kathmandu to Bangkok, although with the lessening of restrictions a stop in Burma can now be added. Once in Thailand, many world travelers head down the Malay peninsula to Singapore and Indonesia.
- An alternative is to explore Indochina, including Laos, Cambodia and Vietnam, and then travel to China, perhaps continuing all the way to Korea and Japan.

5. Oceania

- The standard circumnavigation continues from Indonesia (people usually get as far as Bali or Lombok) to Australia and New Zealand, and then across the eastern Pacific with perhaps a stop in Fiji, the Cook Islands (Rarotonga) or Hawaii.
- An alternative is to cross the Pacific just south of the Equator, starting in northern Indonesia (Borneo, Sulawesi, the Moluccas, Irian Jaya) and continuing to Papua

New Guinea and such island nations as the Solomons, Vanuatu, Fiji, Tonga, the Cook Islands and French Polynesia. A difficulty with this plan, though, is that some South Pacific nations will not let you enter without an onward ticket.

6. Latin America

- A really grand tour would continue the last itinerary further across the Pacific to Pitcairn Island (the only access is by boat), Easter Island and then Santiago, Chile. At this point you could head to Patagonia and perhaps even catch a boat to Antarctica. You could then retrace your steps and go up the west coast of South America to Bolivia, Peru, Ecuador and Columbia. Alternatively, you could cross over to Argentina and ascend the east coast via Uruguay, Brazil and Venezuela. However, if only because of the need to develop a decent understanding of Spanish, South America is usually the subject of a separate trip.
- Lastly, you could travel through Central America to Mexico, or island hop across the Caribbean from south to north. (The onward flight issue can also be a major problem for independent travelers in the Caribbean, since many of the countries there, particularly the smaller islands, cater themselves to tourists. A better option is to get a job crewing and travel by yacht.)

Gathering points

Whatever route you take, you should consider stopping at some of the traditional traveler oases, such as the destinations on the following list:

- Christiania
- Casablanca
- Istanbul
- Jerusalem
- Cairo
- Dahab
- Lamu
- Nairobi
- Zanzibar
- Ladakh
- Manali
- New Delhi
- Varanasi
- Goa
- Kovalam Beach
- Kandy
- Onowatuna Beach
- Kathmandu
- Pokhara
- Chiang Mai
- Bangkok
- Koh Chang
- Koh Samui
- Penang Island
- Kota Kinabalu
- Tioman Island
- Lake Toba
- Jakarta
- Yogyakarta
- Ubud
- Kuta
- Lombok
- Perth
- Darwin
- Cairns
- Sydney
- Auckland
- Queenstown
- Rarotonga
- Fiji
- Buenos Aires
- Rio de Janeiro

You can wile away weeks, or even months, among a fun and ever changing group of like-minded world travelers at any of these locations. There are also trends among independent travelers. One of these is that some locations that formerly were popular, such as Machu Picchu, Kabul and Kashmir, have been off the list in recent years because of civil conflicts. (Machu Picchu should be making a comeback now. Also, you are not a world traveler if you go straight from one hangout to the next and spend all of your time with other westerners smoking pot!)

When to go

The crucial timing issue for a world trip is when to do it? (If you live to be eighty, one year is 1.25% of your life. It's not that much. Go for it!) Traveling before you start a career and establish a family is usually the simplest to arrange. Indeed, the many people who tour the U.S. after college could easily expand their horizons and go around the world. This should not be limited to young people, though, since the older and more educated you are, the more you should appreciate the wide variety of experiences that the world has to offer. Other opportunistic times to take off would include between job and career changes, after your children have left home, and after you retire. In any case, you should definitely find some period in your life to become a world traveler, since it is not that difficult or expensive, and because the pleasures and other benefits are so profound.

More specifically, the question of when to travel is affected by the issues of costs and crowds. For instance, if you want to be in Rio during Carnival Week, you will have to pay triple the ordinary cost for a room and endure monumental crowds. Of course, many people would say that the former is still reasonable for the best party in the world, and that the latter is part of the attraction. One way to avoid crowds and reduce expenses is to travel during low seasons. Accommodation should always be less expensive, and you never need a reservation. You can usually negotiate a better deal on arrival anyway. Indeed, world travelers only need reservations in the highest seasons, or at locations where the accommodation choices are extremely limited. However, if you plan to visit an area during a low season you should check if special activities in which you are interested will be available. Certain activities, such as sports, may not be offered since this is when the specialists who conduct them typically take their vacations.

World travelers usually encounter many different climates, and it is impossible to plan an itinerary where you arrive at a series of destinations always during the seasons when the local weather is most favorable. Overland travelers may also need to alter their routes, if for some reason they are unable to get visas for upcoming countries. In addition, if you are adventurous you might want to stay up-do-date on the political developments in countries that are presently closed to travelers. You should then be able to be one of the first people to visit them when they reopen. For example, Afghanistan may be open soon, and travelers will someday return to Iraq as well.

Seasonal considerations

The following is a list of seasonal considerations and local attractions around which you might want to plan your trip:

- Cultural and religious festivals. (I have been in Thailand for the Surin elephant festival and for *Loi Krathong*. During the latter, the Thai people make floats out of flowers, incense and candles, and then launch them in lakes and rivers as an offering for good fortune in the coming year.)
- Sports and other outdoor activities, both as a participant and as a spectator. The seasons when you should travel for snow skiing or English Premier League soccer may be easy to determine, but what about for surfing, particularly if you want to catch a World-Cup competition - and the great party that surrounds it? In other cases, you should call your destinations just before you plan to arrive, since the availability of some activities may change from day-to-day. For instance, if you want to go scuba diving in northern Australia you will probably want to avoid their summer, which is box jellyfish season. In addition, the tides there are up to thirty feet or more. Because of safety concerns diving is usually only possible on days with low tides.
- Wildlife observation. Wildlife species are generally easiest to observe during particular seasons, such as when migrations are in progress. It is often necessary to make reservations far in advance for accommodations inside parks and sanctuaries at these times. Parks may also be closed to tourism during some seasons. (When I was in India during my world trip, I was unable to visit Ranthambhore National Park to look for tigers because it had just closed for the monsoon.)
- When wildflowers bloom.
- To avoid inconveniences and dangers, such as insect pests and the diseases that they carry.
- To be present during, or to avoid, particular weather conditions.

Weather considerations in the tropics

If your trip will take you to the tropics, and for a world traveler this is inevitable, you should decide if you want to avoid the monsoon. Many countries actually experience two monsoons each year, although only one will typically have severe rainfall. Monsoons last about three months, but they can be highly variable by region and by month. The rainfall may be constant and drenching, or only periodic with sunshine in between.

The disadvantages of traveling during the monsoon include the following:

- It rains a lot! You can forget about getting a good suntan.
- The heat and humidity may be uncomfortable.
- There is increased difficulty in traveling. Roads may be muddy or flooded, and subject to closure from landslides. Trains and ferries are often canceled, and the latter may actually shut down for the entire season. Traveling by boat would probably be unpleasant anyway, since the seas are rougher. Trekking is also more dangerous, and parks may be closed.
- There is an increased number of pests, including leeches and mosquitos.
- Scenic attractions may rarely be visible, because of cloud cover.
- Beaches get washed away.

There are, however, a few advantages:

- The number of other foreign travelers in the country will be at a minimum. Local residents may be less stressed and more friendly because of this.
- Forests will be their greenest and most alive.
- Accommodation and activity costs will be at their lowest levels.

5. SOURCES OF INFORMATION

"*Police Captain Louis Renault:* *'And what in heaven's name brought you to Casablanca?'*
Rick Blaine: *'My health. I came to Casablanca for the waters.'*
Louis: *'The waters? What waters? We're in the desert.'*
Rick: *'I was misinformed.'*"

This immortal quote of Humphrey Bogart, as Rick Blaine in the movie *Casablanca*, illustrates (when taken literally) an enduring point about traveling: visitors to foreign countries are regularly given incorrect or misleading information. In some places, if you ask five people the same question you will get five different answers. There are any number of reasons for this. People almost always want to help, and they may try to assist you even if they do not really understand your question, or are unsure of the answer. They may just not want to disappoint you. On the other hand, many people will deliberately try to mislead you, such as to get you to pay too much for goods or services. A lot of information also quickly becomes out-of-date: timetables change, hotels and restaurants close, and prices go up. A classic example of misinformation occurs with maps. Many maps, particularly of lesser developed countries, are blatantly incorrect. A good policy, therefore, is always to buy the best maps that are available.

Whatever the reason for it, you should learn to recognize misinformation. It is important to evaluate the reliability of all your information sources. For things that you have to be positive about, such as transportation departure times, you should check your information with at least one independent source.

You will need to collect a lot of information to make the most of your trip - both before you depart and after you are on the road. This research will enable you to plan an itinerary that satisfies your interests and needs, and it will also alert you to infrequent events, such as cultural festivals and sports competitions, for which visits might need to be arranged months in advance. Fortunately, tourism is a huge industry and a phenomenal amount of information is available - much of it free for the asking. For example, the government tourism offices of the countries that you would like to visit should at a minimum be able to provide you with information on visa requirements, health concerns, cultural issues, lodging choices and activity options.

It is sometimes worthwhile to ask for personal references from the people who give you travel information. They can be useful in many circumstances, such as to get permission to visit closed or limited-entry areas. There are also different types of references, ranging from the simple right to use a person's name in conversation, to a formal letter of introduction.

The U.S. government

The U.S. government distributes information for Americans who travel internationally, and many such publications are referred to throughout this book. In addition, the following documents contain general and region-specific advice. They are all available from the Superintendent of Documents, U.S. Government Printing Office, Washington, D.C., 20402, (202) 512-1800.

- *Your Trip Abroad*
- *Travel Tips for Older Americans*
- *Tips for Americans Residing Abroad*
- *Background Notes*. These are available for every nation. They present a profile of the country, and describe its history, people, government, economy and relationship with the U.S. Each note also includes a small, but accurate, map.
- *Tips for Travelers to the Caribbean*
- *Tips for Travelers to Mexico*
- *Tips for Travelers to Central and South America*
- *Tips for Travelers to Russia and the Newly Independent States*
- *Tips for Travelers to Eastern Europe*
- *Tips for Travelers to the Middle East and North Africa*
- *Tips for Travelers to Sub-Saharan Africa*
- *Tips for Travelers to South Asia*
- *Tips for Travelers to the People's Republic of China*

Foreign government tourism offices

As mentioned above, a great amount of information is available from foreign government tourism offices. This makes them probably the best place to begin destination-specific research. Obtaining information from a tourism office is simple. You can either go to the office or, if this is inconvenient, call them and request a travel information packet. When you call, you should act as if you are definitely going to visit the country, even if you are only considering adding it to your itinerary. If you have a specific interest, such as for a particular activity, or region in the country, you should request information on it as well. It is also a good idea to ask for a map and a calendar of local festivals. A large envelope full of information will usually be mailed to you the next day.

Most countries have tourism offices in New York City, which are typically separate from their consulates to the U.N. You can call directory assistance for New York on (212) 555-1212, and request the local phone numbers for the tourism offices and consulates for almost any country.

You should be able to narrow down your interests after reading the material in the first packet. Then, if you decide to visit the country, you can contact the office again and ask for further information, such as accommodation guides. You can continue to work with them as your plans become more focused. In some cases, they might even be willing to help you make arrangements for transportation, accommodation and activities.

Guidebooks and other publications

Most world travelers use guidebooks, and of these Lonely Planet and Rough Guides are the best. (There are many other series, but they are directed at tourists.) There are also many excellent independent guides for specific destinations, including nations, cities, parks and other scenic attractions. Guidebooks can be found in most bookstores, but travel bookstores usually have the best selections. They also have the best maps. Rand McNally stores in the U.S. are well-stocked, and Stanfords, which is located in London near Covent Garden, is world-famous. Many sporting goods and camping equipment shops also sell travel guides.

Building a guidebook collection is one of the best ways to learn about the world. Country guides usually describe the histories, religions, cultures, political and economic systems, and geography and scenic attractions of their subject nations. Guides are as informative as encyclopedias, and they are certainly more entertaining.

It is a burden to carry all of the guidebooks that you might use during a multi-country trip. One option is to postpone buying a local guide until you arrive at a destination, although there is a risk that a specific guide that you would like to have might not be available. International book distribution is imperfect, and in a few cases guides are not available because the local governments do not like the writers' views. It is also a good idea to mail guides and brochures home when you leave countries, to cut your baggage weight. (Many travelers give their guides away, or sell them to bookstores.)

Other useful publications include travel magazines, nature and environmental magazines, and newspapers. Domestic papers publish travel information in the form of stories from foreign countries and in travel columns and weekly supplements. Foreign newspapers, as well as the *International Herald Tribune*, which is *the* paper for world travelers, also provide such news and information. In addition, many papers, both domestic and foreign, carry classified ads that list discount airfares which are available from local travel agents. (Some foreign magazines, such as *Time Out* in London, and *Paris Passion*, also contain these types of ads.)

Travel agents and transportation companies

You can also get information from travel agents, although you might have to search for an agent who has in-depth knowledge of the part(s) of the world in which you are interested. Travel agents are usually most helpful when you have a booking to make, so if you need to buy a ticket, or make some other arrangement, this is an excellent time to request other information. Airline and other transportation companies also provide information on the destinations that they serve, including accommodation choices and local transportation options and timetables.

Sources on the road

Your need for information will usually increase exponentially when you are on the road, as you seek to fill the hours and days of your trip with interesting activities. In general, you will find that the quantity and quality of travel information improves after you arrive at a destination. This is particularly the case with special interest guides and maps. An important implication of this is that having better information available may affect your plans, if you learn about more interesting things to do than you originally intended. This is a good reason to allow flexibility in your arrangements. It is also an excellent idea when you travel to collect guides and brochures on nearby destinations that you will not be able to visit, since you can use this information when you return home to plan later trips.

All of the information sources that were described above are available in foreign countries. Indeed, local tourism departments should have even greater abilities to assist you. Other new sources will also be available. U.S. consulates distribute information on local political conditions and health concerns, and you can also ask them if there are any expatriate associations in the area, such as American Clubs, since these organizations often arrange social engagements and in-country tours. In addition, two of the best sources of travel information in foreign countries are other travelers and local residents. If you are outgoing you will regularly meet other travelers, including expatriate workers, who have been where you are going and who can give you up-to-date advice and recommendations. Such people are often very well-informed, and they represent a huge storehouse of information. Their recommendations can lead you to wonderful places, and help you avoid horrible situations. However, you should consider what they have to say with a grain of salt, since they may have different interests than you. Fellow travelers and expats can also teach you about their home countries, and it is not uncommon to receive offers from them to visit their homes and requests to deliver messages or mail. (You should of course join the grapevine and pass on your own information.)

Lastly, local residents can usually answer any type of inquiry. They will know where and when festivals and other cultural performances are being held, and for travelers who are interested in nature they should be able to guide you to the habitats of wildlife species. They are actually one of the most important sources of information, since it would be a shame to visit a town or village and, for want of asking, miss an infrequent event that happened to coincide with your stay, or fail to observe a local endangered species. They can also be used for references to hotels and restaurants. However, having some friendly skepticism is often appropriate at such times, since they might direct you to friends' businesses rather than give you objective advice.

6. BUDGETING

The amount of money that you need for a world trip depends on where and how long you intend to travel, and what your style will be. Furthermore, the range of costs for different destinations and styles can be extremely wide. For example, if you stay in Europe for a month, visit major cities like London and Paris, get lodging in decent hotels (two or three stars), rent cars, take excursions and do a lot of shopping, you could easily spend $8,000 or more. This is roughly calculated as follows:

- Discount air fare - round trip New York to London	$1,000
and London to Paris	500
- Rental cars for ten days	500
- Other public transportation, incl. taxis, buses and trains	3,000
- Accommodation	1,500
- Food and entertainment	1,500
- Shopping	=====
	$8,000
Total:	

On the other hand, if you visit India for the same period of time as a low budget traveler, your total costs might be as follows:

	$1,200
- Discount air fare - round trip New York to New Delhi	100
- Public transportation around India, second class	150
- Accommodation	300
- Food and entertainment	50
- Shopping	=====
	$1,800
Total:	

The major cost of a journey to India is the airfare to reach the country. Once there, it can be incredibly inexpensive, which is an attribute it shares with many other lesser developed countries. A real budget traveler would not even pay this much. You could travel around India for years, assuming you could get the visas, for the cost of a good, but not deluxe, one month European break. (This is not as ridiculous as it might sound. Excepting the somewhat limited availability of modern conveniences, India is certainly comparable to Europe in terms of traveler interest. It is a large and diverse land, with extraordinary historic, cultural and scenic attractions. A proper tour of the country would take a minimum of a year.)

As this example shows, you do not need that much money to visit other countries. Most of the five billion people on the planet live on only small fractions of what Americans are used to, yet they have interesting and fulfilling lives. When you visit their countries, if you are willing to live the way they do - sleeping where they sleep, eating what they eat, and traveling the way they travel - your costs should be the same.

Budgeting review

Budgets are limits, in other words, the upper limits on the total amounts that you may spend for particular items. They are useful in planning, since they force you to calculate reasonable costs for different types of expenses, and in control, since if you follow them you will not exceed these costs. Travel budgeting involves researching the expenses that you will incur during your trip. This sounds simple, but in practice it can be quite difficult. After all, if you have never visited a destination, how do you know how much it will cost? Anyone can call up a travel agent and find the price of a flight to Paris or Sydney, but what about once you are there? How much are rooms and restaurants in *real money*? In addition, what are the hidden expenses that you have no way of expecting, but which can easily add up to large sums?

This chapter answers these questions. It provides information that you can use to calculate the total budget for your entire world trip.

(Many world travelers do not use budgets. They raise as much money as they can before they leave, and then travel for as long as it lasts. This approach is fine, if you have the discipline to control your expenses. However, if you do not you will have a short trip, and you will almost certainly regret this at its end.)

At an extreme, you can plan your expenses using a method called zero-base budgeting. This technique is often used by companies, and it involves analyzing and budgeting for every single expense; for a business this would include everything down to the cost of paper clips. This level of detail, though, is unnecessary for world travelers. It should be sufficient to plan only for your largest expense categories. One approach you can use is to have separate budgets for basic and special travel expenses. Your total basic budget would be the sum of various essential expenses, including transportation, accommodation, food and normal tourist activities. These sub-budgets could be broken down further as appropriate, such as to establish separate limits for air and land transportation. (It is also necessary to include in your basic budget any expenses that you must pay at home while you are away.) A well-planned basic budget should ensure that you return from your trip with your fundamental needs satisfied, and a good level of tourist activity accomplished. The special expense budget would cover non-essential activities. These would typically include participation sports, other major activities and excursions, splurges - where you *break* the budget and treat yourself to some luxury, large souvenirs, and expensive photography.

A simple method for checking your basic budget while you are traveling is to divide the total, net of airfare, into daily or weekly amounts. For instance, if your basic budget is $1,500 a month, this is equivalent to $50 per day. Rather than track all of your expenses by their different sub-budgets, you would only need to check the daily or weekly sums against the planned totals. You would then have to revisit the sub-budgets only if your spending had exceeded these totals, and you wanted to determine exactly why this had occurred.

Expense categories

The following sections discuss appropriate budgets for different types of expenses. The costs are in U.S. dollars and were accurate as of the summer of 1996. However, they will undoubtedly increase as time passes. Prices in lesser developed countries will rise as the nations become more developed and as their tourism increases. Indeed, in a few years the prices in South Asia will approach today's prices in Southeast Asia, which themselves are moving rapidly towards European levels. Inflation is also endemic around the world, although there is one consolation to this. Because the currencies of lesser developed countries often decline over time relative to western *hard* currencies, *real* price increases may only be slight. A guesthouse room in Kathmandu has not increased in price, even if it costs 160 rupees today and 200 rupees next year, if the dollar strengthens by 25% over the period. Of course, the dollar could also decline in value, particularly against other major currencies. If you travel during a period when it is weak, this will obviously reinforce your need to be budget conscious and thrifty.

You will also have to bargain well to get the prices that are listed for lesser developed countries.

Transportation

The cost of air travel is the major item in a transportation budget. With careful shopping, though, the maximum amount that an out and back traveler should have to spend is $1,200, since this should get you a round-trip ticket from any major city to virtually any destination, or $2,000, for a series of tickets encompassing most of the globe. However, you should increase these amounts if you intend to take side trips or scenic flights. In addition, if you plan to take many international flights you should budget for airport departure taxes. These are commonplace around the world, and they cost between $10 and $25 per flight.

The alternative to air transport is to travel overland. People with the time and inclination can circle the globe with a minimum of flights, or even none at all. This is certainly the best way to see the planet. For travelers who take only local public transport, daily expenses are often so low as to be insignificant. For example, in 1991 the ferry from Java to Bali cost a quarter. Even in Europe, $3 to $5 per day should suffice for local transport, particularly if you walk a lot. The only separately budgetable overland expenses would be for long bus, train and ferry rides. (I bought many tickets for long-distance transport during both of my trips, as well as passes for travel around Australia and New Zealand.) In many countries, one way intercity transportation by bus or train (second class) should cost less than $50, except for the most distant destinations. To further illustrate how inexpensive public transport can be, in India an unreserved second class rail ticket in 1994 cost $10 for travel from New Delhi in the north of the country to Trivandrum in the far south (on a straight-through train). This is a rail distance of approximately 2,000 miles. However, I would not want to spend days packed into an Indian unreserved second class car. Travelers who intend to spend a lot of time in cities may want to budget separately for taxis, particularly if they are avid fans of nightlife. Other people may want to budget for rental cars. The lowest rates that are available in the U.S. for economy rental cars are indicative of what you will have to spend in other countries.

Travel documents and insurance

Passports cost $65 if you apply in person, or $55 by mail. Visas usually cost from $10 to $30 per country for the nations that require them. An *International Driving Permit* costs $10. Travel insurance is a large expense; it ranges from $50 to $100 per month of travel.

Medical examination and vaccinations

A pre-trip medical exam will cost whatever your personal physician charges. You should expect the vaccinations for your world trip to cost at least $200.

Accommodation

Accommodation expenses vary widely by country. There are also large differences by season and for single versus multiple occupancy. In low seasons, you should be able to get discounts of from 20% to 50%, if not greater. For instance, I got a 68% discount in June 1991, which was early in the monsoon, at Tiger Tops Lodge in Nepal, although part of this was due to presenting myself as a freelance travel writer who would publicize the lodge. I was also one of only a handful of guests. One consequence of this was that I had my own elephant for wildlife safaris (with a *mahout*, or driver, of course), whereas during the high season they are shared by up to four guests. Multiple occupancy savings can also be dramatic. In many countries charges are per room, so if you share with another person you effectively get a 50% discount.

In Europe, air conditioned (AC) hotel rooms in the two to three star category range from about $60 to $100. Non-air conditioned (NAC) rooms should be at least 25% less. In London, a room without a private toilet at a B&B in the Earls Court area (non-rated to one star) costs from $30 to $50. Hotel rooms in other European cities can usually be found for about $50, although this increases to $60 to $70 in Scandinavia or when the dollar is weak. Prices are much lower in lesser developed countries, and significant differences also exist by region. In most of South Asia, including Nepal, India and Sri Lanka, a hotel room with a fan and private bathroom should cost from $4 to $6 per night. This will double with AC. Fan rooms in guesthouses on Malé, the capital island of the Maldives, however, are at least $15 per night. In Southeast Asia, including Thailand, Malaysia and Indonesia, basic NAC rooms are $5 to $10, and again double for AC, although the least expensive single in Singapore is about $30, and this is for a fan room with the toilet down the hall. Moving on, a basic room in Australia will run from $30 to $50 per night. New Zealand is slightly less expensive.

The accommodations that offer the lowest prices include guesthouses, hostels, backpackers inns and, in lesser developed countries, the inexpensive hotels that cater to locals. (The last are often horrible - small, filthy, hot and bug-infested.) In most locations the following prices would apply to dorm bunks, but in a few places they will get you private rooms. Hostels in Europe cost from $15 to $25 per night. In comparison, budget accommodations in Nepal can be found for $2 or less, particularly on the trekking routes. It is slightly higher, from $3 to $5 per night, in India and Sri Lanka. In Southeast Asia, excluding Singapore, budget accommodations rise to $4 to $8 per night. The difference between the two regions might seem insignificant, since they are both so inexpensive, but for world travelers the higher prices in the latter region will add up. In Australia and New Zealand, a bunk in a backpackers inn will cost from $10 to $15 per night.

Food

Food and beverage budgets should also vary by country. Other factors include the size of your appetite, the quality of restaurant that you intend to patronize, or if you will cook your own food, and your consumption of alcoholic beverages. Excluding cooking for yourself, food and beverage expenses in Europe can easily cost $20 per day. Even if you are on a low budget you will probably want to spend some time in pubs and bars, and the cost of pints of lager and glasses of wine quickly adds up. On the other hand, food in Asia can be incredibly inexpensive. Full meals at basic restaurants should only cost a few dollars, and even less from roadside stands. Beer is also cheap - a dollar or two for a large bottle. With discipline, a daily budget of from $5 to $10 is easily achievable. If you do not drink alcohol, have a small appetite, and live on fruit and local dishes, probably half of this is sufficient. Prices in Australia and New Zealand are higher than Asia, but most backpackers inns have kitchens that guests can use. However, even if you cook for yourself you should recognize that it is common to increase your consumption of beer and wine in these countries, if only to match the locals. Because of this, your food and beverage expenses will probably approach European levels.

Basic travel activities

This category covers expenses for standard tourist activities, such as museum entrance fees, day-long bus and boat tours, and tickets for spectator sports, the cinema and plays. High cost activities, such as participation sports and scenic flights, are not included. For Europe, a budget for sightseeing expenses could be $10 per day or less, if your idea of fun is sitting in cafes or going to pubs. However, if you are a fan of professional soccer, or cultural performances such as the ballet and opera, then you should expect to pay at least $15 per event. This would cover a ticket for a soccer stadium terrace (you might have to stand, but it is the best place to be because of the fan enthusiasm and singing), smaller performing companies, and even the lower priced seats at major cultural venues. On the other hand, orchestra seats for national opera and ballet companies can cost $100 or more.

Activity costs are much lower in Asia, and you should get by on from zero to only a few dollars per day. Lying on the beach, for example, is free. (Your costs will be higher if you visit national parks and go on wildlife safaris.) Australian and New Zealand expenses will be comparable to or slightly less than Europe. You should be aware, though, that both of these countries offer a wide range of more expensive activities that can be hard to pass up, such as naturalist tours, scuba diving, and even sky surfing and bungle jumping. Indeed, the last activity was invented in Queenstown, New Zealand, where it is still offered from a bridge that is two hundred and fifty feet high.

Other costs

This is a catch-all category for other routine expenses, including pharmaceuticals and toiletries, batteries and film, postcards and stamps, inexpensive souvenirs, telephone calls, newspapers and magazines, and cleaning bills. World travelers incur these expenses infrequently, so allowing for a dollar or two per day should be sufficient.

Sample trip budgets

The four most effective ways to reduce your expenses are to discipline your spending habits, take as few flights as possible, minimize drinking alcoholic beverages, and limit your splurges. In addition, your costs will soar if you are constantly on the move or if you do a lot of activities. One of the best ways to reduce your daily average expenses, therefore, is to settle somewhere inexpensive periodically and relax for a week or more. The following budgets should be achievable if you do these things. They are rough examples of daily and weekly budgets for the geographic regions just described. The room charges are for hostels in Europe and Australia (or cheap hotels if shared by two people), and hotels in Southeast Asia (single occupancy). The budgets exclude the costs of travel insurance, visas, vaccinations, expensive travel activities and large souvenirs, and are based on costs that were prevalent during a period when the dollar was weak in comparison to other major currencies. A significant strengthening of the dollar should reduce these amounts.

Europe

Local transportation	70
Room, six nights	150
Food and beverages	140
Tourism and other costs	105
	===
Total per week	$465
Total per day	$66

Southeast Asia

Local transportation	14
Room, NAC, six nights	42
Food and beverages	70
Tourism and other costs	21
	===
Total per week	$147
Total per day	$21

Australia

Local transportation	70
Room, six nights	90
Food and beverages	105
Tourism and other costs	70
	===
Total per week	$335
Total per day	$48

Special activities, splurges and major souvenirs

There are an incredible number of expensive pleasures available to financially-equipped travelers. For instance, a week of snow-skiing or scuba diving, including equipment rental and lift tickets or boat charges, may cost $500 or more. Because of this, your special expense budget should be based on what you can afford. However, even the lowest budget world travelers should try to have at least a few hundred dollars reserved for splurges. It is highly likely that you will become aware of once-in-a-lifetime activity and souvenir opportunities on your trip, and you will probably be loathe to pass them up.

Photography

The major variables affecting your photography budget are the quality of your camera, your choice of film (slide or print), and the duration of your trip. A Nikon outfit with a good telephoto lense will run from $2,000 to $3,000, while an automatic camera can cost less that $100. Slide film costs from $7 to $10 per thirty-six exposure roll, which is two to four times more expensive than print film. Developing and printing charges are also higher for slides, especially if you want enlargements. You should expect to use at least one roll of film per week during your trip, although in scenic environments, particularly if you are a keen photographer, it can be easy to shoot a couple of rolls per day.

Total trip budget

Most world travelers stay on the road for as long as their money lasts. This is easy to understand, since once you experience the freedom and enjoyment of this type of life you will probably want to keep going for as long as you can. For low budget travel, a total of from $10,000 to $15,000 should be sufficient for a year-long trip. Assuming a budget for airfare and travel insurance of $3,000, this leaves from $135 to $231 per week, or from $19 to $33 per day. Travelers must usually spend long periods of time in lesser developed countries to achieve this level of expense. For example, two English friends of mine traveled for seventeen months in 1991-92, through Asia, Australia, New Zealand, the U.S. and Canada. Their expenses for the entire period were only $12,000 per person. They were able to accomplish this by sharing room costs, enforcing each other's spending discipline, and allowing for only a few splurges. They also cooked their own meals and bought cars for transportation in Australia and New Zealand, and worked in New Zealand for almost three months picking apples. Their costs during the latter period were minimal.

My basic budget for extended travel is $2,000 a month, but I always beat it, even in Europe. My total budget is substantially higher, though, because of shopping and splurging.

The total expenses for my world trip were about $30,000. I traveled as inexpensively as possible for most of the trip; however, the total was probably double what it might have been because of the following costs: twenty-eight flights, when nine would have been sufficient; a new camera outfit and the cost of almost 4,000 slide photographs; expenses be damned visits to London and Stockholm; twenty-one elephant safaris; twenty-six scuba dives; a handful of gourmet meals; two months out on the town in Bangkok and Singapore; and souvenir gold and diamond rings, sapphires, turquoise, silks, tailored clothing, tapestries and wood carvings. (The total for my 1994 trip was about $25,000, which included thirty-one flights.)

Budget worksheet

You can use the following worksheet to plan your own trip expenses:

Basic Budget

- Transportation

    - Airplane tickets
    - Airport departure taxes
    - Public intercity transportation
    - Taxis
    - Rental cars
    - Local public transportation

- Documents and insurance

    - Passport
    - Visas
    - Travel insurance

- Medical

    - Examination
    - Vaccinations
    - Pharmaceuticals
    - Toiletries

- Accommodation

    - Resorts and hotels (include service charges)
    - Budget accommodations

- Food and beverages

    - Own cooking (cost of ingredients)
    - Restaurants (include tips)
    - Alcoholic beverages

- Basic travel activities

    - Day tours
    - Entrance fees and tickets

- Other expenses

    - Newspapers, magazines and books
    - Mail, shipping and telephone charges
    - Cleaning bills
    - Batteries and film
    - Inexpensive souvenirs
    - Expenses at home

Total basic budget

- Total amount
- Per week *
- Per day *

* Net of air transport, travel documents and insurance, up-front medical expenses and expenses at home.

Special budget

- Participation sports
- Scenic and in-country flights
- Other splurges
- Camera equipment
- Major souvenirs

Total budget

7. TRIP FUNDING AND FOREIGN EMPLOYMENT

The standard method of funding a world trip is to save for it, and this should suffice for most people. However, there are a few other options as well, such as to sell your house or car! This is only partly a jest - a Swiss friend of mine sold his racing motorcycle to help fund a trip. As another example, I worked with a New Zealand woman who was a *serious* traveler. Whenever she stopped she would buy a small apartment by taking out a mortgage for as close to 100% of the purchase price as possible. She would then get a job for a year or two as a temporary secretary, work overtime whenever possible, and save as much money as she could. She would sell her apartment at the end of this period, and reap the small amount of principal she had repaid and hopefully some inflationary gains as well. Then, it was off around the world again. (She actually began her third major trip while I was still living in London.)

Unless you can get money from someone, or come into an inheritance, you will probably have to save for a number of years. Arranging a world trip is a long-term commitment, paralleling the commitment that you should have to make the most of your life.

The other source of funding is short-term employment while you are on the road. For example, I worked as a bartender, waiter, dishwasher, busboy, cook, bookkeeper, laborer and ski shop salesperson when I traveled around the U.S. after college.

Temporary employment

As a proviso to this section, if you intend to fund a world trip by periodically finding employment, it may be appropriate to reconsider this. Travel jobs often require hard work and long hours, and the wages are usually low. As many people have pointed out to me, it is almost always easier to increase your funds by working for a longer period of time at home, before you start a trip, than it is to make money along the way.

Temporary jobs can of course provide other benefits, one of which is that they are an excellent way to meet people. If you decide that you do want to work on the road, you will probably want a job where you work intensively and make money as rapidly as possible. (A month or two of hard work in Australia or New Zealand can provide enough funds for three or more months of budget travel in Asia.) Some jobs can also fund you in ways other than by paying a wage. Indeed, it is often easier to barter your efforts for goods or services - hostel guests regularly get free accommodation in return for cleaning up or making beds. The best ways to find temporary jobs are to inquire at potential employers, to ask other travelers for ideas, and to check the ads in local newspapers. For the last, newspapers and magazines that are published in resort towns, or which are directed at budget travelers (there are a number of these in Australia), often have extensive listings of available short-term employment. Finally, it is essential to get paid, since there are a lot of sleazy employers out there who take advantage of travelers. You should not work for more than a few days before receiving your first payment.

Teaching English

A common job for world travelers is to teach English, and many Peace Corps volunteers do this as well. To find a teaching job you should inquire at schools, advertise in newspapers, put up signs, or just pass the word among the locals that your talents are available. This is a worthwhile activity even if you are not paid. An American friend of mine, who traveled overland from Guatemala to Brazil, spent two weeks teaching English for free in rain forest villages in southern Columbia. She had many wonderful experiences, so her efforts were certainly not without compensation. Teaching English is also an excellent way to improve your local language skills.

Resort employment

If you have ever been employed by a resort in the U.S., it is a small step to working for one in another country. For instance, many Americans teach skiing during the winter at resorts in the European Alps. Others work there in lodges, shops, restaurants and bars. As another example, when I was in Portillo, Chile, some years ago, most of the ski school staff there were from the Sugarbush ski area in Vermont. Indeed, it is common for activity staff at resorts in lesser developed countries to come from Europe, the U.S. or Canada.

If you want a resort job in another country, all you have to do is apply. In most cases, of course, you should apply in-person. Your potential employer will want to meet you, and you will probably want to see the resort before accepting a position. However, it is not always necessary to apply on-site. For example, I met a Norwegian woman who was a scuba diving instructor at Kanifinolhu Resort in the Maldives. She had already been a qualified instructor in Norway, and had sent letters to fifteen resorts in the Maldives before departing from home to travel through Asia. The resort contacted her parents and paid for her to fly down from Nepal, where she was at the time, for an interview. You should not expect to be this lucky, though. You will probably have to pay your own way. The off-season is the best time to apply for resort work. Many employees quit at this time, and it is when new staff are hired and trained.

Farm and ranch work

From an Israeli *kibbutz* or *moshav* to a New Zealand sheep ranch or fruit orchard, farm and ranch work is a regular employment choice for many world travelers. This type of job usually involves back-breaking work, and only low to moderate pay. However, it can also provide extraordinary experiences - I met one American woman who spent months working as a cook at an Australian outback cattle station. Farm and ranch work is seasonal, so if you are interested in it you will need to learn what times of year work is available. One way to find farm jobs is to ask at local government labor or unemployment offices. You can also inquire directly at the farms, or speak with other workers in local bars. Another option is to ask for advice at farm supply stores.

Fruit picking is a common temporary occupation for travelers in New Zealand. You should technically have both a government tax number and a work permit to be hired for this job, although only the former may be sufficient. (Foreign travelers can apply for a tax number without having a work permit.) Of course, if a farmer loses a picker or two during the harvest, and bad weather is forecast, he or she may employ you even if you do not have a tax number. As I mentioned earlier, two English friends of mine picked apples in New Zealand. They worked in early 1992 at orchards in Motueka, which is located on the northern tip of the South Island. They initially used a fake tax number (one number was sufficient for both of them), which was simply a friend's legitimate number with a few digits changed. However, this is not a viable tactic if you plan to work for the entire season. They then applied for a number in the nearby town of Nelson, and got one free that day. Whenever they were asked for their work permits, they would say they had left them at their accommodation. Foreigners can apply for work permits in New Zealand, but at the time they cost about NZD 150 (USD 89). My friends did not let other orchard workers know that they did not have permits, since the country was in a recession at the time and some of the locals were unhappy about the presence of foreign workers. They could have been deported if they were caught.

They lived at the farm in a rented caravan, which had its own kitchen and cost NZD 87 (USD 52) per week. There were also worker cottages, which cost only NZD 10 per week, but these were already filled. They were picking apples by 7:30 a.m. each day, and usually worked six days a week, although they put in one stretch of nineteen straight days. The orchards ranged from densely fruited bushes to larger trees, and ladders were required for the latter. They filled large plastic sacks that hung around their necks, and emptied the contents into 4X4X3 foot bins.

Apples are picked by variety. High quality varieties, such as Braeburn and Royal Gala, are called *selects*, and these are carefully picked by color and size. My friends, between the two of them, were able to pick three bins of selects per day. They earned NZD 35 (USD 21) per bin pre-tax, and the tax rate was 15% for casual workers. Other varieties, such as Cox Pippen and Golden Delicious, are called *strips*, and can be picked much faster. They managed 7 bins of these per day, and earned NZD 25 (USD 15) pre-tax for each. However, these rates were dropped by NZD 5 if too many apples in a bin were badly bruised, since they could only be used for juice and processed foods. For the season my friends made about NZD 6,000 (USD 3,600) after-tax. While this is not that much money, it did enable them to finish their trip.

Fishing industry employment and yacht crewing

It is also common for travelers to find temporary employment on the high seas, since it is relatively simple to go to a port city or fishing village and hunt for a job. Employment is regularly available on fishing boats and in fish processing plants. Fishing jobs are often seasonal as well. For instance, scallop and other commercial fishing on the northwest coast of Australia usually starts in March. You might also be able to get a job before this by helping to refurbish a boat for the coming season.

One of the most adventurous ways to travel is to crew on an ocean-going yacht. However, it is not always that demanding, since calling in at beautiful ports, having your food and liquor paid for, and throwing outrageous boat parties, are all part of a sailor's life. Yachts travel around the oceans and seas following the weather patterns, and it is not too difficult to find a boat to crew on if you visit a gathering point prior to a seasonal migration. You should ask at marinas and frequent local bars. Being easy going, and having some sailing experience and a limited susceptibility to seasickness, will help. An excellent book on the subject is *The Hitch-hikers Guide to the Oceans, Crewing Around the World*, by Alison Muir Bennett and Claire Davis (Adlard Coles, London). I have a bit of crewing experience, from when I helped an Englishman sail a forty-six foot Beneteau yacht from New York to Florida. We left in late November, which is certainly not the best time to be in the North Atlantic. We had to endure two Force 9 storms, and during one of them a rogue wave knocked the boat over and its mast hit the water. We spent some time in the Intercoastal Waterway after each of these storms, and had wild boat parties to celebrate our survival.

Temporary secretarial work

While it is a bit more mundane, you can look for temporary office work if you are good at word processing. The wages, though, can be excellent. As mentioned earlier, many travelers from Australia and New Zealand replenish their funds doing temp work in London. They do not have problems with work visas because they are citizens of British Commonwealth countries. Many cities around the world regularly have dire shortages of qualified secretaries, and you can ask for job references at local temp agencies even if you do not have a work visa. They might be able to help you get a visa, or find you a job where the wages are paid under the table.

Other temporary employment

Other mainstays of travel employment include construction work, and service work in shops, bars and restaurants. The simplest way to get these jobs is to apply on-site. Another good option is to work for a travel agency or tour company. As a world traveler, you are, after all, an expert. Lastly, if you use your ingenuity you may become aware of more unusual ways to earn money. For example, I met an American woman in Chitwan who was being paid to collect samples of different fungi by a scientist in the U.S. This individual planned to culture the fungi and evaluate it for medical applications. The woman had special Department of Agriculture bags to take the material through customs, and it was interesting to see some of the things that she had collected - one fungus grew on decaying rhinoceros manure!

Travel careers

Once you do a world trip it is not unlikely that you will want to restructure your life so that you can continue to travel extensively or even live abroad. Indeed, this is the next stage in your development as a global citizen. You may want to pursue a career that requires travel, which includes jobs where you live at home but regularly visit foreign countries, and positions where you are based abroad. Another option is to have a job that gives you a substantial amount of free time. For instance, teachers can travel during student holidays, and they can also arrange foreign sabbaticals for teaching assignments or to conduct research. In addition, you should have the freedom to travel extensively if you are self-employed. Independent professionals, such as doctors, dentists, lawyers and consultants, are often able to schedule one or more lengthy trips per year.

The most obvious example of a travel career is to be part of the travel industry itself, such as an airline pilot, flight attendant, travel agent, or cruise ship or resort worker. Other careers that typically involve extensive international travel or foreign postings include:

- Diplomacy
- Scientific and other research
- Peace Corps and other aid associations
- Armed forces
- Shipping and merchant marines
- Other international businesses
- International banking and stockbroking
- Other business services, such as consulting and advertising
- Journalism
- Performing arts, film-making and professional sports, both as a participant and as a member of accompanying staff

A few additional comments are as follows:

- You will have to take the State Department's Foreign Service Exam to become a professional diplomat. However, this is an extraordinarily challenging test of general knowledge - can you distinguish between the Doric, Ionic and Corinthian classical Greek architectural orders? The exam is definitely worth a try, but good luck. (Notwithstanding your performance on the exam, your chances of being accepted should be better if you have strong foreign language skills.)
- If you want to work abroad, you should take a résumé with you when you travel and do some networking after you arrive. It will also help if you research your target job market beforehand. The consulates and trade associations of other countries, such as those which are located in New York City, are excellent places to start. For

example, and as I said before, I decided to move to Sweden after taking a vacation there. I then visited the Swedish Church in Manhattan to inquire about language courses, and happened to meet a trade diplomat. He was impressed by my interest in his country, and introduced me to potential employers. I arranged a second trip for interviews, and this paid off with a job offer from Citicorp.
- A friend of mine has one of the best careers of all for travel, which is international auditing. He does not have a fixed address, and instead travels from one month-long assignment to the next. At the time I wrote this, he was in the Africa, Middle East and Eastern Europe unit of his firm, and his last five assignments had been in Pakistan, the Czech Republic, Zambia, Poland and Côte d'Ivoire. In addition, all of his expenses are paid, so he is able to save his entire salary.
- Finally, you should recognize that the world is a homogenous place. People everywhere demand the same goods and services. If you have a skill, whatever it is, you should be able to make it pay in almost any country. If you are a doctor, nurse, cook, farmer, mechanic, carpenter, accountant or qualified member of any other trade or profession, you should be able to find employment virtually anywhere in the world.

Work and residence visas

You may obtain legal residence and the right to employment in another country by marrying a local citizen or by successfully applying for a work and residence visa. (Illegal employment is simply where you work without having this visa.) Getting a work visa is usually associated with an ongoing career, where you are assigned to a position in another country. If this happens to you, welcome to the world of expatriate workers. This is obviously different from the temporary employment that pleasure travelers typically seek. However, it is worth a note for people who are offered this option, and for travelers who decide that they want to work abroad.

In the business world foreign postings are usually offered to managers and executives, and to people who have degrees in international business, particularly if they are fluent in other languages. All is not lost if you do not possess these attributes, but it will not hurt if you start to develop them, especially the language skill. Even this, however, is not always necessary. I did not speak Swedish when I interviewed for a job in Stockholm, although I did have the MBA. The basic rule for getting a job in another location, wherever it might be, is to go there and find one. It is almost impossible to arrange a foreign position from home. You have to travel to the country for interviews, on your own expense if necessary, to have any chance of success.

You need to have a sponsoring employer for a work and residence visa. Indeed, in some countries, such as England, it is the employer that files the application. In others, such as Sweden, you must get a letter from your prospective employer stating the terms of their offer to you. You then submit this letter with the visa application. The letter should contain two types of information. The first is a description of the position, including its title, responsibilities and salary level. The second, which is more important as far as approval of the visa is concerned, is a statement justifying why you are the best person for the job. It is essential to give reasons why it cannot be filled by a local citizen. You should be imaginative and comprehensive when presenting these reasons. Fortunately, the national immigration offices of most countries will generally not refuse local employers permission to hire skilled foreigners.

You can sometimes increase your chances of having a visa approved by using a local visa consultant. For instance, I received an offer from a small English investment company after I left Citicorp. (I ultimately declined the offer.) I contacted a specialist consulting firm, staffed with former government officials, who assured me that with their assistance I would receive prompt approval of my visa for this new position. They did, however, quote a not insubstantial fee of 750 GBP, which was equivalent to $1,350 at the time. Your employer should pay this fee. In you use a visa consultant, though, you should only deal with an individual or firm that has a good record of success. If you have any doubts about this, you should ask for references from other clients who have actually received their visas. You might also negotiate to pay the majority of the consultant's fee only on success.

Employment contracts

If you accept a career position in a foreign country, your service will almost certainly be the subject of an employment contract. Such contracts usually contain a wide variety of terms and conditions, and it is also common for them, at least in the business world, to provide a number of benefits that are not regularly offered at home, except for the highest executive positions. You should not be shy about what you request. Indeed, I renegotiated my move from Stockholm to London at the last moment when I became concerned about the housing costs there. This enabled me to obtain a substantial housing allowance. Contractual benefits and perks that you should consider trying to negotiate for are as follows:

- Moving expenses.
- An up-front bonus. A small bonus is often given to help a new employee pay the incidental costs associated with his or her relocation.
- Guaranteed bonuses and other compensation arrangements, such as stock options and profit participations.
- An allowance for, and assistance in arranging, local housing.
- Language tutors or schools for yourself and your spouse, and enrollment for your children at a special international school.
- Private health care.
- A company car.
- Low interest loans.
- Life insurance.
- Tax relief. One approach to tax relief is for the company to calculate the taxes on your income and benefits as if you resided in the U.S., and then give you the surplus of the total of your foreign and domestic tax payments over this amount.
- A reduced benefit would be tax preparation assistance, including for both your foreign and domestic filings.
- Club memberships.
- Extended vacations and paid flights home. For example, in Saudi Arabia expatriate workers get up to ten weeks vacation and two round-trip tickets home per year. For jobs in Europe you should only expect the legislated vacation periods, although they are at least four weeks for most countries.

The contract should also specify the circumstances under which you can lose your job, and the severance periods and payments that will be due to you if this occurs. This is particularly important for an expat, since your visa will probably become invalid in these circumstances. If you lose your job you will want to have as much contractual protection and employer assistance as you can get. You should obviously expect more if you are laid off than if you are fired for cause. A year or more of severance pay is not uncommon if you are laid off from an international posting. The company should also pay for employment counseling, to help you in your search for a new job in the foreign country, or the costs of moving you home.

8. PREPARATION

"*Be Prepared*"

- The Boy Scout Motto

The final steps to prepare for your trip are to obtain travel documents and insurance, and to decide on your gear.

Travel documents and insurance

Your passport is your basic travel document. (Individuals with dual nationality have two!) It is sufficient for travel to many countries, although for others you will need a visa and perhaps a special permit as well. Other travel documents include the following:

- *International Certificate of Vaccination.*
- *International Driving Permit.*
- Travel insurance policy.
- Airline tickets. (See the Arrangements chapter.)
- *International Student Identity Card*, which is available from the Council on International Education Exchange, 205 E. 42nd Street, New York, NY, 10017, (212) 822-2600. In London you can get an ISIC from STA Travel.
- Membership in the international youth hostel association. You can get a hostel card from American Youth Hostels: AYH, P.O. Box 37613, Washington, D.C., 20013; or 891 Amsterdam Avenue, New York, NY, 10025, (212) 932-2300.

Passport

If you do not have a passport, you should apply for one today.

U.S. passports are valid for ten years, although for an active traveler they usually start to fall apart after a few years of wear and tear. It is okay to tape them when this happens. Indeed, having a well-worn passport, with a multitude of stamps, should get you a measure of respect from immigration and customs officials. This will minimize your hassles, since they will usually just wave you through.

Passports come with either twenty-four or forty-eight pages. You should request the longer version. You can also get additional pages inserted at any U.S. consulate.

You should have plenty of blank pages when you begin your world trip. In addition, it is a good idea to buy a leather passport cover, which can be purchased at better quality department stores and leather goods shops. This will protect the document, and it also converts it to a wallet which you can use to store important papers.

There are a few countries for which you should avoid having their stamps entered into your passport. This was formerly the case with South Africa, since if you had one of their stamps you would have been refused entry by many other African countries. This will still happen with some Islamic nations if you have a stamp from Israel. In addition, travelers who have Taiwan stamps have been known to have problems with China and its allies. You can request a stamped insert when you visit such a country. This is stapled into your passport when you arrive and then removed on departure. (I got my Israeli stamps.) In addition, a similar issue might exist if you visit one of the countries where U.S. citizens are generally prohibited from traveling, including Cuba, Iraq, Lebanon, Libya and North Korea at the time of this book's publication. You could have a problem with U.S. officials when you return home, since you need either (or both, for Iraq and Libya) State Department permission or a Treasury Department license to make a legal visit to these countries. Information on the latter is available from the Licensing Division, Office of Foreign Assets Control, Department of the Treasury, 1500 Pennsylvania Avenue, NW, Washington, D.C., 20220, (202) 622-2480.

Lost or stolen passport

You can replace a lost or stolen passport at any U.S. consulate. You will need identification that (1) proves you are who you say you are, and (2) that you are a citizen. At least one of these forms of ID must contain your photo. If you do not have ID, it should expedite matters if you obtain a police report for the loss (this will serve as temporary ID while the passport is being replaced), know your passport number and its place and date of issue, or have a photocopy of the signature page. It may take many days to get a new passport if you do not have this information, since you might need to have ID delivered from home. In addition, you may need to contact the local immigration office after you receive your new passport, since it will not contain a visa or entry stamp.

Visas

The State Department publication *Foreign Entry Requirements* describes the entry requirements for Americans for all sovereign nations and their possessions around the world. (These are summarized in the Appendix.) It is available from passport agencies and the Consumer Information Center, Pueblo, Colorado, (719) 948-3334. You can also check on visa requirements, and request applications, by telephoning the Washington D.C. or New York City consulates of the countries that you would like to visit. Visas must usually be entered in your passport before you arrive. You can apply for them in person or by mail, and you should allow at least a couple of weeks for the latter. You will need to send the consulate your passport, the completed application, at least one photograph, and the visa fee. You should also use certified or registered mail, or an independent courier, to ensure the safety of your passport.

Travelers usually apply for tourist visas. Other options are transit visas, which are typically issued on arrival and which are only valid for a few days, and work and residence visas, which were discussed earlier. However, some countries, such as Saudi Arabia, do not issue tourist visas at all. You can only enter them with visitors visas, if you have friends or relatives who live there, or business visas, which require local companies as sponsors. For example, the only way to visit Bhutan inexpensively is to be invited by a Bhutanese citizen, but good luck meeting one outside the country. You can also try concocting a story if you are having problems getting a visa. One way to do this is to *borrow* the stationery of a business, and then draft a letter where you identify yourself as its representative and present a persuasive rationale for why you should be admitted. (You might also need to have a business card printed.) In addition, if you are applying for a visa at a consulate that is extremely bureaucratic, or which is demanding a high fee, you may want to wait until you find a more reasonable consulate for the same nation. For instance, Sweden is a great place to get visas for many lesser developed countries, because of the general ease of the process and since the fees are usually quite low. (Sweden enjoys this advantage because of its traditional good relations with these nations.) Lastly, in some countries you might need to get an exit visa when you want to depart. This was formerly the case with Warsaw Pact nations, particularly for long-term visitors, and the requirement may still be in place in a few countries in Africa.

Tourist visas have two dates. The first is the date by which you must enter the country, and the second defines how long you can stay once you have arrived. (The existence of the first date is the reason why, on my world trip, I waited until I got to Thailand before I applied for an Australian visa.)

You should generally request visas that let you stay as long as possible. (The maximum stay for most countries is usually either three or six months.) It is also a good idea to get visas that allow multiple entries. This means you can enter and leave the country more than once while the visa is still valid. The usual alternative to a multiple-entry visa is single-entry, although double-entry visas are offered by some countries, such as Nepal. Double and multiple-entry visas may cost more. Visas can also sometimes be extended or renewed, although this can be expensive. You should therefore plan your trip carefully, since it would be unfortunate to have to pay for a new visa to stay in a country an extra day or two. An alternative in this type of situation is to overstay your visa, although you will probably have to pay a fine. (There could be more severe penalties!) For example, the visa overstay fine in Thailand is 100 bhat per day (about $4), and there is a desk at the Bangkok airport where you can pay it. (I met a Korean traveler who overstayed his Thai visa by six months! He turned himself in and spent four days in jail as a penalty, and he can never return.) Many people actually live and work there without having residence visas, but they leave periodically to apply for new tourist visas. Penang Island across the border in Malaysia is a common destination for this.

Some visas also specify the airport, port or border crossing which must be used to enter or leave the country. In addition, a few countries that restrict tourism, such as Bhutan and Laos, only let travelers apply for visas through specific travel agents. In other cases, such as trips to Tibet that originate in Nepal, you will have to take a group tour.

Special permits

Some countries have regions that are closed to pleasure travelers, but you may be able to visit them by applying for special permits. This is a routine application in a few cases, such as for permits for the standard trekking routes in Nepal. However, they are usually difficult to obtain, particularly for parks where access is limited to scientific researchers, and for unsettled regions. (People who receive special permits are often required to register with the police at each location that they visit.)

When you apply for a visa you should inquire if a special permit will be necessary for any portion of your itinerary. If you have trouble getting one, probably your best option is to find a sponsor and submit an application or proposal to the government. For instance, you can get permission to visit a local Maldivian island - one that does not have a resort - if you are sponsored by a friend who is from the island. (It is easy to meet locals on the capital island of Malé.) You can submit a proposal without a sponsor, of course, but good luck! During my world trip I tried, and failed, to get a reduced price visa for Bhutan and a business visa for Laos, even though in both cases I used every connection and approach that I could think of. (Restrictions had been relaxed when I visited Laos in 1994, but I still haven't made it to Bhutan.)

Proposals for special permits should generally include the following information:

- A description of who you are, and of your sponsor if you have one.
- A summary of your project, including its objectives.
- What the benefits of your visit will be for the country.
- Your proposed plans and itinerary.
- What support you will need in-country, such as for guides and porters.
- A discussion of your preliminary budget.

You should attach any references that you are able to obtain from VIPs, or else have them send separate letters and make telephone calls supporting and checking up on your application. You should also request an interview with a senior consular officer, and try to get his or her support. In addition, it is generally wise to ask for wide-ranging permissions (ask for as long a stay as possible), although the shopping list approach does run the risk of receiving a blanket refusal.

If you get the permit you should ensure that the central approval authority communicates with officials at your final destination(s), so they expect your arrival. Then, when you show up, you might try to lie about the extent of your permission and act as if you have more.

My greatest success story in getting a special permit occurred in Burma in September 1994. Earlier in the year maximum length tourist visas were increased from two to four weeks, and there seemed to be some momentum to open up the country. (SLORC had started having discussions with Aung San Suu Kyi, the democratic leader and Nobel Peace Prize winner who at the time had been under house arrest for over five years.) I was fortunate to stay in a small hotel in Rangoon which was owned by the father of a senior tourism official. I decided to request permission to visit the top of the country, where an old map showed the existence of a wildlife sanctuary. (It subsequently proved to have been deforested.) I said I was a travel photographer specializing in parks, which was fitting because the organization of a tourist promotional year - *Visit Myanmar 1996*, was just getting under way. I said

I would support this project. (Like hell!) However, after a week of meetings - I did not even have time to visit the huge, gold covered Shwedagon Pagoda, I still lacked Ministry of Intelligence permission. (This is the local equivalent of the CIA.) I had approval from the Ministry of Tourism, the Travels and Tours Office and the Ministry of Defense, but not Intelligence. I decided: this was requiring too much effort, particularly considering the nature of the regime, and changed my flight out of Burma to the next day. Then, that morning, Intelligence came through. (I found out later that the father of my chief liaison, a woman in Travels and Tours, was a Colonel of Intelligence.) In any case, accompanied by a guide (I was required to have one, but like most Burmese he was an excellent fellow), and after arrival in the north by police, immigration and intelligence escorts (who we soon learned how to avoid), it was an extraordinary trip.

In rare circumstances you might be able to get a special permit by surreptitious means. For example, during my world trip I met a trekking couple in Pokhara, Nepal (the man was from New Zealand and the woman from Canada), who got permits on the black market for the recently opened trekking region of Dolpo. (This area was the subject of Peter Matthiewson's book, *The Snow Leopard*.) The primary benefit of getting permits this way was that they did not have to fulfill the normal application requirement, now eliminated, of presenting currency exchange receipts showing that they had legally changed a specified amount of money. At the time, trekkers had to have exchange receipts for $10 for each day of their permit applications. By not having to show the receipts, they could convert their money on the black market at a 15%-20% premium above the official rate (now much less).

A second benefit of getting permits this way was that they did not need to change that much money, because they did not plan on spending $10 a day in Dolpo. I actually met them after they finished the trek, and they told me that a budget of $3 per day proved sufficient. (They cooked their own meals.) If they had gotten the permits legally and then only spent this amount, they would not have been able to reconvert all of the daily $7 surplus into a hard currency, since in Nepal you can only reconvert up to 15% of the total of your exchange receipts. Having extra rupees would typically not be a problem, because there are so many interesting souvenirs to buy there. However, they were on an extremely low budget and did not want to be forced to buy souvenirs or otherwise spend excess rupees.

There was also an interesting epilogue to this story. When they were trekking they went outside the area for which their permits were valid. (Quite a pair!) They ended up about a two weeks' walk from their nearest allowable location, at which point they were questioned by a village policeman. They pleaded that they were lost, and the officer let them go without even paying a fine. They were instructed to get back to where they belonged ASAP! This type of behavior is rarely a good idea, of course, since it can turn nations against travelers, and because of the severe penalties that may be incurred.

How does one get a special permit through *unofficial channels*? Immigration and other officials are unlikely to accept a direct approach, so you will probably have to find someone who knows an official, such as a local businessperson, and ask him or her to arrange it. You should be extremely careful if you ever try this, and it is worth remembering that you may have to give up your passport to get the permit stamp. You might not get it back!

If you simply cannot get a permit, it might be worth trying to visit the closed area anyway. Take overland transport to its perimeter and see if they will let you in. Local officials may not have heard of the restriction, or they may not care, particularly if they see it as an imposition from a central bureaucracy. There are few areas in the world today that do not welcome travelers and the economic contribution that they bring.

As an example of just how aggressive you can be, consider this story about an Italian engineer who was hired to help the project management of a Soviet steel plant in the mid-1980s, which was a frigid period in the Cold War. Unfortunately, he was not met on arrival at the Moscow airport, either by plant officials or the KGB. He did not have a travel pass or permit, or rubles - only dollars, deutsche marks and lira. He did not even know where the plant was, just its name - something like the "*Kirski Project.*" Paying foreign exchange, he took a taxi to the train station, where an english-speaking local told him that Kirski was seven hundred kilometers away. The station would not sell him a ticket, though, so he bribed this man to buy him one - in third class. He actually made it to Kirski, but there was no Project there. Another local then said that it was in a restricted zone, an additional one hundred and forty kilometers away. He tried to get another taxi: for $50 it was no, but yes for $100. Finally, when he arrived, the plant officials were extremely upset. He was not really there, since he was not properly checked in! Heads rolled, at the plant and in the KGB, but not his since he was critical to the project. (This is an illustration of travel with a will, by a person who won't take no for an answer.)

Fraudulent documents

The use of fraudulent documents is common, but it is certainly not recommended since the penalties can be severe. I have actually met two people who spent time in jail because of this. The first was a German traveler who had a forged visa for Canada in his passport. He served six months there on a one year sentence before being deported. (He was a real nut - a skinhead with a swastika tattooed on his forehead.) The second was a Maldivian travel agent who was suspected of helping a group of Chinese refugees obtain false Japanese passports with Belgian visas. They had arrived in the Maldives, and he arranged their onward flight to Brussels. However, they were refused entry there and sent back. The travel agent was then held for questioning for five days, and when he was released the police told him the forged passports had probably come from Bangkok. I have also seen documents forged once, when I watched two travelers change their visa expiration dates from the 11th of the month to the 21st. They used the same color ink as on the visas, and then roughened the changes to obscure them.

Illegal entries and departures

Some travelers who are unable to get permission to visit countries, regions, parks or monuments, or to climb mountains, decide to go anyway - illegally. The classic example of this was Sir Richard Burton, who in the nineteenth century disguised himself as a Muslim and made the *Haj*, or pilgrimage, to Mecca. This was a truly serious undertaking, since the presence of an infidel (non-believer) in Mecca is punishable by death. Illegal entries are actually quite common. The usual motivations are economic, to find jobs, or political, to escape repression and conflict, and such people often intend to become permanent residents. A perfect example of them are the many illegal immigrants to the U.S. However, this type of motivation is rare among travelers, who usually make illegal entries for the thrill of them. For instance, many people have entered Burma from its border with northern Thailand. Indeed, I met two English travelers who made friends with some Burmese rebels who were hiding in Thailand, and then accompanied them on a trip into the country. Their wildest experience was when they were in a rebel village that was shelled by government forces. People also regularly cross remote borders into Tibet, and I met four people who actually rode their motorcycles there. They did not have Chinese visas, but somehow managed to talk their way through the immigration checkpoint at the Nepalese border. (Some people!) They were less lucky at an army barrier further down the road. Rather than stop at the barrier, they just rode around it and continued on their merry way. They were pulled over some miles later by a jeepful of unhappy soldiers, and were interrogated for hours before being thrown out of the country. They were also very fortunate not to have had their motorcycles and luggage confiscated.

You should consider your appearance if you are thinking of making an illegal entry, since you are sure to be stopped on a regular basis if you do not look like a local. In my own case, I have some Thai friends who regularly cross the Mekong River into Laos. During my world trip they invited me to join them, but I declined because I thought the risk was too great. Taking a local guide in such circumstances is advisable for many reasons. He or she can make the arrangements, steer you clear of difficulties, and help resolve any encounters with officials. If you try this, though, you should have a story ready for if you are caught (or a large bribe!).

The likely penalties for an illegal entry are also worth considering. As just mentioned you might be fired upon if you enter an area where unrest is present. (A German traveler was shot and killed when he was caught entering Jordan illegally in the summer of 1992.) You could also be sentenced to jail, and you might be imprisoned for years if they think you are a spy or a mercenary. (Three Swedes and two Brits were each sentenced to seven years in prison in Iraq during the summer and autumn of 1992, after they purportedly strayed over the Kuwait border. They were later released, but only after spending months in jail. The same sequence of events also occurred with two Americans in early 1995.) Confinement would certainly include interrogations, and the attendant possibility of beatings and torture. Other penalties for illegal entries include fines and the confiscation of your belongings. At a minimum, you would be deported.

In rare circumstances, travelers get caught inside countries that close their borders because of civil emergencies. If this happens to you, your only option may be to cross the border illegally. (This happened en masse after Iraq invaded Kuwait.) In addition, you would obviously want to depart from a country illegally if you had entered it this way, since not having an entry stamp in your passport could lead to awkward questions at the border.

Vaccination certificate

You should keep a record of your vaccinations in an International Certificate of Vaccination. This booklet is provided by the traveler health clinics that give the inoculations, and it may be requested by immigration health authorities when you arrive in new countries. Yellow fever is the only vaccination that is regularly required, and then only for specific countries. You may be asked for evidence of a yellow fever vaccination when you visit a country where it is endemic, or when you travel to another country after having recently been in such an area. In addition, if you visit a country where an epidemic of some other disease is in progress, you might be asked for proof of vaccination against it if such a vaccine exists. You could be refused entry if you have not had a required vaccination, be put in quarantine for the incubation period of the disease (six days for yellow fever) or be forced to get the vaccination at the border, possibly under questionable hygienic circumstances. Health officials may exempt some travelers from having vaccinations, such as children under one year of age, and people who have letters from their physicians stating that there are medical grounds for their not having them. "*No vaccinations are required to return to the United States.*" (*Health Information for International Travel 1995*, Centers for Disease Control, page 11)

Some countries now make entry for travelers contingent on proof that they are not HIV positive. This typically applies only to long-term travelers, such as students, and individuals who are making applications for permanent residency. The results of AIDS tests that have been conducted in the U.S. are not always acceptable. Information on which countries require AIDS tests is given in *Foreign Entry Requirements*.

International driving permit

Many countries require visitors who want to drive to have International Driving Permits. There is also an *Inter-American Driving Permit*, which is recognized by most countries in Central and South America. However, in these regions only Brazil does not accept the former as well. You should also take your driver's license with you, since this is required in some countries. Driving permits may be obtained in person or by mail from American Automobile Association offices. The AAA can also tell you which countries require them. The permits are valid for one year and are non-renewable. If you will be away from home for more than a year, you should take along an extra application and send it back when you need a new permit.

Travel insurance

All world travelers should have health and accident insurance. American Express and many of the major domestic insurance companies offer such policies. (Amex will provide travel insurance for trips of up to one year.) Another option, if you are passing through the U.K., is the Lloyds of London coverage that is offered by the travel agency Trailfinders. I used this for my world trip; it was valid for citizens of any country. It was also available for any number of months and could be extended, as I did from Thailand, with a phone call and credit card. Coverage provided by the policy included, among other things:

- Medical and related expenses, including emergency air evacuation, surgery, hospitalization and expenses for repatriation home, including the costs of an accompanying friend or family member. A 24-hour medical emergency help-line was available.
- Personal accident insurance, with benefits paid out in case of death, loss of sight, etc.
- Loss of prepayments from trip cancellation or curtailment.
- Expenses arising from delayed departures.
- Loss or damage of personal money, tickets, baggage and personal effects. (This type of coverage may also be provided by homeowners and credit card insurance plans.)
- Certain legal expenses. A 24-hour legal help-line was available.

You should also check that your policy does not exclude any activities, particularly sports, that you intend to pursue. In addition, if you do require medical care while traveling, you should request an itemized bill that lists all of the different treatments and services that you receive. This will simplify the insurance reimbursement process.

Baggage insurance is worth a further note. If you travel with expensive equipment, such as a sophisticated camera, you may have to get special coverage for it in order to receive a reasonable reimbursement if it is stolen. Increasing your coverage under your house or apartment insurance is one option. The process of making a claim for stolen or damaged baggage can also be quite complicated, and you could easily end up receiving only a fraction of the value of your lost goods even if you thought they were fully covered. You need to understand the general nature of an insurance policy, and the claims process of your particular provider, if you want to get full restitution. The important issues regarding these are as follows:

- What belongings are covered, and to what amounts and/or percentages of value? This will usually be described, including any limits thereon, in the policy's fine print.
- How do you prove their value? This is a crucial issue. It is not enough to have a policy for $1,000 to receive this amount if you are robbed of an expensive camera. You will also need to prove that the camera is worth this much. (It is worth noting that insurance companies are in the business of *not* paying you money.) You should have your purchase receipt, but even then your policy may apply a value depreciation formula that reduces the amount you receive based on the period of time since the item was acquired. It is irrelevant that you will have to pay the full price to replace the camera. Because of this, you should try to get a policy that reimburses purchase prices or replacement values. You should also make sure that you have the receipts that you will need to prove values before you travel and put your belongings at risk.
- Is there a policy deductible, some amount off the top that will not be reimbursed?
- How do you file a claim, and how is the theft or damaged proved? The first is usually a simple process of filling out a form. For the second, a police report is necessary if the belongings were stolen, and it should contain an itemized list of everything that was taken.
- Lastly, do not hold your breath while waiting for the check.

To give you an example of how frustrating filing insurance claims can be, subsequent to my world trip I lost most of my camera gear and a few other items while staying with friends in London. Their house was ransacked while we were out having dinner. I had mistakenly assumed that their home, which was in a nice neighborhood, was safe.

I filed claims under:

1. My homeowners policy.
2. My Amex travel insurance policy. (I had shifted to them for this trip.)
3. The Amex Purchase Protection Plan, for a pair of sunglasses I had purchased with the card within the preceding three months.
4. My friend's U.K. homeowners policy.

The order of the list is important. When there are multiple insurers for a loss they are stacked in order of obligation. Each subsequent insurer will not act until it learns the outcome of the prior claims. (This really slows down the process.)

1. For this claim I received a decent and timely settlement. (Thank you Allstate.) The deductible was small and the depreciation that was applied to the camera gear was less than I expected.
2. I hoped the travel insurance would pay the balance of my loss, since this amount was well within the policy's theft limit. Amex, however, applied draconian depreciation and only paid about half.
3. Fortunately, the Purchase Protection Plan paid for the sunglasses, filling in some of the gap, although they initially refused the claim completely because I did not have a proper (to them) police report. In the case of theft, U.K. police departments will only provide a file reference number and a confirming letter, not an official report listing stolen belongings. I argued the point with Amex, and got the claim reopened by the adjustors.
4. Lastly, my friend's homeowners policy, which had a clause providing for payment of up to GBP 250 for losses suffered by house guests, paid GBP 180.

In the end I was about even, although it took a hellish six months to get there.

Travel gear - what to take with you on your trip

The luggage, clothing and other gear that you take on your world trip should be based on the weather that you are likely to encounter and your planned activities and individual preferences. For example, if you intend to go trekking you will need good boots, warm clothing and a sleeping bag. As another example, if you plan to spend a lot of time in cities, and many nights out on the town, you may want to take an extensive wardrobe.

It is great to travel with jeans and a few t-shirts and nothing else. It is just you and the road, which goes on forever. Traveling this way gives you a taste of absolute freedom - I did it for years and it was fantastic. However, there is an alternative to the travel light philosophy. The two standard views are to take as little as possible or to take anything and everything that you want. If you are a sports person and a proponent of the latter view, you should take your skis, tennis racquet, golf clubs, bicycle, scuba diving gear, surfboard, windsurfer, paraglider, hang glider or kayak. If you are a *bon vivant* you should pack a tuxedo. Why not? You will certainly enjoy your trip more if you have these things. For instance, one of my preferences is to travel with a bottle of cognac or whisky and a box of cigars, since it is a superb experience to have a good drink and smoke in the evening at an exotic location.

The only real limit on how much you can take is how much you can carry, unless you are willing to be dependent on porters. You can also avoid carrying specialized gear by arranging for it to be shipped to the destination where you will need it. In addition, you can always find someplace to store excess gear. Locations that typically have such facilities include airports and train and bus stations. Any hotel or guesthouse that you stay at should also be willing to hold a bag. Before leaving your gear with them, however, you should confirm that access to the storage room is limited to the hotel staff and, in general, you should only leave your bags in places that you trust completely. For example, I met a French traveler who had valuables stolen from a locked bag that he left in the storage room at Transit Center Backpackers, Townsville, Australia. Access to this room was supposed to be limited to the reception staff and, frankly, they did not seem to care that he had been robbed. It is quite possible that one of the staff was the thief. I often needed to find somewhere to leave my gear during my world trip, and this was always possible. I actually left a bag at Ned Kelly's Guesthouse in Kathmandu for ten weeks, at a cost of 1 rupee (2.5 cents) per day, although I did so only after learning that another person had left a bag there for seven months when he went to travel through India. This was a good enough reference for me. (Sadly, Ned Kelly's is now gone.)

During your trip you will probably accumulate souvenirs, clothing, guidebooks and maps, and broken but repairable gear, until you reach the point where you can no longer carry it all. When this happens you should ship a box home. Other options are to throw or give away what you no longer need or want. (Many people give gear to their guides and porters at the end of their stays in lesser developed countries. It is a standard tip in these types of circumstances.)

Deciding on your gear is most challenging when you will visit many different environments. For instance, both of my trips took me to cities, mountainous regions and island resorts, so I needed dressy clothing, warm clothing and lots of specialized gear, not to mention my camera, lenses and notebook computer. It was really difficult to keep the weight down, and on each trip I shipped a parcel home soon after starting, full of items that were too heavy or bulky to justify having now that I actually had to carry them.

Gear commentary

Your sources of gear include what you already own, what you buy before your departure, and what you buy or rent along the way. It is best to start light, although if you take everything you need this should reduce the temptation to shop. You should of course take any gear that will be unavailable or expensive in the countries that you plan to visit. If you take valuable equipment, you should bring copies of the purchase receipts and warranty information.

Another tip is to limit the clothing that you take. One of the joys of world travel is to shop for clothes that are made with local fabrics and designs. They are often inexpensive, and they may be more functional in the local environments. (You can also show them off when you return home.) You should, however, bring any clothing that you will need for special activities. You should also take clothing that complies with local standards, such as the standards of dress for when you meet officials or attend religious ceremonies. In Asia, this means having a dress shirt or blouse and a pair of pants or long skirt. You should not take military style or camouflaged clothing to a country where there is civil conflict, and you should limit the amount of clothing that you take that requires dry cleaning. You should also limit your electrical gear, since it will not work unless you have an international outlet plug and voltage converter. As a final point, you should not take anything that you could not bear to lose, including jewelry, fine watches, other luxury items and personal mementos.

Before my world trip I purchased a new backpack, trekking boots, a gore-tex rain suit, a water filter, camera equipment and a valuables purse. For my second trip I got a new daypack and boots. I bought most of my clothing when I was traveling. I also rented down sleeping bags in Nepal on both trips for trekking. Sports equipment is often available for rent, so you do not always need to take it. However, I took my own scuba gear on the world trip, because I trust it and since my life depends on it.

Luggage and packing

World travelers generally take three pieces of luggage: a main bag, a day bag and a valuables purse. Your main bag should have a large capacity, provide easy access to its contents, and be designed to be carried for long distances - preferably leaving your hands free. The standard option is a backpack, and a model that has a subdivided internal compartment, rather than one large cavity, is better for organizing your gear.

A pack should also have at least one sizeable external pocket, the means to tie on additional gear, and a well-designed and padded suspension system. I used a scuba diving bag for my world trip, because of its massive size and ease of access. I also found that I could carry it long distances by using its shoulder strap, or even by putting it on my head like an Asian porter. On my second trip I used a backpack, since I did not plan on doing a lot of diving.

Suitable day bags include small backpacks, camera bags and purses. (You can wear a small pack across your chest when walking long distances.) For my day bag I use a pack that just meets airline size limitations for carry-on luggage (a total linear dimension of forty-five inches). I also carry all of my heavy gear and books in it on flying days, to stay within the weight limit for checked-in luggage. Options for a valuables purse include a money belt, a neck pouch that fits inside your shirt, or a waist pack or shoulder pouch. I used a shoulder pouch on my world trip, but eliminated it on the second because my new daypack had an internal zippered mesh pocket for valuables.

Your main bag should be lockable, and all outside pockets should have double metal zippers, so they can be secured with small padlocks. (I heard of one traveler who designed the ultimate in theftproof luggage. He welded a metal cage that fit inside his backpack, complete with a hinged and padlocked cover. It also had a chain, so the whole assembly could be locked to something immovable.) Your bag should also be water resistant, and you can further protect your gear, and keep it better organized, by storing everything in plastic bags and nylon stuff sacks. (When you are packing, the basic rule is to position your gear for when you will need it.) In addition, you should leave some room for souvenirs, or else buy an extra bag along the way. One way to make room is to repackage your gear - get rid of any boxes and other packaging material, and carry everything in stuff sacks or reusable plastic containers. Both of these are available from camping equipment stores.

Gear checklists

The following are gear checklists that you can use to plan your own trip requirements. Medical kit and toiletry checklists are included in the Staying Healthy chapter.

Clothing

- Walking shorts
- Beach shorts
- Swimsuit
- Underwear
- Long underwear
- T-shirts
- Jeans
- Dress pants or skirt
- Dress shirt or blouse
- Sarongs
- Belt
- Socks or hosiery
- Sweater
- Rain jacket and pants
- Ski suit
- Parka
- Sun hat
- Wool hat and scarf
- Gloves or mittens
- Bandannas or handkerchiefs

Footwear

- Flip-flops or sandals
- Dress shoes
- Athletic shoes
- Trekking boots
- Climbing boots
- Spare shoelaces
- Gaiters
- Crampons

Additional clothing for visiting cities

- More dress pants, shirts and outfits
- Sports jackets
- Suits and ties
- Tuxedo or party dress
- Trench coat or overcoat

Sports and camping equipment

- Gear for participation sports
- Sleeping bag
- Sleeping sheet or light blanket
- Sleeping foam pad
- Hammock
- Mosquito net
- Binoculars
- Swimmer's goggles

Electronic equipment

- Camera equipment and film
- Flashlight
- Headlamp
- Spare bulb
- Radio/cassette or CD player
- Headphones and speakers
- Music tapes or CDs
- Language tapes

- Snorkel, mask and fins
- Frisbee
- Football or soccer ball and air pump
- Musical instrument
- Traveler's chess, checkers and backgammon set
- Playing cards
- Tent
- Ground cloth
- Segments of cord and webbing
- Climbing rope
- Seat harness
- Gear rack, including carabineers, chocks and slings
- Rock hammer or ice axe
- Helmet
- Stove and fuel bottle
- Nesting pots and pans, cutlery and scouring pad
- Food

Other gear

- Water bottles
- Cup
- Whisky flask or bota bag
- Individual cup filter holder, filters and coffee
- Bag of candy
- Towel
- Watch
- Swiss army knife
- Pen and spare ink cartridges
- Sunglasses
- Alarm clock
- Hair dryer or curling iron
- Calculator
- Notebook computer
- International outlet plug and voltage converter
- Spare batteries

Paper materials

- Guidebooks and maps
- Dictionaries and phrase books
- Star chart
- Novels
- Equipment manuals and warranties
- Personal journal
- Sketch pad
- Sheet music
- Photos and postcards from home
- Stationery and envelopes

Valuables purse

- Passport
- International driving permit
- Extra passport photos
- Travel insurance documents
- Scuba diving logbook
- Your résumé and other documents
- Aspirin
- Tissues or toilet paper
- Jewelry
- Spare padlock keys

- Ski goggles
- Padlocks, keys and key chain
- Umbrella
- Matches and/or lighter
- Sewing kit and safety pins
- Scissors
- Compass
- Altimeter
- Vitamins and nutritional supplements
- Candles
- Incense
- Universal bath plug
- Clothes washing soap
- Tube of silicone lubricant
- Cellophane tape
- Packing tape and felt-tip marker
- Stuff sacks
- Plastic bags

Wallet

- Cash
- Credit cards
- Traveler's checks
- Bank account checks
- Driver's license
- Other licenses and certification cards, such as for pilots and scuba divers
- Blood donor card
- Currency exchange receipts
- Expense receipts
- Addresses and phone numbers of friends
- Business cards
- Receipts for expensive gear
- Gear warranties
- Shipping receipts

Passport cover

- A piece of paper with the following information:
    - Your home address and phone number
    - In case of emergency
        - Your blood type
        - Allergies and other medical conditions
        - Personal prescriptions
        - Name, address and phone number of the person to inform in an emergency
        - Name, address and phone number of your doctor
    - Travel insurance information
        - Company name and address
        - Emergency telephone numbers
        - Policy number
    - Bank information
        - Bank name and address
        - Telephone number
        - Account numbers

- Credit cards
    - Addresses for bill payment
    - Account numbers
    - Telephone numbers to report lost cards
- Plane and other tickets
- Receipts for traveler's checks
- Special permits
- Letters of introduction
- Receipts for safe deposit facilities

9. PSYCHOLOGY

Being a world traveler has profound psychological implications. You can expect to gain many benefits, such as increased self-assurance, but you should also be prepared to deal, regularly, with challenging and stressful situations.

(A few of the points from the beginning of the book, where I talked extensively about the issues of identity and personal growth, are reexamined here.)

Psychological rewards of travel

Travel can strengthen your body, mind and spirit. Many people understand this, and it is one of the main reasons why we take vacations. Annual vacations, though, with some guilt for leaving your job thrown in as extra baggage, are only a temporary analgesic. You cannot resolve the big issues in your life during a week at Disney World or Club Med.

People accumulate so much information during their lives. We meet so many other people, watch so much television and advertisements, and read so many books, magazines and newspapers. We have a tremendous number of experiences and think a phenomenal number of thoughts. Unfortunately, all of this information and all of these ideas can easily grow into a larger and larger jumbled pile. Rather than reach a greater understanding, many people end up more confused. You have to wonder, is it possible to sort out your ideas and make some sense of yourself and the world? The sad truth is that if you stay on the treadmill, busy and under stress, it is quite possible that you will not figure life out, or make peace with it, and that you will go to your grave this way. You will make more mistakes than necessary, miss out on a lot of what life has to offer, and even experience tragedy that could have been avoided.

No one says finding a purpose for or accomplishing change in your life is easy. It takes a vision and a lot of commitment, hard work and time. But where do you get the vision to decide what it is that you really want to do and what will make you most happy? For example, if you are just starting out you should recognize that most people get channeled into their careers. There are very, very few individuals who know at an early age what they want to do with their lives. Your frame of reference is too narrow. It takes years to find out what the opportunities are, and by then you are usually stuck. In today's specialist culture it is almost impossible to jump from one field to another.

This is why world travel is so beneficial. If you take a long trip and think about your life purposefully, you will eventually leave all of the mental baggage behind, escape from the influences that cloud your thinking, and be able to view your life objectively. Only then can you properly consider such issues as your past, your family and friends, your options for a career, and your other plans for the future.

It is also much easier to change if you let the passage of time be your ally. For instance, if you start jogging or lifting weights today, you will be strong in a year. If you begin studying French or Spanish, in one year you will be conversational and in two basically fluent. If you attend night school, you will have a degree in two to four years. The important thing to recognize is that time will pass, these future dates will arrive, and in the process you will have acquired these attributes. You will have changed, and for the better.

As an aside, I worked in New York City for seven years during the 1980s, and like many people there I was often under a tremendous amount of stress. I used to dream of getting as far away as possible, imagining that wherever it was it would have to be better. I had a world map on my office wall, and one day I started daydreaming about the children's story of tunneling through the earth and coming up in China. Where would I arrive if I started digging in Manhattan? After plotting the latitudes and longitudes, I determined that the opposite side of the planet was a point in the Indian Ocean off Perth, Western Australia. Well, I made it to Perth in early 1992, and it was better there! It is a lovely, temperate seaside city with beautiful beaches and relaxed, friendly people, sort of what Los Angeles was probably like in the 1950s.

I think this story demonstrates that there is always room for optimism, and no matter what your circumstances you can change your life if you set your mind to it.

One approach that you can use to understand yourself better is to recall, systematically, different events from your life, including your best and worst experiences. It is also an excellent idea to write your memories down in a journal, as well as your thoughts about them. A few ways to review your life include by year, by structural periods, such as the changing of residences or schools, and by events, such as participation in different activities. Some possible subjects that you might want to begin with are as follows:

- The best thing that ever happened to you
- Your greatest achievement or win
- Other major accomplishments and strengths
- All long-distance or international travel
- First fight won
- First kiss
- First love
- First sex
- Best romantic experiences
- All the people you have loved
- Old friends you have not seen for years
- All moments of bliss and exaltation

- The worst thing that ever happened to you
- Your greatest fear
- Worst failures and weaknesses
- First fight lost
- Worst romantic experiences
- All severe personal injuries and illnesses
- All relatives and good friends who have passed away
- All close encounters with death

In other words, you should remember many of the good things, and some of the bad, that have made your life interesting, enjoyable and unique. It is particularly beneficial to recall your childhood. For example, what is your earliest memory? Your ability at this should improve with practice, and long dormant pearls of experience will spring to mind. In addition to just reviewing your life, you should also question your memories. Why was something your greatest achievement or win, or one of your worst failures? Working your memory like this will increase the cohesiveness of your self-view, and it should have other positive effects as well such as improving your confidence.

A few other psychological rewards of travel are as follows:

- Travel is a wonderful experience for people who are lonely and, conversely, for people who are gregarious. If you are outgoing you will meet an incredibly wide variety of people during your trip, of different nationalities, races, ages, sexes and occupations. (If you are normally introverted you should force yourself to be outgoing - it should be easier in new environments.) Other travelers, for instance, are usually very friendly. One reason for this is that they are away from their normal circles, so they have room for new friends. In addition, in many of the situations where travelers meet there is little of the positional interference, such as background and employment, which obstructs the formation of friendships at home. One consequence of being sociable is that you will develop a worldwide network of friends. You should expect to collect many addresses and phone numbers, and to be regularly asked for your own.

- Travel is a challenge to yourself to remain young. Modern lifestyles take a severe toll on our bodies, and also on our mental health. Career pressure, workaholism and constant competition in all areas of life have had an impact that includes premature grey hair, weight gain, cardiovascular illness and mental strain, in short, premature aging. Taking a mid-life break can be an excellent way to combat and even reverse these trends. In this way, world travel may actually be the proverbial fountain of youth. It is worth noting that almost all long-term travelers, of any age, are in good shape and, furthermore, that youth is synonymous with flexibility - and not just being able to touch your toes, either. Your mind also becomes inflexible as you age, and things which when you were young you would have done without hesitation, later on seem impossible or unacceptable for someone of your age.
- Lastly, and perhaps most importantly, travel is an excellent medium for furthering your spiritual goals. Many of the great religious leaders of history, including Jesus Christ, the Lord Buddha and the Prophet Mohammed, traveled as part of their paths to personal enlightenment, or to preach their teachings. A world trip gives you the time, and also the motivation, to think about the serious issues of life. It provides an ideal environment for a quest for answers to the fundamental philosophical questions, such as the nature of universal and human existence, good and evil, and life and death. Everyone can benefit spiritually from contact with other peoples, from being exposed to the wide range of human experience and belief. Indeed, when you visit lesser developed countries you will probably see instances of extreme hardship, and even tragedy, as well as hope, struggle and joy. It is difficult not to think about the deeper meanings of life after witnessing such events.

Psychological demands of travel

Most people are uncertain about what to expect when they visit new countries, and a few are actually predisposed to expect the worst. Because of this, travelers commonly have a wide variety of fears. However, many people have fears that are out of proportion, or even completely inappropriate, when compared to the real risks of foreign travel. After all, millions of people travel every day without having any problems. Another consequence of dealing with new environments is that it often leads to great amounts of stress. Finally, a combined effect of the fears and the stress is that many people do not enjoy their trips as much as they should.

Understanding the psychological challenges that you will be faced with when you travel will enable you to enjoy yourself more. You should have few difficulties if you are prepared, no matter how exotic the environment. Indeed, there is little reason to worry. The world is a friendly place. Relax, and enjoy it. Even with the difficulties that do exist, many people find that once they start traveling they want to do it more and more. They become more skilled as their experience increases, and they quickly learn how to deal with new situations.

Travel fears

Most travelers share similar fears, including the possibilities of falling ill or being in an accident, or of being robbed or the victim of a terrorist incident. Practical advice on how to avoid health problems and accidents, as well as theft, terrorism and other risks, is given in the Staying Healthy and Risk Prevention chapters. You can gain a proper understanding of travel risks by reading these chapters, and this should help you eliminate unwarranted fears.

Many people also share a general fear or insecurity about dealing with the residents of other countries. This is one of the main reasons why package tours are so popular. A guide, westernized to an extent where he or she is not threatening, provides a layer of insulation from the locals. This is a fear that you should work hard to overcome, and a broad discussion of the relevant issues is given in the chapters on Cultural Understanding and Cultural Negatives. However, this is not a subject that you can learn solely from a book. Your skill and comfort in dealing with people from other cultures is dependent on your experience. There is no substitute for this familiarity, especially in difficult situations, such as those involving beggars, street hustlers and corrupt officials.

I have learned to surmount all of these fears, and others as well. For example, my greatest fear on my world trip was that I would not make it all the way around, that something would force me to return home. To guard against this I tried to be conservative in all potentially dangerous situations, and to keep the goal of a successful circumnavigation foremost in my mind.

Appropriate expectations

A critical step in your psychological preparation is to develop an accurate set of expectations about the countries that you intend to visit. You should be ready for the wide range of experiences, both good and bad, but particularly the bad, that you might have. For instance, I prepared myself to be disappointed when I visited the Taj Mahal. My expectations were extremely high (everyone has seen the photos), and

I did not know how the monument could live up to them. Fortunately, I was wrong in this belief, and I soon learned that no photo can do it justice. Its incredible beauty and serenity can only be fully appreciated in person. I was enthralled.

As this suggests, one of the most fundamental aspects of expectations relates to your senses. The first difference that you will notice on arrival in a new location is its *feel*, or the combined effect of its climate, sounds, smells and other sensory inputs.

I visited Agra, the town where the Taj Mahal is located, on an Indian Tourist Development Corporation day-long bus tour from New Delhi. The bus was virtually empty, but it did have three women passengers from Dallas. (They were the only American women travelers that I met in India during my world trip.) They were completing a five week tour of northern India that had been sponsored and paid for by the Rotary Club. They had been wined and dined by government administrators, judges and businesspeople, and had had one of the best possible introductions to the country. However, all they wanted to do, once they realized they had a willing American ear, was complain. They were upset because they had regularly been harassed by men, and because of the poor sanitary conditions and the bland (to them) diet. It was obvious that when they arrived they had not had a clue about what to expect, and that they had not dealt with their circumstances as well as one might have hoped. (The most severe problem, sexual harassment, is a common concern for female travelers in India, but many women do find ways to minimize it.) I was sympathetic, but after listening to this for hours I felt obliged to redirect the conversation. We were, after all, on a bus to the most beautiful building in the world. Surely they would acknowledge that there were some positive aspects about travel in India.

(If you visit the Taj Mahal the best time to do it is in the early morning, before the tourist line forms. This rules out a single day Delhi-Agra bus tour, at least in the high season.)

Advance knowledge about a destination should enable you to bypass its worst problems, and to react appropriately when they are unavoidable. But how can you know what to expect, if you have never visited it? For a start, a tremendous amount of information is publicly available for all but the most obscure countries. This includes information from the media, such as stories in newspapers and on television, as well as from government tourism departments, travel magazines and guidebooks. You should be aware, though, that these sources are often misleading. News organizations are trying to sell their stories, and tourism departments and private publicists are trying to sell their countries. Bad news sells, so media portraits may be unduly negative, while the tourism information will have a positive bias. Unfortunately, even with this information you will still rarely be able to develop a proper understanding of what a new country is really like, arriving at the airport and then dealing, day-by-day, with transportation, hotels, restaurants and activities. You can never know for certain what the local conditions will be until you get there.

To begin creating some appropriate expectations, you might consider the question of how dangerous world travel can be. Well, you could die on your trip. However, since this can of course also happen at home it is not an issue unless the risk is greater in other countries. Except for the most adventurous travelers, such as people who visit war zones, this risk is no higher abroad than at home. It is extremely unlikely that you would become involved in any type of survival situation. You may hear of such events, though, since in the rare circumstances when they do occur, stories and rumors spread rapidly through the press and traveler circles.

Conditions obviously vary by country, and your expectations should reflect this. For example, Western European countries are in many ways similar to the U.S. There may be differences in language, architecture and attitudes, but they are still modern nations. Education, transportation and health care are all at parity with the U.S. On the other hand, lesser developed countries will present greater objective hazards and challenges to your fortitude. In addition to the horrible toilets, you may witness social problems that either do not exist, or which are rarely in sight, at home. Poverty, destitution and despair are pervasive in some countries. The streets may be populated by cripples and beggars, and you might pass the corpses of dead animals or even people. Of course, if you do end up somewhere this unpleasant, you should always remember - it could be worse - it could be raining. Ha!, and if it is raining, oh well, at least you are at rock bottom.

The changing concepts of responsibility and time

In the U.S., we sometimes differentiate people as having either Type A or Type B personalities. This describes how driven and intent a person is, and a workaholic with a quick temper would be a Type A. In lesser developed countries people are often so relaxed that they would hardly qualify as U.S. Type B. One reflection of this is in a person's sense of responsibility. In many of these countries if you ask people to do things for you, and they say they will, unless it involves giving them money they will immediately forget their commitment. Indeed, they will often fail to do things even when they are to receive payments. Because of this, you should not automatically expect a high standard of responsibility from other people when you are traveling. In addition, the longer you are on the road the more your perception of time will change. You might be able to tell at home, without looking at your watch, what the time is to within a few minutes. After traveling for a while, however, you may be lucky to know the month. One day tends to flow into the next, and weeks just pass by. This happens because you are out of touch with the events that are typically used to note the passage of time. Weekends become irrelevant, and you are unaware of other signposts such as the beginnings of professional sports seasons. Normal separators are replaced by others that are specific to travelers. Once a week you might have to take a malaria pill, or every few weeks you might call home or mail postcards. Perhaps you will even mark time by how often you cut your hair or fingernails. If you are in the tropics, you will not even have a sense of the seasons passing. Your friends at home will be going to the beach, and then seemingly within days, to holiday dinners. All of this will pass you by, and if you do consider it, it will probably seem extremely remote.

Dealing with the exotic

As a traveler, you will regularly encounter environments that are exotic in comparison to your normal frame of reference. Many things will appear strange and wonderful, because they are so different from home. You should condition yourself to openly accept new environments. Indeed, on a world trip you will continually confront the unknown. In making these adjustments, it is worth remembering that to the locals their homes and lifestyles are as ordinary as canned food. To them, the converse holds true. It is you and the U.S. that are exotic.

One characteristic that can be hard to deal with is the view of personal space that exists in much of the world. In general, and on local transportation in particular, many people obviously require very little of it! This is something that you should try to accept, since you certainly cannot change it, although it might be difficult in a van packed with smelly, sweaty people. It is best to be tolerant and to take the local view, which is that there is always room for one more. Of course, you do have a right to some space, and you should demand this. This is especially the case if you have paid more for a ticket than the locals. (In many countries the last few locals that pack onto vehicles travel free.)

Foreign environments can be even more challenging when you are on your own. In some places you might feel like the lead character from the old television show *Kung Fu*: a lone traveler coming into a new town, greeted sometimes with friendship but often with suspicion. Another consequence of continuous exposure to the unfamiliar is that a dose of the ordinary can be quite refreshing. It can be very beneficial to seek out contact with other people, and news and culture, from home.

Being the center of attention

Travelers attract attention in many places. Characteristics such as stature, skin color, clothing and language will make you stand out. You may hardly get a second glance throughout Europe or in Australia or New Zealand, but in much of the rest of the world you will be the subject of great curiosity. This usually increases the farther you get from normal tourist destinations. In some countries, such as India, you will have to get used to rubberneckers. You may feel like you are under a microscope, and you will learn what it is like to be a beautiful woman or a celebrity - looked at by everyone. This type of attention can be difficult to endure. (It definitely helps to be an exhibitionist!) However, you should try not to take offense. In some environments your presence will be a very unusual event. In such places, locals often shout or laugh at western travelers. They might not know how to respond to your presence, especially if they catch your eye, so they will shout hello, or ask you where are you from, or laugh. (This last response is almost always out of embarrassment, not to be rude.) Fortunately, your surprise value will wear off if you stay in a community for a few days. People will get used to you, even the children, and you will fit in like everyone else.

In the worst places there are so many people that someone will always be looking at you, no matter where you are. Privacy is at a premium. Indeed, it is a concept that the people from these countries barely understand, at least from a western point of view. Many of them have been raised in, actually, they probably still occupy, single room dwellings where multiple generations, of up to ten people or more, eat, sleep, make love, fight and die together! You might find yourself, in such an environment, hiding in your hotel room to escape the attention.

It takes a lot of energy to be a world traveler. You can't withdraw into yourself. You have to interact!

Travel stress

There are a multitude of potential sources of stress for world travelers. It often develops on arrival in new locations; when making arrangements; from relationships with other people; when spending money, particularly in expensive areas; when participating in risky activities; and even from leaving behind, if only temporarily, your normal life. With so many sources of stress, you need to manage your trip carefully or you can be overwhelmed. As you push the limits of your experience, you should take confidence from the fact that skilled travelers are able to go anywhere, and do anything, without undue stress.

Symptoms of stress include obsessions with planning, order and cleanliness. More severe symptoms include a quick temper, pessimism, guilt, and even paranoia and depression. To fight stress when traveling, you should consider how you deal with it at home. The creation of routines is the single greatest tool that people use to eliminate stress from their normal lives. What works at home will also work on the road, so you should follow carefully planned routines, particularly in the most stressful situations.

Feelings of stress usually subside after you come to grips with a new environment and eliminate unwarranted expectations. It is very helpful to take things slowly for the first few days after your arrival. Giving yourself extra time also reduces the stress of specific situations, such as when you are catching transportation. Finally, if you cannot get over the stress of a particular environment, you should leave and go somewhere else that you find more relaxing.

Psychological attributes and behavioral responses

Most of the psychological attributes that you need to manage your life at home are of course also useful when visiting other countries. In addition, since it is easy to deal with good experiences, the most important attributes are those that get you through difficult situations.

How you are treated in another country depends on how you behave; if you are easygoing you should receive a better reception and have a more enjoyable time. As this suggests, the most important attributes for world travelers are patience and tolerance. These characteristics are necessary in many situations, such as when dealing with the inevitable transportation delays and with misunderstandings with travel partners and people from other cultures. It would help if we would learn to be more content with what we have and not always demand more. For instance, the joys of travel should easily exceed any material shortcomings. A cheap hotel in India is exactly that, but a trip exploring this fascinating land is sure to yield pleasures that will outweigh any such inconveniences. After time the cheap hotel will be forgotten, or even fondly recalled. Related characteristics, such as maintaining your sense of humor and having perseverance and endurance, are also important. They are particularly helpful when the going gets tough, such as during interminable bus and train rides and when you are exposed to climatic extremes, including freezing cold, scorching heat and torrential rain. In any case, whatever you encounter that you find trying, you should discipline yourself not to complain. After all, you do not want to be taken for a "*whinging POM*" (prisoner of Her Majesty), which is what the Aussies call the Brits, because they think they complain too much. It is better to be cheerful when the going is at its worst. Tell jokes or sing a song. This will make the circumstances easier to bear, and time will pass much more quickly.

The issue of pace has special applicability in endurance situations. If you are on a long and torturous bus ride, which you are told should last five hours, expect it to take eight. Then, when you reach seven hours, prepare your mind, and body, for ten. You should always keep a little strength, and tolerance, in reserve.

Unfortunately, being patient may not be enough in some circumstances. You may also have to use speed, ingenuity or charm. For example, if something goes wrong in your arrangements, such as if a bus breaks down and leaves you stranded, you should quickly evaluate the situation and be the first person to get the best option that is available. In addition, another way to get satisfaction is to be assertive. (This is not the same as complaining.) Patience and tolerance are admirable, but not when people are trying to take advantage of you. While difficult situations are almost always best dealt with in a calm and relaxed manner, if you travel at length through countries that have serious social problems, or where the governments are corrupt, this approach may not always work. There are also many countries, including the U.S., where having the confidence to raise your voice and stand your ground is valued if not praised. If you do not demand attention in these places, you will be ignored. A classic situation requiring assertiveness is where you have tickets or reservations for something, but the people in charge say that no space is available for you. Do not let them take advantage of you. Be firm and demand satisfaction, or go to their superiors and make some noise. It is worth remembering that the squeaking wheel usually does get the grease.

There is a fine line, though, between assertiveness and aggression. The former implies that you are still in control, but the latter means you have lost your temper. You should always avoid doing this, since your judgement will be impaired and you could easily make a bad situation worse. (You are most at risk of losing your temper when you are tired or when you have been drinking.) In my world travels, the worst I ever lost my temper was on a train in India. I was going to Bombay from New Delhi, and decided to take the best class available (first class air-conditioned sleeper) on the Rajdhani, or Raj, Express. Excluding special Maharaja-style tourist trains, this is probably the best train in the country. The local paper reported that the class was sold out for nine days, but the station master in New Delhi did me a favor and gave me a berth for the next day from a special quota. This was in July, at the height of the north Indian summer, and the temperature was 109 degrees Fahrenheit (43 degrees centigrade). I had about one hundred pounds of luggage, and made the mistake of not using a porter. The train was probably a quarter mile long, and I struggled up and down the platform looking for my car. Even though I was in Class 1A, no one from India Rail would give me any assistance. Finally, immensely agitated, soaked with sweat, and with the train about to leave, I managed to collar an official and get him to show me to my car. A notice taped on its side had my name assigned to the lower bunk in a two person compartment, but when I found my room I was indignant to see an obese man lying on the clean linen of my bunk (fat equals wealth in India) surrounded by three of his friends. Standing in the aisle, and being jostled by other passengers, I was ignored by all of them when I asked for some space to put my bags in the room. This was the absolute limit, and I blew my top. Rather than punch one of them, I hit the wall, and to my surprise my fist went right through it. This, and my bleeding hand, immediately got everyone's attention. An official soon arrived, and was kind enough to show me to another compartment, which was larger and for four passengers. The rest of the trip went fine, and I did not even have to pay for the damage. I was a bit ashamed about the hole, though, but my action certainly had an effect. I also have a small scar on my hand, which I glance at now when things go wrong as a reminder not to get too upset.

You should make full use of your self-discipline in potentially dangerous situations, and it is worth noting that this may be as simple as remembering to take your malaria pills. Discipline, however, can be hard to maintain when you travel for a long time, and many people become careless with hygiene or let their insurance lapse. Being wary will also help you avoid problem situations. A classic example of this occurs in mountainous areas. If you are tired, or the weather is changing for the worse, you should stop or turn around and return to somewhere safer. Accidents regularly occur in the mountains because people push themselves too far.

It is important to be prepared when severe dangers are present. One way to do this is to anticipate the worst thing that might happen, and then visualize in your mind how you would respond. This should stop you from *freezing* if it does occur. Visualization practice is particularly useful for planning your responses to situations that involve dangerous people.

If you do have a problem, you will just have to be resilient. If you are injured, you should have faith that your body will heal and be strong again. If you become involved in a survival situation, such as if you get lost in the mountains or are at sea on a boat that has a broken engine, you should try not to panic and you should never give up. Force yourself to think rationally, and then choose your best option and stick to it.

It is amazing what people can survive. When I was in Australia in January 1992, two cases of unbelievable endurance were reported in the press. In the first, an Australian hiker was lost in a snowstorm while trekking in Nepal. He ironically became lost after turning back. He was found alive on a cliff ledge forty-three days later, when his parka was spotted by a rescue helicopter. This was paid for by his sister, who had refused to give up hope that he was still alive. He survived by eating snow, and had lost almost seventy pounds. At about the same time, a boatload of illegal immigrants from China crashed on the remote northwest coast of Australia. They wandered for three weeks before one of them reached a cattle station. All of the remaining passengers were found alive after two weeks of air searches. They had survived by catching fish and young salt water crocodiles. Indeed, many Australians were shocked that they had not been taken by the infamous, man-eating *salties*.

On another level, as in life travel regularly involves dealing with disappointments. One way you can reduce your susceptibility to them is to adopt the Buddhist view that they are a consequence of having unsatisfied desires. By limiting the set of things that you desire to only the most important, for instance, by eliminating your need for luxury goods, you will reduce the number of circumstances in which you might be disappointed. Furthermore, one of the best ways to reduce your desires is to avoid the things that cause them: do not look at any advertisements, on TV or in glossy magazines. Other ways to minimize the impact of a disappointment include to find its silver lining, such as by using its effects to fuel your creativity and further your personal development; to resolve to be less disappointed if the same thing occurs again; and, if what happened was due to a personal mistake, to be determined not to make the same mistake again.

As a closing point on psychological attributes, world travelers must regularly make trade-offs between fun and adventure, and expense and danger. It is usually best to follow your heart, and not your mind, when considering these trade-offs. People who let their intellects dictate their decisions often live too much for the future, and postpone present happiness to this end. It is of course beneficial to have long-term goals, but many people, when they arrive after years of work at their planned for futures, find that they now have new sets of goals which must be accomplished before they can be content. This can become a vicious and never-ending cycle. You should be happier if you predominately follow your heart, and you will hopefully never reach the sad state where you wonder what happened to your life and why you did not achieve your dreams. For your travels, you should do what you *want* to do, not what you *think* you should do, when planning where to go and with whom to travel. You can generally limit following your mind to situations where you need to evaluate specific arrangements or dangers.

Issues for women travelers

The above issues apply equally to both men and women. One point, though, which is the harassment of women by men, deserves special comment. Women travelers are continually subjected to unwanted approaches by local men in many countries. Repeating what many people have told me, the worst areas for this sort of behavior include North Africa, Islamic nations in general, and India. However, almost all developing nations have this problem, because the women in these countries usually have inferior status and limited, if any, rights. You can even be harassed in Europe. Italian men are famous for it.

The following are a few stories from women travelers. They illustrate some of the more severe problems that you might have to face:

- A Swedish friend of mine was living in Saudi Arabia, where her husband worked with a construction firm. Like most expats there they lived in a segregated compound for foreigners. One day she was shopping in a *souk* (bazaar) with some other women from the compound. They were all wearing scarves to cover their hair, although this is not required for foreigners, and *abayas*, or neck to toe robes. While walking through the souk my friend stepped over something and revealed her ankle; she was not wearing a full length dress under the abaya, which is the standard attire. Unfortunately, a member of the Saudi religious police, the *Mutawwa*, saw this.

The Mutawwa approached the group and demanded to know which person had shown her ankle. My friend, at the rest of the women's urging, kept silent, since otherwise she would have been arrested. She also risked being assaulted. Just prior to this a New Zealand woman had been beaten after she was picked up on the street while waiting for her husband. She was accused of being a prostitute. An American woman had also recently been beaten, for sitting in the front seat of her car next to the driver. In Saudi Arabia, a woman cannot sit beside a man unless it is her husband or other family member.

The entire group were taken to Mutawwa headquarters, held in detention for some hours, and interrogated. Their IDs were taken, and they had to sign a paper admitting guilt to the breach of propriety before the documents were returned. (They demanded that this statement, in Arabic, first be translated into English.) They were also fingerprinted, the left hand only, since if you are convicted of theft there your right hand is cut off. Lastly, they were warned that if they were caught again they would be jailed. (Following this experience my friend did not leave the compound for three months. She is now safely back in Sweden.)

The rumor among the expats about the Mutawwa is that they hate westerners in general and western women in particular. They look for any reason to harass them. For example, if a woman is not wearing a scarf, they shout in her face, but only if her husband is not present: "*Cover your hair, woman!*" It is also said that some of them have been students in the west and failed, or have been rejected by western women, or have drunk alcohol. On their return home they have become reactionary, because of their resentment and guilt.

The following quote, further illustrating the plight of women in Saudi Arabia, is from *Princess*, by Jean P. Sasson (Bantam Books, appendix).

"*Why women are forbidden to testify in criminal proceedings.*

1. Women are much more emotional than men and will, as a result of their emotions, distort their testimony.
2. Women do not participate in public life, so they will not be capable of understanding what they observe.

3. Women are dominated completely by men, who by the grace of God are deemed superior; therefore, women will give testimony according to what the last man told them.
4. Women are forgetful, and their testimony cannot be considered reliable."

Wow! What can you say? Earth to Saudi Arabia: join the modern world.

- When I returned to India in 1994, I met a Danish woman who had had a problem in Kashmir. (Even with the danger some people still go there.) The men in a particular village would not let her go to the bathroom. They kept following her into the bushes. She finally had to ask a local woman to accompany her and keep guard.

- I also met an American woman in India on this later trip who had a few stories to tell. Men regularly grabbed her or rubbed up against her on buses. Her usual response was to announce, in a loud voice, exactly what had happened, to the chagrin and extreme embarrassment of the man. (Contrary to what you might expect, sexual harassment is a severe offense in India. You regularly read about cases of it in the press.)

She also had a very serious experience when a man tried to force his way into a shower to rape her. She managed to beat him off and lock the shower door. She then instituted a search for her assailant (she was in a village), and when some other men found him they beat him to a pulp! (In a postscript to this story that is completely at odds with Saudi ethics, the village men asked the woman's companion, another woman, if she could be trusted, before they exacted their punishment.)

Unfortunately, since fundamental change in the worst areas is unlikely to occur soon, these are the types of experiences with which women travelers to these areas may have to deal. Traveling with another woman or two will help, and this is exactly what many people do. You can also travel with a man, of course, if only as a friend. This may well be appropriate in the regions just mentioned. If you do travel with a man, in many countries the presumption will be that you are married, since the locals would find any other alternative inconceivable because of their cultural norms. In some cases it may be best not to destroy this illusion. (Some single women also wear wedding rings to discourage unwanted advances.)

However, you should not be deterred by this abhorrent behavior. The world needs more women travelers. By visiting these countries you are helping to acculturate the local men to accept the idea of independent women travelers. You are also setting an example for other women who would like to travel but who are afraid. Perhaps most importantly, you are demonstrating to the local women the rights that are provided by your own culture, which they can then lobby for as an improvement to their own conditions.

Rejoining the *real world*

A basic decision for a world traveler is when to return home. This should ideally be at the end of a carefully planned and successfully completed trip. However, if you decide after a shorter period that you are homesick, then by all means return. You have the rest of your life to travel again. On the other hand, you should keep going if after doing everything you initially intended you find that there are additional places you would like to visit. You should try not to let a need for cash be the reason to send you home, since it is definitely possible to make money while you are traveling.

You should prepare carefully for your return to the real world, and this may necessitate a substantial amount of psychological and practical groundwork. Basically, you want to close the book on a great trip (in your mind and by getting yourself and your souvenirs home safe), and then get a running start on establishing a new, settled life. To begin with the psychology, you are free when you travel. You answer only to your own whim. A major issue, therefore, is the adjustment that you will have to make to enjoy living again in a situation that places limits on your freedom. Another consequence of world travel is that your home might seem boring. You can suffer from reverse culture shock after a long stay in foreign lands. Travelers get used to dealing with continuous challenges, and often find that they miss them when they are gone. Indeed, many newly returned world travelers rebel at being settled again, and immediately begin planning their next trips. You may also have to make an effort to restart old friendships, since out-of-sight is out-of-mind. Most of your friends will of course be very happy that you have made it back, and be quite interested to hear about your trip. On the practical side, it is wise to plan for the financial, housing, employment and other concerns with which you will be confronted. It is best to do everything that you can ahead of your arrival, such as contacting your family or friends if you will need their support.

Your ability to adjust positively to being home relates directly to how you sum up your trip, to understand what it meant to you. You will continue to benefit from your experiences for years, but it is good to draw some preliminary conclusions: about what you did; who you met; what you learned, about yourself and life; and about how you want to move forward. A world trip should be the foundation for your future, but to ensure that this occurs you will need sufficient time for reflection. You should try to allow a few weeks after you arrive home to do nothing except think about your trip and slowly integrate back into normal life.

The most important concern for many people will be the amount of difficulty involved in resuming their careers. Will potential employers hold your time spent traveling against you? This depends on a number of factors, including what career you have (or are interested in), how senior you are, how up-to-date you have to stay, how difficult entry into the career was in the first place, and how accepting an environment it is for nonconformity of personal interests and background. Primarily, of course, your success will depend on yourself, on how hard you are willing to work to find a job. Some people may be threatened by your daring, but fortunately the world is not a uniform place. Most people will be complimentary of your experience, if not a little envious. You have, after all, completed what to most people is only a dream. In doing so you have exhibited independence, courage, the ability to organize and to think on your feet. All of these qualities are highly desirable to employers, and you want to work for someone who is intelligent enough to understand the benefits of your experiences and who does not hold your successes against you.

In interview situations you should never express any regrets for having traveled. This should be easy, since a world trip should be one of your life's defining periods, a high water mark. Even if repositioning yourself proves to be difficult, it is unlikely that you will regret having had one of the best times of your life. Indeed, regardless of whatever happens in the rest of your life, you will always have this major accomplishment to give you support. You will also know that you can always put some funds together and go traveling again. All of this should give you great personal confidence, and this will be clear to the people you meet.

It is a good idea to rehearse your responses to tough interview questions (you should use a video recorder if you have one), including why you traveled, what its benefits were, why it will not detract from your ability to do a good job, why you can be trusted, and why you will not leave to go traveling again. You will have to be persuasive on all of these points. The last question in particular is a legitimate employer concern, since the restrictions on your freedom may prove too much to bear.

Some rejection will be inevitable during the employment process, and you should of course try to avoid it whenever possible. You can eliminate a lot of rejection by screening your connections and opportunities for signs of receptivity, and then by quickly ending meetings or conversations with people who are negative. You do not need their rejection, so do not accept it. Reject them instead! In any case, it should not be too hard to establish yourself. Most people will be impressed by your accomplishments, and many of them will be happy to assist you.

Form and your return home

To revisit the earlier discussion about form, it is common for world travelers to change during their trips, if only slightly, because they have been away from their normal sources of influence. At a minimum you will become more independent and self-sufficient. When you return, though, these sources of form will reappear. (The TV!) It is important to recognize that they will not understand that you have changed. Frankly, most will not even care. They will only be interested in re-establishing the status quo, in bringing you back under control. You will need to perceive, and reject, the demands that they place on you. This will be difficult, since they will be very persistent. Defend yourself: do not make the first concession! Finally, one key to avoiding form and establishing your own identity can be found in the idea that there is no difference between travel and the real world. There is no return. The attitudes and principles that you learn on the road carry over, you apply them everywhere, in all situations. When you change, you do not change back. You are a world traveler for life.

10. PARTNERS

Many world travelers have partners, since it is great to have a ready social companion and someone to share your experiences with. Indeed, some experiences, such as visits to romantic tropical islands, seem more special when you are with another person. (On the other hand, if you are traveling as a couple many people may assume that you want to be left alone. If this is not the case, you will have to be particularly outgoing to make new friendships.)

Having a partner also provides many practical advantages, a few of which are as follows:

- It can make travel easier, since you can share responsibilities. For example, one person can carry the luggage while the other rushes to save seats on transportation.
- It is usually less expensive, if only because of the reduced per-person cost for shared accommodation. Having a partner also helps enforce spending discipline.
- Travel partners can bargain together very effectively. When you are shopping, or in other situations where people need to be persuaded, you can use the classic good cop/bad cop routine.
- Partners make travel difficulties more bearable. If you are ill, someone is there to care for you. If you are both affected, such as by a delayed flight, at least you have someone to talk to.
- Lastly, traveling with a partner can reduce danger, since two people are less likely to be assaulted or robbed than one.

Having said all that, do not let the lack of a partner keep you from traveling. It can be a challenge to find someone who wants to go to the same places as you. If you cannot, go anyway, on your own. When you arrive at your destinations, you will certainly meet other people with whom to spend your time.

Choosing a travel partner

Sometimes you choose your partners, and other times they are chosen for you. For instance, the latter is what happens when you join a group. Benefits of being in a group include the likelihood that your fellow travelers will share your interests, and also that they are a ready-made source of new friends. In addition, it may enable you to meet new types of people. This can backfire, of course, since you might end up despising other people in your group. However, this is more of an issue if the group stays close together and shares day-to-day responsibilities. As an example of this, a friend of mine from New Zealand spent four months on an overland African truck tour. She said a number of people on the truck were at each others' throats for the entire trip. Probably the ultimate example of a tight-knit group is a yacht crew. If you are going to join a group, you should try to meet the other members before you make a commitment. To generalize further, you should not agree to stay with anyone throughout a long trip unless you already know them well.

If you are on your own you can screen potential partners. It is also usually easy to go your own way if things do not work out. However, it can be difficult to link up with another traveler. This is because most people have carefully made plans. One person will typically have to change his or her itinerary for a pair to form. Travel partners should generally have similar interests, pace and budgets, but this does not mean that you should always travel with someone like yourself. Different types of people can make fascinating companions. Traveling with someone from another country, or from another race or age group, can be very enlightening. Old friends are probably the best travel partners, but they may not be available for your entire trip. If this is the case, you should try to persuade them to take vacations and meet you for part of it.

It is also important to recognize that traveling with another person is a serious undertaking. The responsibilities and obligations that you have to each other are great, and you only want a partner whom you can trust and who understands these obligations. The last person you want to travel with is someone who will leave when the going gets difficult, or when you are in trouble. Because of this, you may sometimes need to reject a potential partner. Such a situation can be tricky to handle, but the honest and direct approach will at least clearly communicate your decision and limit any possible confusion.

In addition, you should understand that your partner may have a major impact on your approach to a new environment. For example, one of my classic groupings occurred during my trip to Laos. I started this adventure by taking the overnight train from Bangkok to Nong Khai. I was at a bar with friends before I left, and I spent the entire night drinking on the train - with the transit police! I then crossed the Mekong River at dawn to get to Vientiane, and on the boat I met a French couple. They asked me how I was, and I responded "*totally drunk.*" What an introduction. Vientiane is like a village, and I soon met them again at the central fountain where everyone drinks Lao beer in the afternoon. Little did I know that they were both hard partiers.

I left a few days ahead of them to travel farther north to Luang Prabang, the idyllic ancient capital at the confluence of the Mekong and the Nam Khan. I met three Tasmanians there, two of whom had just finished two years in Japan (one was an English teacher), and who now had money in their pockets and were raring to go. (If you meet a Tasmanian, the Australian equivalent of a hillbilly, ask him or her where their neck scar is - from their Siamese twin!) Anyway, the day I met them the French couple arrived and we formed a group of six. Rather than do what I had planned and travel farther into the hills, in other words, be an explorer, I spent the next eight days with them in Luang Prabang getting legless in riverside restaurants. (Our record was seven hours in one.) The main fuel was beer and *Lào Láo avec la-sá-bji*. The latter is pots of rice whiskey that are filled with bitter roots, sticks and lizards. After steeping for a few days it turns a deep red, and it is said to have a salutary effect on your appetite and sexuality!

Arranging to meet someone abroad

If you arrange to meet someone it is important to have a series of backup plans so no one is left in limbo and wondering what to do next. I know how this feels from experience, and it is not that pleasant. I once arranged to meet some friends in Aspen in mid-winter. We were going to ski for a few days and then drive in their car to Phoenix. I arrived by bus in the evening, and my only contact method was the telephone number of a friend of theirs with whom we were going to stay. This number proved to be incorrect, and I did not even have the person's name. I ended up hiking into the forest to sleep, but woke up in the middle of the night in a storm, my sleeping bag covered with four inches of snow. I then retreated to a hotel lobby where I slept on a chair. The next morning I didn't know what to do. On a hunch I went to one of Aspen Mountain's many ski-lifts, and by a miracle ran into one of my friends. I now know better than to have such skimpy arrangements, and in recent years have successfully met people in many different countries.

The most difficult meeting to coordinate is when both people will arrive in a country without having planned specific flights or even days of travel. In this case the best thing to do is follow the procedure that spies use and arrange a letter drop. The first person to arrive will visit the drop and, on realizing that the other has not yet arrived - because there is no letter waiting, go and find accommodation. This person should then return to the drop and leave a message describing where he or she is staying. Possible drops include the local post office, by leaving a message at the Poste Restante counter, the nearest U.S. consulate, or an American Express travel bureau.

You should agree in advance the order in which possible drops will be checked. Another method is to agree on your hotel or guest house, and the first person to arrive should take a room there. If it is full, or otherwise inappropriate, they should be able to leave a message with the reception staff with instructions for the second person. Some places are also known for their traveler bulletin boards, such as the Kathmandu Guest House and Nairobi's Thorn Tree Cafe. As a final backup, you can arrange to use someone in another country as a contact point - a person whom either traveler can call for information on the other's whereabouts.

Staying together

Getting along with a travel partner is similar to staying on good terms with friends and family, but with one big difference. Many people in their ordinary lives accept less than ideal behavior from their closest associates. They do this because they believe they do not have a choice. These relationships are important to them, and they hold on to the hope that they will improve. When traveling, though, people often have less substantial ties to their partners. One consequence of this is that if you act selfish or overbearing, you may soon find yourself on your own.

Having mutual respect and a willingness to compromise in decision making are the most important attributes for travel partners. For instance, these characteristics are essential when making travel arrangements. Both partners should be comfortable with the arrangements, but this does not mean that either person will always get exactly what he or she wants. There will be times when one partner will have to give in and respect the other's desires. Difficulties often develop when one person arrives at a destination first and makes arrangements for both, such as by choosing a hotel. When the second person arrives a disagreement about the choice can easily develop. This may be due to this person having an honest desire to stay somewhere else, or it could be a reflection of the tendency that people have to resent having their decisions made for them. A good test of your willingness to compromise is to determine if you have to have the last word in a conversation, just the actual last word spoken. Many people are addicted to having the last word, and it is a nightmare when two of them come together. Their conversations go on and on and on. You should reflect on a few of your most recent conversations and ask yourself, how often did you have to have the last word? If the answer is always, you may be able to improve your ability to compromise by learning to control this habit.

You should also respect your partner's desire to have some time to his or herself. People have varying needs for personal time, and yours may be less than your partner's. Traveling with another person can be more intensive than marriage, since you are often together twenty-four hours a day. It is easy to get on each others' nerves. If you find that your partner is getting a bit testy, it is probably a good idea to give him or her some more breathing room.

In summary, if you retain your flexibility and have a sense of humor, you should have little difficulty with your partners. This also holds, of course, with any human relationship. If you both work at it, it should last. For example, my two English friends who picked apples in New Zealand set off on their world trip at about the same time as I. (We actually met in Bali.) At the beginning of their trip neither of them had much confidence that they would stay together for the entire time. However, they were still together when they stopped off in the U.S. to visit me, just prior to flying home after one and one-half years on the road.

Sharing responsibilities

A complex task like international travel is best accomplished by dividing up at least some of the work. It is therefore a good idea to agree with your partner on who will be responsible for different chores. You will each have preferences, and also strengths and weaknesses, and the assignment of responsibilities should reflect these. For instance, if you are generally more relaxed than your partner, it is a good idea for you to be the one to deal with aggressive individuals such as merchants and taxi drivers. As this suggests, the role of leader may be called for in some situations. Classic examples of leadership positions are yacht captains and the heads of climbing expeditions. Many other situations can also benefit from one person taking charge, and skill and experience should be the deciding factors in determining who gets the job. However, there are substantial opportunities for misunderstandings to develop in these circumstances. Whenever someone is to be the leader, this should be clearly communicated to everyone who will be affected including the fact of who bears first responsibility if things go wrong. Finally, partners have special obligations to each other in dangerous situations. You are responsible for each other's safety and rule number one is that you should always stick together. For example, if one person is slower at hiking, the other should reduce his or her pace. (This rule also holds when you are walking through dangerous neighborhoods in towns and cities.)

Resolving problems

Problems between partners usually center on plans, pace, other people or money. If you disagree on plans or pace, or if another person has become involved in your relationship, this could easily lead to a breakup of your pairing. It is best to avoid letting such problems become too great in the first place. You should be sensitive to symptoms of disquiet in your partner, and if something is wrong it is almost always appropriate to discuss it openly. The importance of having a rational discussion as early as possible following the development of a dispute cannot be overemphasized. It will often be your only chance to diffuse a problem before it becomes too large, and acrimonious, to resolve. When discussing a problem you should try to accept criticism unemotionally. Most people, when they are criticized, immediately become defensive, and this often leads to situations where compromise is impossible. A better practice is to swallow your pride, acknowledge the complaint and show some appreciation of it, and then try to explain your views and sort things out. At such times, it is a good idea to remember that everyone is entitled to his or her own opinion, and that there are always at least two sides to every story.

Sharing expenses

Money problems regularly occur between travel partners, and not only because one of them is cheap. However, such problems can be avoided by scrupulously sharing expenses. They should be divided exactly, since even small differences in amounts paid can lead to great resentment. Pennies count! Keeping a complete expense record, from country to country and accounting for the effects of different exchange rates, will minimize the potential for differences of opinion, and also make them easier to resolve if they do develop. Whoever is most disciplined should be delegated the bookkeeping task, and expenses should be discussed on a regular basis to limit misunderstandings. In addition, you should request separate checks whenever possible. (The bookkeeping process should also help you stick to your budget.)

It is also a nice idea to treat each other from time to time, such as by grabbing checks or giving presents. For instance, when we were visiting a weaving village in Laos one of my French friends bought colorful silk shoulder bags for everyone in the group. They were not that expensive, but the thought definitely helped bring us closer together.

When to stop traveling together

Unfortunately, some travel partners may become constant sources of irritation. When you are on your own you have complete freedom and flexibility. When you have a partner, you have to give this up and compromise. Because of this, many world travelers go through cycles from wanting to be with other people to wanting to be on their own. Knowing when to part from someone is just as important as knowing when to get together. What often happens is that over time you and your partner's interests will diverge. Even if this happens it does not always mean that something is terminally wrong with the relationship, and if you do split up you can arrange to get together again at a later date and place. In addition, if you do not meet again the important thing is not that you broke up, but that you shared some good experiences as partners. You should always treasure the memories of your relationship because of this.

If serious problems develop, or if you just feel under a lot of stress from being with someone, then perhaps it is time to separate. You should certainly never let anyone take advantage of you, particularly on expenses. You should also not keep the other person in suspense while you make up your mind about whether or not you want to stay together. For example, an American friend of mine was traveling in Nepal and was invited by a couple to join them to visit southern Thailand. She agreed to this and changed her plans, whereupon they told her, after checking in at the Kathmandu airport for the flight to Bangkok, that they had changed their minds and wanted to be on their own. What can you say? Some people are jerks!

Fortunately, separation from a partner is usually not that difficult to arrange. When you want to be on your own, you should just say goodbye and head off. However, there is a skill to this. You should try to arrange a party to celebrate your time together, and then make a clean and prompt break. For the latter, if you part at a transportation station, there will only be time for a few choice words and sentiments before one person has to leave.

Lastly, if you travel with a partner for an extended period of time you will usually come to rely on him or her for certain things, not the least of which will be emotional support, When you separate you will suddenly be on your own again, and you will probably miss this support. Many people feel a bit insecure in these circumstances, but they usually regain their bearings and self-confidence after only a few days.

11. CULTURAL UNDERSTANDING

Many of the difficulties that travelers experience involve people from other cultures. Few of us, it seems, are fluent at the intricacies of multicultural situations. This is usually because we have a shortage of the sensitivity, and sometimes the respect, that are necessary in these situations. This chapter examines the issue of cultural understanding, of how you can improve your sensitivity to and respect for, and hence your relationships with, the people that you meet during your trip.

(This is a graduate school-level travel topic. The true sign of a skilled traveler is his or her ability to have good relationships on the road. You should be able to talk to and get along with anyone. One way you can increase your sensitivity is to use the following framework to analyze and compare the different cultures to which you are exposed.)

The difficulty of cultural understanding

What is a culture? What is it that we are trying to understand?

- A culture is simply a social system. (The terms can often be used interchangeably.) They come in a variety of sizes, and are conceptually extraordinarily complex.
- Individual cultures are held together by the shared characteristics of their members, which for the largest cultural organizations are usually geographical proximity, ethnicity or religious belief. Smaller cultural units may be refinements of these groupings, such as regional cultures within a nation, or based on other characteristics, including political beliefs, age, sex, occupation or personal interests.
- In practical terms, a culture is the set of roles that are fulfilled by the members of the social group. In the largest cultures, roles are determined by class, race, age or sex, in other words, they are assigned to smaller social groupings.
- A culture is governed by the principles, laws and decision-making systems that define how the different classes, races, age groups and sexes may relate to each other. These decision making systems, as well as certain other roles, are administered by social institutions, including governments, judiciaries, organized religions, schools, employers and the media.
- To fully understand the breadth of the roles and the complexity of their interrelationships, one would need to observe what different members of a culture did every minute of the day and every day of the year. What routines do they follow,

and how do all of the individual routines fit together to satisfy the needs and desires of everyone in the group?
- In this way, a culture implies a sense of permanence, that some form of social equilibrium has been achieved.
- However, a culture is more than just roles and routines. It also encompasses the wide-ranging beliefs and motivations of the members of the group, as well as the history and traditions that support them (and the language used to express them). What do the members of the culture believe (and disagree about), and how deeply, and why; what are their dreams and aspirations; and how are all of these reflected in their ethics, behavioral standards and other attitudes?
- Finally, to use a traditional meaning of the word, a culture includes all of the forms of artistic expression of these beliefs and aspirations, such as dress and design, festivals and ceremonies, art, architecture, music, dance, drama and literature.

A particularly important aspect of a culture is the means by which it keeps its members and, conversely, how it relates to other groups. The above characteristics unify a culture, and establish a base with which its members can identify. However, they also act as barriers to other cultures and reinforce attitudes of "*it's us versus them.*" It is remarkable how strong these barriers can be. They are the cause of cultural conflicts, as well as xenophobia, racism and sexism. For example, among the most pressing problems in the world today, and which appear to allow for no possibility of rational resolution, are the actions of certain groups of fundamentalist muslims following their belief that all non-muslims are infidels.

Related to this issue are the dimensions, and the degree, of the control exercised by social institutions over individual liberties. How much are these institutions, particularly the government, involved in the daily life of the people, and is this relationship supportive, benign or restrictive? What personal freedoms are allowed, what is prohibited, and to what degree? How are the prohibitions enforced? In other words, how strict, and authoritarian, is the social contract?

Some cultures are more stable than others. Indeed, cultures evolve, and new cultures regularly develop, in response to environmental influences such as civil conflicts, changing economic conditions and the impact of new technology. The development of new cultures also results from the normal process of generational rebellion, where teenagers break with their parents to make their own way and find their own identity. The generation gap is nothing more than a clash of cultures. However, the process of cultural evolution is usually quite slow. For instance, even if the U.S. were somehow able to eliminate instantaneously all of the guns that are now in private hands, it would still require decades, if not centuries, to solve its violence problem. Resolving problems, or at least trying to, by resorting to violence, is an ingrained part of American culture, one of its traditions.

Another aspect of the evolutionary process is that cultures deteriorate. They have a cycle of existence, including initiation, growth, maturity and decline. In the last stage, roles, responsibilities and decision-making systems break down, institutions atrophy, and skills, traditions and memories are lost. (There may be social unrest as well.) As an example of this, one could easily take the view that many of the problems in American society today, such as increasing negativity and intolerance, and the destruction of moral values, are evidence of such a decline. Fortunately, this decline is not necessarily irreversible. The challenge for the U.S. is to find ways to reinvent itself, to begin the cycle anew.

Ironically, a major cause of the cultural decline that is now plaguing many lesser developed countries is the cultural pollution that has resulted from the widespread distribution of our influences, most notably through videos and through such peoples' blind adoption of the profit motive and consumerism as the driving forces behind achieving *the good life*. By emulating us they are proceeding through the cycle much more rapidly.

Given this degree of complexity, it is not surprising that it is extremely difficult to understand other cultures and individuals from them. Our frames of reference are usually too far apart. If you have not had long exposure to another culture, you will inevitably have large gaps in your understanding of it. Even if you live in a country for a year or two, many things that the locals grasp implicitly and take for granted will still pass you by, because you did not spend your childhood there learning these things.

Active travelers must also deal with the fact that there are literally thousands of different cultures around the world, each of which would require an in-depth analysis to reach a proper understanding. Indeed, one of the most important and valuable legacies of the human race is the astonishing diversity of cultures that continue to survive. (The world is actually a collection of cultures, not of nations. The latter is a recent, and artificial, overlay.)

Since the process of learning to understand and appreciate other cultures is long and involved, many people, eschewing this effort, adopt simplistic views that are based on conventional wisdom and stereotypes. Japanese are workaholics, Scandinavians are cold, southern Europeans are fiery and Americans are domineering. As this demonstrates, lack of knowledge is not the only barrier to cultural understanding, since what people think they know about other cultures is often biased or incorrect as well. Such views are usually formed through exposure to the media, which as mentioned earlier is rarely designed to be objective. For example, how often are Asians portrayed in western films as inscrutable and dangerous? Expanding on this observation, lesser developed countries are usually only discussed in the news when they have problems. Because of this, few people would think of them as being nice places to visit.

Negative attitudes are also fostered by politicians, through their policies, rhetoric and propaganda. This can be via direct opinion manipulation, such as when the Ayatollah Khomeini called the U.S. the Great Satan, or it can be quite subtle. For instance, the government of India has a policy of charging foreigners higher prices than locals for air transportation and better classes of accommodation. This is a form of discrimination, and it also encourages many Indians to take advantage of travelers whenever they can.

As this last point suggests, everyone has problems with cultural understanding. The local residents of the countries that you visit will have as much difficulty comprehending you and making sense of your behavior as you will of them. In addition, travelers are usually perceived in the widest possible terms. If you are an American you may think of yourself as a sophisticated New Yorker, or a midwest farmer, or a dreadlocked homeboy from L.A., but to the locals you will be just another "*Yank from the States.*" They will have little appreciation of the social differences that exist at home and which you take for granted.

The degree of mutual understanding will vary, of course, depending on who you are talking to. The range of locals that you meet may be quite broad, from individuals who have never met a westerner before to people who were educated in the U.S. They will also have wide differences in English language ability and their own cultural biases. Since travelers must deal most frequently with members of social systems that are based on occupation, you should take special care to be sensitive to the cultural circumstances of service workers, officials and touts.

Cultural respect

People have a right to their own cultural identity. This is a fundamental human right, and it is wrong for travelers to force their ways on their hosts. A classic example of this occurs regularly in France. In the U.S., one hears again and again of tourists who have not enjoyed their holidays there because the residents *refused* to speak English with them, or in general were rude. However, the tourists themselves were probably to blame. You should look at it from the French point of view. They have one of the most beautiful and elegant languages in existence, of which they are justly proud. Unfortunately, they receive thousands of tourists each year who ignore this and refuse to try to speak it, even by learning just a few words. Instead, the tourists run about shouting in English and become upset when no one understands them. This behavior is very disrespectful, as a reverse example easily illustrates. If a group of European tourists visiting America approached you and refused to speak English, but instead insisted on using French, German, Italian, Spanish or some other European language, how would you respond? Most people would find this type of behavior extremely rude, not to mention stupid, and would probably be rude in return.

Travelers who do not respect people's cultural identities often act as if they believe everyone should be like themselves. One reason why they may do this is that they feel a false sense of superiority. However, people who act like they are better than others usually reveal only their own insecurities. For example, many people denigrate things that are foreign in order to be more content with what they have at home. Everyone should recognize that all cultures have their own merits, and that you cannot judge them and say that one is better than another.

At an extreme, a lack of cultural respect becomes cultural imperialism. This is usually reserved for people from lesser developed countries. For instance, many westerners look down on the inhabitants of countries where traditional rural lifestyles are still the norm. Indeed, farmers in the U.S. continue to be the subject of jokes and ridicule. However, the local residents of a rural area are not simple-minded. They often have a highly evolved and disciplined understanding of how their environment works, and what their role is in it, not to mention a complex and vibrant culture. There is always so much more than meets the eye. What might seem to be a bland lifestyle can be amazingly complicated in practice, representing traditions that have taken centuries or, in the case of some Asian countries, thousands of years to develop. In addition, many cultural events might occur only once a year, or even less frequently. A short-term visitor would witness only a small portion of the full range of such events, and have a limited understanding of the culture's richness and depth. Lastly, rural cultures are inherently valuable as a counterpoint to the modern, technological world, since they are typically more relaxed, and because they are a reflection of our own origins.

The residents of lesser developed countries will, of course, usually not have as much formal education, or knowledge of modern technology, as a typical traveler. Most of these people have not had our opportunities, and you should be sensitive to this. The distribution of human capability is not that great, and we all share a common set of experience and needs. Locals will probably understand as much about life as you do, if not more. Indeed, many travelers learn to appreciate this when they try to bargain with locals. In my own case, I thought I was a skilled negotiator after years in business and investment banking. However, after bargaining for hundreds of items with local businesspeople in Asia, and being bested many times, I reconsidered my ability and have now revised many of my negotiation techniques. Having knowledge of modern technology also begs the question of its usefulness. Is such technology more beneficial than traditional methods, and how many examples of technological progress have had to be reevaluated after all of their consequences became known?

It is also wrong to treat the most ancient cultures as artifacts, fit only for museum displays and assimilation into modern societies. This is cultural genocide, and it is one of the worst crimes of humanity. A particularly despicable example is religious imperialism. Charity from religious orders is admirable, but such good works can be ruined when missionaries proselytize and encourage the destruction of holistic groups in their zeal to reach out to *primitive savages* and increase the number of *true believers* for their particular faiths. Everyone has the right to be exposed to other religious beliefs, as well as to modern education and communications and health care technology, but they also have the right to refuse such exposure. In situations where interactions are inevitable, these peoples should be encouraged to preserve and record their traditional beliefs and practices, rather than give them up in an uninformed grab for the flashy trappings of the modern world. There are few things on earth sadder than the destruction of a group that has lost its cultural identity.

In summary, you should practice "*Least Possible Impact*" traveling. You should minimize exporting your values and culture to the countries that you visit. Instead, you should try to appreciate and enjoy these countries and their residents exactly the way they are.

Getting along with locals

You can improve your relationships with locals by thinking of them as individuals, not as stereotypes, and by respecting their cultures. It is also important to work at communication. If you do this, even just a little bit, your relationships will improve dramatically because the locals will be flattered by your efforts to be considerate and to understand them.

You should also recognize that you cannot change places that you do not like. Making a few friendly suggestions may be appropriate in some circumstances, such as to discourage littering, but in general your efforts will be futile. The locals will not change, and if you keep trying this will only lead to unpleasantness and mutual frustration. Your only options are to leave, or to accept things the way they are and adapt to them as best as possible.

Travel in foreign countries often seems like a continuous series of misunderstandings. This is something you should expect, and the problems are usually small and easy to resolve. Unfortunately, though, both travelers and locals are often ready to assume the worst. People tend to put a negative connotation on things that are said or done, and this can easily cause a situation to deteriorate. Misunderstandings are due to a lack of communication, but you do not want to be misunderstood, and the locals don't either. There is an incentive to get along. If you are open, patient and smile a lot, almost any problem can be resolved. (A common catalyst for misunderstandings in lesser developed countries is the resentment that some locals feel towards you due to the fact that you can visit them, but they cannot afford to visit you.)

The depth of misunderstanding can be unbelievable at times. It is not uncommon in some countries to speak with people who appear to understand English, but who completely fail to comprehend what you are saying. In response to a simple question, such as the directions to the nearest train station, they will stare at you in utter incomprehension or disbelief. It seems that these people assume that they cannot understand foreign travelers, so they simply do not. (If you encounter this, the solution is obviously to find someone else to ask.)

Many travelers make cultural mistakes because they are ignorant of local standards of behavior (see below). It will help if you do some homework before you go so you are not completely uninformed. Many guidebooks have sections on local cultures. You can also buy pamphlets on the language and culture after you arrive, since these are available almost everywhere. Another option is to go to the source and ask the residents for information. You should ask people to explain how things work in their country, and get advice on everything from cultural prohibitions to the best local restaurants, where to shop and what things really cost. In addition, showing an interest will often lead to friendships and increase the pleasure of your trip. If you develop good relationships with locals you may want to take their photographs, get their addresses and send them copies. Similar ideas are to take photographs of yourself, postcards from your hometown, or caps with the logos of your favorite sports teams, to give to new friends.

You can also have a positive impact by channeling your tourist dollars to the local people who need them most. Service workers and entrepreneurs involved in accommodation, restaurants, transportation and activities will think more positively of tourism if they personally receive its economic rewards. For example, many Australians are resentful of Japanese tourism to their country, because the visitors usually stay at Japanese-owned hotels, eat at Japanese-owned restaurants and use Japanese-owned transportation. Tourism is a significant compromise for many cultures, because of the social and environmental degradation that often results. It is not worth it if there is no financial benefit. If you are aware that a choice exists, you should use a locally-owned service instead of one with foreign or government-crony owners. Indeed, you should spread your spending around to multiple lodges and shops. This is a personal form of economic assistance. Contributions to a local economy can also reinforce sound cultural and environmental practices, since the income that tourism provides is a strong incentive for locals to preserve arts and crafts and not to destroy natural habitats.

The importance of language

Learning a foreign language is a great challenge, and this begs the question of whether or not it is necessary for your world trip. It is actually an almost impossible challenge, since you will visit many different countries, most of which will have their own language(s). It is possible to travel around the world only speaking English. It is commonly spoken in British Commonwealth countries, and millions of people in other nations are learning it right now. Wherever you go, both locals and foreign travelers will want to practice their English with you. However, you will certainly miss out on many interesting cultural opportunities if you limit yourself this way. For instance, one of my great travel regrets occurred when I rented a truck and drove along the Pacific coast in Ecuador. This coast is periodically interrupted by fishing villages, and it is rarely visited. I was greeted by the locals with great openness and friendship, but because I could not speak much Spanish our conversations were usually reduced to smiling and charades. I am certain that if I had spoken more of the language I would have had an even better reception, and probably been invited to stay as a guest in many people's homes.

You should definitely try to learn the local language if you visit a country for an extended period of time. In addition, there are some countries where virtually no one speaks English, and if you travel to one of them you will have to acquire a reasonable vocabulary to get around. This is often required to complete transactions and to locate transportation, since in order to catch the right bus, train or ferry you will have to be able to ask for it. Guesthouse staff, shop clerks and guides and porters also commonly do not speak much English. It is useful in such countries, especially if unfamiliar scripts are used, to ask someone who is bilingual to write on a piece of paper the local script for the address where you are staying and the words for water, food or restaurant, and toilet. You can then point to the appropriate words, such as by showing the address to taxi drivers. (This is how I got around Bangkok during my world trip, since few of the tuk-tuk and motorcycle taxi drivers there speak English.) Another option is to get a phrase book, and many guidebooks also include short vocabularies.

It is hard to overestimate the positive effects of learning a few words of the local language. You will immediately earn the residents' respect, and suspicion and mistrust will evaporate. Unfortunately, though, not only will people be friendlier, they will also assume that you know much more of the language than you actually do. Good luck! In addition, if you can speak the language a bit you may be quoted lower prices for goods and services. If you can actually negotiate in it, you should be able to reduce your costs to the local price level.

If you have a strong attraction to a particular country or region, you should begin studying its main language right now. Many U.S. colleges have night courses in a variety of languages, and there are independent language schools in most towns and cities. For obscure languages, government embassies and tourism departments should be able to direct you to tutors. Audio cassette courses are another option, and the best of these are the courses that are published by the U.S. Foreign Service Institute. They were developed to prepare State Department employees for foreign postings, and are available for many different languages. They can be ordered from bookstores and the U.S. Government Printing Office. Courses and tutors are of course also available in your destination countries, and spending a few hours in such a course or with a tutor soon after you arrive should lead to a substantial improvement in your ability to communicate.

As a final point, it may take some time to get used to the local pronunciation, especially for personal and place names. You can learn to pronounce names no matter how strange they initially appear. It is only a matter of learning the intonation and accents. People in a number of Asian countries, in particular, have long given names, but short nicknames are used in conversation because of this. Another tip is to write people's names down, since a little name recognition goes a long way towards demonstrating friendship and respect.

Words to learn

Simple language skills include the ability to convey greetings, farewells and thanks; request information and assistance; express desires and preferences, as well as disagreement; conduct transactions; and make compliments. The following is a brief English vocabulary that when translated into a local language will enable you to have these conversations. (The French translation is given for illustration and reference purposes.) When you travel, you should write the translation for the local language on a piece of paper, which you can then keep in your wallet or pocket. It should only take an hour or two to prepare, and you can do so by finding someone who knows the language or by referring to a dual-language dictionary.

Common terms	French
- I, You	- *Je* or *J'*, *Tu* or *Vous*
- He, She, It	- *Il, Elle, Il* or *Elle*
- We	- *Nous*
- They	- *Ils* or *Elles*
- Yes, No	- *Oui, Non*
- Please	- *S'il-vous-plaît*
- Thanks	- *Merci*
- Excuse me	- *Excusez-moi* or *Pardon*
- I understand	- *Je comprends*
- I do not understand	- *Je ne comprends pas*
- I have	- *J'ai*
- I do not have	- *Je n'ai pas*
- Don't beg!	- *Ne mendiez pas!*

Greetings and introductions

- Good day, Good evening	- *Bonjour, Bonsoir*
- Sir, Madam, Miss	- *Monsieur, Madame, Mademoiselle*
- How are you?	- *Comment allez-vous?* or *Ça va?*
- Fine, thanks. And you?	- *Très bien, merci. Et vous?*
- My name is	- *Je m'appelle*
- What is your name?	- *Comment vous appelez-vous?*
- Do you speak english?	- *Parlez-vous anglais?*
- I do not speak french.	- *Je ne parle pas français.*
- I speak a little.	- *Je parle un peu.*
- Can I speak english with you?	- *Est-ce que je peux parler anglais avec vous?*
- I live in	- *J'habite à*
- Where do you live?	- *Ou habitez vous?*
- Goodbye	- *Au revoir*
- See you soon	- *A bientôt*

Emergency assistance

- I need help.	*- J'ai besoin d'aide.*
- A doctor	*- Un docteur*
- The hospital	*- L'hôpital*
- The police	*- La police*
- I am sick.	*- Je suis malade.*
- I was robbed of	*- On m'a volé*
- There was an accident.	*- Il y a eu un accident.*
- It is an emergency.	*- C'est une urgence.*

Inquiries

- What is this?	*- Qu'est-ce que c'est?*
- It is	*- C'est*
- Where is?	*- Ou est?*
- Who?, Why?	*- Qui?, Pourquoi?*
- I want (would like)	*- Je voudrais*
- I do not want (am not interested)	*- Je ne suis pas intéressé*
- Shall we go?, Let's go!	*- On y va?, Allons-y!*
- At what time?	*- A quelle heure?*
- Which way?	*- De quel côté?*
- Right	*- A droite*
- Left	*- A gauche*
- How far?	*- A quelle distance?*

Transactions

- I like	*- J'aime*
- I do not like	*- Je n'aime pas*
- And, With	*- Et, Avec*
- How much money?	*- Combien coûte?*
- Too expensive	*- Trop cher*
- Okay	*- D'accord*
- One to ten	*- Un (une), deux, trois, quatre, cinq, six, sept, huit, neuf, dix*
- Eleven to twenty	*- Onze, douze, treize, quatorze, quinze, seize, dix-sept, dix-huit, dix-neuf, vingt*

- Twenty-one, twenty-two	- *Vingt et un, vingt-deux*
- Thirty, forty..., ninety	- *Trente, quarante, cinquante, soixante, soixante-dix, quatre-vingts, quatre-vingt-dix*
- One hundred	- *Cent*
- One thousand	- *Mille*

Verbs

- Go	- *Aller*
- Stop	- *Arrêter*
- Sleep	- *Dormir*
- Eat	- *Manger*
- Drink	- *Boire*

Nouns

- Toilet	- *Les toilettes*
- Water	- *L'eau*
- Tea	- *Le thé*
- Coffee	- *Le café*
- Food	- *Les aliments*
- Market	- *Le marché*
- Restaurant	- *Le restaurant* or *Le café*
- Shop	- *La boutique* or *Le magasin*
- Drug store	- *La pharmacie*
- Bank	- *La banque*
- Hotel	- *L'hôtel*
- Road	- *La rue*
- River	- *Le fleuve* or *La rivière*
- Bus	- *L'autobus*
- Train	- *Le train*
- Boat	- *Le bateau*
- Station	- *La gare*
- Airport	- *L'aéroport*

Qualifiers

- Very	- *Très*
- Many	- *Beaucoup*
- Good	- *Bon* or *Bonne*
- Bad	- *Mauvais*
- Beautiful	- *Beau* or *Joli*
- Ugly	- *Laid*
- Quickly	- *Rapidement* or *Vite*
- Slowly	- *Lentement*
- Hot	- *Chaud*
- Cold	- *Froid*
- Big	- *Grand*
- Small	- *Petit*
- High	- *Haut*
- Low	- *Bas*

Dates and times

- Minute	- *Minute*
- Hour	- *Heure*
- Day	- *Jour*
- Week	- *Semaine*
- Month	- *Mois*
- Year	- *Année*
- Now	- *Maintenant*
- Today	- *Aujourd'hui*
- Yesterday	- *Hier*
- Tomorrow	- *Demain*
- Sunday to Saturday	- *Dimanche, Lundi, Mardi, Mercredi, Jeudi, Vendredi, Samedi*
- January to December	- *Janvier, Février, Mars, Avril, Mai, Juin, Juillet, Août, Septembre, Octobre, Novembre, Décembre*

Cultural standards

Every culture has standards for acceptable and prohibited behavior, and it is easy to make mistakes and act inappropriately. Indeed, this is the area where travelers most often fail to show respect, although ignorance, rather than contempt, is almost always the cause. Cultures typically have standards for every aspect of behavior. The most important of these relate to life's defining moments, including birth, sexual and marital union, and death. Furthermore, since these types of standards often have a religious basis, failure to observe them may be interpreted as a serious insult.

You can reduce the number of mistakes that you make by being conservative, and by adopting the local behavior. In potentially sensitive situations, you should ask yourself the following questions: what is the local religion; what are its taboos; and what behavior is probably inappropriate or forbidden? If you are in doubt as to how to act, you should ask a sympathetic local for advice. Travelers should take particular care to respect religious ceremonies. They are not tourist attractions being held for your entertainment. You can visit religious monuments and ceremonies in many areas, but rigid dress codes are almost always in effect. Shorts are usually not allowed, and long-sleeved shirts may be required. In some places, such as churches, bare feet will be prohibited, while in others, including mosques and Buddhist and Hindu temples, you will be asked to remove your shoes. (This also holds when entering people's homes in areas where these religions are prevalent.)

The mistakes that travelers make most often involve actions with respect to another person's body, the display of emotions, the giving of gifts, and food. For the first, many cultures assign varying degrees of importance to different parts of the body. For example, it is common throughout Asia for the head to receive the most respect and the feet the least. Because of this, it may be appropriate to bow your head to an elevation below that of a local elder. Other standards that are common in Asia forbid you to touch someone on his or her head, to touch someone with your feet anywhere on their body, to walk across a sitting person's outstretched legs, or to point your feet at another person while you are sitting. As another example, when Thai Buddhists visit a temple they sit with their knees bent to the side so their feet do not point at the statue of Buddha on the altar. The common western standard of shaking hands when meeting people is also usually unnecessary in Asia.

Proper clothing is regularly an issue in areas where the residents place great emphasis on modesty. This especially applies to women visitors, where showing liberal amounts of skin will meet with severe disapproval. Local men may also consider it an invitation to sex. In such areas you should not go topless or nude on any beach which locals might frequent, and you should avoid public displays of affection. Another issue that can be sensitive is the behavior of male travelers towards local women, and not only because of the rights of the women who are involved. For instance, women in many Islamic countries are cloistered away from public view. If you do come into contact with them, excepting female shopkeepers, it may be an insult if you engage them in conversation before receiving a proper introduction.

There are a tremendous number of people in Asia, far more than in the west, and the congestion in the cities can be unbelievable. Social tensions are inevitable with so many people, and one standard that has evolved in many countries, possibly as a means to diminish these tensions, or perhaps because it is more civilized, has to do with expressing emotions. It is considered to be extremely bad form to lose your temper in some countries, particularly in those that have a Buddhist tradition. It will brand you as a fool, and will be a severe insult to the person you have confronted. Both of you will lose face. (If you are justifiably upset, you should try to find a more discreet method of obtaining satisfaction. Use your ingenuity!) The giving of presents can also be tricky. Good behavior is not considered to be extraordinary in much of the world, so it rarely deserves a special reward. Gifts may also be inappropriate because of their tendency to create mutual obligations. However, in some cases they are appropriate, such as in the U.S., when you bring a bottle to a party or a present for Christmas. Small gifts are also exchanged in some Asian countries, such as Japan, when you first meet people. As another example, if you visit a Buddhist spiritual leader in the Himalayan mountains, you should bring a silk scarf as a present. (They are available locally at a reasonable price.) As mentioned above, if you are ever unsure about what to do, just ask someone who is knowledgeable for advice.

Many cultures also have taboos regarding food. The eating of beef is forbidden in countries that are predominantly Hindu, and the same holds true for pork in Islamic nations. Instead of beef or pork, you will be able to eat water buffalo, or buff for short, in many of these countries. Buff is just another domesticated quadruped, and it can taste excellent. Bon appétit! Also in Islamic countries, public restaurants and shops close during prayers, which occur five times a day. In addition, some food taboos exist as a means of restricting the spread of disease. In many lesser developed countries it is forbidden to use your left hand to eat if cutlery is not used, to touch food with either hand and then give it to another person, and to drink directly from a communal container. For the last, locals are remarkably proficient at drinking without touching their lips to the container. Like using chopsticks, it just takes practice.

Finally, some cultures just want to be left alone, to protect their traditional ways of life. The Amish in the U.S. are one example of this, and it is also the case with many tribal peoples in rain forests and on remote islands. You should respect these cultures' right to privacy. In addition, you should realize that at its worst, you personally could be responsible for the destruction of such a group by introducing a disease for which they have no immunity.

12. CULTURAL NEGATIVES

Understanding and respecting other cultures will increase the ease and general pleasantness of your foreign travels. However, you may sometimes encounter situations where special considerations will exist, and where adjustments to your behavior will be necessary. Many cultures exhibit negative manifestations, which range from environmental destruction to governmental subjugation of all or a portion of their populations. The latter practice, among other reasons, often leads some individuals to violently oppose their governments, to resort to criminal behavior or begging, or to become corrupt if they have an official capacity. This chapter considers these individuals, and the interactions that world travelers potentially may have with them.

Some problems, of course, are caused by travelers. Many people berate locals, and a few engage in criminal activity. All travelers have an obligation to help limit this behavior. For example, if you hear another foreigner insult a local, you should take a moment to tell him or her to stop.

Separatists, revolutionaries and bandits

The United States was founded by separatists. Some of the problems that confronted early American immigrants, such as limited justice and political representation, are the daily lot of millions of people around the world. Some of these people have also decided that their best course of action is to fight for their rights. Because of this, as well as for other reasons, including greed, historical differences, and religious and ideological beliefs, the world is a checkerboard of civil conflicts. Until political representation or the right to self-determination is universally available or, more generally, until people learn to resolve their disputes without resorting to violence, such conflicts will continue to exist. Of course, many political actions are not justifiable. Rebels often undermine whatever moral validity they might have by engaging in unethical activities, such as terrorism and consorting with criminals. Examples of this include IRA bombing attacks in Northern Ireland and England, fundamentalist muslim attacks on tourists in Egypt and foreigners in Algeria, and the Shining Path of Peru's assassination of villagers and association with drug gangs.

The Revolutionary War is an example of one type of civil conflict. There are many others. Conflicts between nations include raw conquest and territorial and border disputes. Internal conflicts include civil wars, ethnic and religious clashes, the actions of separatists and revolutionaries, organized crime, military coups and government repression.

Groups that are involved in conflicts follow a variety of different strategies. Civil wars are fought with traditional battles and guerrilla tactics. Separatists and revolutionaries resort to terrorism, including hit and run attacks, bombings, hijackings, kidnappings and assassinations, as well as election violence and banditry. Repressive governments fire on crowds, and use death squads, imprisonment and torture. Repressed populations respond with demonstrations and riots.

Hijackings and assassinations are the rarest types of incidents. Kidnappings are also rare, but they are becoming more of a risk for travelers. It has been estimated by Control Risks Ltd. of London that in 60% of kidnappings ransoms are paid and the hostages are released, in 30% hostages are released or escape with no ransom payment, and in the remainder they die, often in rescue attempt cross fire. Bombings are also infrequent, although there is a slightly higher risk of travelers being exposed to them. Soldiers are often the victims, although the IRA bombs in London, in particular, were intended for *soft targets* - for innocent bystanders. In general, your chances of being the victim of a bombing in a foreign country are extremely small. As a counterpoint, it is worth noting that the Bureau of Alcohol, Tobacco and Firearms reported that there were 3,199 bombing incidents in the U.S. in 1994. The motivations behind this huge figure included gang and drug-related activity, vandalism and revenge.

Travelers are more frequently exposed to armed attacks on transportation vehicles and at stations, attacks at road checkpoints, often by the people manning the blockades, and street riots, demonstrations and strikes where rebels, police or armed forces open fire. Travelers are also sometimes the victims of armed robberies. Otherwise known as banditry, this is regularly a problem in countries that have severe social problems, such as civil war or famine. Locations where bandits have preyed on travelers in recent years include Kenya (in Nairobi, the northeast and the game parks), Algeria to Mali on the Sahara overland route (from Touareg nomads), former states of the Soviet Union and the nations of Eastern Europe (from out-of-work soldiers and developing criminal classes), northwest Thailand (on the hill trekking routes), Papua New Guinea, the South China Sea (from Chinese and Malay pirates), Peru (near Machu Picchu), Brazil (on the beaches of Rio), and in the cities of the U.S. Indeed, nine foreign tourists were murdered in Florida in 1994.

(Advice on avoiding and, in the worst cases, dealing with these types of situations, is given in the Risk Prevention chapter.)

Touts, con artists and thieves

Welcome to the world of international travel! It is difficult to find a destination these days where you will not have to deal with street hustlers. Otherwise known as touts, they are everywhere, at airports on your arrival, in towns and tourist centers, and on idyllic tropical beaches. At their best, they are simply local lads (most touts are male) who want to assist you in some way, and who may even be able to save you a great deal of time and hassle. At their worst, their only intention is to steal your money and possessions.

Touts will offer you anything that you conceivably might need, and they can in fact be distinguished by what they offer and by where they position themselves. Touts at airports and other long-distance transportation stations will offer to carry your luggage and arrange local transportation and accommodation. Touts on the street and at the beach will offer to show you the local sights; change money; rent beach umbrellas and sports equipment; sell souvenirs, including jewelry, watches, wood carvings, leather goods and clothes; and sell food and beverages, newspapers and magazines, tickets for entertainment, haircuts, shoeshines, massages, sex and illegal drugs. In 18th century England, touts even sold seats to public hangings. (*The Fatal Shore*, Robert Hughes, Knopf, page 34) Touts are most prevalent in countries that have great poverty, and in such countries they are always present in tourist locations. This is because they are attracted by the easy money. Locals rarely use their services, so you will meet less of them if you go to places that are off the beaten track.

The worst touts in my experience were on Legian Street in Kuta, Bali. (Kuta is one of the beach-side towns on the island.) This is the main street there, and in a quarter mile you may be questioned by up to one hundred individuals. This is not an exaggeration - I counted. Unfortunately, many of the bars, restaurants, shops and hotels are located on this street, so it is almost impossible to avoid. Kuta is a real headache, and many world travelers pass it by since other parts of Bali are definitely worth visiting. For example, it is very pleasant in the village of Ubud, which has fewer touts and which is the cultural center of the island. Ubud is surrounded by picturesque rice paddies, and it is home to the best Balinese dancers. Matching Kuta touts for persistence are the touts of northern India. (I have had to threaten touts in Delhi with physical violence to get them to leave me alone.) Criminal touts are prevalent in Asia and also East Africa. For example, a Swedish friend of mine was conned in a black market currency deal in Nairobi, and an American friend was swindled in a souvenir transaction in Moshi, Tanzania. My worst memories of touts from East Africa are of women in a Kenyan village on the border with Tanzania, who persistently screeched at me to buy their crafts.

Touts usually work for commissions. If one of them gets you a taxi, or takes you to a hotel or souvenir shop, they will receive a kickback from the merchant. You should therefore not pay these types of touts separately, since this would mean paying them twice. Using touts will almost always make your travel more expensive, and their commissions may be 25% or greater. However, this could actually lead to a doubling of your expenses, or more, since they often assume that anyone who is stupid enough to use them can also be quoted a ridiculous price. It is not uncommon for the first quote from a tout to be from two to five times what would be a reasonable price. A percentage of touts are also professional thieves, and a good policy is to assume that they all are, at least when you first meet them. The touts to be most wary of are the ones who make illegal proposals, such as black market money changers, but they are all suspect. Few touts would pass up an opportunity to rob you. It is easy for them to justify their behavior - you are so rich and they are so poor. As Lonely Planet's guide to trekking in Nepal put it, "*Many Nepalese consider it their personal obligation to separate a share of a westerner's money from him.*"

Avoiding touts

How you deal with touts depends on whether or not you want to use their services. If you do not need assistance, then your objective should be to avoid them completely. Touts approach people in either an aggressive or friendly fashion. In the latter they bank on a traveler's desire to be nice to people, so if you receive this type of approach you should limit your predisposition to be friendly in return. After all, there is no benefit in being overly pleasant with someone who is only trying to hustle you.

A standard tout opening is the question: "*Where do you come from?*" Other common openings are "*Where are you going?*," "*Hello Mister*," and "*Hello friend*," from people who are not your friends. Answering a tout is an invitation to a stronger approach, so you should not respond. Silence, a grim look, and holding your hand up as a stop sign should get your message across. One of the most effective ways to avoid touts is to wear dark sunglasses. If they cannot see your eyes, they can't establish contact.

Having a travel partner is very useful when dealing with touts, since he or she can divert you from them and help watch your gear. You should never let touts invade your personal space and touch you or your gear. They may be pickpockets or grab and run thieves. If their behavior is such that you feel obliged to talk to them, you should say clearly and forcefully that you do not need their assistance. A variation on this response, which many people use, is to be open and friendly, but at the same time to communicate that you are not going to buy anything. You should say: "*Sorry, I don't have any money*," or "*I'm not going to buy anything, so why waste your time.*" This technique is easier to use with lone touts than with groups of them. In any case, you should avoid being rude or flippant, since this may cause them to become more aggressive.

Hustlers can be overpowering at airports. Arriving in a strange country can be very unpleasant if you are immediately surrounded by a dozen or more touts, all of whom are shouting offers at you and trying to grab your bags. It may help if you recognize that their perspective is that only one of them has a chance to make some money from you, so they need to rush to be that person. If you are approached like this you should raise your voice, tell them firmly that you do not want anything, and then grab your bags and move away. If you act like this they will usually look elsewhere for easier game. You can then survey the situation. If you decide that you do need their assistance, such as to find a taxi, you can approach one of them discreetly. You should also not give in to persistent touts who will not stop following you. This will only encourage them to bother other travelers. One option is to sit somewhere and wait them out - you might have a cup of tea or coffee from a nearby stand. If you do not want to do this, though, you should just go on your way. It is usually easy to outlast touts, although I have had rickshaw drivers follow me for hundreds of yards in New Delhi. If you feel threatened, you should ask for assistance from nearby police or bystanders. Touts are also unlikely to follow you if you walk on the fringe of a busy street, on the road, not the sidewalk, next to the flow of traffic.

Lastly, it is not uncommon for touts to beg, if only as a way to make contact with you and determine if you can be hustled. If they can persuade you to give them some charity, they will try to think of a ploy to get more. Touts posing as beggars should therefore obviously be avoided.

Using touts

All of the above points notwithstanding, some touts actually offer good deals. For instance, I arrived in Tissamaharama, Sri Lanka, when a religious festival was taking place. A few locals who were looking for travelers hopped on my bus before it reached town. They tried to persuade me to stay at a particular guesthouse, but I ignored their offer because I was wary. However, after searching for lodging for an hour with no success, I returned to the bus stop and asked for their help. Unfortunately, by this time the guesthouse was full. Since no other rooms were available, they arranged for me to stay free in the guest bedroom of the house of a local merchant. I stayed in Tissa for a week and we became good friends, although this did not stop me from bargaining hard for jeep safaris that they arranged through nearby Yala National Park.

Touts are a headache, but they can be managed. You want them to respect you as an experienced traveler, not as a bumbling neophyte, since this should cause them to lower their expectations about what they can get from you. Anyone who is familiar with ticket scalpers at sports stadiums and rock concerts should know how to deal with them, since these scalpers are the brethren of street touts worldwide. The first thing to do is evaluate the tout's intentions. Is he just trying to earn a living, and is it a situation where you could actually use his assistance? On the other hand, is the tout disgusting, aggressive and totally untrustworthy? You should shop around and bargain with touts, since the next one you meet may offer a better deal. In addition, it is essential never to accept anything without first agreeing on its price. You should also watch out for touts who use bait and switch tactics, where they attract you with an offer of a great deal, but then increase the price or try to get you to select something more expensive. The golden rule for dealing with touts is never to give them any money, none at all, without first receiving and checking the service or merchandise that they have arranged.

If you plan to stay in a particular hotel or guesthouse, you should not tell this to the accommodation touts that you meet at the transportation station on your arrival, since they will inevitably say that it is already full. You also do not want them to know where you are staying, because they might use this information to rob you. Do not let touts follow you to where you intend to stay either, since they may apply pressure to the proprietor not to take you in. This happened to me when I arrived in New Delhi at the start of my world trip, when my rickshaw driver appeared to pressure the manager of a guesthouse where I wanted to stay to say that it was full.

The driver then took me to a hotel that some of his friends ran, and in my ignorance of local prices I paid probably 40% too much for a room. I would never let this happen to me now. In retrospect, I should have stayed at the first guesthouse and waited for him to leave. As this incident suggests, some touts even run protection rackets against service providers, including guesthouses, restaurants and shops. For example, I saw a tout pull a knife on a restaurant owner at a beach in Sri Lanka, who had refused to pay him a protection fee. Fortunately, friends of the owner intervened and forced the tout to leave.

Using taxis and other forms of local transport is also worth a note. Drivers in many countries refuse to use their fare meters for foreign travelers, or if they do not have meters, to work for the standard rates. You will need to bargain with them to get reasonable prices. It is essential to set the price before you get into the vehicle. If you do not do this, the driver will almost always demand an exorbitant rate after you arrive at your destination. It is just the ordinary course of business for these drivers to have loud arguments with their customers at this point. You should also be certain that the agreed price covers your luggage, or the driver may demand an extra charge. In addition, it is important not to let him pick up additional paying customers after you have agreed on a price for private transportation, at least not without reducing your fare. (Friends of the driver are okay, and in many countries they will often hop in the front for a free ride.) If you cannot agree on this you should get out of the vehicle. I had a particularly nasty argument about this with a taxi driver at a train station in Bombay. After setting a price with him, he stopped to pick up a paying Indian passenger. He would only agree to reduce my fare after I jumped out of the taxi.

Finally, if you have a problem with a tout you should demand that the police resolve the issue. This will almost always lead to a compromise in your favor, since the police in many countries are very hard on touts who try to take advantage of tourists.

Corrupt and bureaucratic officials

Corrupt and bureaucratic officials are prevalent in many countries, and the former sometimes prey on travelers by demanding bribes. However, the incidence of this is quite rare. It has only happened to me twice: once to get a trekking permit in Nepal - "*200 rupees if you want it today;*" and the other time to get a box mailed in Delhi - "*let me keep the change if you want it to get there.*" Corrupt officials may include customs and immigration personnel, as well as police and the military. For instance, in Cameroon, the standard bribe during the day at a road checkpoint is a beer, but at night, when the guards are drunk, they demand whisky. Extortion problems affecting travelers are most prevalent in countries where the national leaders are also corrupt. This is merely a reflection of the fact that imitation is the sincerest form of flattery. From stories I have heard, it appears to be most common throughout Africa, and slightly less so in South America, India and other parts of Asia. (Petty bribery in India, or a few rupees as a tip, is called *baksheesh.*)

Requests for bribes are usually made at border outposts and police and army checkpoints. An official at such a location might say that there is a problem with your visa, or that you are not allowed to enter or leave the area with certain equipment, such as your camera. Other situations where bribes may be demanded include to get on transport, and to resolve charges that are related to trumped-up traffic violations and planted contraband. It is not uncommon for police to set up highway traps, and then pull over all rental cars or cars with foreign drivers. They will say that you are guilty of some infraction, but that you can leave if you pay a fine. If something like this occurs, it may be best just to pay up. I would not bother asking for a receipt, though! As another example, I met an American traveler who had a joint planted on him by the police during a bus search in Sumatra. He got off by paying a bribe of about $30.

The best way to avoid having to pay a bribe is to present yourself as someone who will not stand for it. Officials can be intimidated. It is also important not to flaunt your wealth - keep your cash and expensive equipment well-hidden. If an official hints at a bribe, you should act obtuse and boldface your way through. You might also try saying that you will make a complaint, or that you have friends who are highly placed in the government who will be extremely upset that you have been forced to pay a bribe. (Try dropping the name of someone you have read about.) If you say this, you should also ask the official for his or her name and, for a police officer, for their badge number. It is essential to be patient in these circumstances. If you are at a border you will almost certainly have to wait for hours, and you might be interrogated. You should not let yourself get upset, though, since this may be exactly what the official wants.

If a bribe appears inevitable or expeditious, you should request a private conference with the person in charge. You do not want any witnesses, since you could be charged with attempted bribery. You also do not want to have to pay more than one person. You can initiate this process by making comments like "*isn't there some way we can work this out,*" or "*can I talk to you for a second in private.*" Another possibility, such as when you are dealing with a visa problem, is to ask if there is "*a charge for the paperwork.*" You could even say that you want to make amends "*for the inconvenience you have caused.*" (*The Little Drummer Girl*, John Le Carré, Pan Books, page 274) The amount of the bribe will obviously depend on the circumstances. You should negotiate it, and never overpay - think of the poor travelers who will come after you. Plead poverty, and consider the official's lifestyle and probable salary. How much money should be persuasive? A bribe of $20 or so should be sufficient in many circumstances in lesser developed countries. Finally, a classic technique for paying a bribe is to put the money in your passport. The official can then discreetly remove it. Passing the cash by a handshake is another option.

Officials do not need to be corrupt, though, to cause you problems, as the following two stories, both from Iran, illustrate:

- I met an Australian man who traveled overland from Turkey to Pakistan. He crossed the frozen wastes of Kurdish Turkey and had a one week Iranian transit visa with the entry and exit points specified. Unfortunately, they were transposed, such that it appeared he was to arrive at the border from Pakistan. He did not realize this, though, because the visa was in Arabic.

To compound the problem, the guard at the border acted like a lunatic. He threw the Aussie in a jail cell, and also slashed open tins of cooking oil that were being carried by Iranians in transit - using a machete. The oil spilled all over the floor of the customs house.

The jail cell was in a nearby building. It had no toilet or furniture, and the traveler was given no food. After a day he decided this was intolerable. He started shouting, hoping to attract another official. However, this brought the guard, who threatened him with the machete. The situation appeared desperate, until another person, hearing the commotion, came to investigate. This official berated the guard, particularly about the spilt cooking oil, offered apologies, and arranged for the visa problem to be solved.

This last action actually led the Aussie to a quite original travel experience. He went to Tehran, with the official, and had his case reviewed by a forum of eight bearded, black-robed mullahs. They agreed that in the circumstances his was an honest mistake, let him go, and gave him a three week tourist visa for his trouble.

- In the second story, an Austrian couple drove an old Mercedes van to Turkey and along the same overland route to Iran, Pakistan and India. (They drove because the woman was afraid to fly.) Their Iranian transit visa was for three days and their luggage included a video camera and a pile of old cassettes. At the border the guard insisted on viewing all of the tapes, but since he did not know how to work the recorder the Austrian man had to oblige. During this process the traveler realized, to his horror, that the last tape included ten minutes of a home sex video that the couple had filmed when they first got the camera. It was years old, but if the guard saw it prison would be likely and the woman might be raped.

When he got to the tape he said to the guard: "*Kaput.*" The guard repeated, "*Kaput,*" and the matter appeared resolved. However, he then wrapped and sealed all of the tapes, noting their existence on the visa. The couple were not allowed to use or sell them in Iran, and they still had the risk that an official at the exit point would demand to see them. They drove straight to Tehran and appealed for help at their embassy, which responded, "*Sorry, but it's not our problem.*" They then asked for an extension of the visa, only to be told (shades of the last story) that some writing on it in Arabic stated that it was not extendible. At this point the man put his girlfriend on a plane to Pakistan. (She flew!) He then drove to the border and crossed with no problems, except that he had not slept for sixty hours.

Dealing with officials

Whenever you meet an official you will reduce your chances of having problems if you are well-groomed and dressed in clean clothes. Indeed, doing this at airports and border outposts will persuade many officials not to require proof of financial resources, or to search your luggage, before they let you pass. (I always shave and put on a decent shirt before entering a new country.) Having strong interpersonal skills is also very useful. Contrary to the popular belief, officials are human. One reflection of this is that they can be unpredictable. On one day they will be friendly and polite, and even let you do something that is not allowed. On the next day, though, they will be rude and unbelievably bureaucratic. One sure way to have trouble with an official or, actually, with anyone, is not to show respect in his or her power sphere. This is defined as any place where they are in control. It is essential to have a proper attitude in such environments. You should not be aggressive, but you shouldn't be toadying or subservient either. What usually works best is to act professional and knowledgeable. You have rights too, but only if you claim them, and also only if you do so without impugning the official. You should act like you respect officials even if they are brutal and ignorant slobs, and you should never underestimate their ability to make your life miserable. If delays occur, and they often do, you should force yourself to be patient no matter how long the wait, even if the official tries to goad you. Maintain your self control! Unfortunately, travel delays that are caused by officials are often measured in hours, so if you suspect this might occur you should have a good book handy to help pass the time.

Beggars

Severe social problems are present in much of the world, and one consequence of this is that many people beg to survive. However, you personally are not to blame for their troubles, so you should not feel responsible for helping everyone who is in need. You certainly should not feel guilty when you choose not to give money to beggars. As some people will know from the homeless problem in American cities, there are often more beggars than spare coins in your pocket. There are so many beggars in some places that if you were to give to them all, you would soon join their ranks. In the worst places everyone begs, including the adults, children, cats and dogs. This is, of course, horrible and sad. On the other hand, locals in some areas ask travelers for money simply on the offhand chance that they will receive some, and not because their lives depend on it. It is, after all, very easy to ask.

These points, however, should not detract from the fact that charity is an admirable practice. Many people would be sincerely assisted by receiving even small sums. Religious beliefs also encourage charity, and Christianity is an obvious example of this. Similarly, followers of Hinduism and Buddhism believe that individuals pass through series of reincarnations, and that a person's behavior in his or her present life helps determine the nature of their next one. Being charitable is believed to have a positive influence on this. Buddhism is also well-known for its emphasis on compassion. Whatever your beliefs, if you would like to be charitable you must answer the question: who should you give to? You should of course decide this on a case-by-case basis, but a few guidelines do apply. The personal circumstances of beggars vary widely. You should try to consider these circumstances objectively, and reserve your assistance for those people who are most in need.

The handicapped and desperately poor

People who are handicapped or desperately poor are generally the most worthy recipients of charity. This is because their lives truly depend on it. Many people in the world do not have access to a welfare system, or even to regular health care. If they are born with a disability, or have an accident, they will have to depend on charity for the rest of their lives. This is reflected in the charitable practices of the citizens of many lesser developed countries, who will often find a few coins to spare for handicapped beggars even if they themselves are poor. The countries that have the most handicapped beggars include India, Sri Lanka and Cambodia. (The latter two have many amputees because of the use of mines in recent civil conflicts.) Handicaps can also be mental, of course, but it is rare for world travelers to encounter deranged beggars. (On the other hand, this does occur sometimes in large U.S. cities, such as New York.)

One incident in particular has done the most to increase my sensitivity to the plight of such people. It occurred in India during my 1994 visit. I was in New Delhi for the *Holi* festival, or festival of colors. On this day, in March, people walk around blessing each other on the forehead with brightly-colored pigments, followed by a double embrace. It is exuberant, even rowdy, and you may be hit by balloons full of indelible dyed water, or, as a foreigner, assaulted by groups of excited young men. (Women stay off the streets, otherwise they are subjected to harassment, even attack, which is known and semi-legitimized as "eve-teasing.")

By the end of the day my t-shirt, and face, were technicolor, and I also had a camera full of fantastic images. I was in great spirits. Walking back to my guesthouse, though, I passed the most pitiful beggar I have ever seen. It was an emaciated leper, of indeterminate sex, with no hands or feet. The skin was weathered black, but chafed white in spots. The face was wet, with tears, or infection, I couldn't tell. A cloth, with a few *paise* pieces (fractions of a rupee), lay on the ground.

This unfortunate individual was obviously at life's end, and would soon be just one more body on the streets of Delhi - to be swept up with the other refuse in the morning.

My spirits were deflated, and I could only think of the cry, the shout of joy, at the end of each of the day's blessings: "*Happy Holi! Holi Hai!*" Happy Holi indeed. I now give all of my change, and bills as well, to people who are in dire straights.

Mothers and children

Travelers are regularly accosted in lesser developed countries by mothers pleading for money, and they usually hold out their naked babies to you. While it is difficult not to feel some sympathy, after a while you may find yourself taking a hard view towards people who use their children as occupational accessories. The mothers are rarely starving, although the children may be malnourished. Since overpopulation is the leading cause of social and environmental problems around the world, I personally refuse to support it except in the most extreme circumstances, such as when people are starving due to drought or civil conflict. In addition, if you do give charity to a mother, there is no guarantee that it will be used to help the child. One circumstance where I did give something, though, was in Connaught Place, which is the large traffic circle in the center of Delhi. It was just after dawn, and the streets were not yet crowded. I was there to catch a bus (the bus to the Taj Mahal), and I passed a woman and her two little girls on the way to the stop. They had obviously spent the night on the street, and one of the girls, who was about six, followed me and in an insistent way held out her hand for alms. She was completely silent, unlike almost all child beggars, and my heart went out to her.

Children begging on their own are also a common sight in such countries. The cries of "*Pen, Mister*" or "*Bon Bon, Madam*" are ubiquitous. You should not give presents to children as a general rule, and most certainly not candy. It will rot their teeth, and they will not be able to get dental care. More importantly, a childhood spent begging is unlikely to engender self-esteem or respect for other people. You should not reinforce begging unless the children are desperately in need. Unfortunately, many children are forced to beg by their parents, but this is not always the case. Children in rural villages often have nutritious diets and traditional, fulfilling lives. Begging is just a habit they pick up to see what they can get for free, and if people will give them things, why not? Some children even find life on the streets preferable to life at home. For example, I met two American women in Kathmandu who had taken a beggar into their hotel room to shelter and care for him. He was about ten years old, and his story was that his father beat him and that because of this he had to live on the street. The women decided to put him in a private boarding school at their own, considerable expense. After checking with the local school, though, they found out that he had already been a student there, courtesy of another traveler, and that he did not even have a distressful family situation. He had run away from the school simply because it was more fun, and profitable, to meet and con female foreigners.

Even with this advice, you will still have to deal with hordes of shouting, pestering children. Developing a good reply is difficult, because children who beg are often very clever. A response that usually works is to be good-natured, and then to change the topic by asking them a question, such as for directions. Another option is to turn the conversation around and ask them for a pen or a bon bon. This will confuse them, and they will typically respond by laughing.

Spiritual seekers

It is not uncommon in Asia to be approached by spiritual seekers and pilgrims, who are usually either Hindu *sadhus* or Buddhist monks. They are easily recognizable by their flowing robes and, for the former, long beards. These individuals have renounced the material aspects of life, and are seeking spiritual salvation through an ascetic existence. As mentioned above, they hope the merit that they exhibit in this life will lead to a better reincarnation in the next or, if they are Buddhists and are able to achieve enlightenment (*nirvana*), that they will escape from the cycle of life and death. They subsist solely on charity because of their renunciation of the trappings of temporal existence, and it is worthwhile to give them a few coins as a sign of respect for their task. Many sadhus and monks are also well-educated and conversant in English, and they are often very interesting to talk to.

13. ETHICS

In the opening scene of *Hamlet*, the guard Marcellus says: "*Something is rotten in the state of Denmark.*" If he lived today, he might easily expand this comment to include the entire planet. As a traveler, you should recognize that you have a responsibility not to add to the world's problems. Indeed, we can all make small contributions to improving our home, and behaving decently when we travel is an excellent place to start. This section describes some of the ethical considerations that you should be aware of, and some guidelines that you should try to follow.

Ethics are behavioral screens. In other words, before you do something you should ask yourself if your action will harm other people, the environment, or even your nation. (Politicians, take note!) Your first concern should not always be to satisfy yourself. (There are also personal ethics, such as to make the most of your life.) Not betraying trust is a simple ethic, and a travel situation where it applied to me occurred when I agreed to pay $100 for a helicopter ride in Nepal. I did not have this much money with me at the time, but the man who chartered the helicopter and gave me the ride trusted me to go to a bank, cash some traveler's checks, and return to him with the funds. It would have been easy for me to walk away without paying, but I got the money and returned. This is ethical behavior.

Ethics are often controversial, as a number of examples in this chapter will illustrate. You will have to decide for yourself what is ethical in many different situations. It is easy to accept the golden rule, but does its converse also apply: *Do unto others as they have already done unto you*? If someone takes advantage of you, are you justified in seeking revenge? Do two wrongs make a right? There is often a fine line between justice and revenge, and how you respond should always depend on the specific circumstances.

Ethics regarding people

1. As discussed earlier, you should respect the rights of, and not try to change, people from other cultures.

2. People are often remarkably good-natured and kind, and you should not take advantage of this. It is unethical to hustle people, or to rob them, or to run away from bills.

3. It is unethical to take advantage of people who are in dire circumstances. However, a person's income level is not always an accurate guide to this. It is certainly acceptable to be a hard bargainer, and you are not being unethical if you pay the local prices for goods and services, no matter how low they are compared with the prices at your home.

4. Lastly, you should support the rights of repressed peoples. You should not visit (or do business with or buy products from) countries that are governed by totalitarian regimes. This is a personal economic sanction. You should only travel to such nations if your visits can increase the pressure for positive change. One of the best ways to travel ethically is to be a journalist, and report on the conditions that you observe. This can be beneficial even if you only make a small contribution to your local newspaper. Travel to such a country for other reasons, such as tourism and sightseeing, only serves to support the regime and normalize a terrible status quo. To broaden this point, it is unethical to let your private interests and selfishness undermine the awesome task the world faces in implementing uniform human rights in all nations.

This is a perfect example, however, of an ethic that is difficult to follow. Some countries appear to be quite clear cut, such as South Africa in recent years and, at least into 1996, Burma and Nigeria. You should not travel to the latter two until their military forces turn over power to the democratically-elected leaders. (But look at me - I went to Burma.) Other nations, though, are more problematic. Is it appropriate to visit India, a struggling democracy, even though its caste system perpetuates the dismal plight of the untouchables and other lower classes, or Indonesia, hardly a democracy, because of its annexation of and suppression of dissent in East Timor, or China, if only because of its violent annexation of Tibet?

As an example of the impact that an individual can have, a friend of mine, a teacher of history and culture, went to South Africa while the sanctions and travel restrictions were still in place. He then wrote the first book about apartheid for the Danish school system. Later, during the transition to majority rule, he was invited back by the ANC. His first stop, direct from the airport, was at a stadium where a funeral was being held. There were 50,000 people in attendance, including Bishop Desmond Tutu, and he, and his writing partner, were the only whites present. In a similar vein, a Swedish friend of mine, who was doing research in Malaysia on her university thesis, on opposition politics, had her private papers seized by the police. In such a state, *they* do what *they* want. *You* have no rights.

Environmental ethics

The following sign is located at the entrance to Yala National Park in southern Sri Lanka:

"*Through these gates you enter a protected area. The animals, birds, trees, the water, the breeze on your face and every grain of sand, are gifts that nature has passed on to you through your ancestors so that you may survive. These gifts are sacred and should be respected. Whisper a silent prayer as you pass through for the protection of wilderness around you and ensure that what you see and feel is passed on to the unborn generations to come.*"

This should clearly be our approach to all of the world's ecosystems and species, not just to Yala!

5. We should learn to respect the rights of other species, instead of selfishly caring only about our own. The rest of the life on this planet has been caught in a trap by our rapid population growth and voracious appetites. The seemingly unstoppable evolutionary process of increasing diversity, which has been underway for hundreds of millions of years and which is responsible for the phenomenal natural beauty of the planet, has effectively been reversed. All of the species that have suffered need a respite from our pressure. Indeed, they need our assistance, so that they can quickly regenerate themselves.

As I mentioned earlier, in an ideal world the entire planet would be turned into a park, by which I mean massive expanses of natural habitat would be preserved, subject only to the forces of natural law and the patterns of natural evolution, i.e., without human tampering and interference. The means to this end would be environmental activism, voluntary control of population and consumption, and effective land and industrial planning. Many habitats could even be restored to their former glory, which is already happening in some places, such as Nepal, where relocation of human settlements has enabled the expansion of Royal Chitwan National Park. This habitat can now support larger populations of tiger, rhinoceros and many other endangered species.

(Note to the governments of Brazil, Malaysia, Indonesia, Zaire, China, India, Taiwan, Thailand, Russia, Japan and many other countries, not to mention the World Bank: conservationists are not being imperialistic when they ask you to stop cutting down forests, over-fishing oceans, and destroying other species and indigenous human cultures. They simply do not want you to repeat the mistakes that have been made in the past. The early immigrants to the U.S. cut down the great forests of the northeast, devastated the buffalo herds of the plains, and subjugated the Native Americans. They did this on purpose, or because they did not care, didn't know any better, or were stupid. But these are the 1990s. We now know better, and do not have to be vicious or ignorant any longer. In addition, the first four countries listed control the bulk of the world's rain forests, which in turn control the planet's climate. If deforestation in these nations is not stopped, the earth could eventually become a desert wasteland. This is an issue that transcends national sovereignty, and these countries will have to amend their policies, and restrict the practices of their businesses and citizens, for the good of the world.)

My apologies for the preaching. To return to travel, wildlife and other species, especially in parks and wilderness regions, should be disturbed as little as possible. As the Sierra Club motto says: "*Take nothing but photographs, leave nothing but footprints.*" Some specific guidelines include not to pick plants and flowers, and not to start fires where there is a risk of them spreading or where deforestation is a problem. Animal species should also not be bothered, so they do not need to change their behavior to adapt to the presence of humans. Observing wildlife, however, is ethically acceptable. If more people would do this, we would better understand the beauty, intrinsic value and rights of other species. As a consequence, we would be less inclined to kill them and destroy their habitats.

6. Animals should never be sacrificed to provide thrills for tourists. Live or dead baits are still used in some countries to attract large carnivores, such as the feeding of goats to Komodo dragons in Indonesia. These are appalling spectacles, and you should complain if you visit a location that presents them. The age of the Roman Coliseum has passed.

7. You should never litter anything, not even cigarette butts or matches. You should carry out and properly dispose of all of your garbage. It is also an excellent practice to pick up a few pieces of trash from scenes of natural beauty, such as trails, rivers, lakesides, beaches and parks. You should let the locals see you do this if you can. Actions speak louder than words, and they may learn to have more respect for their environments, or at least feel shame when they next throw things on the ground.

Photographic ethics

8. You should respect other people's desires not to be photographed. If there is any doubt as to a subject's willingness, you should ask if it is okay before you take a shot. However, this is another ethic that is difficult to follow, since you may not have the time, or the language ability, to ask. You should also not photograph airports, bridges or other militarily significant structures in countries where there is a risk of civil conflict. Your film or camera could be confiscated. You might also be imprisoned as a spy. Cultural standards often prohibit photography of religious ceremonies and the insides of monuments, although this is acceptable in some circumstances, such as when you ask or if many other people are taking photos and the locals do not seem to mind. (Permits may be required at some locations.) Lastly, even though it can make for dramatic photography, you should avoid taking photos of human despair, especially without permission. Photos of personal suffering may be acceptable in rare cases for journalistic purposes, to raise the conscience of the world, but they are otherwise inappropriate. It is parasitic to take such photos for a personal collection. It is far more ethical to drop your camera and give assistance.

9. Photographic techniques that disturb wildlife, such as staged fights between and among species, and pressure pads to trigger night photography, should not be used.

In summary, these are the most important ethics for travelers, if not for everyone. They are easy to understand and, if you maintain a little self-discipline, they are not that difficult to follow. Indeed, if more people would follow them the positive effects on human relations and other species would be profound.

14. RISK PREVENTION

"*No worries, mate!*"

- A common Australian saying

Many people overrate the risks that are associated with world travel. Indeed, the risks that people tend to fear the most, such as being in a plane crash, are extremely rare. To consider another risk, among the millions of visitors to the tropics each year, only a few catch endemic diseases and become seriously ill. Some travelers will fall prey to the probabilities, of course, and become ill, or be robbed, or be involved in an accident. Being in the wrong place at the wrong time can happen to anyone. Other people, through their own ineptitude, will make mistakes. Most travelers, though, will not have any significant problems at all.

One of the greatest challenges of foreign travel is to learn about the risks in new environments. Once you know what the risks are, you can take steps to guard against them. For example, visitors are the disproportionate victims of crime in some countries, in part because they are unfamiliar with the methods that are used by local criminals. Unlike the residents, they fail to adopt appropriate preventative behavior. (Travelers may also suffer a greater risk in some locations because they are wealthier and are specifically targeted.)

Risks can be analyzed by what is in jeopardy - either your health or property, by their severity, by their source or cause, and by the environments in which they occur. These factors are considered throughout the review of travel risks, which consists of this and the next two chapters. This chapter continues with a few general comments on risk prevention, an appraisal of the most severe risk - the risk of dying, and reviews of health and property risks from civil conflict, terrorism and armed robbery, and property risks from theft. The following chapters, Staying Healthy and Sources of Assistance, conclude the review with discussions of traveler health concerns and of where you can get help if you do have problems.

General comments on risk prevention

Above all else, you should exercise good judgement to avoid or reduce risks. You should never forget that you personally are responsible for your own safety, and you should be particularly careful in dangerous situations. Taken to an extreme, there are some circumstances where having good judgement is essential. For instance, adventurous travelers often go places where they simply cannot make mistakes. If you are hiking through a remote region, away from assistance and medical care, you cannot afford to have an accident. Similarly, you should not let yourself be caught after dark in a dangerous part of a city or town, unless you are confident in such environments.

I clearly understand the consequences of poor judgement, since I once made a serious mistake by trusting two steel bolts while rockclimbing at Pinnacle Peak, Arizona. (The climbing route was called *Requiem*!) The bolts had been drilled into a sheer granite wall, and although they had been in place for a few years most local climbers thought they were secure. Unfortunately, they were not, and both broke while I was suspended from them waiting for my partner to ascend to my position. I fell one-hundred feet to a talus slope, and almost died. (I was told it was the longest surviving climbing fall in the state to that date, and I made the front page of the *Arizona Republic.*) My injuries included a fractured skull and concussion, compressed and fractured lower back vertebrae, a fractured pelvic bone (my left hip was numb for six years), and broken ankles, not to mention hundreds of stitches worth of cuts. I was not wearing a helmet, and the crack in my skull was so wide that air reached my brain and I was at risk of developing meningitis. I was actually conscious after the fall, but have amnesia from then until the next day when I woke up in a hospital. (What a feeling! When I started to fall, and realized, instantly, that the bolts had broken, I was certain I would die. When I woke up my first thought was: I made it!) My partner was luckier. He fell about fifty feet, landed in a tree, and only broke his wrist.

This accident was a turning point for me. Its silver lining was that I grasped the true fragility of existence, and it motivated me to make the most of myself and to experience as much of life as possible.

Other general preventatives of travel risks include being fit and having a partner. Good personal fitness, in addition to improving your ability to recover quickly from an illness or accident, will also help you in endurance situations. Many problems occur when people are tired, and if you are fit you should be better able to maintain your alertness and good judgement. Having to withstand a long travel day is also easier if you are in good shape. In addition, being fit can intimidate and deter criminals. Having a partner also reduces the likelihood that you will have problems, and provides a ready source of assistance if you do. (After the above accident another friend of ours ran to the nearest phone and called for help. I was evacuated by helicopter.)

Another important issue with risk prevention has to do with the advice of other people with whom you are traveling, including both other travelers and local guides. You should never automatically assume that they have a sufficient understanding of, and respect for, any dangers that might be present. In addition, it is a common superstition that bad luck occurs in threes. There is at least one grain of truth in this. If you have a problem during your travels, or at any time in your life, you should immediately double your vigilance against further difficulties. It is common to lower your guard when a problem occurs, if only as a result of an emotional reaction. If you do this, it could make you more susceptible to other risks, which could also be much more severe. For example, many people have been run down after they got out of their cars to change flat tires.

The supreme risk

At its absolute worst, you could die while traveling. Approximately six thousand Americans die abroad each year, and of these about two-thirds are overseas residents and the balance are travelers. (*Travel Tips for Older Americans*, U.S. Department of State, Bureau of Consular Affairs, page 10) However, this is a very low percentage of the total number of people who live in or visit foreign countries (just think of the many people who go to Canada and Mexico). Given the vehicular accident and crime rates in the U.S., it is probably safer to travel than to stay at home. The most frequent causes of death to travelers are preexisting health conditions and accidents. People are also sometimes exposed to deadly illnesses, but modern vaccinations and pharmaceuticals have eliminated the risks of, or provided effective treatments for, many of these problems. Even if you do have a serious problem in another country, transportation and medical standards are now sufficiently high that you should easily be able to reach life-saving care. On the other hand, a few travelers are killed each year in civil conflicts or by criminals. Death in conflict is unlikely for most people, although the risk is a concern for war tourists and certain types of professional travelers, such as soldiers, journalists and aid workers. In cases of armed robbery, you are at greatest risk if you fight back. You might also die as a result of capital punishment, if you are caught with illegal drugs in Singapore, Malaysia or a few other countries. In general, of course, the risk of being killed by another person is slim. People kill each other out of anger, revenge, jealousy, envy, greed or insanity.

All of these severe emotions and mental problems are extremely unlikely to be directed at travelers.

I have only been in one travel situation where someone died. This was in the Seychelles, when a scuba diving boat on which I was a passenger ran over a snorkeler. This unfortunate individual surfaced directly in front of the boat, which at the time was passing through a wide and empty harbor channel about a quarter mile from a group of small islands. It was a terrible accident, and I still have difficulty believing that it actually occurred. I have also met only one other person, an American in Nepal, who was in a situation where another traveler had died, and in this case it was after the fact. He was trekking on the Annapurna Circuit, and was asked by local authorities to accompany them to the body of an Englishman who had died from altitude sickness on Thorung La (pass), which at 17,650 feet is the highest point on the trek. After twenty years of international travel, and conversations with thousands of other people, this is certainly not that many cases. On the other hand, one does read in newspapers from time-to-time about other travelers who have perished, and a few of these cases are described later in the chapter.

There is also the risk that you will be exposed to situations involving victims who are local residents. This is probably more likely, although it should still be extremely rare. However, if you go to Saudi Arabia you could actually be forced to witness an execution by beheading! This happened to a Swedish friend of mine who lived there (the husband of the woman mentioned earlier). He had also been walking through a bazaar, and was unaware that a public execution was scheduled in a nearby square. The religious police came to the bazaar and forced all of the westerners who were present to accompany them - they were given front row seats. I have also met an English traveler who was in a terrible bus accident in Egypt - the bus crashed at night into a parked, loaded truck (a number of people were killed, and the police laughed at their bodies!), an American photojournalist who saw riot victims in Kathmandu, two German climbers who passed the body of a porter on a high pass near Mt. Everest, and a few other travelers who passed the bodies of people who were killed in traffic accidents in Nepal and northern India.

In summary, the odds are minuscule that you will die while traveling. There is no reason to be overly concerned with this risk.

Civil conflict, terrorism and armed robbery

As a world traveler it is inevitable that you will visit countries which are experiencing civil conflict. England and the actions of the IRA are one of the most obvious examples of this. In general, though, you should not have any problems in these countries. Where military conflicts are in progress, you can usually avoid them just by staying out of the battle zones. You would probably not be permitted to visit them anyway. In other circumstances, such as where rebels or bandits are active, your chances of being victimized are also slim, particularly if you follow the advice in this section. You would have to be traveling through a very dangerous region, make a major mistake or have terrible luck, to become a victim.

Travel warnings

The Department of State issues warnings for countries where travelers may be exposed to severe risks. These can be obtained from the Citizens Emergency Center in Washington, D.C. (CEC - part of the Bureau of Consular Affairs, 202-647-5225), on the Internet (http://travel.state.dove), from passport agencies, and from U.S. consulates. If you decide to visit an unsettled nation you should definitely obtain the warning for it, and go to the nearest consulate when you arrive to discuss the current security conditions and to register your itinerary. If the U.S. is not represented in the area, you might want to obtain security advice from the consulates of other countries - the U.K., Australia, Sweden and Switzerland are widely represented around the world. Local newspapers, as well as the *International Herald Tribune*, are also an excellent resource for evaluating security conditions, since their stories often contain the most up-to-date information available.

However, once again, there is the issue of press bias and even censorship. For example, an Italian traveler was attacked and killed by a gang of Nepali men in a bar in Kathmandu in October 1995. This incident was covered in the Nepali-language press, but omitted by the local English press, notwithstanding complaints by his family and friends.

The following is an example of a State Department warning. I got it during my world trip from the U.S. consulate in Colombo, Sri Lanka.

"Subject: Travel Advisory - Sri Lanka - Warning

1. Summary: The Department of State advises U.S. citizens traveling to Sri Lanka that while the main business and tourist destinations in western, central and south Sri Lanka are generally calm, terrorist bombings of government security targets causing civilian casualties have occurred recently in Colombo. All travel to the north and east should be avoided until further notice. While there is no direct threat to Americans at this time, there is a general risk of being inadvertently caught in or near acts of violence end summary.
2. The security situation remains unsettled and volatile in the north and east of the island of Sri Lanka. Consular services and protection cannot be guaranteed in these areas due to fighting between government security forces and the Tamil extremist group, the Liberation Tigers of Tamil Eelam (LTTE), which continues in all parts of the north and east. Border areas such as Wilpattu and Galoya National Parks, should be avoided. Other border areas, including Yala National Park and the cultural sites of Anuradhapura and Polonnaruwa have not been affected by the fighting; however, caution should be exercised and specific enquiries made before venturing to those areas. Roadblocks manned by security personnel may be encountered and travelers should follow closely any instructions given.
3. The center and south of the island, including the western beaches and the hill (tea) country, are generally calm, and travelers should experience few problems there at present. However, since March 1991 terrorists have exploded several powerful car bombs in Colombo aimed at security individuals and installations. Although no foreigners have been killed in these incidents, several have been injured. Travelers should be alert to the continuing threat of terrorism in the capital.
4. There have also been outbreaks of Japanese encephalitis and dengue fever in part of the island. Malaria is prevalent everywhere outside of Colombo. Visitors should be sure that immunizations are up to date, and use all available precautions to avoid contact with mosquitos.
5. Because the situation in Sri Lanka can and does change very rapidly, all American visitors are urged to register with the embassy upon arrival. The embassy is located at 210 Galle Road, Colombo 3, Telephone 448007.
6. Review date: December 31, 1991.
7. This replaces the previous advisory of June 8, 1991, and is issued to reflect recent terrorist activity in Colombo."

As of June 1996, most of the above warning still applied. The government had taken the town of Jaffna, the Tiger's declared capital of an independent Tamil homeland, but terrorist activity continued in Colombo and the north and east.

In addition to this nation-specific information, general advice on ensuring a safe trip is provided in the following State Department publications, all of which are available from the U.S. Government Printing Office:

- *A Safe Trip Abroad*
- *Security Awareness Overseas, An Overview*
- *Security Guidelines for American Families Living Abroad*
- *Security Guidelines for American Enterprises Abroad*
- *Emergency Planning Guidelines for American Businesses Abroad*

How to avoid becoming a victim

The locations where civil conflict and banditry are a risk are usually easy to recognize. However, the pace of change in some parts of the world can be extremely rapid. Countries or regions may be open and relatively safe, but then events occur, instability develops, and they quickly become much more dangerous.

Instability can also develop slowly, of course. For instance, the security situation in Delhi appeared to have deteriorated between my first visit in 1991 and subsequent trip in 1994. Severe overpopulation, urban migration and poverty, coupled with rising inter-caste tension, had made the streets of the city noticeably more aggressive. There were hundreds of crippled beggars and thousands of families, most with small children, living on the sidewalks and in vacant lots in the downtown area alone. I regularly saw scuffles and shouting matches. (This deterioration is common throughout many of the large cities of Asia, although it is being offset somewhat by the growing prosperity in the region.)

You should avoid current and developing hot spots. (Few travelers would have gone to Beirut in the late 1980s!) Fortunately, there are so many places worth visiting that it is easy to postpone some trips, even for years, until their destinations settle down. It is worth noting, though, that risks can be highly localized. One of the reasons why I went to Sri Lanka was to expose myself to an environment where conflict was present, to research this section of the book. However, I soon learned from the above warning (and other sources) that travel was quite safe in the south of the country.

During my visit I went all the way to Yala, which was secure, whereas a further fifty miles northeast of the park was very dangerous territory.

Conflict often develops during elections, or when governments increase their pressure on rebels. For example, during my first stay in Nepal some locals were killed in pre-election violence. India was planning elections at the same time, and this was when Rajiv Gandhi, the leading candidate for prime minister, was assassinated. The Indian elections were postponed, and I delayed my return there until after the rescheduled date since additional violence was expected. As another example, when the Indian government started an offensive that summer against separatists in the northeast state of Assam, the rebels there took nineteen hostages.

If you travel to a dangerous region you should pay careful attention to your surroundings, and ask trustworthy locals for advice on where it is safe to go. They will usually know which areas and roads are the most secure. You should stay on main thoroughfares and avoid sections of cities and towns that are rebel strongholds - these are typically the slum areas, as well as crowds, demonstrations and celebrations, which are often the scenes of spontaneous or planned violence. It is a good idea to be especially vigilant in airports, and to avoid waiting in their exposed areas. In conversations, you should be circumspect about your local address and travel plans. If you are wealthy, or have an important background, you should be particularly private about this. In general, you want to have *street smarts*. This is a second sense that you can develop, which enables you to tell when danger is present and how to avoid it. In essence, street smarts are a healthy sense of mistrust, coupled with a dose of caution, that you apply in unfamiliar environments. In practical terms, it means maintaining a strict vigilance for the presence of potentially dangerous people. A literal example of street smarts is to walk along sidewalks next to the roads that they border, instead of next to the buildings, to minimize the risk of someone surprising you from an alley or building entrance. It is also important to know when to change your route. If you are walking down a street towards a group of unsavory characters, it may be better to turn around and find another way. This also applies when you are in a vehicle. I was in Ecuador during a period of civil unrest, and when I drove into Guayaquil, which is the country's second largest city and major port, I took a wrong turn and ended up in a bad neighborhood. Rather than try to find my way through, I turned around and retraced my route until I found the correct road.

You should keep a low profile, and try to contact the nearest U.S. consulate, if you are caught somewhere during a coup attempt or other violent incident. It is safest, obviously, if you do not go out, especially at night. A better option is to find somewhere to wait until the situation calms down. If you have to go out, you should not travel alone, and you should always tell someone where you are going, what route you will take, and when you will return or arrive at your next destination. In addition, it is important not to exhibit fear if you must walk through a dangerous neighborhood. You should walk with confidence, even if it is only an act.

It is essential to stay calm in situations where people are armed. Do not let yourself panic. If you feel yourself becoming agitated, breath slowly and deeply and count silently to five. This should help you relax. I was stopped and searched at many army and police checkpoints in Ecuador, and the guards always pointed their machine guns at me, which was very unsettling. I did not speak Spanish, so I just waved my New York drivers license (an International Driving Permit was required!) and bluffed my way through. I had left the bulk of my luggage at a hotel in Quito, and was only traveling with a small bag. This simplified the many searches. Another reason to travel light in such circumstances is that checkpoint guards sometimes help themselves to people's gear. If this happens to you, you should try to negotiate with them. On the other hand, roadblocks can be extremely dangerous since the guards could easily shoot you and dump your body in a ditch. You should turn around if you are approaching what may be a rebel checkpoint. You should also try to stay in your vehicle. Finally, in the movie *Under Fire*, which is a superb film about war journalists in Chad and Nicaragua, a character who is being held at gunpoint says that the theory in such situations is to keep talking. He kept talking, but was shot shortly thereafter! You decide. If you are in a situation where you may come under fire, you should find a safe place to hide and stay as low as possible, or keep your head down and run away as fast as you can - in zigs and zags - not in a straight line, using any possible cover.

If you are caught in an armed robbery, you should not be a hero and fight back. Give your assailant(s) your money and anything else that they demand.

As unlikely as it is to occur, if you are involved in a violent incident you should try to think like a soldier. (It is worth noting that there are no prizes for second place.) If there is a risk that you will be assaulted, you should never be caught sitting down and you should grab anything that can be used as a weapon - before you are attacked. "*A man with a weapon, any weapon, is twice the man without one.*" (*The Night Manager*, John Le Carré, Coronet Books, page 281) You might even want to carry a weapon in dangerous areas, although just having one could cause trouble. It could also be confiscated. I debated for a long time before deciding not to buy a Nepalese kukuri knife for my return to India in 1991, and this proved to be a reasonable decision. However, a Danish friend of mine, who is a martial arts expert, travels with a set of short hardwood fighting sticks. Of course, he can use them for training as well as defense. A friend of mine in the U.S. travels with a can of Mace, and she always carries it when answering knocks at the doors of her hotel rooms. As this suggests, it is a good idea in dangerous areas to think through how you would respond to an attack. If there is no way out, including running away, and even though it is usually safer to be on the defensive, you should consider using the element of surprise and attacking first. If you are attacked, you should try to avoid or block any blows (protect your stomach if your assailant has a knife), and then counterattack when you see an opening. Notwithstanding the above point about not being a hero, if you are assaulted you should fight as violently as possible. Your life may depend on it.

On a separate topic, you should not let yourself be used as a courier for a criminal or terrorist. Never carry anything for anyone on any form of transportation, unless you trust them completely. For instance, I know two Swedish women who were interrogated when they left Israel, on the assumption that they might have made friends with Arab men in the country and agreed to carry something for them. They were also strip searched, and I think the guards just wanted to see them nude! However, it is worth remembering that many people have been caught carrying drugs and other contraband, sometimes as unwitting couriers, and as a result are now incarcerated. "*During 1991, 3,050 Americans were arrested in 105 countries.*" (*Travel Warning on Drugs Abroad*, Bureau of Consular Affairs) Over 40% of these arrests were for drugs.

Lastly, to inject a bit of humor into such a serious subject, the following is an amazing story from a Swedish friend of mine who was working in Tripoli, Libya, on April 15, 1986, the date of the U.S. bombing. He was with an industrial firm and was living in an expats' compound. After the first salvo all of the residents were extremely frightened. They telephoned their embassy, which said: "*Sorry. We do not have a contingency plan for this. We don't know what you should do.*" My friend and two other people decided to take things into their own hands. They went to a nearby construction site and commandeered an earth mover. They then returned to the compound and built a bomb shelter by digging a large hole and burying two ship's containers - only a direct hit would destroy it. After this, whenever a warning came that further bombing was possible, they moved into the shelter. However, they also met another man who was burying his home-distilled spirits. He was afraid of discovery by the Libyans. (Their biggest fears were carpet bombing by B-52s stationed on Cyprus, and that the local situation would degenerate into anarchy.) They persuaded the man not to bury the alcohol, but instead to drink it! They set up a table by the shelter and drank at night, watching anti-aircraft artillery fire at U.S. Blackhawk surveillance planes. What a party, with a fireworks show! Later on, after four days, my friend was able to catch the first flight out: Swiss Air to Geneva. The champagne was opened the second the plane left the ground. When they landed, everyone but the pilots drunk, it was to a media circus. CNN, BBC, ABC, journalists from all over the world, put cameras in their faces and asked: "*How was it?*" "*Wellll, not soo bad.*"

Case examples

To further illustrate the above advice, the following section describes specific incidents of civil conflict, terrorism and armed robbery.

Danish traveler killed in southeast Sri Lanka

A Danish traveler was killed in June 1991, during an attack by Tamil Tigers on a bus in southeast Sri Lanka. He was one of fourteen people who died when the bus was strafed with gunfire. He was the only foreign passenger and was returning from the Lahugale elephant sanctuary, which was considered to be extremely dangerous at the time since it was a known Tiger stronghold. The purpose of the attack was to kill Sinhalese citizens, who are the majority ethnic group. The bus was fired upon on a remote stretch of road bordering the sanctuary, and it is likely that this location was picked because of the escape route the park provided.

Sri Lankan press coverage of such incidents is incomplete, to say the least. Perhaps because of this, there were many rumors circulating about the attack. I heard from some Peace Corps volunteers that the bus was stopped, and that the traveler was given a chance to run for it. When he protested that the attack should not take place, the terrorists lost patience and shot him anyway. In addition, an official at the U.S. embassy in Colombo told me that all of the Tamil passengers on the bus had been alerted to the planned attack and had gotten off at earlier stops, and also that the gunman who actually shot the traveler was killed after the incident by his fellow Tigers as punishment for the murder of a foreigner.

Israeli travelers kidnapped and killed in Kashmir, India

Also in June 1991, seven Israeli tourists, six men and a woman, and one Dutch woman, were kidnapped at night from a houseboat on Kashmir Lake by approximately a dozen armed men. The kidnappers were Islamic separatists who want the state of Jammu-Kashmir to break away from India. Some of the separatists there want the state to be joined with Pakistan, while others want it to become independent. The two women were then released, but the men were marched into a quiet alley and lined up. The Israelis were traveling after having completed their military service, and one of them was able to loosen his bonds. When it became apparent that they were about to be executed, this man jumped the terrorists and managed to grab a gun. One traveler, and at least one terrorist, died in the resulting shootout. During the commotion one of the remaining Israelis lost contact with the others. The group managed to find sanctuary with local police, but this individual was again taken hostage, this time by another separatist group. He was finally released after a week of intensive negotiations involving a Swedish journalist and a number of diplomats. One consequence of the attack, and of other violent incidents that occurred around this time, was that the Vale of Kashmir, a beautiful area that has attracted thousands of world travelers for many years, was rapidly deserted by them.

Swedish engineers kidnapped in Kashmir

Two Swedish engineers were also kidnapped in Kashmir earlier in 1991. They were hostages for three months, before they managed to escape late one night by climbing out of an open window in the house where they were being held. They then walked fifteen miles to another town, to get as far away from their kidnappers as possible, before seeking assistance from the police. The men said they were moved some forty-five times during their captivity, or an average of every two days. It is clear from this that the kidnappers had a substantial amount of local support.

A few other more recent kidnappings are as follows:

- Two British travelers were kidnapped while trekking in Kashmir in June 1994. They stumbled onto a rebel hideout and training camp, but were released eighteen days later after government and journalist intervention. In another incident shortly after this, an American traveler was discovered by chance being held in a building in Delhi. Information given by his captors, once again, Kashmiri separatists, also led

to the release of two other Brits who were being held at another location. (The fact that these travelers had been kidnapped was completely unknown.)
- The big news in 1995 was the kidnapping in Kashmir of six trekkers: two Americans, two English, a German and a Norwegian, by a Pakistan-affiliated militant group, beginning on July 4th. One of the Americans was able to escape almost immediately. A month later, the Norwegian was beheaded. Despite intensive negotiations, the militants refused to release the remaining hostages, and in May 1996 there were reports that they had been killed.
- In addition to Kashmir, another hot spot has been Cambodia, and 1994 was a terrible year: there were three separate incidents. In the first an American aid worker was kidnapped by the Khmer Rouge (KR), but then released in exchange for food and medical supplies. Then, an Australian and two Brits were taken from their car in an ambush. Their bodies were recovered a few month's later. Finally, in a case that got worldwide attention, an Aussie, a Brit and a Frenchman were captured during a KR train ambush which also left thirteen local passengers dead. Their governments refused to pay a ransom, or to halt aid to the Cambodian government, and when the army pressed on the area where they were being held they were murdered. (The KR commander who ordered the execution slipped away.) As a footnote to this incident, it turned out that the Frenchman did not want to make the journey, since he thought it was unsafe. He succumbed to pressure from his friends. (An American woman was also killed in Cambodia, in 1995, in an attack on her tour group at Angkor Wat.)
- As an example of how quickly things can heat up, in January 1996, Costa Rica became substantially more dangerous for travelers. Two people, Swiss and German, were kidnapped from their hotel, and there were also a number of armed holdups of tourist vehicles. At about the same time, seven European researchers were kidnapped by separatists in a nature reserve in Irian Jaya, Indonesia, and seventeen French tourists were taken captive in Yemen. These incidents followed a number of other kidnappings in the southern Philippines. It would appear that rebel groups and criminal elements worldwide are increasingly looking to the kidnapping of travelers and other westerners for ransom and as a source of publicity.

New Zealand traveler killed in northwest Thailand

A New Zealand man was shot and killed a few years ago on a trek out of Chiang Mai in northwest Thailand. His party was ambushed by two bandits on a lonely trail. During my world trip I heard a rumor that when he put up a fight and punched one of the thieves, the other shot him. Two women trekkers who were with him ran into the jungle and were not found for days. In addition, according to this story the guide who led the trek had gambling debts with the bandits, and had actually helped arrange the robbery. (You should get references from other travelers for any guides that you intend to use.) I was also told by another person who has extensive experience in northwest Thailand that a good practice there is to buy souvenirs in hill tribe villages. This economic contribution may reduce the likelihood of your being robbed by thieves from these villages.

This incident was also reported in *Lonely Planet Traveller's Information Update 27* (August 1988, page 31). In a letter to this publication some travelers wrote that they saw the body of the victim, and that they were told that the group of three "*were walking well behind the guide.*" The letter also said that the Kiwi did not have anything to give to the bandits, and was shot because of this, and that the robbery was set up by a rival trekking company. Both of these points conflicted with what I was told, but regardless of what actually happened, I decided not to go trekking in northwest Thailand. (This area is part of the opium-growing Golden Triangle.) I instead visited the northeast plateau of the country, which is called Issan, and which extends to Cambodia and Laos. There are also only a few other travelers in this lovely and tranquil region, in contrast to the large number of people who visit Chiang Mai.

Other incidents involving guns

A friend of mine was robbed in the late afternoon on Broadway and 29th Street in New York City. The thief jumped out of a doorway, pointed a .45 at him, and demanded his wallet. Needless to say, he gave it to him. I also met an English traveler who had to duck gunfire on a bus in northern India. Two men boarded the bus and attempted to take a woman passenger off. This happened late at night, and in fact woke up the person who told me the story. One of the men drew a gun, and in the altercation that followed shot the woman's companion in the shoulder. It appeared that he was of a lower caste, and that the attackers were trying to prevent their relationship. After protestations from the driver and other passengers, the men left without the woman and the injured man's wound was attended to. Ultimately, everyone went back to sleep.

Theft

One of the greatest concerns of many travelers is the possibility of being robbed. However, if you take precautions it is relatively easy to avoid. Visitors are regularly the victims of theft, but this occurs because they fail to perceive when the risk is high and as a result make stupid mistakes. (Witness my thinking my friend's flat in London was safe.) Reading this section should help you avoid doing this. It describes which belongings are most likely to be stolen, who the thieves are, what types of travelers are the most common victims, and which locations have the highest risks and how you can avoid being robbed at them. The section concludes with a discussion of what you should do if the unfortunate does occur and you are robbed.

To begin, it is important to recognize that the residents of many countries are very poor by American standards. They may have no qualms about stealing from people who are so wealthy. (By comparison, even a budget traveler is rich in these countries.) Because of this, you should not tempt them by leaving your belongings unwatched, including baggage in a station, clothes hanging up to dry at night, and valuables on a beach. However, this does not mean that the world is a lawless place. Most countries are trying to develop their tourism, and they understand how much it is undermined by petty robbery. Crime prevention is often effective, and it may include more than law enforcement by the police. For example, one night when I was in Thamel, which is a neighborhood popular with world travelers in Kathmandu, a thief was spotted breaking into a hotel room. Some local merchants chased him down and beat him up, and then handed him over to the police.

Everything that you have may be stolen, but thieves usually have preferences. Money, traveler's checks, credit cards, passports and cameras are at the top of the list. (I saw a man selling stolen cameras out of a cardboard box one evening when I was walking along the beach in Colombo.) Your efforts at gear protection should be proportionate to their value or difficulty of replacement. For instance, I always worry about losing my water filter when I visit lesser developed countries, since I depend on it for my health and because it would be virtually impossible to replace. You should therefore carry such items with you or secure them very carefully.

Perpetrators and modus operandi

Anyone may be a thief. Local thieves include con artists, pickpockets, bag slashers, grab and run thieves, hotel room thieves, people who break into cars, and armed bandits. Officials may also be thieves, and if you are confronted by them in uncertain circumstances you should ask to see their identification before agreeing to anything. For example, a Swedish friend of mine (the auditor) was stopped by an official in Pakistan. As he described it in a postcard to me: "*Imagine a Gestapo type individual in official looking clothes waiving an ID from a car and asking for my passport.*" My friend asked to see the ID, but the man refused and then threatened him. When he insisted, the official drove off. The number plates on the car had been covered, and it seems clear that if he had handed over his passport, the official would have immediately driven away with it.

You may also need to be concerned about other travelers, since some people engage in petty pilfering. Many travelers are young and have limited funds and belongings. Your cash, or jacket, or sleeping bag could be very useful to them.

Armed robbery is rare, since thieves usually prefer other tactics, such as stealth, with pickpockets, bag slashers and hotel thieves, or subterfuge, with con artists. A classic ploy, with many variations, is for a thief to become your *friend*. In the worst case, after lulling you into complacency, he or she will drug you with tampered food or drink. This is particularly common in Asia. For instance, during the 1991 Southeast Asian Games in the Philippines, the Vietnamese volleyball coach was drugged and robbed of his money and jewelry. He was left unconscious in a cemetery, a victim of the "*Ativan Gang.*" I also heard about a French traveler who was given spiked orange juice by a local in Goa. He woke up to find that his money and camera had been stolen, although the thief did leave his air ticket and passport. (This was a very generous gesture.) You should never accept *any* food or drink from people who you do not know well enough to trust, unless the circumstances clearly are such that there is no chance that you will be drugged and robbed. Even professionally wrapped food, such as candy, is suspect. Cigarettes can also be tampered with. If something tastes funny, you should immediately spit it out. Knockout drugs can work in seconds, and while you are unconscious you will probably be robbed of everything that you have. Women victims could easily be raped as well. In a similar vein, you should not go to a stranger's home, no matter how friendly he or she is, especially if it is in a slum. Do not let yourself be persuaded to go for any reason, such as for a party, or for a quick stop to pick something up, or as a way to make some money. This is a common setup for an armed robbery. Lastly, it is important to recognize that some thieves may buy you things, such as meals, to increase your trust, and also that they can be extremely patient. I heard of one local who developed a friendly relationship with some travelers over a period of weeks, including guiding them around sightseeing. However, when his chance came he stole everything that they had.

Actually, friendships with residents can work both ways, since real friends can help you better understand the local risks. In some cases, such as in villages, it is also less likely that travelers who have local friends will be robbed.

Thieves often work in teams. One person will engage you in conversation and misdirect your attention (this is the technique that magicians use), while the other picks your pocket or steals your bag. Common forms of misdirection include bumping into you, spilling food or condiments on you, or dropping coins at your feet. If any of these things happen to you, you should immediately assert your personal space, shouting if necessary to do so, and check all of your gear. You have to be quick if you are robbed this way, since you only have a few seconds to catch the thief. Thieves also work in groups, by crowding around travelers. They have even been known to stage road accidents, and then rob people who stop to help.

To understand how hard thieves will work, consider this story about an English traveler who almost fell victim to an elaborate con in Nairobi. He was twenty years old and, in his own words, "*I looked younger - very naive and innocent.*" (This was his second trip abroad.)

The attempted con had three stages. In the first, he *met* two college-age *students* who said they came from Djibouti. They wanted to talk to him about England. His *first mistake* was to agree to go with them to a coffee shop. While they were talking the students said they needed some money to get home. Could he spare some? His *second mistake* was to give them GBP 5. The students offered profuse thanks and demanded his address so they could send him the money. His *third mistake* was that he gave them his home address.

For the second stage of the con they parted company. He then walked around town for an hour. Unbeknownst to him, he was followed.

In the third stage he was approached on the street by a plainclothes policeman. This man flashed an official looking "*Kenya Police - Nairobi Division*" badge, and asked him if he had recently met two Djibouti students and, if so, would he accompany him to a cafe to discuss it? The traveler's *fourth mistake* was that he agreed that he had met the students. (He should have lied and said he had never met them.)

At the cafe they were soon joined by three other men. The lead conman said that the students had been caught with cocaine, and asked why he had talked to them and why they had his U.K. address. His *fifth mistake* was his failure to realize that this was an extremely improbable series of events, especially in just a couple of hour's time. The conmen slowly started to put pressure on him, implicating him in the students' supposed troubles. They then said that he would need to come with them, but that everything would be okay for a bribe of GBP 200.

The traveler, who by now was very frightened, almost in tears, had also become very suspicious. He refused to accompany them by car. (This was his *first good move.*) He said he would walk to the nearest police station, but not drive. He also demanded to see their IDs again, but they refused. (Other people in the cafe were now aware that there was a problem.) At an impasse, two of the men went to get their car. The other two were on the far side of the table, and the traveler, making his *second good move*, bolted out of the cafe - running as fast as he could.

To give you an idea of his psychology, later that day he was still uncertain if it had been a con or if he was now wanted by the police. Such was the power of their persuasion. Still later, he learned of a warning from the British Embassy about this group of criminals. One traveler had given the gang the money. Another had gotten into their car, and was then driven to the outskirts of town, beaten up and robbed.

A few lessons to learn from this story are as follows:

- Do not make the first mistake; the first concession.
- Demand to see any official's badge and ID. Scrutinize them closely and call the police station or office for verification.
- If you know you have done no wrong, and the officials are not uniformed police in a proper patrol car, refuse to accompany them. Call the nearest U.S. consulate and ask bystanders for help.

How to avoid being robbed

Anyone can be robbed but, as the last story illustrates, thieves usually pick the easiest targets. Single travelers are more likely to be robbed than those with partners. People who flaunt their wealth, or otherwise advertise their presence, are also at greater risk. This group includes gee whiz sightseers, travelers who wear gold jewelry or who keep expensive cameras hanging around their necks (you should keep your camera in a bag until you need it), and people who are intoxicated. In addition, travelers who are looking for good deals are at risk, since many scams prey on a person's desire to get something for nothing.

The behavior that you use to avoid civil conflicts and armed robbery will also reduce your risk of theft. You should keep your guard up, exercise street smarts, control your drinking, and act confident, or even intimidating, when risks are present. Indeed, travelers who act like they can take care of themselves are much less likely to be victimized. You should also not be overly open with locals, at least not with people who start conversations with you, until you get to know them well. Do not tell strangers where you are staying, or invite large numbers of people to your room. Never tell anyone how much money you have. These precautions, and the others that are discussed below, do not take much effort or time, and they will soon become a standard part of your travel routines.

Protecting valuables

As was mentioned before, one of the most important rules for guarding against theft is never to give people money before receiving the goods or services that they have agreed to provide. This is a classic con in black market transactions, and it is also common with souvenir deals. Many travelers have been robbed because they broke this rule, such as my American friend in Tanzania. The thief in this instance was a young boy, who had *arranged* for the traveler to buy a hand-made belt. Money changed hands up front for *materials and the craftsman*. However, there were *production delays*, and the hustler even tried to get more money by pleading *cost overruns*. (You should never underestimate the audacity of these people.) The traveler, though, would not accept that he had been conned. He wanted his character judgement to be correct, and his trust well-placed, rather than acknowledge that he had made a mistake.

You should always minimize the amount of cash that you carry. This is especially the case when arriving at checkpoints and borders in unsettled regions. Instead of carrying a large sum, it is better to get small amounts of funds periodically using a credit card or traveler's checks. You should also carry your cash with you wherever you go, or leave it in a safe or safe deposit box, either at your hotel or a bank. Indeed, you should use such facilities whenever you can. In addition, you should never leave valuables in a hotel room (see below). As for your passport, excepting the countries where it is necessary to carry it with you at all times (some lesser developed nations - people have even spent days in jail in such countries because they were stopped by the police and did not have their passports with them), it is better to keep it locked up along with the bulk of your cash and traveler's checks. (An alternative is to carry photocopies of your passport's identification and visa pages.) If your valuables are put in a safe, as opposed to your own individual box, you should ask for a signed, dated and itemized receipt. Your valuables should also be placed in a separate container, such as an envelope, stuff sack or bag, before going into the safe. You should ideally be able to seal or lock this container and, if you use an envelope, you should sign your name across the flap. Finally, you should inventory your valuables after getting them back. (Some people have lost traveler's checks from the center of a stack, and not discovered it for weeks.)

Travelers are also sometimes asked to relinquish their passports, but you should avoid doing this whenever possible. (Witness the earlier story from Pakistan!) Many hotels will ask for it, but most of them will accept a firm, but polite, refusal.

Most world travelers carry their valuables in a money belt, waist pack, neck pouch or purse. Another option is to sew pockets inside your clothes. (My rain jacket has an inside zip pocket.) In addition, you should carry your camera, film, journal, favorite souvenirs and other expensive gear in a small bag or backpack. Like your money belt or purse, you should never let it out of your sight and easy reach. In questionable accommodations, you should use it as a pillow or put it under your blanket. You should be especially careful about it at night on buses and trains.

The only risks that are associated with this approach are from grab and run thieves and armed robbers. For example, an American friend of mine had her purse stolen in London. The thief drove by while she was walking down a sidewalk and ripped it out of her hands. Her passport, traveler's checks and airplane ticket were in the purse. Using a hotel safe or a money belt would have prevented this loss, but in general the best solution is to remain alert. In addition, if you use a purse you should carry it across your shoulder and on the side away from the street.

There are a few other issues that pertain to safekeeping valuables. If you use traveler's checks you should keep the receipts with the numbers of the checks stored somewhere safe, and separate from the checks, such as inside your passport. (Remember to mark off the numbers as you use the checks.) You might also want to keep a photocopy of the receipts in your luggage, as well as copies of the ID and visa pages of your passport. In addition, it is important to be careful when using credit cards. You should be certain that merchants make only single imprints, and tear up all of the bad copies and carbons. Do not let merchants take your card into back rooms "*to call for charge confirmation.*" This is a common problem in souvenir shops in northwest Thailand. Some merchants there make more than one imprint, and then forge your signature from the one that was used for the purchase. The shops also write in different dates on the imprints, to avoid suspicion and exceeding your daily credit limit. You should always check your bills for extra charges, and by law you have a year to dispute them.

High risk locations

The risk of theft is higher in certain types of locations. For instance, popular tourist destinations often have large numbers of thieves. The specific locations that present the greatest risks are crowds, transportation stations, transportation vehicles and hotel rooms. However, since you can be robbed anywhere, you will have to evaluate the risk in every location that you visit. Travelers who visit Patpong, which is the main red light district in Bangkok, should readily understand that they are in a risky area. A common problem there occurs in upstairs sex bars. Some of these bars are clip joints, where customers are physically prevented from leaving until they pay large sums. In other places, though, the dangers are not so obvious. When I was in New Zealand, the local newspapers reported a rash of thefts from rental cars that were parked at scenic locations. As another example, a few years ago the European press reported a series of robberies on the east coast of Spain. Thieves were acting as if their cars had broken down on empty stretches of road. They would signal passing vehicles to stop, and then rob the passengers by force. You may also be able to judge the degree of danger in an area by the size of the local police presence. If a neighborhood or beach has a regular patrol, you should watch your belongings carefully.

Crowds and stations

Pickpockets and other thieves like to operate in crowds, so you should protect your personal space, and keep an eye on your gear, whenever you are in one. In addition, if you use porters at stations or on treks, you will need to watch that they do not run off with your bags. Many stations have uniformed porters, and they are probably trustworthy. (If they have badges, remember their numbers.) Freelance porters, though, need to be watched very carefully. On a trek you may find that a porter, even when carrying your bag, can hike much faster than you. The last thing that you may see of him, and your belongings, is his back as he walks away from you down the trail.

On transport

Trains, buses and ferries are favorite haunts of thieves. For example, the buses in Rome that are most popular with tourists are plagued by pickpockets. Another problem is that if you put your luggage under your seat, someone could sit behind you, reach down and cut it open, and steal its contents. I also heard an interesting story about women thieves on crowded trains in Calcutta. They wear huge skirts, and if one of them sits next to you she will *inadvertently* spread her skirt over your bag. When she gets up to leave, your gear will go with her.

Lastly, local buses can be fraught with risk, particularly night buses, which are also more prone to armed robbery. It is common in some countries for luggage to be stored on the tops of buses. You should persuade the driver to let you keep your gear with you if people are also allowed to ride on top. Even if this is not allowed, you will still have to watch the roof at every stop to ensure that it is not taken. (This is difficult to do on night buses.) It is probably acceptable if your luggage is tied down under a tarp. Storage compartments under buses are better, but you still have to be alert at stops to see that your bags are not removed. In a risky situation, you should take your luggage onto the bus, even if it cannot fit in the overhead rack or under the seat. You can leave it in the aisle, or put it up front next to the driver. (I was never stopped from bringing my dive bag onto buses in Asia, which I did whenever I thought there was a risk of theft from the roof.)

Case examples

A Swiss friend of mine was almost robbed by a team of two thieves when his train pulled out of a station in northern India. One of them had entered his compartment well before the train's departure, and struck up a conversation. When the train was getting ready to leave, this person asked him to move his bag from the floor to the overhead bunk, which he did, although he left its straps hanging in his peripheral vision. As the train started to move, the thief increased his conversation, drawing my friend's attention away from his bag. The second thief, who was standing in the aisle, then reached up and grabbed it. Fortunately, my friend quickly noticed that it was gone and, after racing the length of the car, managed to grab it and boot the man off the moving train. When he returned to his seat, he found that the first person had also jumped off. As another example, a Singaporean friend of mine was robbed on a Garuda Indonesia flight from Bali to Jakarta. She was on a flight that was boarded, but then canceled for mechanical reasons. Her bag did not show up on the carousel after deplaning, and the ground staff argued that it had been sent to Jakarta on another flight. This was impossible, because no other flight had departed, but she could not get any satisfaction. (I would have gone to the airport police.) When she arrived in Jakarta on the next day's flight, the staff there said that they had never seen her bag. It was finally returned two weeks later after a trace was put on it. The lock had been broken, and a gold chain, earrings and other items were missing. It seems clear that following the cancellation of the flight, the ground staff in Bali had opened the bag, if not others as well, to see what they could steal, and then concocted a story to cover their crime. There is little that you can do to combat this type of theft, except to carry your valuables with you. (This is reinforced by the fact that by international convention an airline's maximum liability for lost luggage is $20 per kilogram.)

Hotel rooms

To prevent theft from hotel rooms it is essential to understand that you cannot hide anything in them, and that they are never secure, since duplicate keys always exist. Any good thief, and you have to assume that he or she will be good, can search a room in a few minutes. You should not take a room if it cannot be securely locked, with reasonable assurance that duplicate keys will not be used. Indeed, for budget accommodations, the safest rooms are those that have doors with fittings that will accept your own heavy gauge padlock. (If the door takes a padlock and the hotel supplies one, use your own instead.)

Okay. As a matter of practice you will end up trusting many hotel rooms, if only by leaving the bulk of your gear in them, but be cautious!

After taking a room, and the point about the impossibility of hiding things notwithstanding, you should unpack and spread your belongings around. This will reduce the risk of losing everything.

If your only option is a room that has questionable security, you should not leave your belongings there when you go out. (This is often the case with dormitory accommodations.) It is safer to leave them in the hotel's office or luggage storage room, in a locker, or with someone you trust. Even the most luxurious hotels are suspect. For instance, jewelry valued at $500,000 was stolen in July 1992 from the room of an American woman at the Ritz Hotel in Paris. Also that month, $60,000 worth of jewelry was taken from the room of an American golfer while he was playing in the British Open. It is remarkable that neither of these individuals chose to use their hotel safes.

As these points suggest, you should always look at a hotel room before accepting it. Are the front and other door locks sturdy, can the windows be forced, and is there any other possible entrance? For example, I have stayed in many guesthouse rooms in the tropics that had attached outdoor bathrooms, but refused others where I thought thieves might have been able to climb over the walls.

Rooms are also sometimes robbed while their occupants are asleep. This is a frightening thought, and it is an excellent reason not to take a room if you mistrust its security. (If a room does not have an inside bolt or chain, you should put a wedge under the door.) If there is any chance that your room might be entered, you should put your valuables under the bed linen, in your sleeping bag, or under the mattress. You should also lock all of the windows, even in areas that have a hot climate. You can always cool down with a shower. You may even need to protect your belongings in rooms that have barred windows, since thieves have been known to use poles with hooks to pull bags close to windows for pilfering.

An example of the night-entry problem occurred while I was staying at a hostel in Dublin during my current trip. I was in a room with twelve bunks, in a basement with a door and window that opened onto a staircase below the street. (I put my pack in the luggage room, and carried my day bag with me.) One night, when returning from a dance club, I saw a man in the distance climb out of a basement well over a pointed bar fence at street level. He joined another man and walked off and, as I crossed the street, I saw him stuff a woman's purse, which he had obviously just stolen, inside his jacket. Then, as I walked up the street, I realized he had come from my room!

Inside the room the window was open (we had been warned by reception to keep it locked), but a mattress with a quilt was below it and a person's shape seemed outlined underneath. How strange that they hadn't woken up?

Anyway, I climbed into bed, but couldn't sleep. After a while, at about 3 a.m., I heard the window move, and a man's head poked into the room. (I had an upper bunk in a dark corner with a direct view.) He kept still, and his eyes glanced around. He didn't see me, but why did he come back? Or was it a second thief?

Not wanting him to climb in, and as he would hear me if I left my bunk (I wanted to give his head a whack with a baseball bat!), I shouted a warning: "*Hey man. What the f... do you think you're doing?*" He stayed motionless for a second, and then jerked his head back. The window closed with a crash.

The shape on the mattress didn't move. It was obviously just a quilt. (In the morning, I found out that nobody else in the room had heard any of this.)

Still later, at about 4 a.m., voices entered the room - two men and a woman. Suddenly, the woman's voice rang out: "*Where's my pocketbook?*" All hell broke loose. Drunk, she started bitching and moaning about her loss, which it turned out was just a vinyl bag, toothbrush and bus ticket. (Now I knew why the thief came back.) She woke everyone up and demanded to know if we had taken her bag. Then she mentioned that *she* had opened the window (it was her mattress on the floor), putting us all at risk, to dry her bloody towel.

After about an hour of this, at one point she actually started pounding her head against the wall, she finally shut up. In the morning, she kept up her complaining to the manager, so he threw her out. (Accept the loss, lady. It happens.) It was a high point in hostel living.

Other locations

If you are in a motor vehicle, you should keep its doors locked and windows closed. (In November 1995, a thief in northwest Thailand tossed a grenade threw the open window of a tourist van, decapitating the driver.) In addition, you should never leave anything valuable inside when you park, not even in the trunk. There is also no excuse for being robbed at a beach. You should never take valuables to one and, except at deserted beaches where there is limited risk, you should always be able to find someone who will watch your belongings while you go swimming or take a walk. This is also a good way to make new friends. Finally, you should be careful when walking along beaches at night, since they are a common setting for muggings.

What to do if you are robbed

You should not let yourself become overly upset if you are robbed. It can happen to anyone, and it is not the end of the world. There is no good reason to let it ruin your trip. You should also assume that you will not get anything back. This way, if something is returned, it will be a bonus. Nonetheless, you should work hard to get the thief caught and your belongings returned.

If you are robbed, you should complete the following procedure:

1. Collect the bulk of your funds and the backup photocopies of your important documents from the safe locations where you stored them.
2. Contact the police as quickly as possible, and obtain an official report that itemizes everything that was taken. You should continue to visit or call them if you lost something important, to ensure that they are still working on the case.
3. Check local lost and found offices, since the thief may discard some of your goods. You should continue to check them for weeks after the theft, such as by telephone if you have moved on or returned home.
4. If the theft was substantial, contact the nearest U.S. consulate and ask them to put pressure on the police to solve the case. The consulate will also reissue your passport if it was stolen, although this may take a few days if you do not have any identification left.
5. You may want to contact the local media, including newspaper and television reporters, to publicize your loss. This will also keep pressure on the police.
6. Report any lost credit cards, traveler's checks and airline and other tickets, and request replacements.
7. Lastly, it is wise to travel with insurance that covers theft. After you have the police report, you should call your insurance company's hotline to initiate the claims process. You should also retain copies of the police report and the insurance form for your own records.

15. STAYING HEALTHY

As a world traveler, there are many health issues in which you should be interested. Those that will be most important will depend on your destinations, travel style and planned activities. This chapter is a broad presentation of these issues, and it is organized as follows:

- On-going health care
- Vaccinations and malaria prophylaxis
- Life-saving first aid
- Traveler accidents
- Traveler health problems
- Medical kit and toiletries

On-going health care

It is wise to have up-to-date knowledge of the state of your health before you begin your world trip. An examination will make you aware of any medical conditions that you have, and if there should be restrictions on your activities because of them. In addition, specialized exams are called for before undertaking certain activities. For example, you should have a lung x-ray and a check-up for asthma if you plan to learn scuba diving. It is also a good idea to request prescriptions from your doctor for any pharmaceuticals that you would like to take. Another concern is that it is important to have up-to-date dental care. It is better to solve a minor problem at home, where excellent care is available, than be forced to use an unknown dentist to treat a more severe problem. Lastly, all world travelers will require a number of vaccinations, and people who visit the tropics may also need to take malaria pills.

Few people become seriously ill during their visits to foreign countries, so appointments with local doctors are rarely necessary. However, if you do develop a severe problem, or a problem of unknown origin, you should obtain local medical assistance as quickly as possible. It is unwise to postpone treatment until you return home, since with the delay it could easily become worse. You may also have contracted an illness that is most prevalent in your specific location. If so, it is probably best to treat it there, where the medical knowledge should be greatest. On the other hand, few problems are so immediately life-threatening that you cannot be transported, so another option is to cancel the balance of your trip and fly home. It is worth noting, though, that this is rarely required. A better option may be to obtain care locally, and then find somewhere pleasant and inexpensive to recuperate. For instance, I met a man who caught hepatitis A in India. He checked into a local hospital for immediate treatment, and then went to Sri Lanka to rest for a few weeks at a tranquil beach village. In addition, if you require emergency dental care, and the quality of the local care is uncertain, you should only get a temporary filling or crown and postpone the permanent work until you return home. (You know the quality of care is bad if the standard treatment for a toothache is extraction!)

It is sometimes worthwhile to visit a doctor or clinic in another country even if you do not have a problem. You might want to do this to get information on local health concerns or to update your vaccinations or medical kit.

In addition, it may be appropriate to have a medical exam soon after you return home, if you were ill during your trip or if you traveled extensively in regions where severe health problems were endemic or epidemic. Some illnesses have long incubation periods and take weeks or more to become symptomatic, and it is usually much better to treat them in their early stages. You should be especially observant for health problems during your first few weeks home. If you have an exam, it may be advisable to include a stool test, to check for intestinal parasites and worm infestations, a blood test, to determine if you have a low-grade or unusual infection, and a check for skin cancer, if you have had a lot of exposure to the sun. A dental exam and cleaning will also probably be in order.

Personal hygiene and fitness

World travelers must regularly endure hygienic conditions that are well below western standards. One consequence of this is that there is a greater likelihood that you will be exposed to disease-causing organisms. Maintaining strict personal hygiene, including regularly washing your hands and taking showers, will improve your defenses against these organisms. As an example of how extreme hygienic problems can be, the newspaper *The Rising Nepal*, in an editorial dated June 30, 1991, stated that the Nepalese mortality rate could be reduced by 40% if the people there would simply wash their hands before eating meals.

Good fitness also provides protection from health risks, and it generally enables a more rapid recovery when a problem does occur. Unfortunately, travel is often detrimental to your conditioning. To counter this, you should discipline yourself to include training in your daily routines. There are innumerable opportunities to exercise during a world trip. You can visit gyms, which are available in most cities, and which usually have exercise machines, free weights and aerobics classes. (Gyms are also excellent places to meet locals.) For informal exercise, there is always jogging and calisthenics. Many activities, of course, also maintain or improve fitness, including hiking, bicycling, swimming and other sports.

Water, food and medical hygiene

You should always evaluate the safety of your water and food supplies. In some situations, such as with dirty tap water, or fly-covered, open-air food stands, hygienic risks will be obvious. At other times, though, there will be no evidence of contamination. You should remember that many countries do not have sophisticated, or even separate, water supply and sewage systems. Indeed, rivers in lesser developed countries often fulfill both roles. A local river may be the sole source of water for drinking and food preparation, yet it will also receive sewage and industrial runoff and be used for personal and clothes cleaning. The safety of food storage and preparation is also inconsistent. The following sections are intended to help you better understand the risks of water and food contamination. Standards of medical hygiene are also discussed, to provide guidance for people who require such care.

Water contamination

Water may be contaminated with many disease-causing organisms. For example, E. coli bacteria is a common cause of traveler's diarrhea. Other diseases that may be spread by water include amoebic dysentery, giardia, bilharzia, hepatitis A, typhoid fever and cholera. It is impossible for an ordinary traveler to determine if water is safe, since you would need professional training and a microscope to be certain. It is therefore appropriate to err on the conservative side when considering the safety of water supplies.

However, if water from a particular source does not taste good, this does not necessarily mean that it is contaminated. The water from municipal treatment systems and desalination plants often lacks a pleasant taste, but it is usually safe. Water supplies in most Western European countries, Australia and New Zealand, Japan and Singapore, and many large cities in other countries, should be safe. Water sources in lesser developed countries and outside of cities should be assumed to be bad, unless you have dependable assurances otherwise. You can make an impromptu survey of water safety by observing the habits of the locals, although this cannot always be trusted. Many residents of lesser developed countries regularly drink untreated water, but significant percentages of them also have intestinal parasites, or contract other illnesses, as a result. Contaminated water supplies are a major cause of the lower average life expectancies in these countries. You should also never drink untreated stream water in rural areas, no matter how clean it looks. You should always assume that there is a village or domestic or wild animals above you which are polluting it.

The following are a number of specific water safety guidelines:

- Drink or otherwise use only sterilized water and other beverages in all circumstances where the safety of the local water is questionable.
- Do not use ice in your beverages.
- Drink directly from bottles, rather than use potentially unhygienic glasses or cups.
- Avoid diluted juices, and any other non-boiled beverages that might contain local water.
- Brush your teeth with sterilized water.
- Avoid swallowing shower water.

Unfortunately, even after following these guidelines it is still almost impossible to avoid consuming some local water. You will be exposed to it if you get water in your mouth while showering, and from using restaurant dishes, glasses and cutlery that have been washed in it. You could protect yourself completely by sterilizing a sufficient amount of water for bucket showers and for cooking and cleaning, but this is an extreme course of action and it is certainly rarely appropriate.

Water sterilization

Methods of water sterilization include boiling, iodine drops and purification tablets, filters, and chlorine treatments. The trade-offs between them are effectiveness, the time that is required to purify the water, taste and cost. For instance, sterilization methods that are based only on chlorine will not kill some organisms, such as amoebic cysts, and are therefore less satisfactory.

Boiling water is a reliable method of sterilization, although it should be left to boil for a few minutes at high altitudes. Water treated with iodine is also safe, but it does not taste very good. In addition, it is not recommended for children, pregnant women and people with thyroid problems. The standard iodine treatment is five drops

(.25ml) of 2% tincture of iodine per quart or liter of clear water. This should be allowed to stand for thirty minutes before use. You should add ten drops for cold or cloudy water, after filtering out as much sediment as possible (use a coffee filter or a piece of cloth), and let it stand longer - for several hours if possible. For iodine tablets, you should follow the manufacturer's directions and again double the standard quantity for cold or cloudy water. (*Health Information for International Travel 1995*, page 177)

Filters are another effective means of water sterilization. They are manufactured with microporous substances that allow molecules of water to pass through, but which strain out larger organisms. Some filters are also impregnated with materials that kill the trapped organisms. I use a Katadyn Pocket Filter, which is the filter of choice for the staffs of the International Red Cross, the World Health Organization, and many other groups. While it is the most expensive from the perspective of up-front cost, which is about $250, it is the cheapest per liter of sterilized water, because it lasts so long. (Katadyn also makes a Mini Filter, which costs about $150.) You need two containers to use a filter, one to hold the potentially contaminated water and the other to receive the purified water. My filter will sterilize a liter of water in about two minutes (others take substantially longer), and this proved to be very useful when I was trekking, since I needed to drink about a liter of water per hour to prevent dehydration. The cost disadvantage of filters compared to iodine is reduced by the fact that you do not need to buy beverages when you want a change from the taste of iodine-treated water. This also proved to be advantageous when trekking, since bottled water must be carried to mountain villages by porters and often costs a dollar or more per liter. Water filters must be used according to their instructions to avoid inadvertent contamination, and they need to be cleaned periodically.

(The *Magellan Catalog* is a good source for a variety of different water filters. It can be ordered from Box 5485, Santa Barbara, CA, 93150, (800) 962-4943.)

Alternatives to water sterilization

An alternative to sterilization is to buy bottled water. It is available in most lesser developed countries and is usually inexpensive. However, you should examine the seals to ensure that they are intact, since unscrupulous shops have been known to refill bottles with tap water. Bottles that are purchased in restaurants should be brought to the table unopened. In tropical countries, another option is to drink coconut water. (Vendors on trains in Sri Lanka will open a fresh king coconut for you, and the cost is minimal.) Collected rain water is a final safe supply, and it is easy to set up a funnel with a piece of plastic or cloth. Alternatives to water include boiled and bottled beverages such as tea, coffee, Coke, Pepsi and other locally bottled sodas.

Food safety

Travelers regularly experience minor stomach discomfort from eating contaminated or spoiled food, or as a consequence of exposure to new diets and spices, perhaps coupled with the effects of jet lag, exhaustion and stress. Indeed, the latter factors are probably responsible for most of the stomach problems that Americans have in Europe. On the other hand, the risk of food contamination and spoilage can be severe in lesser developed countries, because of inadequate food storage and poor food worker hygiene. Electrical generation in many of these countries is inconsistent, and networks occasionally, or even regularly, suffer brownouts. Some merchants, instead of throwing spoiled food away, keep trying to sell it. It is also common for vendors to turn off their refrigerators at night to save on electricity. Food that is left out during opening hours can also spoil, or be contaminated by flies and other pests. Finally, food workers who have dirty hands and bad habits can be a problem. You get the idea, and as the above reference to Nepal suggests, hygienic standards can be very low.

You will inevitably develop traveler's diarrhea or food poisoning if you eat contaminated or spoiled food. Some more severe diseases, such as hepatitis A, are also spread this way. Your basic means of protection is to pass up questionable stands and restaurants. You can try to extrapolate the quality of food safety from the cleanliness of a restaurant or its kitchen, but this is an imperfect test. In risky locations, you should discipline yourself not to eat suspect food, and to avoid items that spoil easily, including meats, dairy products and fish.

The following are additional food safety guidelines that you should practice, depending on the risk of contamination:

- Eat only fully cooked foods.
- Avoid salads.
- Peel all fruit and vegetables yourself.
- Avoid unpasteurized dairy products, including milk, cheese, eggs and ice cream.

- Be wary of seafood, especially from street vendors. Some species of fish and shellfish have or collect toxins in their flesh, and these persist even after cooking. All seafood may also harbor bacteria and parasites. For example, sidewalk vendors of *ceviche* (raw seafood salad) have been linked to the spread of cholera in Peru.
- As this suggests, you should always be careful when eating at outdoor stands.
- Avoid low-cost alcoholic beverages in lesser developed countries. They are sometimes tainted with dangerous chemicals that can cause poisoning and other health problems.
- Eat canned or packaged foods, or cook for yourself.

Medical hygiene

The safety of blood supplies is suspect in many countries. Indeed, hospitals and clinics in lesser developed countries often do not test blood supplies for AIDS. According to the Centers for Disease Control (CDC - a part of the U.S. Department of Health and Human Services), blood should be transfused into a traveler only when it is absolutely necessary. Plasma expanders should be used instead or, if the patient can be transported, he or she should be evacuated to a medical facility at home. If a transfusion is essential, the attending physician should be prevailed upon to make every effort to screen the blood for AIDS and other transmissible diseases. Syringes may also be inadequately sterilized. You should insist that a new syringe be used in any circumstance where an inoculation is required. Indeed, some people, including many traveling physicians, carry syringes in their medical kits to be prepared for situations where good hygiene is not guaranteed.

Toilet and shower standards

The final hygienic issue has to do with psychological adaptation. Toilets and showers around the world are often disgusting, and this section reviews some of more unpleasant conditions that you might encounter so you can begin to make the necessary mental adjustments.

Toilets are uniformly of the seated flush variety in only a few developed nations, and at high standard hotels in lesser developed countries. This means that you will regularly have to use floor toilets. (It is a bit of an acquired skill to use a squat toilet; I hope your legs are strong, although on the plus side you do not have to worry about cleaning the seat.) However, in some areas even these presumably civilized conditions go right out the door - literally. Using the toilet in many places means going to the designated field or beach. For the latter you let the tide do the work, and plan carefully where and when you go swimming! More generally, you will encounter flush toilets without seats, which are a budget restaurant and train station standard, or squat toilets with filthy floors and without doors or even roofs. (You will be happier if you are wearing boots!) The worst situation, which is a bit hard to accept, is when you have to visit one of these pits from hell under less than ideal circumstances, in other words, when you have Montezuma's Revenge, the Kathmandu Quickstep or Delhi Belly. This is horrible, of course, but it is nothing that a little fortitude won't get you through. It might also help if you think of it as a character-building experience.

Moving on to other bathroom fixtures (please excuse the puns), in lesser developed countries shower pressure is often weak and hot water non-existent. You will not even have a shower in some places. For instance, in Indonesia you use a *mandi*, which is a basin full of clean water with a ladle. You stand on the floor next to the mandi (don't get into it!), and sluice the water over your body. As another example, the standard shower when trekking is a bucket of cold water from a tap or stream. This has a real influence on your sensitivity to dirt, especially at high elevations in the cold and wind. I did not take a shower for ten days (of hard exercise) on the Annapurna Circuit trek. (I did wash my hands.) The locals there never do, but they do benefit from the fact that built-up body grease protects you from the cold. Taken to the other extreme, salt water showers are sometimes the only option in tropical countries. For example, some resorts in the Maldives pump salt water into their guests' bathrooms. Fresh water for drinking is available separately from desalination systems, and is provided in pitchers. Salt water may smell bad when you first run the tap, because of sulfur deposits, but this will clear up after a few seconds. Showering in salt water also leaves you a bit sticky, but you should get used to it.

Tropical bathrooms are often inhabited by a variety of interesting creatures, including huge spiders, millipedes and other large bugs. You should not be afraid of them, though, since they will not bother you if you do not disturb them. It is also wise to watch out for snakes. (We found a viper near an outhouse in Burma.) Lastly, you will probably encounter some curious plumbing systems in your travels. I still remember the first time I saw a *bidet*. (What the heck is that for?)

Vaccinations and malaria prophylaxis

Vaccinations have been developed for many of the diseases to which travelers may be exposed. Although "*no vaccine is completely effective or completely safe*" (Ibid., page 79), they do offer from partial to virtually complete immunization and are therefore highly recommended. Indeed, you should maintain an awareness of developments in the field, since improved vaccinations are regularly being licensed. (A vaccine for malaria is reportedly undergoing preliminary tests.)

You will need expert advice on the vaccinations for your trip, including on alternatives and contraindications, or reasons that might make having a particular vaccination inadvisable, such as preexisting medical conditions, potential allergic reactions and other side effects. Few doctors, though, can provide this advice, or have access to the actual vaccines. A better option is to visit a travelers health clinic, and your physician can direct you to one. Vaccinations can of course also be obtained abroad. (I got the vaccinations for my world trip in Sweden and England, both of which were less expensive than the U.S. In London, you might want to try Trailfinders Medical Advisory and Immunisation Centre on Kensington High Street.)

In the U.S., the CDC is the best source of information on vaccinations. It publishes a book called *Health Information for International Travel*, which lists the recommended vaccinations for every country. This book can be ordered from the Government Printing Office, and it is also an excellent source of information on many other traveler health concerns. (The descriptions of many of the issues and problems that are reviewed in this chapter are in part drawn from it.)

The CDC also has an International Traveler Information Hotline. This is a recorded service that provides information on a wide variety of health concerns, including disease outbreaks. It is accessible as follows:

- (404) 332-4559	Traveler's hotline
- (404) 332-4555	Main CDC information service menu
- http://www.cdc.gov	CDC Internet homepage

Vaccination issues

A few other general comments on vaccinations are as follows:

- You should keep a record of all of the vaccinations that you receive in an International Certificate of Vaccination.
- Most vaccinations are based on *live attenuated* (altered, but still living) or *whole killed* (inactivated) virus, or inactivated bacteria. The tetanus vaccine, though, is a toxoid, or a bacterial toxin that has been rendered harmless. All of these substances work by stimulating the body's production of antibodies. Gamma globulin, which is sometimes used for protection against hepatitis A, is an injection of a sterile blood product that is already rich in antibodies.
- You can usually receive many of the vaccinations that you require in one doctor or clinic visit. A few of them, however, must be received separately to maintain their full effectiveness.
- Some vaccinations are given orally, but most require inoculations. Some vaccinations also require series of doses, which must be received following specific timetables to achieve maximum effectiveness. (The series for a particular vaccination may vary by the country in which it is received, both in number and spacing, since different vaccines may be used or because of varying recommendations from the public health authorities.)
- Vaccinations often cause localized pain and swelling, and feelings of nausea.
- Vaccinations may need to be postponed for people who are suffering from febrile illnesses (accompanied by fever).
- People who have immunodeficiency diseases may be at risk of contracting the illnesses that the vaccines are designed to prevent.
- Some vaccinations should not be received by pregnant woman.

Description of vaccinations

For my world trip, I had vaccinations for tetanus, typhoid fever, meningococcal meningitis, polio (OPV), and rabies (HDCV), and an inoculation of gamma globulin. I had previously had the vaccination for yellow fever, and since then I have had the vaccine Havrix for hepatitis A.

Cholera

Cholera is an intestinal disease that is usually spread by ingesting contaminated water or food. Transmission can also occur through interpersonal contact, but this is rare. The disease tends to occur in epidemics. For instance, an epidemic of cholera began in South America in January 1991, and by the end of that year almost four hundred thousand cases had been reported. It is believed that the epidemic started in Peru, and in February 1992, seventy-five people contracted the disease by eating seafood salad on a flight from Buenos Aires to Los Angeles that made a stop in Lima. Cholera is a disease of poor sanitation, so the water and food safety recommendations that were listed earlier should be followed carefully in any country where an epidemic is in progress.

Cholera causes rapid dehydration due to continuous diarrhea and vomiting. Left untreated, it can kill in a day. Travelers to epidemic regions who develop severe watery diarrhea, even after leaving (the incubation period is five days), should immediately seek medical attention. The disease responds well to replacement of fluids and electrolytes and to antibiotics.

"A vaccine for cholera is available; however, it confers only brief and incomplete immunity and is not recommended for travelers." (*Cholera Prevention*, CDC/NCID leaflet). The vaccination is no longer required by the World Health Organization's International Health Regulations.

(There is a new cholera vaccine, made in Switzerland and consisting of two oral doses separated by a week. It is available in Europe.)

Hepatitis A

Hepatitis is a liver disease. Hepatitis A is normally transmitted by contaminated food or water, but it can also be spread by person-to-person contact. Its symptoms include pain in the liver, fatigue, fever, nausea, deep orange-colored urine, which will not lighten regardless of how much fluids are consumed, and jaundice, the classic yellow skin and eye syndrome. The virus is inactivated by boiling water or cooking food, although food can of course become recontaminated from handling. A vaccine for the disease, Havrix, first became available in 1994. The initial version required three inoculations, but this has been reduced to two. The first provides immunity for over a year, and the second, which should follow the first by at least six months, extends the protection to ten years. (A second vaccine, Vaqta, became available in May 1996.)

There is no cure for hepatitis A. If you get it, you should find a relaxing place to recuperate. It is best to eat plenty of green vegetables and fruit, drink lots of water and take vitamin B supplements. You should avoid alcohol, cigarettes and beverages that contain caffeine.

Hepatitis B

Hepatitis B is spread between individuals via the exchange of blood or blood-derived fluids, including through sexual activity and the sharing of syringes. Inadequate sterilization of tattooing, acupuncture and medical and dental equipment can also lead to its transmission. A vaccination produced through recombinant DNA technology is available, and consists of three inoculations. The second should follow the first by one month, and the third should be received five months after this.

Japanese encephalitis

Japanese encephalitis is spread by mosquito bites. It is usually contracted during the summer and autumn in temperate regions of Asia, and during the monsoon in tropical Asia. Most people who catch the disease do not develop symptoms, but of those who do the fatality rate may be as high as 30%. The risk is highest where rice culture and pig farming are practiced. There are a number of vaccines for Japanese encephalitis, and the version licensed for sale in the U.S. consists of three inoculations on days 0, 7 and 30. A booster is necessary every three years. The vaccine is appropriate for people who are planning to travel extensively in rural areas in the endemic regions. Protection against mosquitos should also be used.

Meningococcal meningitis

This disease causes inflammation of the membranes that surround the brain and the spinal cord. There are three separate serogroups that can cause epidemics, and a vaccine that provides immunity against the two most common forms is available. Only one inoculation is required, and the protection appears to last at least three years.

Plague

Plague occurs periodically in rural rodent populations, and fleas may transmit the disease to humans. However, the efficacy of the plague vaccine has not been demonstrated in a controlled trial, and it is rarely considered necessary. Travelers who are in areas where plague epidemics are in progress, such as India in late 1994, may want to take the prophylaxis, which is 500 mg of tetracycline, four times a day, during the period of possible exposure.

Poliomyelitis

World travelers should be vaccinated against polio. Most adults in the U.S. have had the primary vaccination series as children, but boosters are recommended before embarking on a foreign trip. There are two different vaccines for polio: trivalent oral polio vaccine (OPV) and enhanced-potency inactivated polio vaccine (IPV). In rare instances, OPV has been associated with paralysis in both recipients and their contacts. "*No serious side effects of IPV have been documented.*" (*Health Information for International Travel 1995*, page 139)

Rabies

Rabies is a viral disease, and it is fatal if not treated. It is almost always caused by a bite from an infected dog, monkey, vampire bat or other animal. (It is rare for the disease to develop from a non-bite exposure where an animal's saliva comes into contact with an open wound.) All animal bites and scratches should be vigorously cleaned with soap and water, and rubbing alcohol if it is available, since this will significantly reduce the risk of infection. ("*Immediate cleaning with soap and water has been shown to protect 90% of experimental animals.*" *The Sanford Guide to Antimicrobial Therapy 1996*, Antimicrobial Therapy, Inc., page 119) It is also a good idea to carry a stick in areas where dogs or monkeys are present. If you are in a vampire bat habitat, it is worth knowing that they like to bite the exposed toes of sleeping campers. You should definitely close your tent!

The advanced symptoms of rabies include fever, insomnia, anxiety and maniacal behavior, fear of water, difficulty swallowing, excessive tearing and salivation, and convulsions. You are done for if it gets this far.

Having the rabies vaccination simplifies the treatment for people who subsequently may have been exposed. Preexposure immunization consists of three doses of human diploid cell rabies vaccine (HDCV), or rabies absorbed vaccine (RVA), on days 0, 7 and 21 or 28. Postexposure treatment for people who were previously immunized is two doses of either preparation, on days 0 and 3. For people who were not previously immunized, one dose of rabies immune globulin (RIG) is required along with five doses of HDCV or RVA, on days 0, 3, 7, 14 and 28. A dose of RIG can cost over two hundred dollars. It is also important to note that HDCV may have reduced effectiveness if it is received in conjunction with malaria pills. This vaccination series should be completed before you begin malaria prophylaxis.

Tetanus, diphtheria and pertussis

Tetanus and diphtheria are common around the world, but are prevented in people who are adequately immunized. Pertussis (whooping cough) is a children's disease, and it is also prevented by vaccination. Combined vaccines for the first two are administered to adults, and for all three to children. A booster for tetanus and diphtheria is necessary every ten years.

Typhoid fever

Typhoid fever is transmitted by contaminated food or water, and there are three alternative vaccines. The oral version consists of four doses over a seven day period, and the entire series should be repeated every five years. Typhim Vi requires one inoculation, and a booster every two years. The final version consists of two inoculations four or more weeks apart, with a booster every three years. "*All three vaccines have been shown to protect 50% to 80% of recipients, depending in part on the degree of subsequent exposure.*" (*Health Information for International Travel 1995*, page 149) This means that even with the vaccination there is still a significant risk of contracting the disease. Good food and water hygiene should therefore be followed. (Typhoid responds well to treatment with antibiotics.)

Yellow fever

Yellow fever is endemic in tropical and sub-tropical Africa and South America. The vaccination for it consists of one inoculation, and a booster is required every ten years. (People who are allergic to eggs may be allergic to it.) It is the only vaccination that is regularly required by the regulations of the World Health Organization.

Malaria prophylaxis

Malaria is transmitted by the bites of mosquitos that are hosts to any of four related protozoan parasites. It is endemic in most tropical and sub-tropical regions, and travelers to rural areas are at greatest risk. (People who stay in cities or at resorts probably do not need to take the pills.) Symptoms of malaria include severe headaches, fever, chills, and sweating and fainting spells. They may develop from a week to months after the initial infection.

Unfortunately, in many of the endemic areas the protozoa have become resistant to the traditional prophylaxis of chloroquine phosphate. This happens when they survive contact with the blood of people who are taking the prophylaxis. If a mosquito draws blood from such a person, any protozoa that survive may have offspring that are resistant to the drug.

The following options are the currently recommended malaria prophylaxis:

- In areas where no resistance is reported, a weekly dose of 300 mg of chloroquine (500 mg in some preparations), beginning one to two weeks before arrival in the risk area and continuing for four weeks after departure.
- In areas where resistance has been reported, a weekly dose of 250 mg of mefloquine (Lariam), taken for the same period as for chloroquine.
- An alternative to mefloquine is to supplement chloroquine with proguanil (Paludrine - it is not available in the U.S.). A daily 200 mg dose is required for the latter, and you should start taking it one or two days before arrival and continue for four weeks following departure.
- Resistance to both mefloquine and proguanil has been reported in the Thailand/ Cambodia border region. In this area, the recommended prophylaxis is a daily dose of 100 mg of doxycycline, for the same period as for proguanil.
- Two of the four types of protozoa can persist in the liver, and cause relapses of the symptoms for up to four years. Taking daily 15 mg doses of primaquine phosphate during the last two weeks of the prophylaxis should reduce the frequency and severity of such relapses if one of these forms of the illness is contracted.

Malaria prophylaxis can have serious side effects, including hallucinations with mefloquine and vomiting (and hair loss) with proguanil. You should stop taking the pills if you have these reactions. (On my second trip I took Lariam, but after a couple of months my dreams became extremely strange - unusually vivid and depressing and involving people whom I had not thought about for at least ten years. I have also met people who started having these types of dreams after their first pill.) In addition, an "*overdose of antimalarial drugs can be fatal.*" (Ibid., page 128) Perhaps most seriously, and as the above point on primaquine implies, you can still catch malaria when taking the pills, and if you do the treatment can be more complicated and difficult.

Malaria may be fatal if treatment is delayed. If prompt medical care (within twenty-four hours) is not available, presumptive self-treatment consists of a three tablet dose of Fansidar, with the prophylaxis continuing thereafter. It is imperative that this also be followed by a professional diagnosis (a blood test is required), and additional treatment. "*Mefloquine should not be used for self-treatment.*" (Ibid., page 126) In addition, it should not be used as a treatment concurrently with quinine or quinidine. The specific full treatment for malaria depends on which form of the protozoa is present, and the severity of the symptoms. Life-threatening malaria requires treatment with intravenous drugs.

Life-saving first-aid

In rare circumstances you may need to give first-aid to victims of medical emergencies. The most severe life-threatening situations are where a person has a breathing obstruction or where his or her breathing has stopped, where the heart has stopped beating (cardiac arrest), or where severe bleeding is present. First-aid for these and other health crises are described in the following sections. This information should ideally be supplemented with instruction from medical professionals, particularly for people who engage in high risk activities. (The American Red Cross regularly offers inexpensive courses in basic and advanced first-aid, and many hospitals have similar programs.)

If you are in a situation where someone requires any of the following procedures, you should immediately send another person for professional medical assistance. If you are alone with the victim, you should shout for help to attract passersby and send one of them. Victims of any of these problems should also be treated for shock (see below).

Breathing obstructions

The first-aid for a person who has an obstruction in his or her throat, such as unswallowed food, is called the Heimlich Maneuver. To administer this you should stand behind the victim, wrap your arms around them, and make a fist with one hand, holding it above their navel but below the bottom of their breastbone. You should then grab your fist with your other hand and pull sharply into the victim with an upward thrust, repeating this until the object in the victim's throat is coughed out. If you are choking and no one is present to assist you, you should perform the maneuver on yourself (by punching your fist into this spot), or else lean over and press your stomach sharply against a solid object such as the back of a chair. If this does not work, you can also try to jolt the object free by throwing yourself forcefully to the ground, either onto your stomach or back.

Artificial respiration

A victim who has stopped breathing, which may be due to near-drowning, electrocution, an allergic reaction or some other cause, must be given artificial respiration. The procedure for this is as follows:

- Shout for help, and send someone for professional medical assistance.
- As a proviso, if the victim may have a spinal or serious head injury, he or she should be moved as little as possible during the procedure.
- Carefully place the victim on their back, and push their chin up to tilt their head back and straighten their throat.
- Place your ear next to their mouth and listen, and also watch their chest, for signs of breathing. Artificial respiration should not be given if the victim is breathing.
- Check for a pulse in the cartoid artery. This is located on the neck next to the adam's apple. People who have stopped breathing may have a weak pulse. If the victim does not have a pulse, which means that their heart has also stopped, they should be given CPR (see below).
- If the victim is not breathing, use your fingers to clear any obstructions in their mouth, and check to see if they have swallowed their tongue. If the latter has occurred, you will have to pull it out to its normal position.
- If the victim has an airway obstruction that you cannot clear with your fingers, crouch on their legs and, with the heels of your palms, thrust upward sharply into their stomach just above the navel. (This is like the Heimlich Maneuver.) Do this five to ten times, and then try again to clear the obstruction.

- After clearing their breathing passage, pinch their nose, take a breath and, after sealing your mouth around theirs, breathe slowly and deeply into them.
- Look at their chest, and listen, for signs of breathing.
- Give them one breath every five seconds.
- Continue to check for signs of breathing and, every minute or so, repeat the check for a pulse.
- Continue this until the victim begins breathing on their own, or medical assistance arrives.

Cardiac arrest and CPR

Cardiac arrest is most often caused by a heart attack, the symptoms of which include chest pains, shortness of breath, sweating and nausea. Any suspected victim of cardiac arrest should be checked for signs of breathing and a pulse in the cartoid artery (see the above section). If a victim is breathing or has a pulse, then his or her heart has not stopped and CPR should not be performed. In addition, since CPR can cause broken ribs and a bruised heart, it should ideally be administered only by someone who has been properly trained. The procedure for CPR is as follows, and it is important to note that it varies depending on if you must administer it by yourself, or if someone is present to assist you:

- Shout for help, and send someone for professional medical assistance.
- Follow the procedure for artificial respiration and give the victim three full breaths of air.
- If you are by yourself, slide your fingers along their lowest rib to the point where it connects to the end of their breastbone.
- Place the palm of one of your hands on the victim's breastbone, about an inch above this point. Then, place your other hand on top of this hand.
- Lean forward and, with your arms held straight, compress the victim's breastbone by 1 and 1/2 to 2 inches. Repeat this smoothly *fifteen* times, counting out loud as you do: *1* (when you press) *1000* (when you release), *2 1000*, *3 1000*, ... It is not necessary to bare the victim's chest of clothing unless it interferes with the CPR.
- Give the victim two breaths of air, and check the cartoid artery for a pulse.
- If two people are administering the procedure, the first should give the artificial respiration, followed by *five* compressions of the chest by the second.
- Continue the cycle of compressions and two breaths of air until there is a pulse and breathing, or medical assistance arrives.

Severe bleeding

Severe bleeding should be controlled by applying firm and direct pressure to the wound. However, because of the risk of disease transmission, you should use a barrier such as a bandage when applying the pressure, and then wash well afterwards. For arterial bleeding, where a wound is spurting blood, it may be necessary to reach into it and pinch or press the artery closed. A wound on a limb should be elevated so that it is above the level of the heart. Applying pressure to the locations on the limbs where arteries are close to the skin, which are called pressure points, can also help control bleeding if a pressure point is located between the wound and the heart. There are pressure points on the underside of the wrist below the thumb, on the inside of the arm under the bicep, and in the groin on the inside of the leg. They can be located by feeling for a pulse, and you should apply pressure to them with your fingertips.

Burns

Burns are classified as first degree, if they are red and dry; second degree, if they are blistered, mottled and swollen; and third degree, if they are brown and charred or if underlying body tissues are exposed. Burns should be cooled with water or wet cloths until they are no longer warm to the touch. Ice should only be used with first degree burns. Open second degree and all third degree burns have a high risk of infection. You should gently clean any open blisters of second degree burns with soap and water, and apply an antibiotic ointment. Third degree burns are life-threatening and require immediate medical attention. You should not clean them, apply ointments, or remove stuck clothing. Severe burns should be covered with loose sterile bandages, and the victims should be treated for shock.

Poisoning

It is unlikely that you will ingest or otherwise be exposed to poisons during your world trip. However, two possible exceptions to this are spoiled food and tainted alcoholic beverages. For example, a Swiss friend of mine became very ill after eating spoiled prawns in Goa - the restaurant that served them had inadequate refrigeration. Food poisoning typically clears up after the food is expelled from the body, and medical attention is only necessary if weakness and fever increases or persists. Tainted alcoholic beverages are often the cause of blindness and death in lesser developed countries, since methyl alcohol and other dangerous chemicals are sometimes used in their preparation. Indeed, over two hundred people died in the Indian state of Orissa in May 1992, after drinking a spirit that contained methyl alcohol. The problem with preventing this type of poisoning is that drinking with locals, particularly their home brews, can be a tremendous amount of fun. You can minimize the risk by avoiding the cheapest bottled spirits and by carefully questioning the safety of any home brews. Poisoning that is caused by the bites or stings of snakes, insects and sea creatures is covered later in the chapter. Medical assistance should be sought immediately in all other cases of poisoning, such as from breathing or swallowing dangerous gases or fluids.

Shock

Injuries are often aggravated by shock, when the body responds to the trauma by reducing blood circulation. Shock can cause death, and its symptoms include fast breathing, a fast and weak pulse, cool, moist and pale skin, and thirst, nausea and vomiting. If these symptoms are present, you should lie the victim on his or her back, or on their side if they are vomiting. You should also raise their legs by about a foot, unless they are broken or if there is evidence of head or neck injuries. Restrictive points on their clothing, such as the collar, cuffs and waist, should be loosened. In addition, it is important to prevent them from becoming chilled or overheated.

Traveler accidents

Accidents are probably the most common serious health risk for world travelers. There are many different types of accidents, and they generally vary in severity by activity and locale. For instance, accidental causes of death usually involve transportation, drowning or adventurous sports. The risk of being involved in an accident is also higher in lesser developed countries and certain topographical regions, such as mountain ranges. In the latter, travel on foot or by vehicle can be extremely dangerous in areas that are exposed to avalanches and rockslides.

General advice on accident prevention

A few general points on accident prevention are as follows:

- Minimize or forgo drinking alcoholic beverages. This is particularly important for people who will be driving vehicles or participating in sports. If you are part of a group that is out socializing, one person should abstain and act as the designated driver.

- Travel with a partner.
- Plan your activities and arrangements carefully, and allow sufficient time in your schedule to complete them.
- Limit your activities when you are tired.

As an example of the first point, and as proof that accidents can happen anywhere and to anyone, consider the following story of a car crash in which I was involved. I was in Scotland in December 1993, in the village of Durness, which is at the far northwest corner of the country. I had been traveling all day by post bus to get there, and was the only customer in the only open restaurant in the village. (I was also the first traveler there in weeks!) I had a nice fish and chips dinner, and as I finished it a local woman walked in for, as she put it, "*a quiet pint.*" It seems the pub down the road was teeming with four or five other people.

She bought me a dram of whisky and a pint and, to make conversation, I asked her about highland games and *ceilidhs* ("kaylees"), or dances. Before I knew it she made a phone call and we were off. Apparently there was a ceilidh that night in a pub in the nearby village of Melness. It was a retirement party for a local man, with a full buffet and a band (accordionists, and acoustic and bass guitar). There were about fifty people, done up in their Sunday best.

It was a great party. We went straight to the bar, and in seconds people were buying me pints. (Highland Scots are rugged and direct, but also warm and friendly.)

Well, the party went on and on. (I found out later that ceilidhs often last all night.) I became exhausted, and escaped to my friend's van to take a nap. She finally came out, at 4 a.m., but was in a bad mood from having had an argument with another woman about a horse.

We then drove off, only to wreck about a mile down the road. The weather had changed for the worse (this can happen in five minutes on the north coast), and the road was covered with black ice. We hit a patch, and the rear wheels lost their grip. We slid to the right, then back to the left - crunch!, as we hit the stone wall bounding the one lane track, back to the right - bam!, as we hit that wall, back to the left again - at a sharp angle - slam!, as we hit one more time, and then, that sickening feeling, over we went. Fortunately, our speed was such that the van only tipped onto its side. My friend was above me, hanging in her seatbelt (I had insisted we wear them), followed by her sheep dog and then me, by the door and the ground.

Another departing guest soon pulled up and helped us out. We were shaken - wow - what an adrenaline rush, it lasted an hour, but the only damage was to the car. We could not turn it over so we went back for help; all done quickly and quietly so as not to alert the village constable. Finally, in another person's car, we drove back to Durness - in a blizzard. I got out at my B&B at 7 a.m., completely shattered, and without even a kiss from my bonny lass to show for it.

The lesson of this story should be obvious: don't drink and drive, and don't trust anyone else who does, either!

Transportation accidents

You should evaluate the air, road or seaworthiness of all the vehicles that you intend to use, and change your plans if you have serious reservations about them. However, you will have to discipline yourself to act on your concerns, since the general tendency in such circumstances is to ignore the risks and go along. This is particularly true when you are part of a group and there is peer pressure. (Remember the Cambodian kidnapping.) Accidents do happen, and it is your life that is in danger. As another example, I heard of a surfing tour that left Bali to visit a remote island. The boat was poorly maintained, and its engine failed on the way and could not be repaired. It drifted with the ocean currents, and after eight days another island finally came into sight. Two of the surfers paddled to it and then hiked through a jungle for days before finding a village. They were then able to arrange for the rescue of the other people on the boat, who by this time were in very bad shape. You should also avoid vehicles that are overcrowded (think of all the ferries that sink and buses that crash), or where the drivers have been drinking or are otherwise untrustworthy.

Other tips on transportation safety, by mode of travel, are as follows:

- Avoid flying in bad weather, including storms and fog. This applies at both your departure point and destination. (You can get the latest report on the weather conditions at the arrival airport from your airline.) This is especially true with small planes and in mountainous areas. For example, two jetliners crashed in 1992 during their approaches to Kathmandu, which is surrounded by hills. Both flights were attempting to land during monsoon rainstorms. It is also worth considering, if you do take a flight in bad weather, or on a small plane in rugged terrain, that the safest seats are generally the aisle seats in the very last row.

- Avoid using airlines that have poor safety records, such as Aeroflot and CAAC, and also the airlines that fly over Afghanistan (Aeroflot and Tajik Air), since the combatants there have surface-to-air missiles.
- Sit in the rear cars when traveling on trains.
- Avoid traveling at night on local buses and trucks, particularly in mountainous regions where the roads are bad. If you must do this, your life is in the hands of the driver, and it is probably safest to ride by the door, since you can make sure the driver stays awake, or in the back of the vehicle.
- For automobile travel, always wear a seatbelt, only let other people drive if they will do so defensively, and do not let anyone drive who has been drinking. You should also drive only when you are well-rested, during the day if you can, and stop periodically for breaks. Lastly, it is important to watch out for children, bicyclists, motorcyclists and animals on the road.
- On boats and ferries, check for the presence of life vests, life boats or rafts, and two-way emergency radios, and be aware of quick and clear routes to the side railings. You should also keep an eye on any moving boat rig, particularly the boom on yachts. If you are at the helm, you should maneuver your boat slowly and carefully through waters that are shallow or where reefs may be present, that are congested with other boats, or where people may be swimming, snorkeling or scuba diving.
- As a bicyclist or motorcyclist, always wear a helmet, be wary of every vehicle that overtakes you, and watch for vehicles and pedestrians entering your path from side streets.
- If you are on foot, walk on the side of the road towards oncoming traffic and be prepared to jump out of the way.

Drowning

Drowning is one of the most common accidental causes of death for travelers. However, it is usually easy to prevent. It sometimes occurs due to cramps, and the prescription of waiting for an hour after eating before going swimming should of course be followed. The greatest risk when swimming, though, is from water currents, which vary in strength by the time of day and month according to the lunar tides. Currents tend to be strongest during the changing of tides, in channels around and between islands, in lagoon and atoll entrance channels, and along beaches that have steep underwater dropoffs. Surface water movements, which sometimes result from wind, can be misleading and disguise strong currents. You should always test for currents when you go swimming, and this can be done as follows: walk into the water, but not so deep that you have to swim, and then turn around and walk back to the shore. How difficult is it? If this is not a problem, let yourself float off of your feet and try to swim back. Can you do it, and how strong is the current? It is important to check for currents regularly if you do not want to be swept away, particularly as you get farther from the shore.

A special form of current, called a riptide, may be present at any beach where there is surf. Riptides are channels that move surf water back into the ocean or down the beach. You should assume that there are riptides at any beach that has rough surf, and not go swimming unless it is patrolled by lifeguards who say that it is safe. (It is of course a good idea not to swim at unpatrolled beaches, especially if you are alone.) If you are caught in a riptide, and are unable to make headway against it back to the shore, it is better to swim parallel to the beach to find a location where the current is less strong. It is also a good idea to wear goggles, since if you are in a situation where you have to swim through rough surf to reach the shore, they will enable you to see underwater and avoid rocks and coral.

Whirlpools are another type of hazard, and they occur when currents collide or when other sources of turbulence are present, such as submerged rocks. To escape from a whirlpool you should get a good breath of air, and then dive down through its vortex, under and away from it. You should not try to swim away at the surface. For instance, I met a local man on Hudhuveli in the Maldives, who was trapped in a whirlpool with another swimmer. He survived by diving under it, but his friend drowned while struggling at the surface. Both were young, strong swimmers, and the whirlpool had formed less than fifty yards offshore, on a sharp corner of the island where a strong current passed by.

Lastly, many people have drowned when they tried to rescue other people who were in trouble. You should be very cautious when approaching a struggling individual. Swim up to them from behind, and with one arm grab them over the shoulder and across the chest. You can then support them on your hip and swim away using a side stroke. It is also a good idea to take a life-saving course, particularly if you are active in water sports. Such courses are offered by the Red Cross and at public pools.

Orthopedic injuries

Travelers regularly suffer orthopedic injuries, ranging from strains and sprains, such as twisted ankles and *trekkers knee*, to bone fractures. For the former, treatment includes resting the injured body part and caring for swelling and pain. Swelling can be reduced by applying ice, to cool the injured area and restrict blood circulation, and then elastic bandages or braces. Ice packs should be applied for a maximum of fifteen minutes, although they can be reapplied after allowing some time for circulation to be restored. Anti-inflammatory drugs should be taken if the swelling is severe. Over-the-counter anti-inflammatories include aspirin (buffered aspirin is easier on the stomach), ibuprofin, Motrin and Advil, and they should also reduce pain. Prescription pharmaceuticals for reducing swelling are also available, such as diclofenac sodium (Voltaren), although they should only be taken with meals.

Bone fractures are classified as simple or compound, depending on whether or not the broken bone has pierced the skin. Treatment for bleeding is required for a compound fracture, and all fractures should be immobilized while medical attention is sought. A splint can often be improvised from available materials, such as sticks and bandages or cord. It should be padded as well. The victim of a fracture should be moved as little as possible if there is severe trauma, particularly if there is an injury to the head or spine. In such a case, it may be necessary to hold, or otherwise support, the victim's head and neck to prevent movement while other first aid, such as the control of bleeding, is accomplished.

Adventure travel and high-risk sports

If you are an adventurous traveler you should anticipate, and practice, how you will respond if an accident occurs while you are engaged in a high-risk activity. In addition, you should always carry any emergency gear that might be required, such as extra food, water and warm clothing, a rope and carabineers, a light, both for illumination and as a means of signaling, and an extensive first-aid kit. It is worth remembering that accident situations often become much more serious if immediate responses are not possible. You only have to consider the penalty if someone is buried in an avalanche while skiing, but is not wearing a radio transceiver with which to be located. As a less dramatic example, if you twist an ankle while hiking, your problems should be limited if you have an elastic bandage in your medical kit.

Common aspects of adventure travel accidents include a remote location, limited availability of medical aid, a victim in severe pain, and a need for great endurance on the part of everyone involved. Because of these factors, it is essential when you are engaged in high-risk activities to use good judgement, know your limits, and not make mistakes. You should not force yourself to keep pace with someone who is more skilled or in better shape. You should also be extra cautious if you are tired, and if you are faced with a choice to go on or turn back, it is almost always better to return. As an example of this, I once cracked my right hip when I fell while skiing in the French Alps. I had been skiing all day on *Les Grandes Montets* tram in Argentière (there was superb powder on the Argentière Glacier), and on the last ride up I met some people who invited me to join them. In retrospect, this was a mistake. We skied *Le Pas du Chevre* (the Goat Path) off-piste ski run, which falls some 9,000 vertical feet to the town of Chamonix. The snow conditions at the top were great, but it was very heavy lower down. I became exhausted, and fell a few miles from the end of the run after hitting some rocks while skiing across a chute on the thinly covered *Mer de Glace* glacier. (I hit the rocks when I skied around a person who had fallen in the main track; I should have waited until he was clear.) I continued to ski, on one leg, until the snow ran out, and then, using my poles as a crutch, walked the rest of the way into town. It was extremely painful. As another example, I met a traveler from New Zealand who dislocated his shoulder while rafting the Sun Kosi River in Nepal. He had to leave the river and walk for two days to reach a road where he could get to medical care. Finally, a friend of mine took a lead fall while four of us were rockclimbing on Granite Mountain near Prescott, Arizona. He snapped his femur, although it was not a compound fracture, and we were one hundred feet up the cliff at the time. Fortunately, a stretcher was left at its base by the state mountaineering society. (We would have had to improvise and make a rope stretcher if it had not been there.) We had to descend, haul the stretcher up, tie him on, lower him to the ground, and then carry him three miles down a rugged trail to the nearest road.

Accidents that are caused by avalanches and rockfalls are also common in the mountains. According to the Swiss Alpine Club, one hundred and forty-nine people died in the mountains in Switzerland in 1991. Of these, thirty-four people died in avalanches, thirty-two in ski accidents, often off-piste, and the others while climbing or hiking. More than half of the victims were non-Swiss. You should always wear sturdy boots in the mountains, and have clothing to withstand extreme cold, snow and rain. Careful routefinding is also essential to avoid becoming lost, and to minimize your exposure to slide paths. A compass may be required in remote areas; if you do not have one you should locate a landmark each time you change directions. (You might also want to leave a marker.) You should never travel alone in avalanche country, and the safest routes are on ridges and among thick stands of forest. In addition, when a hiking, skiing or climbing party comes to a slide path, its members should spread out in a line, if possible roped-up and wearing helmets, and then cross carefully, quietly and quickly. (It is also wise to rope-up for river crossings.) One person should cross at a time in extremely dangerous locations, and it is also best to traverse them in the morning, when the ground or snow is more stable.

Lightening storms also regularly occur in the mountains, and if one develops in your area you should quickly retreat to a lower elevation. In addition, you should move away from tall and solitary objects such as trees and fences. "*Should you feel the hair on your head, neck or arms stand on end, lightening may be about to strike. 'Immediately' kneel down, bending forward with your hands on your knees, to become as small a target as possible.*" (*Ann Landers column*, Philadelphia Inquirer, July 18, 1992)

If you are inexperienced in mountainous terrain, it is a good idea to hire a guide or to join a larger party. (Guides are available in many areas, and they are also useful in rain forest and desert environments.) It is also wise to develop your mountaineering knowledge by reading books and taking courses on routefinding, climbing and belay skills, and avalanche theory. For example, I took a course on snow safety at the American Avalanche Institute in Wilson, Wyoming. Two excellent books on this and related topics are *Avalanche Handbook* (The Forest Service, U.S. Department of Agriculture), and *Mountaineering, the Freedom of the Hills* (The Mountaineers, Seattle).

Traveler health problems

This section covers other health problems that are associated with world travel. Some of them are very serious, but fortunately most of these are also quite rare. Unless you pursue adventurous activities or spend long periods of time in rural environments, without being careful, your chances of having them should be minimal. You can further protect yourself by not visiting areas where epidemics are in progress. Epidemics are often highly localized, and they are sometimes seasonal as well, such as the outbreaks of cholera that occur during monsoons. Some travelers, of course, act as if they are immortal, and they are often the people who do have serious accidents or catch exotic diseases. For instance, I have seen many travelers drink unsterilized water, even in the most unhygienic environments. They rely on their *karma* to get them through, and if they have a problem, that's fate!

If the symptoms of a problem are severe, or if there is any doubt as to its cause, you should obtain a professional diagnosis and treatment. It is also a good idea to stay up-to-date on standards of medical care, since this will alert you to new treatments and alternatives to the suggestions that are presented here. In addition, while this section does refer to pharmaceuticals, it for the most part does not cover issues of dosages and contraindications.

Readers who have a deeper interest in health problems, or who are suffering from unknown ailments, are advised to buy *The Sanford Guide to Antimicrobial Therapy* (*GAT*) from Antimicrobial Therapy, Inc., 8000 Towers Crescent Drive, Suite 270, Vienna, Virginia, 22182. This booklet, which is primarily intended for physicians, is a collection of tables listing suggested treatments and other issues for a wide variety of diseases.

The following organization is used for the balance of the section:

- Common health problems
    - Jet lag
    - Motion and seasickness
    - Stomach distress and traveler's diarrhea
    - Skin infections and rashes
    - Sunburn and skin cancer
    - Dehydration, heat exhaustion and heat stroke
    - Colds and other respiratory illnesses
    - Ear and eye problems
- Mountain-based health problems
    - Hypothermia
    - Frostbite
    - Snow blindness
    - Altitude sickness
- Dangerous fauna
    - Insects and other pests
        - Mosquitos
        - Leeches
        - Bedbugs, lice and chiggers
        - Stinging insects
    - Dangerous animals
    - Snakes
    - Crocodiles, alligators and other lizards
    - Marine species
        - Sharks
        - Other vertebrate species
        - Other sea creatures
- Other health problems
    - AIDS and sexually transmitted diseases
    - Amoebic dysentery
    - Bilharzia
    - Dengue fever
    - Giardia
    - Leishmaniasis
    - Worms

Common health problems - jet lag

Jet lag is typically more pronounced after flying from west to east, and you can reduce its severity by resting during your flight and by guarding against dehydration. The former is easier if you avoid caffeine (do not drink tea, coffee or soft drinks that contain it), or if you take a sleeping pill such as Halcion or Valium. You can avoid dehydration by drinking plenty of water, and by limiting your consumption of alcoholic beverages. If you do become exhausted after your arrival, you should take a brief nap and then force yourself to stay awake until the earliest time that the locals ordinarily go to sleep. (Now is the time for the caffeine.) It is also helpful to spend some time in the sun, since this will quicken the process of resetting your internal clock. (Taking melatonin, which is available in health-food stores, also reportedly has this effect.) Perhaps the best advice I can give is just to ignore jet lag. This is what many active travelers do, and you can get used to it.

(A more radical system, which I used for the New York - Shannon/Ireland flight at the beginning of my current trip, was to drink all night on the plane, have a pint of Guinness on arrival, and then sleep for a day with a meal in the middle. The following day I was fresh as a daisy.)

Motion and seasickness

Dramamine and antihistamines both provide relief from motion or seasickness. Another option is scopolamine, which is available in transdermal patches that are applied to the neck behind the ear. You should wash your hands before and after applying a patch. This drug is powerful, and it can cause drowsiness, light-headedness and blurred vision. You should remove the patch if the effects are too strong. (You might also try one-half of a patch.) All of these treatments should preferably be taken before traveling or the onset of symptoms. For seasickness, other traditional forms of relief include drinking tea, herbal remedies such as ginger, staying on deck in the fresh air, keeping active, staring at any fixed point that can be seen in the distance, and wearing a snug band around each wrist. (This last remedy is an ancient mariner's cure.) You should also try to keep eating on a regular schedule, no matter how poorly you feel.

Stomach distress and traveler's diarrhea

Mild forms of stomach distress include indigestion and constipation. They are often caused by a disruption of normal eating habits, coupled with the effects of jet lag and stress. You can minimize having these problems by eating slowly, by not overeating, by avoiding heavy exercise after meals, by taking nutritional supplements such as fiber tablets and vitamins, and by limiting your consumption of alcoholic beverages. It is also a good idea to accustomize yourself slowly to foreign diets, particularly to spicy food and hot chilies.

Diarrhea is usually caused by ingesting food or water that is contaminated with fecal matter containing pathogenic bacteria or other organisms such as intestinal parasites. It can be prevented by consuming only hygienic food and beverages, although in some places this will be impossible to ensure. If you do develop diarrhea, you can assume in most cases that bacteria are responsible and that the problem will clear up after a few days. Common bacterial pathogens include E. coli, shigella and salmonella. If the diarrhea is severe, or if it is accompanied by blood in the stool or high fever, then there may be another cause such as amoebic dysentery. Professional medical care should be sought in these circumstances, and you will need to have a stool exam for a proper diagnosis. A series of exams is sometimes required, spread out over a few weeks, to ensure that one test is conducted during a detectable stage in the organism's life cycle.

Temporary relief of diarrhea, such as on days when you must travel, is provided by the following agents: loperamide (Immodium), Lomotil, codeine phosphate and bismuth subsalicylate (Pepto Bismol). The first three work by freezing the bowel with a narcotic, and should only be taken after symptoms develop. If taken as a prophylaxis, they may actually cause diarrhea to occur, although Pepto Bismol may have a prophylactic benefit. According to the CDC, the first three should also not be taken if the symptoms include high fever or bloody stools. Traveler's diarrhea responds well to antibiotics, and both ciprofloxacin and norfloxacin (fluroquinolone antibiotics) are effective in only a day or two. However, it is a good idea to take them for at least three days, to avoid relapses, and also only for serious problems that are caused by bacteria, not the spicy food variety. (You'll know!) The treatment is 500 mg of the former or 400 mg of the latter twice a day. Other antibiotic treatments include doxycycline and trimethoprim/sulfamethoxazole (TMP/SMX - Bactrim). In addition, according to the CIWEC Clinic in Kathmandu, and contrary to general traveler lore, there is no evidence that treating a stomach problem with an antibiotic will make you more susceptible to a subsequent infection. (*Understanding Diarrhea in Travelers*, David R. Shlim, M.D., page 4) It is better to cure a problem in the quickest and most efficient manner, rather than let your body weaken as it fights the illness on its own.

Bananas and yoghurt are good foods for when you are suffering from diarrhea. Meats and other hard to digest foods should be avoided. A home remedy is garlic soup, which is also supposed to be good for altitude acclimatization. (It is very popular on Nepalese treks!) It is particularly important to replace lost fluids and salts, so you should increase your consumption of water and other beverages. (If you think you have food poisoning, you should force yourself to drink liters of water to flush your body out.) It will help if you add an oral rehydration solution to the water. They are available in powder form from pharmacies, and they are also an excellent treatment for the dehydration that is caused by strenuous exercise.

If you regularly have stomach problems, another option is to avoid the local food completely. You can do this by eating only canned or packaged foods. Similarly, if you find a restaurant that has food which does not make you ill, you can take all of your meals there. You should of course avoid any restaurants that you suspect made you sick. In addition, it is best to develop a psychological tolerance to these problems. Stomach distress is a common traveler's complaint, particularly in lesser developed countries. It is part of the price that you pay to visit them.

Skin infections and rashes

All wounds should be cleaned vigorously and regularly. This is particularly important in the tropics, where they often take a long time to heal. You should use lots of soap, and preferably sterilized or bottled water. Rubbing alcohol or alcohol swabs should also be used if they are available. After cleaning, an antiseptic and a protective bandage should be applied.

An infection may develop if you do not keep a wound clean, and a topical antibiotic, such as Neosporin, which contains polymyxin B, bacitracin and neomycin, should be applied if this occurs. In addition, if a wound seals over with an infection still present, blood poisoning or gangrene may develop. It is usually necessary to lance this type of wound to clean out the infection, and it may be appropriate to take an oral antibiotic, such as amoxicillin or cephalexin. (These drugs are related to penicillin, so they should not be taken by people with this allergy.)

Skin rashes are sometimes caused by contact with dangerous plants, such as poison ivy. However, in foreign countries it is unlikely that you will know which local plants are safe and which are not. For example, I brushed against some nasty variety of plant when I was jungle trekking in a singlet and shorts in Chitwan. It caused a bumpy rash on my side and arm, itched terribly, and took over a month to heal. Protective clothing would have prevented this, and I now understand why the park rangers there wear pants and long-sleeved shirts. In addition, any clothing that has touched a poisonous plant, including shoes, should be washed thoroughly before being worn again.

Prickly heat is another type of rash, and it occurs in hot climates. Small red blisters form on the skin, because the sweat glands are unable to cope with the heat. Its cure is to lower your level of activity and to find a cool environment. Skin infections and lesions may also be the symptoms of other ailments, such as leishmaniasis (see below). In addition, it is not uncommon in the tropics to develop fungal infections, and the standard treatment for them is an anti-fungal cream such as miconazole (Micatin) or ketoconazole (Nizoral).

Many rashes are accompanied by itching, and temporary relief is provided by oatmeal bath, astringent powder (it should also dry out the rash), hydrocortizone or mometasone furoate (Elocon) cream (both steroids), antihistamines such as Benadryl, which is available in both oral and cream forms, and cold showers. A physician can also prescribe more effective oral treatments, such as prednisone, or give inoculations of other stronger and longer lasting steroids.

Sunburn and skin cancer

Your susceptibility to sunburn and your ability to tan are based on the amount of melanin in your skin. A fair-skinned person who does not have a base tan can only take about thirty minutes of strong solar radiation before being seriously burned. (Pain and peeling will result.) Sunburn is a precursor to highly wrinkled skin later in life, and also to skin cancer, which is becoming much more prevalent. For instance, I read an advertisement for a dermatological clinic in Sydney which said that two out of three Australians will develop skin cancer at some point during their lives. This is due to their outdoor lifestyles, and the ozone depletion in the southern hemisphere, which is enabling higher levels of ultraviolet radiation to reach the earth. Ozone depletion is occurring in the northern hemisphere as well, and all people who regularly expose themselves to solar radiation without adequate protection, regardless of their amount of melanin, are at risk. Medical research has also shown that people who have had severe sunburn as children have a higher than normal probability of developing skin cancer.

There are three basic types of skin cancer including, in declining order of life-threatening danger, malignant melanoma, squamous cell carcinoma and basal cell carcinoma. (I have had the last.) Malignant melanoma often spreads to other body tissues through a process called metastasis. The latter two types, however, rarely spread if they are promptly removed. Cancerous moles are most commonly located on the face, although they may develop on any areas of the body that have been exposed to the sun. If you are in the sun a lot you should check yourself regularly, particularly for moles that have grown or otherwise changed their appearance, such as by bleeding or developing scabs. Itching is also common with malignant melanoma. It is essential to have a physician examine any suspicious mole.

You can protect yourself by using a sun cream, preferably with an SPF of 8 or higher. Tans that are built on a good base will also last longer. It is important to reapply tanning creams frequently, and to get out of the sun if you start to turn noticeably red. It is also wise to wear a hat, and to use a very high SPF cream, to protect your face.

Dehydration, heat exhaustion and heat stroke

Dehydration and overheating are caused by exposure to the sun or to other hot environments. In such circumstances, you are probably dehydrated if you do not need to go to the bathroom for a long period of time, or if your urine turns bright yellow or orange. Headaches are also a common symptom. Dehydration and related problems are exacerbated by strenuous exercise. They can be minimized by wearing loose fitting, light colored clothing, and a hat and sunglasses, by drinking plenty of fluids, and by resting periodically. It is also helpful to take regular swims or showers. If you are hiking, it is best to start early in the morning and finish by, or rest during, the hottest part of the day. You should hike at a comfortable pace (do not force yourself to keep up with someone who is faster), and take regular breaks to rest and rehydrate yourself. A good rule of thumb is five to fifteen minutes of rest for every hour of exercise, depending on the conditions and your level of fitness.

If dehydration and overheating are not treated, they may worsen and lead to heat cramps, heat exhaustion or heat stroke. Heat cramps are muscle spasms, and they usually occur in the stomach or legs. If you get them, you should rest and lightly massage the cramped muscles. Symptoms of heat exhaustion include moist, cool and pale skin, headache and nausea. With heat stroke, which can be life-threatening, the body's cooling system shuts down and sweating stops. The skin is dry, hot and red. Severe symptoms include a high body temperature, a rapid, weak pulse, and rapid, shallow breathing. Victims of heat exhaustion or heat stroke should lie down out of the sun, and be cooled with water or wet towels and by fanning. They should rest and slowly rehydrate themselves by drinking small amounts of water or other fluids.

Colds and other respiratory problems

Colds and other respiratory problems, such as coughing, sinusitis and bronchitis, are a common traveler's complaint. (Almost everyone who does a Himalayan trek develops a cough at some point.) Respiratory problems are usually caused by exhaustion, coupled with exposure to other people who are ill, bad weather, or dry and dusty environments. You can alleviate the symptoms of a cold by resting, drinking plenty of fluids, and taking acetaminophen (Paracetamol or Tylenol), aspirin, or decongestants such as Sudafed (pseudoephedrine hydrochloride). Throat lozenges and numerous cups of tea should be an effective treatment for a cough, but if it persists you might want to try codeine linctus or tussi cough syrup. Lastly, if a mild respiratory problem develops into a more serious infection, it will be necessary to take a suitable antibiotic, such as ampicillin, erythromycin, azithromycin or loracarbef (Lorabid).

Ear and eye problems

Travelers sometimes develop ear infections, and antibiotic ear drops are the usual treatment. If this happens to you, you should gently clean your ears and then use drops containing polymyxin B, neomycin and hydrocortizone four times a day. If you get a bug in your ear, you can get rid of it by pouring in a few drops of mineral oil. Some travelers also develop conjunctivitis (rheumy eyes), especially in the tropics. Antibiotic eye drops should be used if this occurs. (In Laos, I contracted what the locals called *red eye disease*. My eyes hurt and itched terribly, but drops worked in three days.) An object that has become lodged in the eye should be flushed out with water.

Mountain-based health problems

Travelers in mountainous regions are subject to a number of additional health risks, as follows:

Hypothermia

Hypothermia is a lowering of the body's temperature, and it is usually caused by prolonged exposure with inadequate clothing to cold temperatures. (Remember to account for the wind chill factor.) Of course, you can also speed up the process by falling in an icy river. Symptoms of hypothermia include shivering, numbness, weakness, impaired vision and judgement, decreased pulse, and drowsiness. If a victim has the last symptom, you should not let him or her fall asleep, at least not until after they have been warmed, since they may never wake up! Hypothermia is aggravated by injuries, drinking alcoholic beverages, smoking, wearing wet clothing, and fatigue. Treatment for it involves getting the victim to a warm environment, and giving them dry clothing, blankets or a sleeping bag, and warm beverages. An additional tip is that if you are stuck in the cold for a long period of time, such as in a tent during a snow storm, you should periodically dry the perspiration off your body.

Frostbite

Frostbite is the freezing of body tissues from exposure to extreme cold. The skin turns red in mild frostbite, but it will whiten as the freezing becomes more severe and underlying tissues will feel hard to the touch. Large blisters will form after thawing if moderate frostbite has occurred. In the most severe frostbite, tissues die and turn black after thawing. It is common for infections, which can lead to gangrene, to develop at this point. Amputation is often necessary after severe frostbite. For example, many climbers in the Himalayas and other high mountain ranges have had to have their frostbitten toes and fingers amputated using knives or scissors. As this suggests, it occurs most frequently in the extremities, since as the body cools the blood circulation is reduced to preserve the warmth of the head and trunk. One of the best preventatives, therefore, is to wear many layers of clothing on your torso and a warm hat. Frostbite is exacerbated if the circulation is restricted, such as by tight gloves or boots. The face, especially the nose and ears, is also susceptible, because it is directly exposed to the cold. It is important in sub-freezing temperatures to wear ski goggles and a scarf or bandanna. Frostbite often causes permanent damage to blood vessels, so body parts that have been frostbitten in the past tend to freeze more quickly in subsequent exposures to the cold. Frostbite will also become more severe if a body part is frozen, thawed, and then refrozen. Treatment for frostbite involves getting the victim to a warm environment, and immersing the frozen areas in warm (not hot) water. In addition, the injured areas should not be massaged.

Snow blindness

There is a high risk of developing snow blindness when walking, climbing or skiing on sunny days in snow covered terrain. It occurs when solar radiation that is reflected off the snow burns the corneas. This causes the eyes to swell and close, and it is extremely painful - it has been described as feeling like sand is being ground into your eyes. Prevention is to wear sunglasses or ski goggles, and you should check that everyone with whom you are traveling has protection, since it would be a burden, or worse, to be with someone who was temporarily blind. Protection can be improvised by cutting a slit in a bandanna or a piece of cardboard. If you do get snow blindness, you should keep your eyes closed, or gently bathe them in cool water. Eye drops may also provide some relief.

Altitude sickness

Altitude sickness develops when you ascend to high elevations without taking sufficient time to acclimatize. People with heart and lung problems are especially at risk. The symptoms of altitude sickness are as follows:

Mild

- Headache
- Insomnia
- Swelling of the face and fingers
- Loss of appetite and nausea

Severe

- Rapid breathing, coughing and shortness of breath
- Blue lips
- Rapid heart rate

- Loss of balance and coordination
- Loss of judgement
- Delirium

If altitude sickness is not treated, it may lead to fluid collecting in the lungs or on the brain, which are called pulmonary edema and cerebral edema, respectively. If the symptoms include coughing and shortness of breath, it is probably the former; if they include loss of balance and coordination, it is likely the latter. (*Mountain Sickness and Other Hazards in the Nepal Himalaya*, Himalayan Rescue Association leaflet) If either develops, and the victim is not taken immediately to a lower elevation, he or she will probably fall into a coma and die. The onset of life-threatening symptoms may only take a few hours, and many trekkers and climbers have died as a result of ignoring the early warning signs.

If you are below 10,000 feet, and the only symptoms are headache and sleeplessness, it is probably reasonable to limit the treatment to aspirin and allow yourself additional time to acclimatize. However, if you are at a higher elevation, particularly for a multi-day period, or if the symptoms worsen, then you should descend. You may even feel okay when you arrive at a particular altitude, but then feel terrible a short while later. No matter what the hour of day, if the symptoms worsen you should descend to an elevation where they disappear. A descent of 1,000 vertical feet, or less, is often sufficient for this, and you should spend a day or two at the lower elevation before reascending. If someone in your party has severe symptoms, it may be necessary to force them to descend if their judgement is impaired, and anyone who descends because of altitude sickness should be accompanied by another person who is well. If the victim is incapacitated, they should be carried down. Victims of altitude sickness should also be kept warm, since their conditions will quickly worsen if they become chilled. Indeed, wearing suitable clothing, and following a nutritional diet, may help delay the onset of symptoms.

Taking acetazolamide (Diamox) can accelerate the process of acclimatization. (Taking sleeping pills may slow it.) A conservative course of action is to carry Diamox in your medical kit, but not use it, and instead let yourself acclimatize naturally. It can then be used as an aid if severe symptoms develop. You should descend if the symptoms persist after taking it. In some locations, such as at Himalayan Rescue Association (HRA) mountain clinics in Nepal, plastic, tent-like recompression chambers are available to treat victims who have the worst symptoms.

Many cases of life-threatening altitude sickness have occurred because the victims were traveling with other people, and chose to ignore their symptoms rather than slow everyone else down. This is particularly common with groups that are following tight timetables. For instance, in the early years of Himalayan trekking hikers in organized groups would sometimes die because they became incapacitated and their groups continued anyway. There was even one case of an ill trekker who was put on a pony and carried over a mountain pass to keep him with his group, rather than use the pony to take him to a lower elevation. He fell into a coma and died. In such circumstances, the group should do what is best for its weakest member. (Signs of altitude sickness in other people include their skipping meals and their being the last to arrive at different stopping points.) In addition, as a doctor told us in a talk at the HRA post in Manang on the Annapurna Circuit trek (elevation 12,500 feet), a Himalayan trek (or similar activity) is an adventure of a lifetime for most people. Why not go slow and enjoy it? After all, what does it matter if you take an extra day or two, especially if you have all the time in the world?

Elevation gains should be carefully planned. One rule of thumb is to hike high but sleep low. Another is that you should not gain more than 300 to 400 vertical meters a day, or approximately 1,000 vertical feet. Even this, though, will be too much for some people, since everyone responds to altitude gains in their own way. (Contrary to what you might expect, people who are very fit are often highly susceptible to altitude sickness.) Unfortunately, treks and climbs do not always have convenient stopping points that are consistent with this guideline. For example, in Tanzania, trekkers who join organized groups ascend Mt. Kilimanjaro in three and one-half days (five days round-trip). It is 19,000 feet high, and stops are made at 9,000, 12,000, and 15,500 feet. Almost everyone suffers from the altitude, except the local guides and porters, of course, who are fully acclimatized. Many trekkers do not make it to the top because of the accelerated schedule. I made it to the top, at least to Gilman's Point on the rim (18,800 feet), although I felt terrible beginning at a rest stop at 17,000 feet when I became chilled from the extreme cold. This occurred in the middle of the final midnight to dawn ascent of the crater. I warmed up when we started hiking again, and felt better after about an hour. Feeling bad, however, did not lessen the thrill of seeing the starlit sky from the top of the mountain. (The summit of Mt. Kilimanjaro, along with the summit of Mt. Chimborazo in Ecuador, at 20,500 feet, are probably the best nighttime observation points on earth, because they are the highest elevations near the equator.) I could see about one thousand times more stars than the starriest night that I had previously witnessed, which was in the winter in the middle of the northeast Arizona plateau. You could probably have counted

100,000 or more individual bright stars. In retrospect, it would have been better to have done the trek independently in a week or longer, and then spent a few nights looking at the stars.

Acclimatization plan for the Mt. Everest trek

The following example of an acclimatization plan is the one that I used for the trek to Mt. Everest:

Village	Nights	Altitude	Change
Luckla	1 *	2850 m	
Phakding	1	2652	(198)
Namche Bazaar	2	3446	794
Tengboche Monastery	1	3867	421
Dingboche	2 **	4282	415
Lobuche	2 ***	4930	648
Pheriche	1	4252	(678)
Tengboche Monastery	1	3867	(385)
Namche Bazaar	1	3446	(421)
Luckla	1	2850	(596)
	=		
	13		

* This plan starts from Luckla, which is a village that many trekkers fly to from Kathmandu. It envisions a round-trip of thirteen days, which is certainly not that long to see the highest mountain in the world. It does, however, presume that you can fly at will into and out of the Luckla airport, where multi-day delays are actually quite common. It also assumes a certain amount of prior acclimatization, such as having first done another trek (I did the Annapurna trek before Everest), or the hike to Luckla from the roadhead village of Jiri (five to seven days). If this is not the case, adding one or two days in the stretch up to and including Namche Bazaar would be advisable. In addition, the one day altitude gain to Namche Bazaar of 800 meters is probably too great for many people, even considering that it is only 600 meters higher than Luckla two days earlier, hence the recommendation to spend two days there.

** This is an excellent extra day to hike up to the base of Ama Dablam, or even all the way to the slopes of Island Peak.

*** Two nights spent here cover one night prior to the hike to the Kala Pattar Mt. Everest viewpoint (5623m) or Base Camp (5400m), and a second to rest afterwards before beginning the descent. Planning for a second night at Lobuche also covers the circumstance where visibility is poor on the first day.

Dangerous fauna - insects and other pests

Insects and other pests regularly cause travelers discomfort. Biting pests include mosquitos, leeches, flies, ants, ticks, fleas, chiggers, lice and bedbugs. The stinging variety includes bees, wasps, hornets, spiders and scorpions, although some of these can give you a nasty bite as well. This section gives general advice for protecting yourself from such pests, and some additional comments for a few specific species. The most effective forms of protection are proper clothing and insect repellents. The former includes durable pants (good jungle pants have drawstrings at the ankles), a long sleeved shirt, preferably that can be closed tight at the neck, sturdy shoes or boots, long socks (you can pull them over your pants for additional protection), and a hat. This type of outfit will also protect you against snakes, but it will be uncomfortable in hot environments. You will have to choose between protection and comfort. It is interesting to note, though, that such outfits are almost always worn by park guides and naturalists, even in the tropics. Insect repellents are available as liquids, creams and sprays, and the most effective contain N,N diethylmetatoluamide (DEET). They should be applied to exposed skin and the edges of clothing. (Clothes can also be sprayed with permethrin-based repellents for additional protection.)

Mosquitos

Mosquito nets, coils, electric repellant systems and fans should be used for protection in hotel rooms and other enclosed areas. Many guesthouses supply mosquito nets, so having your own is unnecessary unless you intend to travel extensively in rural areas. (The best nets for travelers are the type that require only one suspension point.) Mosquito coils are readily available in tropical areas, although some types contain DDT. They are also inexpensive, and are often provided by guesthouses and hotels. Two intertwined coils come together, and because of their fragility they must be separated carefully. They also come with a small metal support, and are lit like incense. Instead of coils, some guesthouses have electric systems, where you put a small wafer in a bedside holder each night. These are very effective. Mosquitos will also avoid air currents, so you should not be bothered if a fan is blowing over your bed. In addition, you can fight mosquitos by taking daily vitamin B supplements, since this reportedly causes the body to secrete a substance that repels them. (A similar tip is to try eating papaya seeds.)

Leeches

"If there's anything in the world I hate, its leeches!"

- Humphrey Bogart, in *The African Queen*

Leeches thrive in many different tropical and sub-tropical habitats. Land leeches range from lowland rain forests to mountain cloud forests, and water leeches live in rivers and swamps. Leeches are dark brown or black, and they move like inchworms. They may be quite thin and small before feeding, perhaps only one to two inches in length, but they can grow to be disgustingly fat and long after meals. Land leeches are found in the greatest quantities during and just after monsoons. They often inhabit grasses alongside trails, and they sense their prey by its motion and body heat. A leech can support itself horizontally from a blade of grass to reach towards a passing animal, and walking down a trail and seeing one suspended this way is quite a sight. Leeches inject an anti-coagulant when they bite to make the blood of their hosts flow freely. This is rarely painful; indeed, there is sometimes a localized cooling sensation. The only sign that you will usually see of a leech is the blood spot that is left after it has dropped off. Leech bites should be cleaned well, to stop the bleeding and to prevent infection.

My first contact with leeches was at an altitude of 10,000 feet on Poon Hill, which is a famous viewpoint in central Nepal for the Mt. Annapurna range. I was there at dawn just at the beginning of the monsoon. Unfortunately, I developed a rather severe case of stomach distress after climbing to the top of the hill. I had to retire quickly to some nearby bushes, and while I was there I noticed many small, liver colored inchworms in the grass rapidly making their way towards me. After a few latched themselves onto my hand, I realized what they were. Leeches! Ugh, and very unsporting of them to pick on me at such a time. I have been leeched many times since then, and they do not bother me that much anymore. The idea of them does take a bit of getting used too, though.

Finding protective clothing for leeches is a great challenge. Leech country is often very warm, and even if you wear a shirt and pants, or a lightweight gore-tex suit, they can still get to you at the neck. They are also adept at crawling down the insides of socks and under pants legs. Wearing a pair of shorts, and boots and gaiters (also useful for muddy trails), works reasonably well. You can see the leeches inching up the gaiters and then flick them off. In addition, successful attacks are concentrated at knee height, since once they find some skin they will usually stop. Some people put wads of tobacco in the tops of their socks, or spray insect repellant on their clothes. I also met one traveler who had a unique way of dealing with leeches, which was to ignore them! He was a bush guide from Zimbabwe, and a hard man to be sure. He hiked in leech country in shorts and bare feet, and would only stop from time-to-time to pick them off. At the end of a hike his feet would be bloody. If you have been to Thailand's Khao Yai National Park, where I met him, and been attacked by seemingly thousands of leeches in just the first few feet of a forest trail, you can appreciate the fortitude that this required.

Whatever leech protection you use, you should stop periodically to check yourself, and if possible have someone examine your back and pack. In addition, if you are hiking down a trail with other people you should try to be at the front. The first person down the trail will alert nearby leeches, and subsequent hikers are more likely to be attacked. (In Periyar Tiger Sanctuary in southern India, we would run through shady, wet portions of forest trails, and then stop in dry sections to pick the leeches off our boots.) Finally, if you get a leech on you, you can scrape it off with your fingernail or a knife. This is what the locals do, but you should make sure that you get all of the leech, since otherwise it could lead to an infection. Touching leeches with a match or cigarette, or with salt, will also cause them to drop off.

Bedbugs, lice and chiggers

A wide variety of insects may inhabit hotel and guesthouse rooms, including bedbugs, lice, cockroaches, water bugs and spiders. Bedbugs and lice are most prevalent in the low budget guesthouses that are used by local travelers. Indeed, accommodations in lesser developed countries at remote border crossings are often notorious for them. In the rare circumstances where you cannot avoid lodgings that have vermin, such as when it is raining and there is only one hotel, you can get some protection by enclosing yourself in a sheet or a sleeping bag. If you are exposed to lice, there are special hair and body shampoos that you can use to get rid of them. These shampoos are readily available from pharmacies. Lastly, if chiggers or other insects burrow under your skin, they are easier to remove after first making an airtight seal around them for a day or two using clear fingernail varnish and a Band-Aid.

Stinging insects

The stings of some insects, particularly certain species of spiders and scorpions, contain strong poisons. Life-threatening spiders include the *black widow*, which is related to the *red back* in Australia and the *katapo* in New Zealand, and the *funnel web* of eastern Australia. Black widows make their webs in sheltered locations, but the strands of a web can extend for some distance. Disturbing the strands attracts the spider, which interprets this as a sign that prey has been caught. Funnel webs are aggressive, and they will actually rear up on their hind legs and charge people. Scorpions, as well as snakes, often hide under rocks or in brush piles. To prevent stings and bites, it is wise in suspect environments to be very careful about where you put your hands, and to shake out your shoes and clothing before dressing.

For bees and hornets, if you are caught in a swarm it is essential to control yourself. Do not flail about - this will only anger them and cause more attacks. Instead, crouch down to make yourself a small target, cover your eyes, and move quickly to a nearby shelter or body of water.

Common effects of stings include localized swelling and significant pain and tenderness. Some people are also susceptible to allergic reactions. Minor reactions can be treated with antihistamines and steroids (creams, oral forms like prednisone, and inhalers). The symptoms of severe reactions include rapid swelling around the sting and of the face, lips, tongue and throat, itching and hives, fever, nausea and vomiting, numbness and tingling of the face, muscle spasms, and pronounced wheezing, coughing and difficulty breathing. Travelers who are susceptible to allergic reactions of this severity may want to carry adrenaline in their medical kits. It is available as epinephrine in pre-loaded syringes, which are marketed in the U.S. as Ana-Kit and EpiPen. Treatment with either should keep a victim's breathing passages open. If such materials are not available, it may be necessary to administer artificial respiration.

The first-aid for most insect stings is limited. You should seek medical attention if a poison may have been injected, and apply a wide and firm bandage, perhaps with an ice-pack, to slow blood circulation around the wound. Elastic bandages are ideal for this. A tourniquet should not be used. You should also not take aspirin, since it increases circulation. If you can, you should determine what creature was responsible for the sting, since this information will be useful if a specific antidote is available. (An antidote is available for funnel web bites.) In addition, since most poisons are proteins, they can be broken down by rubbing meat tenderizer or green papaya skin onto the wound. (You should first make a paste with the tenderizer and baking soda.)

Dangerous animals

"Lions and tigers and bears. Oh my!"

- Dorothy, in *The Wizard of Oz*

Rhinos and tigers and sloth bears, not to mention leopards and crocodiles, are prevalent in Chitwan, and when I was jungle trekking there I used to chant this variation of the famous quote. Indeed, we actually found a human skull on one trek. My guide thought it was probably the remains of a poacher from a nearby village, and if so, then good riddance.

The world contains thousands of different animal species, and we should all work to ensure that they continue to survive. Many of these animals are also potentially dangerous to humans, but only because we have chosen to occupy their habitats. Any wild animal may attack a human, but some of the more dangerous species include tigers, lions, jaguars, leopards, cougars and other wild cats; bears; wolves, coyotes, hyenas, jackals and dogs; rhinoceros, hippopotamus and elephants; bison, buffalo and other horned animals; and monkeys. Different reptile species, such as poisonous snakes and crocodiles, are also dangerous. Even birds can be threatening, such as when they are protecting their eggs or young.

However, wild animals will rarely attack humans. This is because we do not fill a role in their natural ecology, and since they have learned that they cannot win against us. They will actually go to almost any lengths to avoid contact. You should respect animals (and their habitats). If you do not confront and harass them, you should not have any problems. With some species, though, it may be dangerous to walk alone in their territories. It may even be appropriate to carry a stick to defend yourself against an attack. For example, I was hiking with two guides in Chitwan when we accidently approached a rhino very closely. The animal was out of sight on the far side of an earthen dike, and the breeze was coming towards us. When we reached the dike, perhaps twenty feet from the rhino, it suddenly sensed us and ran around to confront us. It was a dramatic situation, and a charge appeared imminent. One of the guides raised his bamboo staff over his head, to appear larger, and shouted at the rhino while we slowly retreated. This fortunately worked, because the animal did not charge. As another example, having a stick is essential in areas where you may be attacked by dogs or monkeys.

If you spot a potentially dangerous animal, you should freeze, and then do the following:

- Look at the animal to see what it is doing. It will probably be looking at you. If so, you should avoid direct eye contact, since this may be interpreted as a challenge. However, if you spot a tiger, it will usually return your glance for a few seconds and then turn and walk away.
- Look around for possible weapons, and nearby shelters such as buildings, rivers or climbable trees.
- Do not exhibit fear, and do not run away. A wild animal will almost always chase you if you run, and they are usually much faster. You will have to tough it out.
- If you have a camera, take a photo.
- Withdraw quietly.
- If you are charged, climb a nearby tree, and good luck if it is a leopard, bear or other tree climbing species. (A rhino will drop its head and take a step back before charging.) Another option is to jump into a nearby body of water, although this might not be a good choice if you are in a crocodile, alligator or hippo habitat.
- Drop something if you are charged, such as your hat or camera, since the animal might stop to smell it.
- Some animals have poor eyesight, and rely on their hearing. For instance, if a rhino hears you, and you freeze, it may not be able to see you. If so, instead of charging it will stop and listen for your movement. You can also reportedly avoid a charging rhino by running in and out of trees, since with their bulk they develop too much momentum to change directions quickly. (The issue of eyesight is also the reason why you should be still when confronted by an angry dog. A dog's eyesight is much more attuned to sensing movement, rather than stationary objects.)
- If there are no means of escape, grab any available weapon and shout aggressively at the animal. It is essential to be the first to strike if it attacks. You should hit it sharply, preferably on the eyes or nose. Wild cats are also sensitive about their feet. In such situations you can take some hope from the fact that there have been amazing cases of survival. For example, a member of the staff at Chitwan's Tiger Tops Lodge

was able to fight off a tiger with a hand sickle that he had been using to cut grass. He survived, although he was severely mauled.
- Finally, if you are mauled, try playing dead. This has actually worked in a number of grizzly bear attacks.

To expand on the above points about tigers, it is extremely rare for healthy animals to attack humans. Most tigers who turn to human prey do so only after they have been wounded and are unable to kill their normal food. (A healthy tiger's hunting success rate is only one out of every ten to twenty attacks.) The wounds are caused by fights with other tigers, or other animals such as porcupines, or, as happened frequently earlier this century and in the last, by being shot but not killed by humans. If you somehow happen to enter the territory of a man-eating tiger, "*the greatest danger, when walking into the wind, is of an attack from behind, and to a lesser extent from either side. When the wind is from behind, the danger is from either side. In the same way, if the wind is blowing from the right the danger is from the left and behind, and if blowing from the left the danger is from the right and behind.*" (*The Temple Tiger and More Man-Eaters of Kumaon*, Jim Corbett, Oxford University Books, pages 161-162) Tigers do not like to attack from the front, or to chase. They prefer to wait and pounce, or stalk and pounce.

Snakes

Unless you are skilled at identification, you should assume that all snakes are dangerous. Most habitats that have harmless varieties also have poisonous ones. For instance, the U.S. has many poisonous snakes, including rattlesnakes, coral snakes, copperheads and water moccasins. Snakes often inhabit brush piles, and they may also be found on steep slopes and cliffs (particularly on sunny days). When you are in snake territory, it is important to wear boots and tear resistant long pants, and to watch where you put your hands.

First aid for a snake bite is similar to the treatment for a scorpion or spider bite. You want to slow, but not stop, the blood circulation around the wound, and a broad and firm bandage should accomplish this. The wound should not be washed, since if the snake was poisonous a venom swab may be able to identify it and simplify the treatment. You should also not incise and suck the bite to try to draw out the injected venom. The victim should be kept lying down and as still and calm as possible. They should not be given aspirin, and medical assistance should be sent for immediately to arrange for an anti-venom if one is available. Anti-venoms have been developed for the bites of many different poisonous snakes. They are available from hospitals, and also from the serum institutes where they are produced.

Crocodiles, alligators and other lizards

Since the treatment of a wound caused by a crocodile, alligator or other large lizard is never the preferred option, this section concentrates instead on the prevention of attacks. Fortunately, this is quite simple. You should never walk or swim through, or walk next to the shore of, any body of water that may be their home. (Some dangerous lizards live on land, such as Komodo dragons, other species of monitor lizards, and poisonous Gila monsters. You should be careful in their habitats and carry a stick.) In northern Australia, it is also important to be alert at ocean beaches and inlets, since they may be inhabited by salt water crocodiles. Their proper name is estuarine crocodile, and they live in both fresh and salt water. You should definitely keep a few feet clear of any *billabong* that might have salties, as was aptly demonstrated in the movie *Crocodile Dundee*. (Billabong is the Aussie term for an enclosed body of water, such as a swamp or pond. They are often the remnants of dried-up rivers.) If you need additional motivation, it might help to know that salties like to drown their victims and then tuck them under submerged logs for a few days to let them rot. This makes them easier to chew. I saw many salties on the naturalist tour at Yellow Waters in Kakadu National Park, including one that was fifteen feet long. I also heard an incredible story there about two German travelers who on a dare swam across one of the park's billabongs. This was unbelievably stupid behavior, since salties do regularly kill people. (A buddy of mine lost a good friend to a crocodile on the South African side of Victoria Falls. He was walking on a path, and slipped and fell in the water. In an instant he was taken by a croc. His mother and sister watched it happen, and his body was never found.)

Marine species

Oceans and reefs are home to many creatures that can cause injury. A few general safety tips for these environments are as follows:

- Inform yourself about which species are present in the locations that you visit.
- Never taunt any marine creature, or touch anything underwater unless you know that it is safe.
- Wear goggles to improve your underwater visibility.

- Wear shoes, such as old sneakers, when walking on reefs.
- If you are a diver, wear gloves and a wetsuit.

Sharks

Thanks to the movie *Jaws*, many people are aware of, indeed, are overly concerned with, the risk of shark attacks. Actually, there has been an increase in the number of attacks on humans around the world in recent years. Some people believe this is due to drift-net fishing by Japan, Taiwan and South Korea, which is eliminating the schools of deep-ocean fish that the more dangerous species traditionally hunt. This is forcing them to do more of their feeding in areas that are populated by humans, including shallow waters along coasts and in reef areas.

Only certain species of shark are ordinarily dangerous to humans. However, "*with sharks the behavior of identical species may differ widely from locality to locality and ... the 'safeness' of any particular type can never be guaranteed.*" (*Beyond the Reefs*, William Travis, Arrow Books, page 192) The most dangerous species include great white sharks (called white pointers in Australia), tiger sharks, mako sharks, blue sharks, bull sharks, lemon sharks and hammerheads. The waters that they inhabit are generally well-known. (White pointers regularly attack a few surfers and divers each year off the east and south coasts of Australia and the east coast of South Africa.) It is highly advisable to learn which shark species are present in local waters before you go swimming, and to avoid swimming in unknown waters. Advice on the risk of attacks should be available from life guards at any popular beach. Many predator fish, including sharks, are most active from dusk to dawn, and the majority of attacks on humans probably occur in the late afternoon. Sharks may come very close to the shore when hunting, so it is wise not to go swimming at night in known habitats except in lagoons that are protected by shark nets.

You should also not splash around in shark-inhabited waters, since this will attract them. If you see a shark, it is best to face it since they prefer not to make frontal attacks. Some divers also carry clubs to fend them off. Lastly, sharks that are hunting make quick, jerky movements. If you are swimming or diving and meet a shark that is acting like this, good luck!

Other vertebrate species

Other dangerous vertebrate species include stonefish, scorpion fish, lion fish (also called fire fish or turkey fish), moray eels, stingrays and sea snakes. Most of these species are limited to warm waters. Stone fish can be a significant risk for travelers, because they have excellent camouflage and inhabit reef shallows. They have poisonous spines along their back, as do scorpion fish and lion fish, and are a good reason to wear shoes in the water, or at a minimum never to put your feet down without first checking what is underneath. Moray eels inhabit small holes and hollows in reefs, so it is important to watch where you put your hands when snorkeling or diving. They can give a nasty bite. Stingrays can cause severe wounds with the spines in their tails, but they are easy to avoid because they are not aggressive. Sea snakes are often well-camouflaged, and they have a venom that is more potent than a cobra's. Fortunately, they are usually slow moving, and they also have small mouths that cannot open very wide.

The first-aid for a sting from a poisonous vertebrate is generally the same as for a snakebite, although you should not bandage the wound until you have removed any spines that are present.

In addition, all sizeable fish should be treated with respect. They are often protective of their territories or caches of eggs, and they may also be unpredictable. For example, I was bitten by a rogue titan triggerfish on the island of Ellaidoo in the Maldives. This particular fish was mature, about twenty inches long, and probably weighed from six to eight pounds. Titan triggerfish have opposing sets of two teeth on very strong jaws, which they use to break open shells. My dive partner and I had just finished a wall dive on the house reef, and were ascending to shallow water. I saw this fish swimming near us out of the corner of my eye, but thought nothing of it. (Fish in the Maldives are often curious about divers, and will approach them quite closely.) Then, while I was swimming backward watching my partner surface, I was hit on the head by what felt like a large hammer. I immediately turned around, wondering how I could have run into coral without seeing it, and right in front of me was this rogue fish. In a bit of a panic, I jerked around and fended it off with my fins. The fish then attacked my partner and bit completely through one of his fins. I found out later that this particular fish had *gone bad* in recent months, and had bitten a number of other people including one snorkeler severely on the toe. The dive shop had been unable to kill it because spearguns are illegal in the Maldives. I was upset about not having been warned about the fish in the dive briefings, and was concerned that children swimming in the lagoon might be attacked. In my case, if the bite had been a few inches lower it would have taken off my right ear. As it was, the puncture wounds bled slowly and continuously for about six hours, eliciting a variety of humorous comments from other divers at the beach bar, such as "*had I dyed my hair?*" Very funny. Vigorous scrubbing and daily treatment with an antiseptic helped me avoid an infection, but the wounds took months to heal completely and I now have four small scars on my scalp.

Other sea creatures

Other dangerous sea creatures include sea urchins, coral, fire coral, jellyfish, anemones, starfish, cone shells and octopi. The first two can cause bad punctures and cuts, and the rest may have powerful stings or bites. Spines from a sea urchin should be removed using tweezers or by lancing. Along with coral cuts, they often develop infections and take a long time to heal.

Some of the other species are very dangerous, particularly box jellyfish, which are also called sea wasps. Its sting can cause severe scarring, paralysis and death. Jellyfish trail long, transparent tentacles that contain stinging cells. Prey that swim into the tentacles are immobilized, and then drawn up to the creature's mouth. Jellyfish often swarm during particular seasons, and you should avoid swimming at these times. Divers should of course also be careful, although a full wet suit will provide protection. Box jellyfish are present in the waters off northern Australia, and they swarm during the wet season there which is from October to March. The beaches are closed to swimming during this period. Medical attention is essential for a severe jellyfish sting, and taking antihistamines may provide some relief from an allergic reaction. Tentacles that are still stuck to a victim should not be removed until their remaining unfired stinging cells have been deactivated. Liberally applying vinegar will do this, and some people in northern Australia actually take vinegar with them to the beach. Cone shells can fire deadly, poisoned barbs, so you should not pick them up. Octopi have sharp beaks in the center of the underside of their bodies, and they can inflict nasty bites. Certain species also inject poison. Indeed, a bite from a blue-ringed octopus, which is present in the waters of Indonesia and northern Australia, can be fatal in minutes. It is so named because small, bright blue rings appear on its body when it feels threatened.

Other health problems

This section covers a few other problems with which some travelers might need to be concerned.

AIDS and sexually transmitted diseases

AIDS (acquired immunodeficiency syndrome) is caused by the human immunodeficiency virus (HIV). It is spread by contact with contaminated blood, blood-derived fluids, or blood products. The disease destroys the body's immune system, and people who die from AIDS actually die from other fatal diseases that they contract after their immune systems have deteriorated. Transmission of AIDS can occur through any of the following: unprotected sex; use of shared syringes and other needles, including needles that are used for tattooing, ear piercing and acupuncture; medical and dental procedures; contaminated blood transfusions; and from women to their unborn children. (You should also demand that a new blade be used when getting a razor shave from a barber.)

"*HIV is not transmitted through casual contact; air, food, or water routes; contact with inanimate objects; or through mosquitos or other anthropod vectors.*" (*Health Information for International Travel 1995*, page 78)

Symptoms of AIDS include persistent low-grade fever, weight loss, skin lesions, loss of energy and nausea. Examples of sexually transmitted diseases (STDs) include gonorrhea and syphilis. Symptoms of STDs include genital discharge, pain, rashes, lesions and itching. Both AIDS and STDs can be asymptomatic, with the latter particularly the case among women. People who believe that they may have been exposed to HIV or an STD should have a blood test or medical examination.

AIDS and STDs are preventable. You should not contract AIDS if you use only hygienic sources of medical and dental care, other procedures that involve needles, and transfusions of blood and clotting factors; if you do not take illegal intravenous drugs; if you use latex condoms during sex (the virus can penetrate lambskin condoms); and if you avoid sexual contact, particularly anal intercourse, with people who are likely to be infected. Preventative behavior for STDs includes using condoms and avoiding sexual contact with people who are likely to be infected.

There is no cure for AIDS, although available treatments such as AZT may prolong the strength of the immune system. There are effective treatments for STDs, although some forms of gonorrhea are resistant to certain antibiotics.

Amoebic dysentery

Amoebic dysentery (amebiasis) is a not infrequent nightmare for travelers in lesser developed countries. Transmission occurs by ingesting amoebic cysts in fecally-contaminated food or water. Symptoms include high fever, chronic diarrhea, limited stool, which may contain blood and mucus (in advanced cases there can be a lot of blood), abdominal cramps, nausea and weight loss. A stool test is required for an accurate diagnosis. Amoebic dysentery can be very difficult to cure, since the cysts can survive anywhere in the digestive tract. Many travelers have taken treatments that would eradicate the illness in the stomach, only to have recurrences because it persisted in the intestines. According to the CIWEC Clinic, a treatment which accounts for this is to take 2 grams of tinidazole (Tiniba) once a day for three days, followed by 500 mg of diloxanide furoate (Furamide) three times a day for ten days. An alternative treatment, which is one of the options recommended by *GAT 1996*, is 750 mg of metronidazole (Flagyl) three times a day for ten days, followed by 650 mg of iodoquinol (Yodoxin) three times a day for twenty days or 500 mg of paromomycin (Humatin) three times a day for seven days. All of these drugs can have powerful side effects, and alcohol should not be consumed when taking either Tiniba or Flagyl. (CIWEC says the side effects are less serious with Tiniba.) In addition, some of the drugs "*are not available or are difficult to obtain in the United States. Information and drugs may be obtained from the Parasitic Disease Drug Service, Division of Host Factors, Center for Infectious Diseases, Atlanta, GA 30333.*" (*The Sanford Guide to Antimicrobial Therapy 1996*, page 83)

Bilharzia

Bilharzia (schistosomiasis) is a parasitic fluke. It lives in fresh water snails, and larvae released by the snails can penetrate unbroken human skin. It is estimated that some two hundred million people around the world suffer from the disease. You should not wade through or swim in bodies of fresh water in tropical and sub-tropical countries where the parasite is present. This is especially important in areas that have poor sanitation, and you should vigorously towel yourself off if you are accidently exposed to suspect water. Bathing water, including from wells and streams, may also be contaminated. It can be sterilized by heating to fifty degrees centigrade, or by treatment with iodine or chlorine. Other options are to strain water for bathing using a coffee filter, or to let it stand three days. Bilharzia cannot be contracted in salt water. Symptoms of the disease develop two to three weeks after the initial infection, and include fever, abdominal pain, loss of appetite, nausea, weight loss, headaches, blood in the urine, diarrhea and cough. Stool or urine exams will reveal the presence of the fluke's eggs six to eight weeks after the initial infection. According to *GAT 1996*, the treatment for bilharzia is praziquantel (Biltricide, Cesol).

Dengue fever

Dengue fever is a viral tropical disease that is transmitted by mosquito bites. The number of cases around the world has been increasing rapidly in the last twenty years, and it usually occurs in epidemics. Symptoms include high fever, severe frontal headache, joint and muscle pain, nausea and vomiting. A rash on the body and face may develop three to five days after the onset of fever. There is no specific treatment or vaccine for dengue fever, but "*the disease is usually benign and self-limited, although convalescence may be prolonged.*" (*Health Information for International Travel 1995*, page 101) For instance, an American friend of mine caught dengue in Koh Samui, but he was better after a week in the hospital in Bangkok.

A more severe form of the disease, called dengue hemorrhagic fever, is often fatal. The most important risk factors for it suggest "*that most international travelers from nonendemic areas such as the United States are at low risk for severe dengue infection.*" (Ibid.)

The risk of contracting dengue fever is slight if an epidemic is not in progress. Nevertheless, the type of mosquito that carries it is common near human habitations. If you visit an endemic area, you should closely follow the recommended measures for protection from mosquitos.

Giardia

Giardia (giardiasis) is transmitted by exposure to fecally-contaminated food or water. Its symptoms are generally similar to amoebic dysentery, and indigestion, flatulence and bad smelling burps are also common. Fever and vomiting are rare. A stool exam is needed for confirmation of the illness and, according to CIWEC, its treatment consists of a single 2 gram dose of tinidazole (Tiniba). This is reported to be 90% effective. (I have caught Giardia twice in Nepal, and Tiniba cured me both times.) This treatment is also listed in *GAT 1996*, and other options are either 250 mg of Flagyl, or 100 mg of quinacrine, three times a day for five days.

Leishmaniasis

Leishmaniasis is a parasitic disease that is found in tropical and sub-tropical regions. It is spread by the bites of carrier sandflies. The cutaneous form of the disease manifests itself through skin sores, which may not develop until weeks after the initial infection. The internal form causes enlargement of the liver and spleen, but this might not become evident until months or even years after the infection. Sand flies bite at night, and if you are in their habitat you should use a mosquito net with a fine weave (sand flies are minute), protective clothing and DEET.

Worms

In rare circumstances, travelers are exposed to different types of roundworms. (Always wear shoes or sandals in villages and huts.) Such infestations are often noticeable in the stool and, according to CIWEC, the treatment is 100 mg of mebendazole (Vermox) twice a day for three days. (Certain types of worms require longer treatments.)

Medical kit and toiletries

Every world traveler needs a medical kit, and the contents of yours should be based on your plans and personal needs and preferences. For example, you will need a wide variety of supplies if you intend to travel extensively in rural areas, and adventure travelers, such as sailors and mountaineers, will need to be completely self-sufficient. (One other reason to carry an extensive medical kit is that you can use it to assist other people.)

Issues with pharmaceuticals

- You should ideally use only pharmaceuticals that have been prescribed by physicians. As with vaccinations, most drugs have contraindications, which range from the possibility of severe and even life-threatening side effects to prohibitions against drinking alcoholic beverages or taking other medications. An example of the last is that you should not take an antiacid within an hour of taking an antibiotic, since

this will reduce the latter's absorption. Many pharmaceuticals should also be taken only with meals or large glasses of water.
- Some drugs that are available in foreign countries have not been licensed for sale in the U.S. In a few cases this is because they failed domestic testing procedures. It may also be that testing is still in progress, or that the drugs were never submitted. Local remedies of probably limited usefulness are also commonly for sale. If you need treatment, but only unfamiliar medications are available, drugs that are produced by international pharmaceutical companies should be preferred. It is also important to read the manufacturers' information sheets, which are available from the pharmacists or enclosed in the packaging.
- Drug stores are easy to find in other countries, although they often have different names, such as *chemists* or *apoteks*. They usually sell many of the medications that are available at home, although the brand names may be different. It is important, therefore, to know the generic names. You will not even need prescriptions to buy drugs in lesser developed countries. The prices there are also generally very low, although you should check the expiration dates.
- It is a good idea to stock up on medical supplies when you visit cities, since their availability may be greatly reduced in towns and villages. In particular, if you will be traveling for a long period of time in a rural environment, you should carry a range of antibiotics for different types of infections, or a broad spectrum antibiotic such as tetracycline. For instance, during my 1994 visit to India I went to Kanha National Park, which is in a remote section of the central state of Madhya Pradesh. I developed a severe case of tonsillitis from the hot days and cold nights there, coupled with exposure on jeep safaris to the park's fine dust. What started as a sore throat quickly developed into a high fever, and I was actually delirious during the worst night. If I had not had a suitable antibiotic, I could have been in real trouble.
- Lastly, the following section includes a list of drugs that you can use to treat different illnesses and health problems. However, you should not take them without first becoming informed about their contraindications. Issues will also exist with regard to proper dosages and the duration of treatments, which can vary by the weight and age of the person being treated and by the severity of the problem.

Medical kit checklists - pharmaceuticals

- Malaria	- Mefloquine (Lariam), chloroquine, proguanil (Paludrine), doxycycline, primaquine, Fansidar
- Painkillers	- Aspirin, acetaminophen (Paracetamol, Tylenol), acetaminophen with codeine, codeine phosphate, meperidine (Demerol)
- Motion sickness	- Dramamine, antihistamines, scopolamine
- Sleeping aid	- Halcion, Valium
- Diarrhea	- Loperamide (Immodium), Lomotil, codeine phosphate, bismuth subsalicylate (Pepto Bismol), ciprofloxacin, norfloxacin, TMP/SMX (Bactrim), doxycycline
- Skin infections and rashes	- Antiseptic, topical antibiotic (polymyxin B, bacitracin and neomycin - Neosporin), miconazole cream (Micatin), ketoconazole cream (Nizoral), amoxicillin, cephalexin
- Respiratory problems	- Aspirin, acetaminophen, decongestants (pseudoephedrine hydrochloride - Sudafed), ampicillin, erythromycin, azithromycin, loracarbef (Lorabid)
- Cough	- Throat lozenges, codeine cough syrup
- Itching	- Hydrocortizone cream, mometasone furoate cream (Elocon), antihistamines (Benadryl), oatmeal bath, astringent or prickly heat powder, prednisone
- Anti-inflammatory	- Aspirin, ibuprofin, Motrin, Advil, diclofenac sodium (Voltaren)
- Altitude sickness	- Acetazolamide (Diamox)
- Allergic reactions	- Antihistamines, prednisone, steroid inhaler, epinephrine (Ana-Kit, EpiPen)
- Amoebic dysentery	- Tinidazole (Tiniba), diloxanide furoate (Furamide), metronidazole (Flagyl), iodoquinol (Yodoxin), paromomycin (Humatin)
- Giardia	- Tinidazole, quinacrine hydrochloride, metronidazole
- Nausea and vomiting	- Metoclopramide, promethazine suppository
- Worms	- Mebendazole (Vermox)

Other medical supplies

- Katadyn or other water filter
- Iodine drops or water treatment pills
- Spare glasses or contacts, prescriptions thereof, and cleaning supplies
- Alcohol swabs or pads
- Band-Aids
- Butterfly bandages
- Larger sterile bandages
- Surgical tape
- Moleskin
- Ace bandages
- Eye drops
- Ear drops
- Condoms and other contraceptives
- Tweezers
- Body thermometer
- Syringes
- Snake anti-venom
- Antiacids
- Laxatives
- Sun tan cream
- Cream for sunburn, such as skin milk or aloe vera gel
- Lip balm
- Baby powder
- Packets of rehydration powder
- Vitamins and fiber pills
- Insect repellant (DEET, permethrin)
- Mosquito coils and coil holder

Toiletries

- Toilet paper
- Soap and soap dish
- Shampoo
- Comb or brush
- Pocket mirror
- Toothbrush, paste and dental floss
- Shaving cream
- Razors
- Foam ear plugs
- Nail clippers
- Makeup and perfume
- Other hygienic products

16. SOURCES OF ASSISTANCE

Travelers sometimes require assistance to resolve certain types of problems. These might range from inconvenient hassles, such as losing your passport, to life-threatening emergencies. Fortunately, wherever you are, many different sources of assistance should be available. Which will be most suitable will depend on the nature and severity of the problem, including the speed with which a response or treatment is required and your own ability to help yourself. This last point, in particular, deserves special emphasis. If you hike down mountain trails after dark, swim by yourself in ocean currents, or engage in similar risky activities, you will have to be entirely self-reliant. Your life may depend on this, and it also demonstrates the need to keep other people informed of your whereabouts. Otherwise, no one will recognize that you are not on schedule and may be experiencing difficulties which you cannot deal with on your own. Finally, if you have a severe problem, you should try to clear your head and calmly think through your options. Then, after you decide what to do, you should tough it out and persevere until your situation improves, no matter how difficult this might be.

Emergency assistance

The most critical situations are those where your life is in danger. These include accidents, severe illnesses, and attacks from other people or dangerous animals. If any of these has occurred, you should immediately determine if assistance is available from any of the sources listed below. In almost all cases, one or more of them should be present and willing to help, by giving you first aid, by taking you to the nearest medical facility, by arranging an emergency evacuation, or by providing any other assistance that is required.

Travel partners, other travelers and local residents

Travel partners are obliged to help each other in times of need, and if you have one, he or she is your first source of outside assistance. Good Samaritans also exist, in the form of other travelers and local residents, both of whom are often willing to help people who are having problems. Local residents can always be asked for directions, and perhaps transportation, to the nearest doctor, clinic or hospital. In addition, many travelers do have minor problems in foreign countries, and they can usually give you a lot of practical advice. Lastly, other travelers and friendly locals can sometimes be prevailed upon for small emergency loans. For example, I still remember an

American traveler, a disabled vet from the Vietnam War who I met years ago at a free Hare Krishna feast at the sect's farm on Kauai, who gave me a few dollars when I was broke. It kept me fed for two days, until my flight back to the mainland.

Help from home

Family and friends back home may be able to help in some situations. For instance, they might be willing to send you a money order if you have an emergency need for cash. (Ask them to send a Postal Service IMO or a bank foreign draft, or if you need the cash immediately use Western Union.) Your family should also be able to provide you with identity documents if you need to replace your passport. In extreme situations, such as if you have trouble with the local authorities, your family or friends can contact helpful officials at home. This should include the Citizens Emergency Center (see below) and your local congressperson.

In medical emergencies it may be useful to call your doctor for advice. It might also be appropriate to arrange transportation home if you need treatment for a severe health problem. Your family and friends, in consultation with your doctor, should be able to assist you with this.

The U.S. government

"*The Secretary of State of the United States of America hereby requests to whom it may concern to permit the citizen/national of the United States named herein to pass without delay or hindrance and in case of need to give all lawful aid and protection.*"

As the first page of your passport says, the U.S. government stands behind you when you travel abroad. This means a substantial amount of assistance should be available almost anywhere, although the specific types of aid that you can request may vary by your location. For example, large embassies, such as the U.S. embassy in London, might only be willing to help with certain types of problems, because they have to deal with thousands of travelers. However, embassies or consulates in remote countries, which are only visited by a few Americans, may go to great lengths to help with almost any type of problem. For instance, the U.S. embassy in Kathmandu has a 24-hour emergency telephone number and distributes a *Handbook for Americans in Nepal*. The services that are described in this booklet, and which should generally be available from any embassy or consulate, are as follows:

*"**Protection and Welfare of U.S. Citizens***

1. Missing Persons/Emergency Messages: The Consular section is frequently called upon by relatives or friends to locate an American believed to be in Nepal...
2. Trekking Safety...
3. Helicopter Rescues: If you are seriously ill or injured while trekking in a remote area, helicopter rescue from Kathmandu is possible.
4. Financial Emergencies: The Consular Section can assist you in obtaining funds from family or friends in an emergency...
5. Medical Emergencies: ...In a medical emergency, the Consular Section can assist you in locating treatment, notifying family or friends, and obtaining funds to cover expenses. The Consular Officer will make every effort to visit you in the hospital. If your illness or injury is such that treatment elsewhere is recommended (such as Bangkok, New Delhi, or the U.S.) the Consular Section can assist in arranging transportation and a medical escort, if needed. The Consular Section is also ready to assist Americans who are suffering severe mental or emotional problems in similar ways.
6. Arrests: When you are in Nepal, you are subject to Nepalese laws...The Consular Officer can do the following for you:

Visit you periodically in jail...
Provide you with a list of local attorneys...
Notify your family and friends...
Relay requests to them for financial or other assistance...
Maintain contacts with Nepalese authorities to monitor the progress of your case...
Intercede with local authorities to ensure that your rights under Nepalese laws are observed...
Protest mistreatment...
Provide emergency medical and dietary assistance if you have no funds and nowhere else to turn; and
Attend your court hearings as an observer.

The Consular Office cannot provide bail money, serve as your legal counsel, or intercede on your behalf in any court proceedings.
7. Deaths: It may not be pleasant to think about, but it happens, even in Nepal. If an American citizen dies in Nepal, the Consular Officer will:

Notify the next-of-kin by immediate cable;
Dispose of the remains in accordance with the wishes of the next-of-kin...

Take possession of the personal estate of the deceased...
Provide an Official Report of Death of an American Abroad which can be used for insurance, estate and other legal matters...

8. Onward Travel from Nepal: You should be sure to reconfirm plane reservations at least 72 hours in advance of departure from Nepal. In addition, your Nepalese visa must be in order at the time of your departure...

Services of the Consular Section

1. Registration of American Citizens: ...These cards can be used as confirmation of American citizenship in case you need to replace a lost or stolen passport. In addition, they are invaluable in helping the Embassy relay emergency messages to or from you...
2. Passports: The Consular Officer can issue U.S. passports. If all supporting documents are in order, a passport can be issued in 4 working days...
3. Registration of Birth of U.S. Citizens...
4. Marriage of U.S. Citizens...
5. Loss of U.S. Citizenship...
6. Notarial Services: Consular Officers can notarize or certify documents...
7. Visitors' Mail: Americans in Nepal can have their mail sent care of the American Embassy...
8. Travel Advisories: The Consular section maintains a book of advisories on international travel...
9. Income Tax Forms: The Consular Section has federal income tax forms but no state tax forms...
10. Absentee Voting Ballots: For federal, state and local elections in the U.S., you may register for absentee ballots through the Consular Section...
11. Selective Service Registration...
12. U.S. Customs Information: Available in the Commercial Section of the Embassy...
13. Social Security: Application for a Social Security Card may be made through the Consular Section...
14. Business Complaints: The Embassy is limited in its ability to resolve complaints from Americans who are not satisfied with the service from local merchants. In cases involving shipment of an item which has not been received by the American, the problem can often be resolved by a telephone call from the Embassy. However, if the merchant proves to be uncooperative, the Embassy can only refer the matter to local authorities...

15. Protection of Property: A Consular officer cannot take possession of the property of an American citizen (except in death cases) and cannot be financially responsible for such property...
16. Information Handouts: The Consular Section has a variety of free information handouts for American citizens. Among them are a health and medical information sheet for Nepal, a brochure on your Trip Abroad, and a List of Attorneys in Nepal...
17. American Visas..."

The Citizens Emergency Center, in Washington, D.C., serves as the domestic focal point for problem situations involving U.S. citizens in foreign countries. They can be contacted at (202) 647-5225 from 8:15 am to 10:00 pm Monday through Friday, and 9:00 am to 3:00 pm on Saturday. Outside of these hours, you should call (202) 634-3600 and ask to speak to the CEC duty officer. The CEC "*provides emergency services pertaining to the protection of Americans arrested or detained abroad, the search for U.S. citizens overseas, and the transmission of emergency messages to those citizens or their next of kin in the United States.*" (*Travel Warning on Drugs Abroad*, U.S. Department of Consular Affairs) Additional information on the above services is available in the following brochures, which can be obtained free by sending a self-addressed, stamped envelope to: CA/PA, Room 5807, Department of State, Washington, D.C. 20520-4818.

- *U.S. Consuls Help Americans Abroad*
- *Crisis Abroad - What the State Department Does*
- *The Citizens Emergency Center*
- *Travel Warning on Drugs Abroad*

Finally, the embassies of certain nations have been contracted to handle inquiries from American citizens in the few countries with which we do not maintain diplomatic relations. For example, U.S. interests in Cuba are handled at the Swiss embassy. In addition, you may be able to obtain assistance from the consulates of other countries in these places.

Local officials

Local officials will often provide or expedite assistance, and they are usually highly motivated to ensure that travelers survive their countries and have as few problems as possible. However, it may be wise to avoid the military or the police in countries that are experiencing civil conflict, since they may be the source of problems rather than the solution to them. A further difficulty with local officials is that in many countries they will not be skilled at English. If this is the case with the first person you meet, you should immediately ask if there is another individual available who is better able to speak the language. An even better option is to bring someone with you who is bilingual to act as a translator. Local police are the obvious choice for assistance in cases of theft, since you will need a report from them to file an insurance claim. In addition, special tourist police departments have been established in some locations, and the police in these units often have better English skills. They also tend to be more knowledgeable about the local criminals who specialize in victimizing travelers.

Local medical professionals

Most nations have large numbers of well-trained physicians. However, the quality of hospitals and clinics, with regard to their hygienic standards and the range of diagnostic and treatment equipment that is available, is less consistent. Standards are generally better in developed countries, and in facilities in cities. Of course, in an emergency you will have to use whatever is available. There are also many specialized clinics around the world that have western funding and staff. For instance, during my world trip I went to the CIWEC Clinic to get a vaccination, to the Himalayan Rescue Association to get advice on the prevention of altitude sickness, and to the Swiss Air Rescue Service in the Maldives to get information on their emergency evacuation and medical care services for the victims of scuba diving accidents.

Travel insurance companies

You should never visit a foreign country without having insurance that at a minimum covers medical care and emergency evacuation. Travel insurance companies typically have 24-hour toll-free or collect telephone numbers that are staffed by experts who can provide advice and assistance for any of the problem situations that are covered under their policies. They should be able to refer you to a qualified physician almost anywhere. They may also be able to expedite local sources of assistance. Unfortunately, if you require medical care that is covered under your policy, you will probably have to pay for it on the spot and then file a claim. While this may not be the intention of the policy, which might say that the local medical care provider should file the claim, you are, effectively, always at the local party's mercy.

Hotels and travel agents

Local companies in the tourism industry are usually willing to assist travelers, such as with references to medical care or the police. Large hotels, in particular, can always refer you to doctors, and may even have them on their staffs. Reception desk personnel can also be helpful with other types of requests, and in some places they will assist you even if you are not a guest.

Credit card companies

American Express, Visa and other credit cards can be used to obtain funds almost anywhere in the world. With an Amex card and a personal check from your bank account at home, you can get cash or traveler's checks in over one hundred and twenty countries from their Travel Service Offices. (This is how I get funds during my trips, by periodically cashing a check to get a new batch of traveler's checks.) There should also be a bank in virtually any town that will give you a cash advance on a Visa card. In addition, Amex and Visa cards can be used in many foreign ATM networks, which are rapidly being expanded in population centers around the world. (You will need a PIN for this.)

American Express also provides a wide range of other travel services. The company has 24-hour telephone numbers that cardholders can call for assistance with medical, legal and other traveler emergencies. Amex also offers flight insurance, damage or theft insurance for items that are purchased using the card, broad coverage travel insurance and rental car insurance. In addition, Amex offices supply travel information and can help you make reservations and other arrangements. If you do get one of their cards, it is a good idea to ask for a copy of *American Express Traveler's Companion*. This booklet describes their full range of services, and lists the addresses for all of their offices worldwide.

Special emergency situations

Lastly, the following types of travel emergencies deserve special comment:

- Search and rescue situations
- Kidnappings

In rare circumstances, travelers require assistance because they have become lost in remote areas, such as mountains, deserts or at sea, or because they have been kidnapped. If you are aware of people who are involved in any of these situations, you should immediately request assistance for them from both local and their home government officials. This presumes, of course, that you are not the victim. If you are the victim, unless someone knows that you are missing you are on your own. Good luck!

In the case of a kidnapping, if these sources of assistance are unsuccessful in securing the victim's release, there are a few other options that you might consider. Some kidnappings have been resolved because diplomats and journalists from neutral countries, such as Sweden and Switzerland, were kind enough to intervene and assist in the negotiations. If you arrange for a situation to be publicized in the press, you may be able to attract such assistance. There are also private security companies that the victim's family and friends might be able to hire. You should look in telephone yellow pages for listings that advertise *advisory services*. The primary clients of these companies are corporations, and their services, because of the risks that may be involved, can be very expensive. Examples of such firms include Control Risks in London, Kroll Associates in New York, and International SOS in Philadelphia. Of course, you might also be able to find freelance mercenaries - just ask Ross Perot, but remember, Caveat Emptor!

17. MONEY

This chapter discusses how you can save money during your world trip by finding the best exchange rates and by learning to bargain well. It also includes a review of some shopping issues with which you may be confronted.

Foreign exchange

The best foreign exchange (FX) policy is to keep your funds in dollars, and only do a conversion when you need more local money. You would only benefit from changing a substantial amount of funds on arrival in a country if you thought that its currency was going to strengthen, such that you would get a poorer rate at a later date. Exchange rate movements, however, are extremely difficult to predict, even for market professionals. For example, movements of the dollar against other major currencies are highly variable, and since lesser developed countries generally have higher inflation than the U.S., their currencies often weaken, month after month, against the dollar. (An exception to this occurs when a country *fixes* its exchange rate relative to some other currency(ies), and then lets a lengthy period of implicit value depreciation pass before realigning the currency through a *devaluation*.) You should especially limit your holdings of local currency in countries that have high inflation rates, or when devaluations may occur. At an extreme, in hyperinflationary economies, local currencies effectively lose all of their value and you should only change money when you need to pay for things. It is also common in these circumstances for separate pricing systems to develop that are based on dollars and other major currencies. Having said all this, though, it is worth stocking up on local currency if you are at a location where you will have to pay a high commission for each conversion, or if you find a particularly good exchange rate. Indeed, it is a wonderful feeling in a lesser developed country to change a few hundred dollars into a roll of local currency, and know that it will last for weeks.

You should shop around at a number of money changers, since there are frequently wide differences in their rates. (Avoid the facilities at airports, or only change enough money to get to town.) In general, banks offer better rates than specialist exchange companies. There may also be large differences in commissions and fees. Money changers often add a number of service charges, and since these can run to $5 or more per transaction they are definitely worth trying to avoid. In many locations, if you shop around you should be able to find an institution that does not add any extra charges. The governments of some countries also add their own charges, which are called *stamp taxes*, and all legal exchange organizations are obliged to collect them. Finally, you should not accept all of the local money in large bills. It is wise to ask for some smaller notes, particularly in lesser developed countries where getting change might be difficult.

You can also change money at hotels, although you will always get lower rates than at banks. However, in remote locations, or during weekends, they may be your only option. You can sometimes change at hotels even when you are not a guest, particularly in areas where there are few official money changers. You can even use merchants, although this is easiest when you are making a purchase. If you are not, you should expect to get a terrible rate or to pay a high fee.

Lastly, it is important to reconvert unused currency of lesser developed countries before you depart, since only poor exchange rates will be available outside of them. For instance, when I changed my excess Indonesian rupees in Australia, the rate was 16% below what I had been getting in Bali a few days before. Some currencies are actually unconvertible outside their countries, and I had $50 worth of Indian rupees left over after my world trip because of this, although I used them on the later visit.

Black markets

Many countries around the world have black markets for foreign exchange. These countries typically share certain characteristics, which include extensive corruption in government and industry, the existence of black markets for other goods and services, an inefficient tax collection system, and foreign exchange controls. The presence of the first three means the local residents are saving substantial sums of money outside their legal banking systems. However, these conditions are also highly inflationary, so the domestic currencies will usually be weakening over time. The locals, therefore, have a powerful incentive to convert their money into stronger currencies, but they are unable to do so legally because of the FX controls.

Foreign visitors are a natural source of other currencies. Indeed, when the supply of visitors is limited, and the local demand is great, this will drive black market prices far above the official rates. (The black market rate is a much more accurate measure of a currency's true value, in an international context, than its official rate.) The amount of the premium is a function of the pervasiveness of the corruption, or how much local currency is waiting to be converted; the rates of inflation and currency depreciation, or how rapidly the stored funds are losing value; the degree of tolerance of the black market by government officials, which will usually be based on their own degree of involvement; and the amount of foreign exchange that is available from travelers, which depends on the general attractiveness of the country, and also on the benefits and risks of doing black market deals or, in other words, all of the earlier factors.

Countries that have currency black markets often have sophisticated nation-wide collection and distribution networks. In some cases they may function as virtually legitimate secondary banking systems. Bills and traveler's checks denominated in dollars and other major currencies are collected in greater and greater amounts at higher and higher levels in such a system. They are ultimately smuggled out of the country for deposit in foreign banks, although the money is also sometimes used to buy gold and silver, which is then resmuggled back.

Using a black market

You can get better exchange rates in many countries, and also avoid service charges, by using black markets. However, it is only worthwhile if the rate advantage is sufficient to compensate for the risks, which include being robbed or arrested. Typical black market FX premiums are 10% to 20%, but many such countries are already so inexpensive, by western standards, that it is simply not worth it. However, the rate differentials in other countries might be 100% or greater, such that using black markets will be the only way to make travel in them affordable. (The black market rate in Burma in 1994 was twenty times the official rate!)

Black market deals are available from merchants and touts. You should always avoid the latter, though, because they are usually thieves. Even if they are not, they will have to find willing merchants to do the deals, and they will be looking for good deals for themselves (high commissions), not for you. This could also involve leading you on a long walk around town. They might even be undercover police, although this is unlikely. Some touts also offer local currencies at unbelievable rates, to set up unsuspecting travelers for robbery. This would rarely be by mugging, though, unless you stupidly followed them to a ghetto shack or back alley. In most cases they just want you to fall for a con where you give them your money, and then wait while they collect the local currency elsewhere. They will say emphatically that they will return, but they will not! After all, why should they, since they already have your money? A variation on this con occurred to my Swedish friend in Nairobi who was mentioned earlier. This tout took her to a local restaurant, supposedly to meet a contact with the cash. He bought her a cup of tea, excused himself to go to the bathroom to meet the source, and then ran out a rear exit. She was in shock when I met her later, because she was an experienced traveler and could not believe that she had been so stupid. Touts might also try to short change you, or give you an envelope that is supposed to contain the local currency, but which is only stuffed with paper.

To repeat a point made earlier, and which is particularly important when dealing with black markets, you should never hand over your cash until you have first received and checked your purchase. You should demand that FX dealers give you the local currency, and then count all of it in front of them before handing over your money. (You should have a sufficient amount in your pocket, so you do not have to pull out your wallet.) If the amount that you are given is short, you should give it back and then recount it after it, supposedly, has been made complete. You should ignore any protests that the dealers make to hurry, such as "*the police are coming*." Many people have been robbed because they did not follow this procedure, and they could hardly go to the police to complain. Every rule of thumb has an exception, of course, but you should beware of breaking this one. I have only done so twice. In the first instance, a restaurant manager in Arusha, Tanzania, offered to do an exchange for me, but said he could only get the local currency after I gave him my money. I refused. However, while having lunch in his restaurant I struck up a conversation with some Danish travelers at a nearby table. They told me that they had changed money with him an hour earlier, and that they had given him their money first. They received the entire amount as negotiated. Having a confirmation of his honesty, I called him over and we arranged the deal. We met in the restaurant's bathroom fifteen minutes later, and I received the agreed amount of Tanzanian shillings. I also followed a similar procedure a few days later with a pharmacist in the nearby town of Moshi. The black market rate at the time was twice the official rate, and it was clear that a well-established system was in place in the area.

As this illustrates, local merchants are the preferred intermediaries for money deals. Their main advantage is that they are much less likely to try to rob you. Indeed, this is usually just another business to them, and it may even be more important than their actual trade. They may also be the people who have the illegal savings, in which case they might offer better rates. For example, the local carpet sellers in Kathmandu are an excellent source of currency. You will of course have to bargain well to get the best rates, and shopping around will help. Black market rates, like legal rates, change day-by-day. As with all bargaining, you should not allow a price to be changed once it is agreed. Black market money changers regularly try to lower FX rates by a small amount at the last moment. They also often accept both cash and traveler's checks, although cash, preferably high denomination bills, typically gets the best rate.

Bargaining

During your world trip you will frequently encounter situations where it is appropriate to bargain, and being good at it can have many positive effects. It will obviously enable you to save a lot of money, but it is also useful in situations where there are power conflicts, such as with travel partners or officials. Indeed, being skilled at negotiation, including knowing when to compromise, is applicable to many areas of life. While this section concentrates on bargaining as it applies to price-setting situations during foreign travel, and where you are the buyer, the ideas can also be adapted for any position and type of negotiation.

Why bargain

Many people do not like to bargain. They view it as a hassle, and would prefer to accept a reasonable fixed price. For instance, Americans have traditionally been taught to pay *good money* for *good value.* As a consequence of this, we tend to believe that a product or service must be of suspect quality if its price is too favorable - it has to be expensive to be good. We even sometimes feel guilty accepting excellent deals, as if we do not deserve them. This puts us at a psychological disadvantage to people of other nationalities, since the rest of the world has been taught to pay *as little as possible* for *good value*. Bargaining for goods and services is the norm in many, many countries.

It is easy to pay more than you should, and you will certainly not be stopped from doing so. You can only get the best prices if you learn to bargain well. It is also inappropriate to pay too much because it is inflationary. Poor bargaining by tourists has actually driven up the cost structures of some countries. Merchants are usually rational, and if they think they can make greater profits by selling to incompetent foreigners, they will raise their prices for everyone. This not only hurts the tourists, but also the local residents and travelers who have less resources. If you are with people who do not like to bargain, you should ask them what they are willing to pay and then bargain for them. You might also be able to split the savings with them as compensation for your services.

You should evaluate the bargaining potential for all of your purchases, and devise strategies for getting reduced prices whenever it is appears possible. There will obviously be less room to bargain in a boutique in Paris than at a bazaar in India, but it does not hurt to try. Indeed, it is amazing where you can get discounts. At a minimum, you should always consider the bargaining possibilities for taxis, at hotels and guesthouses, in souvenir shops, with guides and porters, and for anything that is offered by sidewalk merchants or touts. Other rules of thumb are to bargain for all expensive items, and for volume purchases.

The theory of negotiation

Many people consider negotiation to be an art, with the consequence that you are out of luck if you do not have the talent for it. However, it is actually an eminently rational process, which anyone can learn. An effective negotiation is comprised of three stages. The first is the research stage, where you determine the value of the good or service that you would like to buy. The second is the purchase, where through charm and perseverance you get the other party to accept a reasonable price. The final stage, which is only necessary in some circumstances, is to have the willpower to walk away when an unreasonable price is being demanded. Doing this will often cause the other party to reconsider and, if they will not, it protects you from making a bad deal.

Preliminary research

The first stage is the most important. As a world traveler, you will encounter many situations where you will be uncertain about local price levels. You will be at the mercy of the merchants in these situations unless you research their markets and learn the normal prices for their goods and services.

In addition, there are both objective and subjective perspectives on value. The objective value of something is its market price (or range of prices). This can usually be determined by surveying what different merchants are charging. The subjective value is the psychological importance that you and the other party attribute to whatever is being negotiated. If you *have to have* something, you obviously place a very high value on it. Subjective values are particularly important when objective price information is unavailable or difficult to evaluate. If this is the case, you should carefully consider the motivations both of yourself and the other party.

You can obtain price information from local residents, such as hotel staff and waiters, from other travelers, and by shopping around. Indeed, if you do a lot of research you should begin to understand the entire local value system. This is comprised of the prices for all goods and services, and the relationships between them. For example, what are the quality and price differences between first, second and third class for transportation, hotel rooms and restaurants? In addition, how do prices compare across expense categories, such as for public transportation, a budget restaurant meal and a guesthouse room? When you are evaluating these relationships, you should ask yourself if they are consistent with what you would expect? When they are not, it means that you do not fully understand the market, or that bargains are available.

Another factor affecting objective values is the cost of production, such as the income level of a local resident who supplies a good or service that you would like to buy. A shrewd negotiator will calculate the cost of production, and then offer a price that represents a small profit. (The offer could even represent a loss, if the buyer knows that the merchant has to make a sale.) For instance, a beautiful wood carving might cost $100 in an art shop at home, but how much should you pay the actual artist in his or her home village, if he or she has a daily cost of living of $3, can make one carving every two days, and has dozens of carvings unsold. In such circumstances, an offer of $8 to $10 might be appropriate or even generous. The price will increase at each level in the distribution system, so in this example you should expect to pay $12 or more for the same souvenir at a local shop, and add a further premium if you buy it at a fashionable store in a nearby city.

Many travelers assign incorrect values to goods and services because they think of them in terms of their home country price levels. You should always strive to get good deals within the local value contexts. The difference between accepting an asking price for a good of $10, or bargaining it down to $5, might seem insignificant to many people. Indeed, it could be a superb deal at either price relative to what you are used to paying at home. However, you should recognize that you are only wasting your money if you pay the higher price. You are not providing charity to an impoverished merchant. He or she only expects a reasonable price, and if you pay more you will only be viewed as an ignorant tourist who likes to throw their money away. You may as well burn the extra five dollars. Small price differences also add up to large sums over many transactions, and only the wealthiest travelers can afford to ignore this.

The amounts of supply and demand also affect objective and subjective values. For example, if there are many merchants selling similar goods, one of them can hardly take the view that his or her particular goods deserve higher prices. There are often dozens of merchants in tourist locations, so you should definitely be able to find one who will accept a reasonable price. However, merchants also understand that some people do not like to bargain or are poor at it, and that others are highly skilled. They will usually demand inflated prices at the start, but lower their expectations once they recognize they are dealing with an expert.

Finally, to complete the research task you should locate at least one backup merchant. You can then use the first to set the price, and the second to close the deal. You can also follow a more sophisticated strategy if there are many competing vendors. You should start by demanding a price that is so low that the vendor will not accept it, even by calling you back after you walk away. You can then use other vendors to inch up to what is the best price in the market. In addition, even if one vendor refuses your offer, another may not. Different merchants have different personal situations, which will affect their own subjective perspectives. The next one you approach may really need a sale. (Another consequence of having a number of options is that it should reduce your emotional attachment to any one of them.)

The deal

The actual transaction should be easy if you have done the above research. You will know the value of the good or service, what you are willing to pay, and that the merchant should accept this price.

You should prepare for the deal as follows:

- Be positive. You can get what you want for a reasonable price. At its best, bargaining is an enjoyable price setting exercise between two friendly and accommodating people. At its worst, it is only a contest of wills.
- Remember that you do not have to buy anything. Do not let yourself be pressured. If you cannot get a good price, forget it. Have the discipline to walk away. Control your buying lust.
- Carefully plan when to make the purchase. Try to find a time when few other customers will be present, and do not leave it to the last minute before your departure.

- Consider your appearance. Do not look or act wealthy or unconcerned with the price. (Take off your expensive watch and jewelry, and put your camera in your bag.) Avoid displays of enthusiasm for the goods or services that you want to buy.
- If you are bargaining with a partner, outline and rehearse beforehand the roles of good cop and bad cop.

You should use a friendly approach to begin the negotiation, and try to charm the merchant into being reasonable and respecting your right not to pay an exorbitant amount. This is particularly important if you have not been able to develop a good understanding of local values. You should also be alert to, and reject, standard merchant ploys such as bait and switch tactics. Some other positions that merchants regularly take are to protest that what is being bargained for cost them more than what you are offering, that it will be gone the next day or, for a souvenir, that it is an antique. You should reject all of these gambits out-of-hand. More generally, you should ask yourself in negotiation situations what the other parties want from you. This would obviously be a higher price or a larger sale from a shopowner, but it could be many other things in other circumstances. This is actually a blind spot that most people have; few of us are able to think like chess masters and understand the perspectives, motivations and likely actions of other individuals. One way you can improve your awareness of bargaining opponents is to spend some time with them making small talk, interspersed with a few pointed questions, and in the process look for clues about what they seem to want. You should also try to anticipate, and then inquire about, what you are purposely not being told.

You should always force the merchant to set the opening price. This is your prerogative as a buyer, and it establishes a basic parameter to which you can respond. It may also reveal a weakness in the seller's position. (On the other hand, if you are informed about values and do not want to deal with a long haggle, you can use a firm approach and quote the price that you are willing to pay. This is simply a fixed price sale where you set the price.) There is no valid rule of thumb for the percentage reduction that you should make to the merchant's asking price for your first counter offer. The variability of quotes that you will receive in different situations is too great. (However, I often try to get a 10% discount in situations where bargaining is really not expected, particularly for expensive items.) Your first counter offer should be based on the merchant's initial price and the objective value of the good. For instance, in many lesser developed countries, if a merchant takes you for a rube he or she might ask for a price that is five times the regular amount. You should be aware that many people in these circumstances have a psychological resistance to making counter offers that represent greater than 50% reductions. They think that if they do this they will be rude, or appear ridiculous. Merchants anticipate this disinclination, which is why they quote such high prices. Indeed, they will often respond with shock and indignation to customers who are bold enough to make reasonable counter offers. You need to be firm in such a situation, and it is worth remembering that it is only a psychological game. To continue the example, you would want to counter with an offer that was only 10%-15% of the initial asking price, to leave room to settle at the reasonable price of 20% of it. As this suggests, you should set your first counter offer at a level that enables you to move up in small increments two or three times, before agreeing to a deal.

I had to bargain with this type of merchant when I helped a friend buy two elaborately costumed wood puppets at a shop in Kuta, Bali. The merchant asked 80,000 Indonesian rupees for each (about $40), and I countered with 24,000 (a 70% reduction). He said this was absurd, since the puppets were antiques. (They were not!) We haggled for a while before I made a final offer of 28,000, and said that if he did not take it we would go to another shop down the street. He refused, but then called us back as we were walking away. My friend, who had been prepared to pay the full price (she was leaving Bali in a few hours, and had to have the puppets), was kind enough to buy me a nice meal for my efforts.

Difficult negotiations

Bargaining is more difficult when you do not understand the local values, when you are dealing with a recalcitrant merchant and, worst of all, in those rare circumstances when you have to make a deal. The first problem of uncertainty about values can only be remedied by additional research. In other words, you have moved to the bargaining table too soon.

The obvious course of action with a stubborn merchant is to walk away. Another option is to point out similar or lower prices that are available from competing merchants, and threaten to buy from them. (If the competitors have lower prices, they are presumably for poorer quality merchandise.) In addition, many people act unpleasantly during negotiations. They want their opponents to feel uncomfortable, and to react emotionally and suspend their good judgement. If you are dealing with this type of individual and you feel under stress, you should speak slowly, or take a break to consider the situation. This will cause you to appear in control, and it should also help you avoid making stupid mistakes. (If a problem develops in a complex negotiation, you should excuse yourself and go to another place to rework your position.)

A similar concern has to do with the pace of the negotiations. If you are quick-witted, you may be able to use this to your advantage to close a deal before the other party understands your weaknesses or fully comprehends all of the transaction's consequences. On the other hand, if you require more time to understand a transaction, you should force the other party to slow down and adjust to your pace. In addition, if you are negotiating in a situation where a number of people are involved, you should focus your persuasive efforts on the key decision maker, or on the person who stands to lose the most if the deal is not completed.

Issues of pace often develop in multicultural negotiation situations. It is important to recognize that different nationalities have different ways of doing business and reaching decisions. For example, in the industrial world Japanese businesspeople are known for their slow negotiating pace, since they place great emphasis on achieving consensus within their own ranks. Different nationalities also relate to each other in varying manners, in some cases reflecting longstanding cultural sensitivities and biases.

Lastly, if you have to make a deal, you should first examine if this is truly the case. It is extremely rare that there will be no other option. If your back is against the wall it is imperative not to let the other party know this, since if they find out they will probably try to take you for everything that you have. You should be circumspect, and even devious, and never signal your true situation or intentions. It is particularly important not to say too much, since this "*is the sign of an uneasy conscience.*" (*The Little Drummer Girl*, John Le Carré, Pan Books, page 88) (This also applies in job interviews.) For instance, Americans have a disadvantage in this regard, because we tend to be open about our opinions and positions. This can be a major liability in negotiations. On the other hand, the British are known for their tendency to dissemble. For them, "*the first response at any unexpected event is to suppress the spontaneous reaction.*" (*The Secret Pilgrim*, John Le Carré, Hodder & Stoughton, page 154)

It is useful to prepare like an actor for a difficult negotiation, since you will be much more convincing if you know your lines. (It takes practice to be a good liar!) You should analyze the strengths and weaknesses of your position, and decide how you will respond to pressure on the latter. In general, you should refuse to accept or even acknowledge that they exist, and you should never apologize. (You should of course also analyze the strengths and weaknesses of the other party.) Finally, you should recognize that you have the right *not* to answer questions, to change the subject, and to give answers that allow for multiple, and conflicting, interpretations.

Closing the deal

When you are close to completing a deal you should consider using the line: "*Is that the best price you can give me?*" You may be able to get another reduction this way. Merchants also regularly say this, and it is the buyer who often sets the final price. This is either accepted on the spot, or after you have left their premises when they call you back and agree to the terms. Indeed, for purchases in many lesser developed countries, if a merchant accepts your price in his or her shop this means you have paid too much. If they do not accept it, you should be firm and say: "*Sorry, but that's all I can afford,*" or "*That's all I will pay.*" If you have been reasonable, nine times out of ten they will call you back after you start to walk away.

A deal is not necessarily completed after the price is set. For example, if you actually want to buy two or more items, you can reopen the negotiation to request a further volume discount. This is simply good, hard bargaining. You should also consider reopening a negotiation if there is a delay between agreeing to and settling the transaction, if a material event has occurred in the interim.

It is essential to agree on any other terms of the deal before paying, since these may have to be negotiated as well. Some additional provisions that are common in purchase of goods transactions include:

- Are there any other payments that will have to be made?
- Are there any additional parts that are included?
- What is the return and servicing policy?
- Is a warranty included, and what are its terms?
- Is packing and/or shipping included?

You should never allow the price and conditions to be modified, unless this is entirely reasonable, such as if the circumstances change and warrant the provision of additional services. An example of this might be where you hire a guide, who ends up assisting you for a longer period of time than was originally intended. *You should also never sign any legal agreement without reading, and understanding, every word of it!* It is unbelievable how many people ignore this common sense precaution, because they are too lazy to exercise their minds and read the fine print. You should ask for explanations of any provisions that you do not fully understand, and change or delete anything that is unacceptable, *before* signing the contract. In addition, if a merchant packs your purchase for you, you should check that everything is included and then get your receipt and count your change. For the last, attempts at short-changing are common, and many people are also very poor at arithmetic.

Other perspectives on bargaining

A few other tips for bargaining situations are as follows:

- Make a regular habit of turning down merchants' prices. This will make you a tougher negotiator, and it is also anti-inflationary. If you make merchants feel the pain of lost income, this will discourage them from raising their prices.
- Be aware that some people will try to get you to compromise on small things early in a bargaining situation, to soften you up for later, and more substantial, concessions.
- Learn to spot leading questions. Do not not let them take you where you are meant to go.
- If you give a merchant the impression that you will buy more of his or her goods in the future, this may increase your leverage in the present transaction.
- Bargain in cash, since merchants usually have to report credit card payments to the local tax authorities. Merchants are often willing to give substantial discounts for cash.
- Do not allow touts to participate in your deals, since this will usually increase your costs.
- Sleep on every big purchase (not literally, of course). Give yourself a day or two to consider it: do you really want the item; can you afford it; and are the terms the best that you can get?
- For complicated deals, use negotiation checklists to keep track of important issues.
- Lastly, effective bargaining does not have to result in a zero-sum situation, where one party has obviously won and the other has lost. Everyone should compromise, if only a little, and at a minimum leave the transaction with a feeling of accomplishment.

Shopping

"*Caveat Emptor*"

- Let the buyer beware

You will probably need to shop for a wide variety of goods and services during your world trip, ranging from simple items such as toiletries to once-in-a-lifetime souvenirs. The following are some general tips for shopping situations:

- Shop around!
- Shop during sales.
- Do most of your shopping in countries that have weak exchange rates.
- Buy in volume when low prices are available.
- Shop in lesser developed countries that have manufacturing plants built under license with multinational corporations. These manufacturers want to make substantial local sales, but they can only do so if they reduce their prices to what the markets will bear. For instance, properly licensed music cassettes that are for sale only in Indonesia cost $3 in 1991 in the central department store in Jakarta. Conversely, such well-known shopping locations as Singapore and Hong Kong are actually quite expensive, because of the relative wealth of the local populations and the large numbers of tourists and businesspeople who pass through. (You can find bargains for some goods at them, such as electronic gear, if you shop around.)
- Finally, be opportunistic. Travelers are periodically offered extraordinary bargains, and you should obviously take advantage of them. (Be on the lookout for con artists, though.) Indeed, I learned about missed opportunities the hard way, when I met a man from the Indonesian island of Ambon in the Jalan Jaksa traveler's neighborhood in Jakarta. He was in the capital trying to raise money to start a commercial pearling business at home, and he had brought a few sample oysters and pearls with him. I spent a long time talking to him about how to make presentations to investors and banks, and in return he offered to sell me one of his largest pearls. I gathered he was low on funds, but I was wary, since I did not have any idea of what it was worth. I ended up passing on his offer. Later in my trip, though, I visited the town of Broome in northwest Australia, which is also a pearling center. I saw similar pearls there in jewelry shops that cost $1,000 or more apiece. More commonly, many people take advantage of the excellent deals that are available in Asia for knock-off goods, such as clothing and music cassettes. However, you should beware of shabby quality. Cassettes may only cost a dollar or two in Bangkok, but they may not last very long.

Warranties and servicing

"*This IBM portable system comes with something no portable should be without - a warranty backed by IBM and thousands of IBM Authorized Dealers or Remarketers worldwide so that you are never far away from service and support.*"

- *IBM International Hardware Warranty Service*

It is important to understand the terms of any warranties that come with your foreign purchases, particularly whether or not repair services will be available where you live. If your goods break and you have not chosen carefully, you may find that replacement parts are not available, or that the warranties are only valid in the countries where the goods were purchased. You should read the warranties carefully, and good luck! For example, the above warranty from IBM appears to be quite straightforward. It came with a notebook personal computer that I bought in Singapore. Since it is common there to get only a local warranty on electronic goods, I bought an IBM because of the geographic coverage that was provided. (The warranty lists telephone numbers of service locations in ninety-two countries.) I also wanted to *Buy American*. The IBM representative in Singapore confirmed that I would have no problem getting the machine serviced in the U.S. Of course, I assumed, after all, it was manufactured there. Unfortunately, when I returned home the computer was unable to print because of a hardware problem. Imagine my surprise when I was informed by local IBM service personnel that it had actually been made in Japan, and was designed to a different standard than U.S. products. It could not be repaired in the U.S., and the warranty was not even valid. The fine print revealed the catch: "*International hardware warranty service is available for those customers traveling to countries* ***in which this product is sold.***" When I bought the computer, I should have asked in how many of the ninety-two countries this particular machine was sold. Since it was not sold in the U.S., it would have to be sent back to Singapore for servicing, at my expense. ("*so that you are never far away from service and support*"!) I did not want to send the machine halfway around the world to get it fixed, so I searched for other assistance and was fortunate to find a local expert who was able to reconfigure the computer's programming and bypass the problem.

As a postscript to this story, the machine's power controller board failed a few months later. I could not even turn it on. This part was only available from IBM-Japan, and IBM-USA refused to provide any assistance in contacting them. Thanks a lot, IBM!

Souvenirs

One of the most enjoyable travel experiences is to shop for souvenirs. They are great for display cases or to hang on walls, and you will treasure them forever. Each time you look at a souvenir, it will remind you of the places you have visited and the people you have met. You may even feel like the early explorers: you have traveled to remote and exotic lands, and returned with their produce and other products. Traditional souvenirs include foods and spices; wines and liquors; pearls and jewels; textiles, including silks, cottons, woolens, tailored clothing, t-shirts, hats, baskets, purses, carpets and wall hangings; art, carvings and religious objects; furniture; electronic equipment; and automobiles, motorcycles and boats. More unusual souvenirs are also available at many destinations. For instance, in Namche Bazaar, you can buy second-hand climbing equipment, sleeping bags and tents that have been used on expeditions to Mt. Everest.

There are also many small souvenirs that are fun to collect, such as matchbooks, coins and currency, stamps, seashells, postcards, beer mats and bottles, performance programs and tickets, and other memorabilia. I have a Dutch friend who actually collects the air sickness bags of different airlines, unused, of course. He has over one hundred bags, and is a bit eccentric, as you might imagine. Lastly, because of the nostalgia it stimulates, travel photography may be the best souvenir of all.

The major restriction on what you can buy is your budget. You should of course always try to get good deals, but you should also probably buy souvenirs that you really like, even if they are a bit too expensive, rather than regret not having gotten them for the rest of your life. Size, however, should not be an object, since you can always ship a purchase home. You should be especially alert for souvenirs that are available, worldwide, only in the locations that you are visiting. In addition, you should try to shop where goods are actually manufactured. Stores in towns are usually willing to tell you where craft villages and factories are located, and the savings that the latter offer should outweigh the costs of getting to them. They also typically offer facilities tours, where you can observe the employees at work and learn more about your purchases. The selections should be much better as well. For example, the wood carving industry in Bali is centered around the village of Ubud, and the selection and prices there are much better than in the tourist towns of Kuta, Sanur and Nusa Dua. Finally, if you can, you should visit factories with local friends (real friends, not touts), since they should be able to get you additional discounts.

(During my world trip I went shopping with friends in rural Thailand, and we got excellent deals on handwoven silk, pottery and silver jewelry.)

Certain types of souvenirs present additional complications, such as customs issues, and these are reviewed in more detail in the following sections.

U.S. customs regulations and duties

According to the government brochure, *Know Before You Go, Customs Hints for Returning Residents* (this is available from U.S. Customs, P.O. Box 7407, Washington, D.C. 20044), "*You must declare all articles acquired abroad and in your possession at the time of your return. This includes:*

- *Articles that you purchased.*
- *Gifts presented to you while abroad.*
- *Articles purchased in duty-free shops.*
- *Repairs or alterations made to any articles taken abroad and returned, whether or not repairs or alterations were free of charge.*
- *Items you have been requested to bring home for another person.*
- *Any articles you intend to sell or use in your business.*" (page 2)

Furthermore, "*Articles totaling $400 (based on the fair retail value of each item in the country where acquired) may be entered free of duty, subject to limitations on liquors, cigarettes, and cigars, if:*

- *Articles were acquired as an incident of your trip for your personal or household use.*
- *You bring the articles with you at the time of your return to the United States and they are properly declared to Customs....*
- *You are returning from a stay abroad of at least 48 hours....*
- *You have not used this $400 exemption, or any part of it, within the preceding 30-day period....*
- *Articles are not prohibited or restricted....*" (Ibid., page 5)

Some other provisions of U.S. customs regulations are as follows:

- If you fail to declare an article, it is subject to seizure, and you could also be forced to pay a penalty and be subject to criminal prosecution. If you understate the value

of an article, you may be forced to pay a penalty along with any duty that is due.
- Gifts for other people that accompany you must be included in your personal exemption. Gifts that are mailed from abroad are free of duty up to $50 in fair retail value.
- Other articles that are free of duty include: personal belongings of U.S. origin; foreign-made articles taken abroad, provided you have proof of prior possession such as purchase receipts; automobiles, boats and planes that were taken abroad for non-commercial use; household effects and tools of trade; and articles that fall within specialized trade arrangements, such as the Generalized System of Preferences (see the customs booklet *GSP & The Traveler*), the Caribbean Basin Initiative, and products from Israel, Mexico and Canada.
- Articles that are prohibited or subject to restrictions, a few of which are covered in more detail below, include: automobiles that were manufactured abroad; biological materials; unlawful copies of copyrighted articles; ceramic tableware that contains lead; cultural property; drug paraphernalia; firearms and ammunition; food products; fruits and vegetables; gold; meats, livestock and poultry; medicine and narcotics; merchandise; money and other monetary instruments; pets; plants; textiles; trademarked articles; and wildlife and fish.

"*Articles imported in excess of your customs exemption will be subject to duty unless the items are entitled to free entry or prohibited. The inspector will place the items having the highest rate of duty under your exemption, and duty will be assessed on the lower-rated items.*" (Ibid., page 10) A flat rate of duty, usually 10%, is applied to the first $1,000 worth of goods in excess of your personal exemption. After this, specific rates are applied to different types of articles.

Customs duties can be paid in cash; with a personal check from a U.S. bank; with a government check, traveler's check or money order, if it does not exceed the duty amount by more than $50; and with Discover, MasterCard and Visa credit cards (only at some locations).

Antiques and art

Many objects are falsely sold to travelers as antiques, to demand higher prices. In addition, if you buy something in a foreign country that actually is an antique, or an important work of art, it may be necessary to obtain local government permission to bring it home. These types of restrictions are also sometimes enforced on the receiving end. For instance, pre-Columbian art is not allowed into the U.S. unless you have an export certificate from its country of origin. Additional information on this is available from the U.S. Information Agency, Washington, D.C., (202) 619-4700.

Endangered species and wildlife products

Many countries have restrictions on importing or exporting wildlife species and their products. The primary sources of regulatory protection in the U.S. are the *Endangered Species Act*, which prohibits the importation and exportation of endangered and threatened species, the *Lacey Act*, which prohibits the importation of species that have been possessed in violation of foreign law, and *CITES*, which is a wildlife treaty that has been signed by over one hundred nations.

It is difficult when you are traveling to know for certain if a good has been made from a protected species. In general, you should not buy the following:

- Reptile skins
- Tortoiseshell
- Coral and other marine creatures
- Ivory
- Birds and feathers
- Butterflies and other insects
- Products made with exotic leathers
- Animal furs

"*A Final Word. The United States is the world's largest consumer of wildlife, followed by Japan and Western Europe. Despite strong prohibitions, a large percentage of the wildlife trade in these countries still involves protected or endangered species. Consumers like you can play a significant role in curbing this illegal trade. Combatting the problem requires not only increased enforcement efforts but also better informed consumers and travelers.*" This quote is from *Buyer Beware!*, a booklet that is published by the U.S. Fish and Wildlife Service, Department of the Interior, Washington, D.C. 20240. They also publish the booklet *Facts about Federal Wildlife Laws*. In addition, information on the trade in endangered species is available from TRAFFIC (USA), World Wildlife Fund, 1250 24th Street, NW, Washington, D.C. 20037, (202) 293-4800.

Gems and jewelry

Travelers are regularly swindled on purchases of precious gems and jewelry. Unless you are an expert, you should only buy them for personal adornment or as gifts, and never on the presumption that they can be resold for a profit. Gem identification and valuation is extremely complicated, and it is easy for an amateur to be tricked. (This is also true with the identification of gold.) You need a gemological education, and substantial practice with a jeweler's *loupe*, to know what you are doing. Sophisticated laboratory tests are also regularly required. If you visit a country where precious gems are available, such as Sri Lanka, Thailand, South Africa, Brazil or Columbia, it is best to buy only from recognized dealers. This does not mean that you should not bargain with them, though, since the mark-ups on precious gems are huge. In addition, it is wise to have any gems that you want to buy authenticated by an independent testing agency. For example, Sri Lanka has a government testing office in Colombo that anyone can use.

A gem's value is dependent on its scarcity, which is determined by the following characteristics:

- Weight. This is measured in *carats*, and one carat equals 200 milligrams. Precious gems, which are called *stones* in the trade, are priced per carat, and larger stones cost more per carat because they are rarer.
- Color. Gems should have deep and consistent color. For instance, the best sapphires have a color that is referred to as *corn-flower blue*, while the best rubies are *pigeon-blood*. Diamonds are also rated by color, and *D Flawless* is the highest rating.
- Clarity, transparency, and inclusions and other imperfections. The last includes cloudiness, which is called *silk*, fractures, bubbles and other flaws. (Star sapphires and rubies are prized for their regular patterns of silk.)
- Shape and cut. Some cuts, such as *brilliant*, are more expensive because they have more facets, and since it may be necessary to cut away more of the natural stone to achieve them. The facets on cut stones should ideally be perfectly symmetrical. (Another type of cut is *cabochon*, which is dome shaped.)
- Luster. This is the shine or gleam of high-quality, well-cut gemstones.

Some legitimate gems, to increase their prices, are sold as if they are from the most prized sources. For example, Sri Lankan sapphires may be sold as Kashmiri, and Vietnamese rubies as Burmese. In addition, "*to produce clean salable gems, almost all rubies and sapphires (and many other colored gems) are heated to enhance their color and clarity.*" (*Rubies and Sapphires*, Fred Ward, *National Geographic*, October 1991, page 116) The gems are heated in special ovens at temperatures close to their melting points. It is "*a long accepted practice.*" (Ibid.) Heat treatment is usually done at the source, or in Thailand, which controls much of the world market for colored gems. Professionals say that such stones have been *burnt*, and non-burnt stones command the highest prices. However, there is no good reason to shy away from the treated variety. Some stones, which are called *synthetics*, are actually grown in laboratories. While they may be chemically and structurally identical to gems that are mined, they are definitely not as valuable. Travelers are also regularly tricked into buying fake gems and jewelry. Some semi-precious stones are sold as precious varieties, and another common occurrence is for fake gems to be manufactured from glass or plastic. Lastly, you should recognize that if you are offered gems by a tout, it is extremely unlikely that they are genuine, or at least of high quality. If they were, they would have been sold to dealers while still in rough form. (*Sri Lanka*, Insight Guides, page 277)

Motor vehicles

"*Automobiles imported into the United States must conform to Environmental Protection Agency (EPA) emission standards and Department of Transportation (DOT) safety, bumper and theft prevention standards. Other than models required to meet theft prevention standards, vehicles may be entered conditionally to be brought into conformity.*" (*Know Before You Go, Customs Hints for Returning Residents*, page 16) Almost all vehicles that are imported to the U.S. will require modifications to meet domestic standards. Additional information is contained in the Customs booklet *Importing a Car*, and the EPA brochure *Buying a Car Overseas? Beware!* The latter is available from the EPA, Attn: EN-340F, Washington, D.C. 20460.

18. ARRANGEMENTS

If you are reading this in a foreign country, congratulations! You have acted on your dreams. However, you are probably finding that there are many new things to deal with, for which your life at home has done little to prepare you. Among these, and the subject of this chapter, are the basic arrangements that you will have to make during your trip, which are for transportation and accommodation.

General advice on making arrangements

All travelers will have personal requirements and preferred ways of doing things. However, the following guidelines should be appropriate for anyone:

- Your life at home is organized around various routines, including work and/or school, shopping, cooking and watching television. Your life on the road should be ordered as well. One of your first tasks, therefore, is to create a set of travel routines that work for you.
- It is easy when you are traveling to forget different things that need to be accomplished, but if you periodically make a checklist of them, such as in your journal, this should ensure that at a minimum nothing important is forgotten. Having a to-do list is most useful when you arrive in a city or at a large hotel. For example, you can use a hotel for confirming reservations, souvenir shopping, buying guides, magazines and newspapers, and for having your clothes cleaned and gear repaired. They are also good places to get haircuts.
- If something needs to be done, it is best to do it at the first opportunity. Chores tend to accumulate, and you must stay on top of them if you want to make the most of your trip. You should research travel options, reserve and pick up tickets, and clean or pack your gear whenever you have a spare moment. The chances are that you will be short of time later on.
- If something affecting you is inadequate, such as if a piece of furniture in your room is broken or some expected service has not been provided, you should demand that the problem be fixed. You have paid good money for these services, so you should get them as advertised or otherwise expected. Small inconveniences should not be your problem. If you cannot get satisfaction, you should ask for a refund and take your business elsewhere.
- You should react quickly and decisively in situations where the choices are limited.
- Finally, making arrangements is like trying to figure out a puzzle that has many different solutions, some of which are better than others. In almost any situation, if

you make the effort you should be able to find new ways to accomplish something or to reduce your expenses. At other times, though, making arrangements is a major exercise in problem solving, where even one solution will not be readily apparent. If this is the case, it can be very useful to have general knowledge of a wide range of travel options.

Transportation

Arranging transportation is one of the most time consuming travel chores. For instance, I took one hundred and ninety-three different pieces of transport during my world trip, excluding taxis and public transport in towns, and all of it had to be arranged! I also used an extremely wide range of transport, including some types that were quite unusual, which is illustrated by the itinerary for my two week visit to Chitwan:

1. Power rickshaw from Thamel to Kathmandu's airport.
2. Flight to the Bharatpur airstrip near the park.
3. Van to the Rapti River.
4. Canoe down the river.
5. Elephant ride from the river to Tiger Tops Lodge.
6. Three days with morning and evening elephant safaris and afternoon jungle treks.
7. Elephant ride to the Rue Khola River.
8. Canoe down the river.
9. Ox-drawn cart from the river to a local Tharu village.
10. Jeep to the Narayani River.
11. Canoe down the river to Island Jungle Lodge.
12. Five days with elephant safaris, and afternoon canoe safaris or jungle treks.
13. Hike to the other side of the island.
14. Canoe across the river.
15. Elephant ride to a nearby road.
16. Local bus to Narayanghat.
17. Local bus to Sunachuri.
18. Elephant ride to Machan Lodge.
19. Four days with elephant safaris, and afternoons at the *machan* (watch tower) or on jeep safaris.
20. Elephant ride back to the road.
21. Hitched ride with a van back to Kathmandu.

This trip was one of the best experiences that I have ever had. You should try it, at least for part of the itinerary, if you visit Nepal. It is least expensive during the monsoon.

The primary considerations for choosing transportation are price, speed, comfort and safety. For example, in many countries if you have to decide between a bus and a train, both will probably have about the same price, but if you can find an express bus it will usually be much faster. However, the train should be more comfortable, have better scenery and be safer, since they are less prone to accidents. You will also regularly need to choose between public and tourist transportation. The latter is always more expensive, but it may be faster and include certain amenities, such as stops at scenic viewpoints. At other times, though, there will be few differences between the two, and if this is the case you should use the public transport to save money. One example of this is in the Maldives, where a private *dhoni* (the local type of boat) from the airport island to Malé costs five times the regular service for the locals.

A few other general transportation tips are as follow:

- Try not to view making arrangements as an unpleasant task. It can be fun to work out complicated itineraries, and in the process you will often meet interesting and helpful locals.
- Transportation is regularly delayed or canceled, so you should not get upset when it happens. Common causes include equipment problems, employee strikes and bad weather. For instance, of the four flights that I planned with Royal Nepal Airways during my world trip, two were canceled and the other two were each delayed by about four hours.
- It is usually best to wait until you are ready to leave a location before you arrange onward transportation, rather than reserve it before you even arrive. This is because there will probably be more options available than you were aware of, and some of them may be better suited to your needs. You might also be able to look at the vehicle before buying a ticket, to check that it is safe and comfortable.
- Buy tickets that can be changed or refunded if you alter your plans or become ill.
- Confirm that any timetables that you are using are still accurate, even if they are within their dates of validity. They may have been changed anyway.
- Try to be well-rested for long travel days. This will make them much easier to endure.
- Leave for stations early, to anticipate the inevitable traffic jams along the way.

- When you arrive at the station, find your vehicle and ask how long it will be before it departs. In some countries buses do not leave until they are full, which may take hours. If there will be a delay, it might be better to look for an alternative.
- If you do not have a ticket for reserved-only transport, you will have to be ingenious, fast or persistent if you want to get a seat. You might need to persuade an official to assist you, or be the first person to get his or her name on a standby list.
- Do not throw away tickets after boarding, because you may need to show them again when leaving the vehicles or stations.
- Lastly, it is useful on travel days to have the following items in your day bag: a water bottle, snacks, Immodium or Lomotil, aspirin, prescription medications, earplugs, a book or magazine, camera and film, cassette or CD player, extra batteries, rain jacket or umbrella, sweater, clean shirt and shorts or pants, and a flashlight if you will be arriving after dark.

Air transport - tickets

As a world traveler, you will have to decide what tickets to buy at the start of your trip. Many people would probably consider buying *round-the-world* tickets, which offer a series of flights linking one country to another all the way around the globe. Buying one of these, though, would almost certainly be a mistake. (I bought tickets for eight flights at the start of my world trip, with substantial stretches of overland travel between them, but I now recognize that even this was stupid.) They are expensive, and your money is tied up when it could be earning interest in a bank. There is no valid reason for buying all of your tickets at the start of your trip, since you can arrange inexpensive onward flights in most major cities along the way. (Good luck in Cairo and Tel Aviv, though.) World travelers also usually want to go overland as much as possible, since you are not experiencing the planet when you are flying above it. Perhaps the most important reason for not starting with a series of tickets is that it limits your flexibility. Travelers often decide to change their plans, to shorten or lengthen stays, to visit other areas, or to join other people. You might not be able to do this if your itinerary is fixed by your tickets. Finally, whatever tickets you buy, they should ideally allow free and unlimited changes of their departure dates. For instance, during my world trip I changed the date of my Quantas flight from Bali to Perth six times, as I continued to extend my stay in Asia. Tickets that can be changed are usually valid for a year, and although they are rarely available for discount fares in the U.S., they are commonly offered by travel agents in other parts of the world.

The following discussion assumes that you want to obtain tickets as inexpensively as possible. Indeed, you should never have to pay the full economy fare. Due to the nature of the airline business, discount tickets can almost always be found. This is because a high percentage of an airline's costs are fixed, including aircraft depreciation, maintenance, fuel and staff. One of their main objectives, therefore, is to fly with as high a *load factor*, or occupancy percentage, as possible. Each additional ticket that is sold, even if it is sold at a deep discount, helps cover these fixed costs.

Airlines follow a number of different strategies to ensure high load factors. Some airlines, such as charter operators, sell all of their seats at low prices. Other airlines set aside blocks of seats to be sold at discount. In the U.S., these seats are usually only available well in advance of departure dates, and they may also apply only to specific days of travel. This type of promotion is a common strategy in fare wars, and it also functions as a bait and switch tactic. This is because it persuades many people to call the airline, and some of the callers purchase tickets even after all of the discount seats have been sold. You will have to plan your trip well ahead of your departure date if you want to take advantage of this type of offer.

It is essential to shop around for airline tickets. Promotional programs are periodically announced by the major carriers, and new niche airlines, which serve specific destinations, are regularly established. The former are advertised in newspapers, but you can also get information on them, and on the fares of smaller airlines, from travel agents. In addition, you should always check the fares of the national carrier of your next intended destination, and Virgin Airways and Icelandic Air for trans-Atlantic flights. Some carriers for long-distance destinations, including Kuwait Air, Gulf Air and Air India, also offer good prices for trans-Atlantic flights. They can do this because they are exempted from the regulatory monopoly enjoyed by U.S. carriers and the national carriers of Western Europe.

The least expensive international flights from the U.S. depart from New York, Miami, Los Angeles and San Francisco. If you are in another part of the country, it will probably be cheaper to connect through one of them than to fly directly to your first foreign destination. Low cost airfares are easy to find in these cities; just check with local travel agents. For example, the New York weekly newspaper, the *Village Voice*, has many ads from agents for inexpensive tickets. Also in New York, you might want to try Air Hitch and Council Travel.

In Europe and much of the rest of the world, airlines sell discount tickets right up to the day of departure. Indeed, it is usually easy to get an inexpensive ticket with only a few days notice. These tickets, however, are available only through specific agents, which are referred to as *consolidators* or *bucket shops*. (The latter term is used because seats that are still unsold close to their departure dates are said to go *into the bucket* for sale through these agents.) Airlines often have preferred agents, so you should contact a number of them if you are in a city that has bucket shops. This way you can find discount prices for every airline that flies a particular route, and ensure that you have located the least expensive fare.

Some cities that are well-known for bucket shops include London, Amsterdam, Istanbul, Bangkok, Sydney and Auckland. In London, you should check the ads in the *Evening Standard* and *Time Out,* and in the weekly backpacker and temporary secretary newspapers and magazines. You should also try Trailfinders and STA, which are probably the leading discount travel agents in the world. Both have offices near the Earls Court section of town.

Bucket shop ads are easy to spot, since they only list destinations and prices. However, you should beware of the small print; the prices are often one-way based on the purchase of a round-trip ticket. You may have to pay more if you only need a one-way flight. You should also inquire if there is a booking fee. In any case, the fares that bucket shops advertise rarely correspond to what they offer in their offices or on the phone. Indeed, they regularly offer lower rates, and the differences occur simply because the fares change so frequently.

You should be cautious when dealing with bucket shops, since there have been many cases where they have taken advantage of travelers. One way to guard against this is to confirm with the airline that you have a seat reservation before you pay for your ticket. You should also use a credit card to pay for the ticket if the agent accepts them, since you can then cancel the payment if there is a problem. (You may have to pay a small surcharge with a credit card, but another advantage of using one, at least with American Express, is that flight and baggage insurance is included.)

Airfare discounts are also sometimes available for specific types of travelers, including students, people who are under (or over) a particular age, and individuals who have purchased discount cards from travel organizations. In addition, reduced fare domestic air travel plans are offered by the national carriers of many countries, although you must usually purchase them before your arrival. For instance, Indian

Airlines had a deal in 1991 where foreigners could buy twenty-one days of unlimited domestic travel for $400. However, you should only get a package like this if you are certain that it will be beneficial. These programs may limit your flexibility to stay places that you really like, since you generally need to fly every few days to get the most from them. In addition, ordinary tickets for domestic flights are usually inexpensive, so the savings may not be that great.

Ticket restrictions and lost or stolen tickets

You should ask if there are any restrictions on the tickets that you intend to buy. Some of the more common types of restrictions are as follows:

- The tickets must be bought well in advance of their departure dates.
- They are only valid for travel on certain days.
- They are only valid for trips of specific duration.
- Stopovers are not allowed in connecting cities.
- They do not allow for changes or cancellations. Alternatively, there is a charge for each change, or you do not receive a full refund for a cancellation. For example, *Advance Purchase Excursion* (*APEX*) fares in the U.S. usually cannot be changed or refunded, and they are only valid for round-trip tickets.

You should also inquire about the procedure for replacing your tickets if they are lost or stolen. I learned about this the hard way when I lost two of my world trip tickets. One was for the Quantas flight from Bali to Perth, and the second was on United Airlines, from Sydney to Auckland to Los Angeles. I obtained a police report to document the loss, and then asked the two airlines to reissue the tickets. The local Quantas office sent a telex to their home office in Australia, and reissued the ticket two days later for no charge. The United Airlines procedure, however, was a major hassle. The first thing I had to do was buy a full fare economy replacement ticket, at a cost of over $2,000. I then had to apply for a refund of this amount, which took three months to process and which was supposed to cost $50 for a service charge. However, when the refund arrived it was for only $1,900, so my total cost was over $100. I also could have had to pay the funding cost for the $2,000 for this period, but I was able to get around this because I bought the replacement with my American Express card. (I would have had to pay cash if I had not had a credit card.) I asked Amex to delay paying United until I paid them, which I told them I would be unable to do until I received my refund. (I now avoid United Airlines because of this policy.)

Flight reconfirmations

You should reconfirm all reservations for international flights two or three days before their departure. This is also a good practice for domestic flights in many countries. Indeed, it is wise to reconfirm several times with smaller airlines in lesser developed countries, to reduce the risk of being bumped from their flights.

Canceled flights

All airlines cancel flights from time to time, because of bad weather or for other reasons. However, they are a regular occurrence with the carriers of some lesser developed countries. Mechanical reasons are often the cause with such carriers, since they rarely have backup aircraft available if problems develop. Flights may even be canceled because of military conflicts. A similar problem that travelers sometimes experience is to be bumped off. This could happen if you arrive late for an overbooked flight or, once again, with smaller carriers, where you might lose your seat to an official or other person with influence. (I met a traveler who was forced off a Merpati - Indonesia flight this way.)

You should seek redress from the airline if your flight is canceled, or if you otherwise lose your seat. Unfortunately, with some carriers it may be difficult to get reasonable assistance. If you encounter resistance, you should force them to understand that they are responsible for you! (While this may not be the case legally, it certainly holds if the airline wants to preserve its reputation.) You should demand to see the manager if the counter clerks are not helpful, and you should never leave the airline's airport office until they provide any of the following services that are appropriate in the circumstances:

- Book you on the next available flight.
- Rebook any connecting flights that you will miss, including on other airlines.
- Give you a voucher for a free flight if you willingly agreed to be bumped.
- Return your checked-in luggage, or initiate a lost luggage search if it was mistakenly sent on another flight.
- Arrange and pay for your accommodation until your new flight, as well as for transportation to and from the airport.
- Allow you to make any necessary telephone calls at their expense.

To give you a feel for what you might request, a friend of mine and his family were on an American Airlines flight from Tahiti that was delayed because of a local fuel shortage. They were provided with accommodation and meals for a week, and then upgraded to first class when flights were resumed.

Flying standby

You may be able to get on a fully booked flight by flying standby. This is rarely possible in the U.S, but it is commonly allowed in other parts of the world. If you would like to try it, you should telephone all of the local airlines that have flights to your destination, to see if any of them allow it, and then ask for your name to be added to their standby lists. You should also get to the airport early for such a flight, to confirm, and if possible improve, your location on the list. Standby lists are often reordered just before departure. In addition, you should have your luggage pre-checked by the airport security staff, so you are ready to board immediately after standbys are called. For instance, a Swiss friend of mine and I were the first to arrive at the airport in Goa before the morning flight to Kochi. However, two German travelers who arrived later got their bags checked before us, and were the first standbys allowed on. (There fortunately was room for us as well.) It may also be worthwhile to go to the airport even if the airline does not have a standby policy, since pleading desperation to the counter manager may get you a seat if one is available.

Hitching flights

Lastly, it is sometimes possible in remote areas to hitch rides at local airstrips. You should check at them for general service bush pilots, and planes that are carrying mineral exploration personnel, aid workers or missionaries, in other words, for anyone who is flying. You might even be able to get rides on military transport, or with smugglers. For example, an English friend of mine hitched a ride to Bogota from Tabatinga, which is in the Amazon basin near the border of Peru, Columbia and Brazil. After being told at the airstrip that there were no commercial flights that day, it was suggested that he speak with some independent pilots in a local cafe. A quick $30, and no questions asked, and he had a ride. As another example, a Danish friend of mine hitched a ride with a U.S. cargo plane from the coast of Eritrea to Addis-Ababa - during the Ethiopian civil war. You can probably get a free ride in many of these circumstances, or by buying a round of drinks in the local bar. However, it is usually good form to offer to pay. My only experience with hitching a flight occurred when I arrived at Luckla after completing the Mt. Everest trek. I learned while hiking down that a plane had crashed on the runway two days earlier. No one was killed in the accident, but flights would not be possible for a week because the wrecked aircraft had to be dismantled and removed. This was terrible news, since I had intended to fly out rather than continue trekking to the nearest roadhead. However, I spotted a helicopter coming into land as I walked into Luckla. I ran through the village to the airstrip, and saw a twenty passenger French Super Puma jet helicopter sitting there, surrounded by men in military uniforms, a number of local villagers, and a couple of other westerners. I approached the last group, and asked them if they were flying to Kathmandu and if they knew if there was a spare seat. After a quick check, the person in charge said that they had one seat left and that I could have it. Joy! I took a photo of the wrecked plane, and a few minutes later was airborne. The helicopter had been hired from the Nepalese air force by an Austrian aid organization, which was building a mini-hydroelectric plant in a nearby village. I offered to pay for the ride, and we settled on $100, which was only $13 above the cost of the flight. (I was able to get a full refund for the latter.) To top it off, I ran into some friends from the trek six days later in Kathmandu, who had just arrived after being stuck in Luckla for the entire time. They had actually hiked to the village before me and had seen the helicopter land, but had not thought to ask if any seats were available.

Road transport - buses and vans

Non-private vehicle road transport includes buses, vans and trucks. (The latter two are common on routes where the roads are too rough, or the demand is insufficient, for buses.) Road transport is also differentiated between vehicles for tourists and for the general public. Tourist transportation around the world ranges from luxury guided tours in air-conditioned Mercedes buses, complete with hostesses, meals, videos and toilets, to the large trucks that are used by adventure travel companies for overland journeys across Africa. It is also common in many tourist areas for local entrepreneurs to arrange buses and vans to transport travelers inexpensively between towns, to airports, and to scenic attractions.

Public transportation is usually much cheaper than tourist alternatives, and it can provide wonderful cultural experiences. However, it can also be unbelievably slow and crowded, and the risk of theft is higher, particularly in cities. Public buses in lesser developed countries will also generally stop anywhere to pick up or drop off passengers, and this can be frustrating if you are on board for a long trip. It is a good idea to inquire if there is an express alternative if you are on a well-traveled route.

In addition, it is often necessary to take more than one bus to reach a destination. One interesting option, especially when you are short on time, is to take a long-distance night bus. This can be an excellent way to travel in areas where the risks of accident or robbery are slight, since you can presumably sleep through the trip, and because you save the charge for the night's accommodation.

Bus tickets and seat assignments

You usually buy bus tickets from station ticket offices or on the buses themselves, although they are also sometimes available from travel agents. With the former, your first requirement is to learn the location of the station or stop for the bus to your destination; it might just be an unmarked street corner. Hotels and guesthouses are good places to ask for these directions. (If a bus stops in your vicinity at a number of locations, you should find the first stop and board there.) Finding the right bus after you arrive at a station can also be a problem, if the destinations are written in a foreign script or are not labeled at all. If this is the case, you will have to ask someone for assistance. However, it is quite common to be misunderstood and misinformed at such times, and if you think this has happened you should ask another person. Crowds of locals often form around foreign travelers who are seeking directions, and if you ask for assistance in a loud voice there is a good chance that someone walking by who actually understands English will hear you and tell you where to go. You should also confirm the destination of any bus that you board with the driver and/ or ticket collector.

As a separate point, when you ask people for directions you should not ask questions that can be answered with a simple "*yes*" or "*no.*" It is better to phrase your questions such that detailed responses are required. Do not ask: "*Is this the bus for so-and-so?*" Instead, ask: "*Where does this bus go?*" (Another use of this approach is to ask: "*How many robberies have there been at this hotel?,*" rather than: "*Is this place safe?*")

If you purchase a ticket from a station office or travel agent, you should find out if specific seats are assigned. If so, you should make sure that you get a seat reservation and that its number is written on your ticket, since if it is not you could be forced to stand for the entire trip. The best seats in buses in some countries, such as Nepal, are in a separate compartment up front with the driver, and they are often given to foreign travelers. Otherwise, window seats are nice for watching the scenery, and for the breeze if the windows open. Indeed, they are much more comfortable than aisle seats on buses that do not have air-conditioning. You will also have more room in a window seat if the aisle is packed with people or goods. On the other hand, if you are traveling through areas where the roads are bad, you might have to watch out for motion-sick locals lunging across you to use your window. (Buses in the Himalayan foothills have rice-splattered sides.) You also probably remember from school that the rear seats in buses give the bumpiest rides, but this is where you tend to meet the most interesting passengers. For instance, some friends of mine and I once caught a bus from Taveta, which is a remote town on the border of Kenya and Tanzania, to Mombasa, which is some eight hours away. Seats were assigned, and as the last people to buy tickets we were given places near the back. When the bus arrived, though, the driver refused to let us sit in our assigned seats, which were also broken, even though we protested that it was okay. He forced some local travelers in the front of the bus to change with us. Their seats were much more comfortable, especially since the ride was incredibly bumpy and dusty. (It was also extremely noisy from the rattling windows. Earplugs were essential.) However, we stopped in the middle of the bush after about an hour, and a Masai warrior and eight Masai women, in full traditional clothing, boarded the bus and went straight to the back to seats around where we had been assigned. By moving up, we missed what could have been a fascinating cultural experience.

As was mentioned earlier, in lesser developed countries people are sometimes allowed to ride on top of buses. (I spent a lovely, sunny day doing this on a bus from Pokhara to Kathmandu.) You can watch your luggage if it is stored there, and if the road is dangerous you can presumably jump off if the bus heads over a cliff. You should take a jacket with you, though, particularly if there is a chance of rain. Finally, you are at the mercy of the driver if you take a long-distance bus that does not have a toilet. You should limit your intake of fluids before and during the ride (it is better to be dehydrated!), and use the bathroom at every stop.

Cross-border buses

Tickets for bus trips from one country to another are commonly sold in overland traveler centers. However, there are a few issues to consider if you plan to take one of them. The first is if you really want to travel through the region so quickly, since these buses rarely stop at interesting locations. Such a ride can also be a major test of endurance. You should look at the vehicle, or at least at a photo of it, before buying a ticket. Air-conditioned buses are obviously more comfortable, if you can afford them. It is also rare in lesser developed regions for a bus to be allowed to cross a border and continue into the next country. (You might not be told this when you buy your ticket.) You will have to change buses at the border, which could mean a delay of a few hours while all of the passengers clear immigration and customs. (Foreign travelers are often waived right through, but locals may be screened very carefully.) If you suspect that this will occur, it is probably better to buy a ticket to the border and arrange onward transportation there, since there will almost always be a number of other buses, vans and share taxis headed in your direction. On the other hand, if you do buy a ticket that covers the second country, you should be certain that you are dealing with a reputable agent and that you get the actual ticket, and a seat assignment if possible, for the onward transportation. Do not fall for the con where you are to collect the onward ticket at the border; this breaks the rule of not giving money until you have received a service. You should also get precise directions on how to locate the vehicle.

A related issue is that for a trip that begins in a city, you may have to take a taxi or local bus to get to the main long-distance terminal. You should get instructions on how to find your vehicle at the terminal, or demand that the agent accompany you to show you to it.

Public carrier trucks

Commercial trucks are the only public transportation in remote areas of many lesser developed countries. For example, many trucks are signposted as *Public Carriers* in rural India and Nepal. If you need a ride from a truck, you should flag one down or approach drivers who are stopped in towns or villages. You will usually be expected to pay, so you should agree on the fare before getting in. (It may cost more to ride up front with the driver.) Public carrier trucks also typically transport both passengers and freight, often in highly excessive amounts! For instance, when I did the Annapurna Circuit trek I took a mixed tourist/local bus from Kathmandu to Dumre (eight hours), and then a truck from Dumre to Besisahar, where the walking began. The truck was about a two ton model, with a metal frame over its back, and the driver estimated that we would reach our destination in three hours. Ha! We stopped every hundred yards. We started with ten people in the back, plus three more up front, but as the ride progressed it became more and more crowded. Passengers were soon piled on top of each other, hanging onto the back, and riding on top of the metal frame and cab. We also stopped a number of times to pick up or deliver freight, including about twenty pieces of metal sheeting and huge bales of wool and sacks of grain. Everyone had to get out of the back at each of these stops. The road was a narrow mountainside jeep trail, with sheer drops on one side. As you might expect, a thunderstorm started at nightfall and we were soon driving along in a downpour in the dark, with our way periodically illuminated by cracks of lightning. The driver threw a tarp over the top when this happened, and everyone squeezed inside. It was absolutely packed. (A little girl, who was very frightened, fell asleep leaning against me.) We pulled into Besisahar seven and one-half hours after leaving Dumre, with some seventy people in the truck. (I counted.) To top it off, the locals who were hanging onto the back started singing Nepali Congress Party songs as we arrived. (It was two weeks before the country's first democratic elections.) They had beautiful voices, and listening to them was slightly unreal at the end of such a torturous journey. It must not have been so bad after all, nothing that a shower and good meal couldn't fix.

Private vehicles

Travelers also have the option of renting or buying vehicles, including cars, jeeps, vans and motorcycles. Having your own vehicle obviously provides the greatest flexibility, but with gas and insurance it will cost a lot more than public transport. You can reduce your expenses by renting a vehicle for only a day or two, to make a rapid tour of the local sights, or by sharing the cost with other travelers. The least expensive rental is a motorcycle. You will need a drivers license and/or International Driving Permit to rent a car, but perhaps not for a motorcycle, particularly in traveler centers in lesser developed countries. In any case, if you are pulled over by the police they will definitely ask for your license, and if you do not have one you will probably have to pay a fine.

If you want to rent a car, it is usually best to use one of the major suppliers, such as Hertz, Avis or Budget. (They all have offices in many different countries.) Their vehicles should be well-maintained, and it may be easier to resolve disputes with them. It is important to understand all of the rental terms, so you should read the contract carefully. For example, two friends of mine and I rented a jeep in Bali for a day, but then found out that the contract was only for twelve hours. Still, for $14, plus $5.50 for gas, it was not too bad. There is wide variability in rental terms around the world, such as if you will be charged for mileage, or if you will have to return the vehicle to the location where you rented it. In addition, you should always get insurance, since without it you are at the mercy of the rental company and the local police if you have an accident. For instance, I rented a Mitsubishi truck in Ecuador from Budget, and drove it on some of the worst roads that I have ever seen. Unfortunately, the truck was not a match for them, and by the end of the trip the driver's door and window would not open, the cable to the distributor had become disconnected, which I had to reattach in the rain, and, worst of all, the tailgate fell off and was lost. Budget, needless to say, was appalled, but because I had insurance my only extra charge was for another day's rental to cover the minimum period necessary for repairs.

Another option is to hire a vehicle with a driver, and this is an inexpensive way to get the services of a guide. (I once hired a car and driver in Bombay for four hours to do a whirlwind tour of the city.) Drivers are also used on jeep and van safaris in wildlife sanctuaries. It is usually easy, and inexpensive, to find a local who has access to a vehicle and who will take you through a nearby park.

Lastly, having your own vehicle is an excellent option in countries where you intend to travel long distances. This is especially the case if you can share the cost. You will need your driver's license and international permit, the vehicle's registration certificate and inspection sticker, and insurance. If you plan to visit a number of countries, you may also need to have an international license plate and a *carnet*, which is a document that you use to avoid paying duties when crossing borders. Further information on this is available from the AAA, and from similar organizations in other countries. There are also specialist road travel guidebooks, and the informal accounts of people who have made such trips. (The classic is the crossing of the Sahara Desert.)

Australia is one country where world travelers regularly buy cars. For example, I have a number of friends who have done this, and one couple, my apple-picking friends from England, actually bought two. They arrived in Perth in the winter of 1991, and bought a Ford Falcon for AD 2,000 ($1,500). The vehicle had six months left on its registration certificate, which includes third party injury insurance. (If you are interested in this you should understand that there are numerous regulatory differences between the various Australian states. You do not need a WOF, or Warrant of Fitness, which is similar to an inspection sticker in the U.S., to drive a car in Western Australia, whereas you do need one, and perhaps additional insurance as well, such as third party property insurance, in New South Wales.) My friends usually slept in the car, to save on accommodation, and gave rides to other travelers to share the cost of fuel. Both are common practices, and the first is simplified by the fact that cars which are sold among backpackers in Australia often come equipped with tents, stoves, blankets and other gear. Unfortunately, the car had mechanical problems while they were crossing the Nullabor Plain to South Australia, which is the longest stretch of straight road in the world. They finally made it to Adelaide, after jury-rigging repairs, and traded it in for another Ford Falcon. The additional cost was AD 1,100 ($825), and the second car also came with six months of registration. They ultimately sold this vehicle in Sydney for AD 2,200 ($1,650 - the sale only took two days to arrange), so their total cost for three months of travel, excluding fuel, was AD 900 ($675). Many travelers have actually funded their visits to Australia, at least in part, by buying vehicles in the west or north of the country, where they are inexpensive, and then selling them in Sydney or Melbourne, where the prices are higher.

As this story illustrates, some knowledge of mechanics can be very useful if you have your own vehicle. (It may also be appropriate to join the local equivalent of the AAA.) Indeed, a Swiss friend of mine who bought a car in Australia had to change its rocker cover gasket, to eliminate an oil leak, and its water pump. (He drove thirty thousand kilometers in three months!) My English friends also bought a car in New Zealand, and it needed new tires and breakpads before it qualified for a WOF. (They could have bought a forged one in a pub for NZD 20, or $12.) They bought a Morris Minor for NZD 800 ($476), plus NZD 500 ($297) for the parts, for a total of NZD 1,300 ($773). They drove the car without insurance, and sold it after four months for NZD 900 ($536). In addition, the cost to ferry the car from the North Island to the South Island and back was NZD 120 ($71) each way.

Share rides and hitchhiking

The least expensive forms of road transport are share rides and hitchhiking. Share rides are usually advertised on traveler bulletin boards in guesthouses and restaurants. They are also regularly arranged in conversations in bars. You are responsible for a portion of the gasoline bill during a share ride, and also perhaps for other expenses such as food.

Hitchhiking, on the other hand, is free, and it is a great way to meet people. It may also be your only option in some circumstances.

There are a lot of different ways to hitch a ride. For instance, you may be able to get one if you are alert when friends or acquaintances who have vehicles are discussing their travel plans. Many hitchhikers also go to truck stops early in the morning to arrange rides with friendly truckers. Finally, you can of course stand on the road with your thumb out. It is a good idea if you do this to make a sign with the name of your destination using a felt-tip pen and a piece of cardboard. However, you should not write the name of a far distant destination, since some people might be willing to give you a ride, but not if they will be stuck with you for days. Some locations are also better than others for getting rides. You should usually get out of a city or town using public transport before starting to hitch. You should also avoid rides that will leave you at remote locations. For example, the town of Three Ways in Australia's Northern Territory is a classic outback crossroads, and many hitchhikers have been stuck there for days. If you do hitch in a remote region, you should carry plenty of food and water, warm clothing, some sort of rain shelter, and a sleeping bag.

Hitchhiking, though, can be very dangerous. Women should never hitch without male companions; even two women hitching together are still at serious risk. In any case, when a vehicle stops you only have a few seconds to determine if it is a safe ride. You should *always* politely refuse a ride, no matter how long you have been waiting, if you have *any* doubts about it at all.

Train transport

Trains are a lovely way to travel. Most people have heard of the Orient Express, but what about the trans-Siberian railway, the Darjeeling toy train, or the trip from Dar es Salaam, Tanzania, to Cape Town, South Africa? The world is simply full of extraordinary rail journeys, which offer relaxation, excellent scenery and ready opportunities to meet locals and other travelers.

Classes and tickets

Trains in most countries offer a number of different classes. For instance, the following are available on long distance trains in India:

- 1A	First class air-conditioned sleeper
- 2A	Air-conditioned sleeper
- 1	First class sitting
- CC	Air-conditioned chair car
- 3T or SL	Three-tiered sleeper (padded bunks)
- 2T	Two-tiered sleeper (hard bunks)
- 2	Second class sitting

(India needs a lot of classes - for the different castes!)

Class names, though, can be misleading. Air-conditioning might mean a proper refrigeration unit, or it could just be a fan, and sleepers may be private, or they could have multiple bunks. In addition, the price differences between classes, and also on different trains, such as express versus local, can be substantial. Second class should be satisfactory for short trips for most people, but on longer or overnight journeys you should determine exactly which class is most suited to your needs and budget.

Tickets are always available at train stations, although travel agents can also arrange them in a few places. You will have to inquire which is the correct station for a particular train if you are in a city that has more than one. As with buses, it is wise to reserve seats. Indeed, it is sometimes necessary to make reservations before you can buy tickets, and these often have to be made before the day of departure. For example, for a trip across Java you need to make a reservation at the dispatch office at the Gambir station in Jakarta. You should telephone or visit stations to inquire if reservations are required, particularly for trains that you suspect will be full. If a train is reported as being sold out, however, this does not always mean that all of the seats are taken. The passenger rail systems of many countries save seats until departure for distribution under quota systems, and there is sometimes a separate quota for foreign tourists. The best way to get this type of seat is to ask the station master. You should look presentable, be friendly and professional, and plead a story of extreme need. Lastly, you should confirm that the reservation covers the entire journey. For instance, a friend of mine was woken at 4 a.m. on a train in northern India, because his reservation had expired and someone else had his bunk from then on. He ended up sitting on the floor for the last ten hours of the trip!

If you are waiting at a crowded platform for an unreserved train, you will have to push your way on to get a seat. You should definitely not be shy in these circumstances. You may also have difficulty getting a seat if you have to change trains, but do not have a reservation on the connection. You should rush to the connecting train if this is the case, since a little effort at this point is preferable to standing for hours. (Another option is to ask a porter to run and get you a seat.) There is also the issue of finding the right car for your class. For example, I made a mad dash to get a seat on a train at the Hikkaduwa station in Sri Lanka. After smiling at the other passengers who had also been quick enough to get seats, and feeling quite pleased with myself, I realized I was in third class, instead of second class which I had paid for.

Hopping freight trains

Travelers can also hop freight trains in countries that have rail freight networks. For instance, I have ridden freights from Winslow, Arizona to Southern California and back. If you would like to do this, you should just go to the nearest freightyard and jump into an open boxcar on any train that is heading in your direction. It may also be okay to ask railyard workers which train to catch. However, one time a worker told my friends and I that we could ride in the last of five engines that were pulling a long train. It was interesting to listen to the crew on the intercom (they were in the front engine and the caboose), but we got booted off in Needles, California. This is regularly the hottest spot in America, and we were there on a summer day. We had the last laugh, though, since we rode the rest of the way in a breezy boxcar.

Water transport

Since most of the earth's surface is covered with water, you will obviously have to rely on ferries and other boats for transportation in many areas. Water transport ranges from the small ferries that cross the fjords of Norway, to the large inter-island ships that sail around the archipelagos of Indonesia and other regions of the Pacific. Arranging water transport is similar to catching trains, and you can usually expect regular departures. (There should also be a range of classes on larger vessels.) However, you should get a copy of the local ferry or ship schedule if you will be traveling in remote seas, since sailings may be as infrequent as once every few weeks. In addition, ferries often cease to operate during rainy seasons, when the seas become too rough.

If you would like to travel long distances by sea, you may be able to pay or work for a bunk on a pleasure yacht or cargo ship. Yacht crewing was discussed earlier. For the latter, you should check for a ship heading to your destination in the scheduled departures section of the local newspaper. You can then inquire at the ship's local agent, or go to the docks and try to persuade the captain to take you. This is not as unlikely as it sounds, since many ships will have a spare bunk or two for the right price, which could actually be quite low. However, you should not expect the Queen Elizabeth II, especially for your meals. (It is a good idea to bring a personal larder to supplement the ship's menus.) In addition, if you sign on for a *working passage*, you should expect to work very hard. Yacht charters are also available in many areas, with or without crew. (The latter are called *bareboat* charters, but they are only available for experienced sailors.) Finally, it is possible in some places to travel by raft, canoe or kayak. Indeed, they are often the only options in rain forests. For example, it is necessary to build a bamboo raft on some of the treks in northwest Thailand. Rafting trips are offered by outfitters in many locations around the world, and they are usually inexpensive. Canoe and kayak rentals are also widely available, but you may have to demonstrate your proficiency if you want to rent one without a guide.

Other transport

You can rent or buy an animal for transportation in many countries. Some travelers, for instance, join multi-day horseback trail rides. These are offered in Spain and Ireland, and they are supposed to be superb, although you should be prepared to ride for six to eight hours per day. Argentina would be another natural destination for this, but there are many others as well. A friend of a friend of mine bought a horse in China and rode it around the country for six months! If you are adventurous enough, you can even travel by camel or elephant. The former is possible in North Africa, from Morocco to the Sinai, western India, and Australia, and the latter can be arranged in a few parts of northern India.

Lastly, you can propel yourself, by walking or by riding a bicycle. This is actually the best way to see the world close-up. Walking is the only means of transport in many places, including most mountainous regions, where it is called trekking, although if you have a mountain bike you can also go almost anywhere. However, if you do go touring, you should take your own bike, panniers, spare tires or inner tubes, and repair gear, since good equipment is rarely available locally. Western Canada, Norway, Switzerland, France, Ireland and New Zealand are all popular with bicyclists. New Zealand's South Island, in particular, has magnificent scenery and very little traffic, although rain gear is a must. If you have no commitments, you could even repeat the journey of one French bicyclist that I heard of, who spent five years riding around the world. (*Lonely Planet Newsletter*, August 1986, page 2)

Accommodation

As with transportation, the range of accommodation around the world is incredibly wide. If you are an active traveler, sooner or later you will stay everywhere from dirt-floored huts to international quality resorts. The characteristics that distinguish accommodation include location, security, cleanliness, furnishings and temperature control, other services and activities, and cost. These variables are discussed below, and checklists to help you evaluate specific lodgings against them are included at the end of the chapter.

Location

Accommodation centers have been developed in many countries, usually in areas of scenic beauty or close to services of interest to travelers, such as transportation and nightlife. Beach resorts along the Spanish Costa del Sol and in Bali are examples of the former, and city neighborhoods such as Earls Court in London and Kings Cross in Sydney of the latter. However, some of these centers have become tourist ghettos, and staying in them may increase your exposure to crime and limit your contact with the traditional local cultures. For example, the only contact that many tourists to Bali have with authentic Balinese culture is through brief performances that are staged by their hotels.

Travelers tend to exhibit a pack mentality, and this is not only limited to tourists. Indeed, I noticed when trekking in Nepal that other hikers would often patronize only one *bhatti* (tea house) in each village, while others would languish for a lack of guests. I regularly stayed in one of the other bhattis, even as the only guest, to regain the feeling that I really was in an extremely remote part of the world. It was also easier to make friends with the locals this way. For instance, there are only two huts in Leder, which is a stopping point high on the Annapurna Circuit. I was the only guest at one, while the other was packed with some ten other trekkers. During my first night there, the man who ran the lodge treated me to bottles of *chang*, which is the local rice beer. We sat by the fire and talked for hours, drinking, chewing raw ginger, and listening on a small radio to chanting monks across the border in Tibet. I also returned his friendship by delivering a letter to his father, who lived in southern Nepal. As another example, backpacker inns in Australia that are well-known in traveler circles are often crowded and run down from overuse, while newer ones in the same towns are clean and empty. This is also true with guesthouses that have been written up in Lonely Planet and other guides, which in addition frequently raise their prices as a result of the publicity they have received.

The noise level in a hotel is also partly a function of its location. Accommodations on busy streets are obviously going to be louder than those on side streets. If you choose the former, you should ask for a quiet room at the back of the building or on a high floor. Sound proofing also derives from the quality of construction.

Unfortunately, the walls in many hotels are thin, and you can clearly hear the guests in the adjoining rooms. They can of course also hear you. It is difficult to be certain about soundproofing if you arrive during the day, since the rooms next door will probably be empty. You should consider the thickness of the walls, and if the room has a solid ceiling or if sound can travel through a crawlspace above it. If a room is noisy you should ask for another. Even with these precautions, though, the sounds of traffic and barking dogs can be inescapable in many areas. This is another good reason to travel with earplugs.

Security

Security should be the most important factor in choosing a hotel, and a typical check begins with the premises and staff. Since room thieves are often hotel employees, you should ask yourself if the staff appear trustworthy. Another issue is if there are entrances that neighborhood thieves can use to enter the premises unseen. If the accommodation is acceptable from these viewpoints, you should ask to see a room and consider the following questions. How strong are the doors and locks? Is there outside access to the room from a balcony or ledge, and are the windows barred? Will you feel comfortable leaving your belongings in the room when you are out, and could it even be robbed while you are asleep? If a room fails any of these checks, you should reject it and ask to see another. You might also want to find another hotel.

After you check-in, you should store your valuables in the hotel's safe or one of its safe deposit boxes. If the room security is especially doubtful, you should put the bulk of your gear in the hotel's luggage storage room or office.

Room security also includes the issue of fire prevention and safety. You should preferably choose hotels that have concrete construction and metal doors, overhead sprinklers, well-positioned fire alarms and extinguishers, and numerous staircases and other options for emergency evacuation.

Cleanliness and pests

A quick examination will usually tell you if a room is clean, but a few hints on what to look for might be useful. In a budget hotel, you should check the walls for bloodstains from bugs or mosquitos that were squashed by other guests, under the mattress for bugs, and on the floor and in the bathroom for cockroaches. Rooms that have screened windows are the best in areas that have mosquitos. Other reasonable protection includes mosquito nets and strong fans. You should also check if the toilet and shower are in the room, down the hall, or outside. Finally, you should check the water in the basin and shower. Is it clean, is it hot, and how strong is the pressure? If the pressure is poor, you might want to ask for another room.

Furnishings and temperature control

The minimum acceptable furnishings in a budget hotel room are a bed, table and chair. Everything else is a luxury. Of course, budget hotels sometimes have extraordinary furnishings. I have stayed at a number of old world hotels in Asia that had large rooms and massive antique mahogany furniture, not to mention beautiful views or gardens. They usually cost less than $10 per day. In a dorm room there should be a bureau with drawers that can be padlocked, so you have somewhere to leave your valuables. If this is not provided, you will have to carry them with you or leave them in a locker or at the office. Lastly, you should turn on the fan or air-conditioning unit to its highest setting, to test its cooling power and noise level.

Other services and activities

Hotels regularly offer a wide variety of services. Indeed, many services can be arranged by the front desk even when they are not formally offered. For example, you should be able to get food delivered to your room and clothes washing done in almost any hotel. In remote areas, it may actually be wise to base your decision on where to stay on which accommodation has the best food. If you require specific facilities, such as for sports, you should research this ahead of your arrival to ensure that you find a place where they are available.

Cost

Cost is the most important consideration for many travelers, and it should obviously be a function of the other factors, since you should expect more as the price rises. With budget accommodations, this would mean moving from a room with a fan, and the toilet down the hall, to one with air-conditioning and an ensuite toilet and shower. Further up the price scale, you should expect larger rooms, better furnishings and perhaps a hotel pool. However, accommodation standards vary widely by country, and you will not always get these improvements, particularly if you do not know what the standards are and demand them. For instance, I use a simple check, which I call the *soap* or *towel test*, to evaluate budget accommodations in different countries.

The gist of the test is to determine how expensive hotels have to be before you can expect to get soap or towels in your rooms. In cities in India, you should expect to get soap in a room that costs only a few dollars worth of rupees per day, and a towel in the $10 range, while in Australia this might increase to $20 or greater for both.

A good philosophy on accommodation costs is to spend as little as possible for a room. This is because the only time you will normally spend in it is to sleep, and when you are asleep your body does not know the difference between a $10 hostel and a $1,000 suite. It is better to save your money for restaurants, activities and shopping. Nights in nice hotels can then be reserved for periodic splurges. (You will also appreciate them more because of their rarity.) In addition, the number of travelers that you meet tends to be inversely related to the cost of your accommodation. You will usually meet many more people in guesthouses and hostels than you will in deluxe hotels.

Discounts on room prices are almost always available for shrewd travelers, and you can get them by shopping around and by bargaining. The ease of getting a reduced rate also increases greatly during the off-season, and by location. For example, in traveler centers guesthouses in small lanes, or short walks from nearby beaches, are usually the least expensive. (They may also be more relaxed and friendly.) I once arranged to stay at a guesthouse like this on arrival in the Seychelles. (The airport accommodation desk actually made the booking.) It had six rooms, and was located a short walk down a jungle trail leading away from the main beach. It was a lovely place, and cost about 20% of the price of a nearby resort on the beach. I then spent my time using this resort's dive shop and beach bar. I also made friends with some Swiss travelers in a similar fashion. They had rented an inexpensive bungalow in Mauritius, which is a beautiful island east of Madagascar and south of the Seychelles, and then used the facilities of the resort where I was staying with some friends as a splurge after roughing it in East Africa.

Other issues with hotel management

Some hotels require deposits for the room keys, which are then returned to you when you leave. This is common with hostels in New Zealand. However, you might not be able to get the deposit back if you have to leave early in the morning before the reception desk opens. You should request alternative arrangements if this might occur. In addition, there is wide variability in the willingness of hotels to allow guests to take friends to their rooms. In some places the room rates cover any number of guests, but at other times they are per person. For instance, it is often forbidden to bring friends to a hostel dormitory or room. This is because it is common for people to smuggle them in to cut costs. If you want to try this, you should find a hostel that has multiple entrances.

Arranging accommodation

Most world travelers never make room reservations, because they want total flexibility to change their plans. You often have to give a deposit when you make a reservation, and you will probably lose it if you arrive late or cancel. In any case, you can always find a place to sleep.

It is an enjoyable challenge to fly somewhere, even during a high season, and on arrival solve the problem of finding accommodation. (I have done this many, many times, and the results have always been excellent.) If you think the choices will be limited, you can use the airport's accommodation desk or follow the recommendation of a tout or taxi driver, at least for the first night. Otherwise, you should just go to the neighborhood where you would like to stay. (You can determine this by reading a guidebook.) When you arrive there, you should find someplace to leave your luggage if it is heavy. Options for this include a station's left luggage office, or with a travel partner in a restaurant. You can then walk around and shop for decent lodgings. It is usually best to compare a number of different hotels or guesthouses before making up your mind. This is because there are often huge differences in price, quality and friendliness. In addition, you should ask to see rooms in different price ranges, to ensure that you understand the local price/quality relationship. You might also want to ask other travelers that you pass if they know of good places to stay. Finally, if you want to arrange accommodations at park or island resorts, you should visit the reservation offices that they have in nearby towns. In any case, wherever you want to stay, you should always try to bargain, and you should never accept anything until you are satisfied that you have gotten a good deal.

Budget accommodations

Budget accommodations include small hotels, guesthouses, bed and breakfasts, farmhouse accommodations, *pensions*, *losmen*, backpackers inns, Himalayan tea shops, YMCAs and YWCAs, and sailor and youth hostels. The least expensive of them offer dirt floored shacks or concrete cubicles, with single beds, candles for light, and toilets outside or down the hall. However, once you adjust your expectations, they are not that bad. They are excellent value for money, and should only cost a couple of dollars per night in lesser developed countries. Indeed, budget accommodations are regularly fantastic. For example, I stayed at the Exmouth Caravan Park and Backpackers on the northwest coast of Australia. The town of Exmouth is on a peninsula that is also home to the Ningaloo Reef, which has excellent diving. The host of the backpackers was very friendly, and he had a free fish barbecue the night I arrived. He also reduced the per-person room rate from AD 10 to AD 7 after I showed him a circular from a competing backpackers that advertised the lower price. This was for a four person trailer home, with kitchen, which I shared with a Danish friend. To top it off, the owner invited us to go deep-sea fishing on his new twenty-five foot boat, and then took us in his jeep to a deserted beach in the nearby Cape Range National Park. We went there at night, under a full moon, and sat around drinking beer and watching sea turtles come ashore to lay their eggs.

Accommodation at the lowest price level is usually in dormitories. They are also the only facilities available in some remote areas, such as the Himalayan trekking routes. Dormitories typically have kitchens that you can use, and they may be the only feasible option in some countries because of the high prices of other alternatives. For instance, you can get a dorm bed in an Australian or New Zealand backpackers for about one-fourth the price of a basic hotel room. A bunk at AYH's facility on Amsterdam Avenue in New York City is also the least expensive accommodation there, although there are some other good options downtown. Dorms are much more pleasant in the off-season, when there are fewer travelers around. Indeed, you often get private accommodation at this time by being the only guest in a particular bunkroom. (In high season, bring earplugs to cut out the sounds of snoring!)

Resorts

Few world travelers can afford to stay at resorts, other than as a short splurge. However, if you are able to visit a beach or island resort, a few of the more refined issues that you might want to consider when making your choice include:

- How beautiful is the beach? Is it an idyllic, palm-fringed lagoon, with white-coral sand like powdered sugar, clear, calm water, and lovely swimming and snorkeling, or is it located on the windward side of the island, with choppy, cloudy water, and littered with trash and debris?
- Is it a private beach, or is the public allowed as well?

- Does it have, or is it free of, such nasties as mosquitos, sand flies and sea urchins?
- Does the resort have a unique or traditional style, or is it common international grade with a standard layout and facilities?
- Are there any characteristics which set it apart from other resorts, particularly features that appeal to you? Is it special, or just one more nice place to stay?
- Lastly, does it offer well-designed t-shirts?!

For resorts that offer wildlife observation opportunities, such as lodges in national parks, a few important issues are as follows:

- How attractive is the park, considering its location, size, topography, variety of habitat and diversity of wildlife?
- How much of the park is open to visitors and how easy is the access?
- How crowded is the transport that is used for game viewing - how many people ride in each jeep or boat or on each elephant?
- Does the lodge have a private concession for a particular area inside the park, or any other special privileges?
- Are the people who guide you trained naturalists and do they speak English? Are they really interested in finding wildlife, or are they only going through the motions?
- What is the quantity, and quality, of normal wildlife observation opportunities? For example, for the former, what are the odds of seeing a rare mammal or bird during a one day visit? How about during a seven day visit? For the latter, will you see the animal from ten yards or from one hundred?
- Is the lodge inside the park?
- Can you arrange to spend a night in an observation tower? (Like a tented camp, this is a truly original experience.)

Rentals and shares

You might want to become a local yourself if you find a spot that you really like, since it is usually easy to find a house, apartment or beach bungalow to rent or share. For instance, when I traveled around the U.S. after college I stopped for from a few weeks to several months wherever I wanted. Finding short-term accommodation was never a problem. This can also be done internationally, and rentals are actually preferable to hotels because of their lower per-night costs, their privacy, and to get your own kitchen. Most people are familiar with the procedure for finding an apartment, and it does not vary much by country. You can locate rentals and shares by checking newspaper advertisements, or by asking residents and other travelers if they know of anything that is available. Long-term accommodation is often priced per-week, but to get a room you might have to give the impression that you are planning to stay a few months, even if you only intend to stay a few weeks. The precise terms of any deposit requirement should obviously be considered carefully if this is the case.

Free accommodation

The cheapest way to travel is to get accommodation free, and many people do this by staying with friends. This is also another good reason to be outgoing, since it is common in many countries to be invited to stay by the locals. However, you should usually offer to pay. Another option is to go to a local university and make friends with the students, and the best way to do this is to frequent the nearest pubs. (University dormitory rooms are also sometimes rented at low rates during student holidays.) You can of course sleep free if you have a tent, and you should always be able to find suitable campsites in fields or forests or at beaches. If you do this, though, you should keep the site of your tent well-hidden, or only set it up at night, because of the security risk. Travelers are also regularly allowed to pitch their tents on the lawns of guesthouses, especially if the latter are full or if you will eat at their restaurants. (In Asia it is possible to sleep on the roofs of some guesthouses for only a nominal charge.) Other free accommodation is available from religious orders, including at Buddhist temples, Sikh temples and Hare Krishna farms. You can also sleep rough, which is fine if you are prepared with warm gear and rain protection. Indeed, it is wonderful to be tucked into a sleeping bag on a deserted beach under a starry night. Finally, if you are really cost-conscious you could even emulate one traveler that I heard of, who as an ideological point refused to pay for shelter. He disciplined himself to find somewhere to stay free every night, or else he just slept outside.

Accommodation checklists

The following checklists can be used to evaluate (or to establish!) any prospective lodgings.

Hotel location and guests

- In an accommodation center
- Near a transportation station
- Near the center of town, restaurants or entertainment
- In an idyllic area: near a river, lake, beach, mountains or other area of natural beauty
- Attractiveness of the specific location
- Away from busy streets, bars and discos
- Types and number of other guests

Hotel management and staff

- Hotel popularity and reputation: in guidebooks and with locals and other travelers
- Friendly, helpful and trustworthy
- Extent of office hours
- Willingness to make wake-up calls
- Check-in and check-out times (some hotels specify times, while others operate on a 24-hour basis, which means if you check in at 7 a.m. you will have to leave by this time on the day of your departure)
- Frequency of room cleaning and change of linen

Premises

- Security, including presence of hotel guards and floor staff
- Quality of construction (refurbishment in progress?)
- Cleanliness of buildings and grounds
- Elevator
- Bar and restaurant
- Pool, gym, athletic courts, golf course, dive shop and other sports facilities
- TV, video and games lounge

- Library or common bookshelf
- Kitchen that can be used by guests
    - Size
    - Cleanliness
    - Refrigerated food storage available
    - Pots, pans and utensils available

Other services

- Hotel safe or safe deposit boxes
- Secure baggage storage room (who has access?)
- Free transport from and to stations
- Telephone, in the room, International Direct Dialing (IDD)
- Office services, including telefax, courier and secretarial
- Room service
- Clothes cleaning and valet services
- Assistance in arranging activities and transportation (are any discounts available?)
- Other freebees - bicycles, sporting equipment, and activities and excursions

Room security

- Access for non-guests to the room's door from a side or rear entrance
- Strength of all doors
- Strength of outside door lock
- Likelihood of duplicate keys
- Outside door bracket for your own padlock
- Inside push bolt or chain
- Wooden or plastic wedge for under the door
- Door peephole
- Access to the windows or balcony
- Barred windows
- Security of access to any connecting rooms
- No surreptitious peepholes (check in budget accommodations)
- If a dormitory room, can it be locked, and how many beds
- Fire warning system, sprinklers, extinguishers and exits

Room cleanliness

- Bed
- Floor or carpet
- Walls
- Toilet and shower
- Evidence of pests

Other room characteristics

- Size and layout
- In a building or a freestanding bungalow
- Balcony or porch
- Scenic view or private garden
- Away from the lobby or hotel bar
- Sound protection from the hallway and adjoining rooms

Room contents - furnishings

- Bed, linen and blankets
- Closet and hangers
- Bureau
- Table or desk, and chair or stool
- Mirror
- Table and chair on the balcony or porch
- Clothes drying rack
- Trash basket
- Pitcher and glasses
- Ashtray

Room contents - other

- Electric lights, or candles
- Temperature control: air-conditioning, fan or windows
- Mosquito control: screens, fan, mosquito net, mosquito coils or electric pad repellant
- Working electrical outlets

- Television: antenna, cable or satellite? The hotel's own dish or a borrowed signal (fuzzy)?
- Radio and intercom
- Pen and stationary
- Coffee and tea available
- Chocolates on the pillow (!)
- Minibar

Toilet and shower

- Type and location of toilet
- Location of shower
- Hand basin
- Water cleanliness and pressure (can you drink the water without sterilization?)
- Hot water
- Bucket for cleaning clothes
- Towels
- Soap
- Shampoo, skin lotion, sewing kit and other items
- Toilet paper

Room cost

- Basic price (are discounts available?)
- Costs of meals and activities
- Room deposit requirements and conditions for forfeiture
- Key deposit
- Service charges and taxes (should be avoidable in budget accommodations)
- Payment terms, such as settlement in advance or on departure
- Credit available on the last day of your stay, or do you have to pay cash
- Accept credit cards and traveler's checks
- Will do currency exchange

19. REDUCING YOUR EXPENSES

This short chapter lists the ideas that were presented throughout the text, and a few others as well, on how you can reduce your travel expenses.

Trip planning

- Plan your trip intelligently, be flexible, research the expenses at your destinations, and try to anticipate charges that can be avoided. For example, when my friends and I returned from Mauritius to Nairobi to connect through to Europe, we arranged our connecting flight for the next day. This meant we had to pay two additional taxi charges, into and back from the city, the cost of a hotel room, and, most irritatingly, a second $20 departure tax.
- Prepare a detailed budget, and stick to it.
- Spend most of your trip in inexpensive countries.
- Never take package tours, particularly expensive adventure tours to inexpensive lesser developed countries.
- Arrange flights and accommodations in advance only if extraordinary bargains are available.
- Use tourism offices and travel agents in foreign countries. They will often know of additional opportunities and discounts.
- Join traveler organizations. For instance, there are backpacker clubs in Australia and New Zealand that give discounts on hostels and transportation.
- Limit making expensive splurges.
- Limit the amount of luggage that you take.
- Delay making payments for as long as possible. (Businesses call this cash management.)
- Get things free! It is easy to get many things free, including transportation from friends or by hitchhiking, accommodation from friends or by roughing it, and food and drinks.
- Live like the locals and reduce your expenses to what they pay.

Shopping and bargaining

- Stock up on local currency whenever good exchange rates are available.
- Change your money using black markets.
- Bargain whenever possible, and learn to do it well (and in the local language).

- Have a travel partner enforce your shopping discipline, and learn to bargain as a team.
- Discipline yourself to ignore the bankroll in your pocket in the early days of your trip.
- Shop around and only buy items when you can get them inexpensively, such as during sales, at the source to eliminate middlemen, in countries that have weak exchange rates, or to take advantage of other opportunities.
- Ask for volume discounts.
- Get refunds on VAT, or shop duty-free.
- Wait a day or two before making large purchases, to give yourself a chance to change your mind.
- Limit incidental expenses, particularly in traveler centers; they are usually full of interesting things to buy.
- Do not take your credit cards if you cannot control yourself.
- Get local friends to negotiate your purchases in places where travelers are charged more.
- Use a story. For example, you can negotiate discounts in many situations if you say you work in the travel industry and that your visit will lead to publicity for the merchants. This is particularly effective when bargaining for discounted rates at resorts. If you claim you are an independent travel agent, guide, photographer or writer, you should be able to negotiate large price reductions. (You will of course have to be convincing.)

Transportation

- Limit your number of flights.
- Shop around for tickets, particularly in places that have bucket shops.
- Take advantage of advance purchase promotions.
- Ask if discounts are available if you are a young traveler, a student, or elderly.
- Take public transportation whenever possible.
- Travel in second or third class on trains.
- Share rides with other travelers, such as the costs of airport taxis.
- Buy vehicles in countries or regions where you intend to travel long distances.
- Hitch rides and flights and hop freight trains.
- Crew on yachts.
- Walk a lot.

Accommodation

- Pay as little as possible for a room - stay in hostels and dorms.
- Travel in low seasons (when large discounts are available).
- Try to negotiate a discount whenever you stay at a location for more than one night.
- Rent an apartment, house or bungalow for stays of a few weeks or longer.
- Share rooms with other travelers.
- Travel at night.
- Stay with friends or locals.
- Camp out.

Restaurants and food

- Cook your own food, using your guesthouse or hostel's kitchen or your own stove.
- Use a water filter or iodine drops to sterilize drinking water, instead of buying bottled beverages.
- Get accommodation plans that include meals. (The rates of many guesthouses include breakfast.)
- Eat only one or two meals a day.
- Eat from street stalls.
- Become a vegetarian.
- Go on a diet.

Entertainment

- Do what the locals do for fun.
- Buy beer, wine and liquor from stores, and do most of your drinking in hotel and hostel lounges and rooms.
- Take advantage of bar happy hours.

Communications and shipping

- Read newspapers and magazines from restaurant racks and at libraries.
- Call using IDD.
- Make calls from the apartments of friends.
- Arrange to receive calls from home.
- Never make international calls from hotels.
- Ship by surface mail.

Other ideas

- Get your vaccinations and pharmaceuticals outside the U.S.
- Clean your own clothes.
- Be a conservative tipper.

20. ROMANCE

"*To be able to fill leisure time intelligently is the last product of civilization.*"

- The philosopher Bertrand Russell, as quoted on the cover of the Transit Inn's guest book, Malé, Republic of Maldives

(As you travel around the world, you will find innumerable activities in which to participate. It is impossible for any single book to cover them all. The remaining chapters of this book will therefore concentrate on a select few: romance for world travelers, observing wildlife and travel photography.)

Love and romance, or even just sex, is a great concern for most people, if not their major preoccupation. If this is the case with you, it is unlikely to change when you visit other countries, what with all the attractive and even exotic people that you will probably meet. You might as well think about it and be prepared. Socializing abroad is different. You cannot just visit your favorite bar, or go to a friend's party, to meet someone new. How does one have a love affair in a foreign land? Perhaps this is not what Bertrand Russell had in mind, but what about you? Inquiring minds want to know!

Unfortunately, the odds are stacked against you if you want to have a relationship during your trip, unless you bring your lover with you. Other travelers, for example, who are one possible source for a partner, are often wary of whom they meet, and in any case the logistical problems are usually too great. You rarely have time for intimacy to develop. Everyone has their own plans, and the chances are that the one person that you meet and are attracted to will be leaving the next day. On the other hand, what you lose in quantity you can expect to make up for in quality. When people who are traveling do drop their guard, they often let go completely. Many people feel free to act out their fantasies once they are far from home. They can leave their inhibitions behind, and turn into sex kittens and studs.

A Danish friend of mine was in Agra, and he visited the Taj Mahal on a night when there was a full moon. He went with a German girl from his guesthouse, whom he had just met, and they found a secluded part of the lawn with a view of the main dome. The effect was magic - the Taj *glows* under a full moon, and in the intensity of the moment she turned to him and asked: "*Would you make love to me?*" He was worried that someone would walk by - there were hundreds of people about, but, needless to say, he obliged. (What would you do?)

If you would like to be with someone in a foreign country, your options include bringing your lover from home, other travelers and locals. Meeting another traveler is an obvious choice, since many people would like to have a holiday romance. Sharing experiences together is great, but finding love and passion as well is fantastic. Relationships formed this way are often so strong that they last for years, if not forever. However, it is a challenge to find someone. You might be the only traveler in some locations, such that there are no opportunities at all. (This is a downside of being an explorer.) Because of the difficulty, if you are attracted to someone you should not waste any time. Let them know how you feel and see if they respond. Unlike at home, it is rare to get a second chance. Indeed, perhaps your best option is to focus on other travelers from home. There is a natural feeling of relief when you meet such a person, and communication is easy.

Another important issue with connecting with another traveler can be *the person left behind*. People that you meet on the road will often have boyfriends or girlfriends back home. You might as well. For the former, perhaps the person that you met is only looking for fun. I would not advise starting a serious relationship, opening up too much, if they say "*this is just sex.*" On the other hand, they may have grown away from their relationship, or are even using the trip as a non-confrontational way to break up. Your prospects are better in this case, but you can still be hammered if they decide to return to their old flame - after you commit yourself. The question is: should you go forward or not? This can only depend on the circumstances, on the signals that you receive (beware of the mixed variety!), and on your level of desire and self-confidence. Good luck!

If it is you who has left someone behind, you should be sensitive to their degree of loneliness and jealousy. For the latter, they may be highly suspicious of what you are up to and extremely manipulative to get you to change your plans and come home early. (You should be honest about the fidelity issue when you leave: will you stay faithful to each other or not? A warning, though, this can be difficult to do - on both ends.)

If you do meet someone during your trip, how do you know if they are interested? Generally, besides the obvious evidence of touching and kissing, you know you are on the right track if you can make them laugh. In addition, they have to be truly interested in you, and if they do not ask you questions about yourself, they're not. You also need to understand what they are really saying, no matter how hard this might be to accept. Everyone knows that the classic line: "*I have to wash my hair tonight*," means "*I don't want to go out with you.*" Similarly, if someone says: *I think I'll hang around town for a few days*," this could easily mean "*I don't want to go traveling with you.*"

Starting a relationship with a local is different. They are not going anywhere, so you have more time. But they are also less likely to be impulsive. Having an affair with someone who is just going to leave is a losing proposition to most people, regardless of his or her attractiveness. Some locals, though, want the adventure, or just let their feelings hold sway. The country you are visiting can also have a large impact on your potential for romance. For instance, it is easy to meet locals in Europe. We share a cultural frame of reference, so it is not too difficult to relate. This is provided, of course, that there is no language problem. Since many Europeans are already fluent in English, and most of the rest know a bit of it, you should be able to communicate. In addition, if you make an effort to learn their language, you will greatly increase your chances. (You should get the target of your affections to be your tutor, and guide.)

The cultural differences that exist with locals from other parts of the world are often much greater, and they typically act as barriers to relationships. Indeed, they can be actual, physical barriers, such as in India and Islamic countries where, for a man, simply meeting local women is almost impossible. People from such localities can also be very difficult to read. For example, does someone like you, or are they just being friendly? You must also adapt to the wide variations that exist in the norms of courtship. In some places a local might be willing to hop in bed with you after only a brief meeting, while in others it will be ages before your first kiss. On the positive side, people from many lesser developed countries are often attracted to Americans. They may only want passports to better lives, but there are other reasons as well. Women from countries that are fundamentally sexist, meaning most of Asia - if not the world, appreciate the consideration and the belief in the equality of the sexes that many American men exhibit in their behavior towards women. The local men in many countries will of course also be very interested in meeting American women.

Many potential relationships, however, will mix races or ethnic or religious groups, and such pairings remain a pervasive cultural taboo. One consequence of this is that if you feel strongly for someone, you may have to demonstrate this for an extended period of time before their conservative instincts will relax. You should also expect to have many minor misunderstandings, because of the differences in your backgrounds. In addition, you may need to persuade both of your families of your sincerity. For these reasons, relationships where substantial cultural differences exist should always be approached with care. Fortunately, the power of love is great, and if you do find it you should definitely work to overcome any obstacles that might be in the way.

Not to kiss and tell, but in all my years of traveling I have of course met many women, from all sorts of countries, and have had a number of incredible relationships. But I've also had some tough ones, both on the giving and receiving ends. It is hell to leave someone behind because they are a local and you are committed to finishing a world trip, as I did in Singapore, or to fall for another traveler who then goes home to her boyfriend.

I met a wonderful girl on my second trip, in Bangladesh, of all places. We hooked up after she changed her plans and decided not to go to a meditation course in India (because of the plague outbreak at the time). We went trekking in Nepal (the Annapurna Sanctuary), and then relaxed on the beach at Koh Phi Phi in southern Thailand. She was a great travel partner, really strong and competent but also very feminine and loads of fun. When she headed home (she was at the end of her trip and out of money) and got together again with her long-term boyfriend, I was devastated.

This actually taught me one of the hardest lessons that life has to offer, which is that you can do anything in the world *except* make someone fall in love with you. This can only come from them.

Parties

You can of course meet romantic partners anywhere, but some places do stand out because they are specifically designed to provide these opportunities. Obviously, foremost among them would be parties and bars.

World travelers can attend many different types of parties. At the top of the list would be the major national festivals, such as *Octoberfest* in Germany, or *Bastille Day* in France. (On my first trip to Europe I met a French girl in Paris on Bastille Day, at the Eiffel Tower, while watching the fireworks!) Indeed, most countries have a number of celebrations each year. For instance, the national parties in Sweden include *Midsommarfest*, *Kräftfest* and *Surströmmingfest*. The first celebrates the summer solstice, and the latter two the seasons for crayfish and fermented herring. The smell of surströmming is unbelievably foul, but the taste is okay. All of these parties also involve a liberal consumption of *schnapps* (spiced vodka).

Other types of parties include invitation-only events, such as dinner parties, and informal get-togethers. You may need a strategy to get invited to the former. In other words, you might need to think like a social climber to break into restricted cliques. For example, I used to do this when I lived in London. I got the manager of a club that I joined to get me invitations to charity balls, including a couple that were attended by Princess Diana. The best party that I ever went to, though - I was invited by a friend, was the *Fairy Tale Ball* in Brussels. It was held by the *stagiaires* (college-age trainees) at the European Community headquarters. They come from all over Europe and, once a year, at the end of their internships, they hold a masked ball in a nearby chateau or castle. The ball that I attended was a nightlong bash. It was quite civilized at the start, with champagne and Strauss waltzes, but became much wilder later on.

Embassies and consulates are another source of parties. For instance, most U.S. embassies have Thanksgiving Day and Super Bowl parties, and American travelers are usually welcome. They also hold many other social engagements during the year, some of which you might be able to attend. If you are interested in this, you should visit the embassies when you arrive in new locations (use a pretext to see a consular officer), and request invitations to whatever is coming up. (Ask about the parties of expatriate organizations, such as the local branch of the American Club, as well.) Embassy Marine Corps guards also regularly hold parties. For example, when I lived in Stockholm the marines there would have a party every other week. If you could get an invitation to one, you could go to their house, drink American beer for a dollar a bottle (one-sixth the local price), and meet and dance with the local women who were invited. These parties were usually excellent, and sometimes exciting, such as when the marines got to show off and throw out local men who got drunk and rowdy.

Impromptu get-togethers, though, are the most common type of party for world travelers. They occur when from two to twenty people, often of many different nationalities, collect in bars, hotel or hostel lounges, or rooms. They are a fixture around the world, and they are certainly one of the best ways to have fun, meet people, and find travel partners and lovers. (If you have a portable stereo with speakers, not just earphones, you can host a party anywhere. Bring some good dance tapes or CDs!)

It is important not to be shy if you are on your own and pass such a party. You should just introduce yourself and join in. They are almost always the more the merrier. The traveler hangouts that were listed earlier offer some of the best opportunities for this type of socializing. Of these, Goa and Koh Samui are also known for their full moon parties.

It's fun to hang with a bunch of cool travelers, just talking about your plans and telling stories. At other times, though, particularly at beaches or in mountain huts, it can be a blast to play drinking games, and a few that you might want to suggest (other people are sure to know lots more) are as follows:

- *Toasting game.* This is an easy game and, although it does not last that long, its effects can be severe. (It is an excellent way to start a party!) In a group, each person in turn leads a toast with a salutation from a particular country, such as *skoal, prost, salut, santé, nastrovya, iechyd da* (Welsh), *keepis* (Finnish), *chinchin* (Chinese), *kompai* (Japanese), *chook dee* (Thai), *mingalaba* (Burmese), etc. You drink at every toast, and keep going until no one can think of another.
- *Clapping game.* The first player in this game picks a number less than ten. He or she then claps once, followed in turn by each person to the left. The rule of the game is that the direction of the clapping must change each time the base number occurs, including as a digit in a higher number or as its multiple. For instance, for the number 7 changes of direction would occur after 7, 14, 17, 21, 27 and 28. You must take a drink every time you make a mistake and clap when you should not, or fail to when you should.
- *Who am I?* In this game you write the name of someone famous on a piece of paper and then stick it on the forehead of another person in the group. Your goal is to discover your own new identity by asking the group Yes/No questions, such as: am I human?, an animal?, fictional?, alive?, a celebrity?, on TV?, etc. You continue to ask questions until you get a No (now is the time for a drink), and then it's the next player's turn.
- *I went to a sex shop.* (There are no penalty drinks in this game; it's just best to play it when you are intoxicated.) The first person in the game announces that he or she went to a sex shop and bought something, such as a leather teddy. The next player then repeats the phrase and adds their own purchase, as in "*I went to a sex shop, and bought a leather teddy and a box of condoms.*" Each participant has to repeat the

entire string of purchases and add something new. If someone forgets one, or names them inaccurately or in the wrong order, they are out of the game. (We have made it to sixteen items; at that point it's hard to think of new things to buy!)

Another option at a party is to sing drinking songs. For example, when I flew from London to Delhi at the start of my world trip, some friends saw me off with a traditional Swedish party called a *Sill Frukost* (herring breakfast). This is a simple party where everyone sits around eating marinated herring with boiled potatoes and hard, flat bread. You also sing a lot of drinking songs, and down a shot of schnapps at the end of each. Beer is used as a chaser. A good party will have many different types of herring and four or five different types of schnapps. My favorite Swedish drinking song is called *Helan Går*, or *The Whole One Goes*, and if you are ever stuck somewhere with some Swedes and a good supply of alcohol, you should definitely ask them to teach it to you.

Bars and dance clubs

Bars and dance clubs are familiar ground for most people, and the variety in foreign countries is magnificent. You can find U.S. style street corner bars, English pubs, wine bars, beach bars, karaoke bars, trendy bars, private clubs, dance clubs, performance clubs, after-hours bars and illegal bars. A few of them are simply pleasant places to have a drink and some quiet conversation, but most provide that wonderful combination of loud music and uninhibited people. Indeed, bars showcase all of the different music scenes around the world, including house (techno, trance, ambient, jungle), rap, alternative, hard-core, metal, oldies rock, pop, disco, jazz, blues, reggae, salsa, calypso and all of the different local styles of music. (Some of the most original music that I have heard includes the *sega* dance music of Mauritius, the *gamelan* orchestras of Bali, and the songs of *chanteuses* in the nightclubs of Southeast Asia.)

Many of the best bars offer an interesting mix of travelers and locals, and if you find one you can fulfill any latent Hemingway/Bogart fantasies that you might have. I know I do. I love these bars, for their mystery and exoticism and, in some cases, for their danger. I like to visit them again and again, get to know the bartenders, and carouse with the regulars. For instance, one of the classic traveler bars is Harry's in Paris. Ernest Hemingway actually drank there. The bar has wood paneling, and is decorated with dozens of U.S. college team pennants. They also have a special cabinet, which is never opened, that contains perhaps a hundred old bottles of bourbon and other whiskeys, some of which have been there since World War II. (Fifty year old Jack Daniels!) On the other end of the scale, I was at a great bar in the ill-lit basement of a pool hall in Victoria, the Seychelles. It was full of sailors and hookers, and the patrons were searched for weapons when they entered. Drinks were dirt cheap, and the music alternated between the best house music from London and superb Seychellois rhythms.

Like parties, it can be a real challenge to get into some bars. Having the right style and attitude is essential, but even this may not be enough. You may also need a bit of *chutzpah*. For example, a large portion of the social life in London revolves around private clubs. As a traveler there, you may want to find out which clubs are currently hot and then try to get in. Locals and taxi drivers can tell you where to go, and a number of different approaches may get you inside. The simplest option, of course, is to be invited by a member. This is how I got into Tramps, which was a notorious club frequented by celebrities, arms dealers and models. On the other hand, a friend of mine and I got into Annabels, which is one of the most exclusive clubs in the city, by acting as if we were members when we approached the door. We were well dressed and just marched in, ignoring the doormen. (Annabels doesn't expect to get crashed!) Another option is to ask if temporary memberships are available. Even if they are not, if you fit the club's style and are persuasive (you might discreetly give the doorperson a large tip), they might let you in. As another example, I met an American man and a couple of English women during a holiday in Monte Carlo, and we decided to go to Jimmy's, the disco in the basement of the Sporting Club, which is the high roller's casino. We went to the outdoor entrance at about 3 a.m., but were refused admission by the doorman, who said the disco was closed. Sure. My reputation for being able to get into any club was on the line, so we went inside the casino to try the entrance there. When the little window in the door opened (really! - it was right out of the movies), I concocted a story about being a friend of Prince Albert's from his days at Morgan Bank in New York. (I had read about this when I lived there.) We got in.

Bars often have short life cycles, so any list of them will rapidly become out-of-date. You should ask locals, particularly the bartenders and other customers at places that you like, for recommendations on which other places are popular. Nightlife magazines are also helpful, although you should be careful to avoid the tourist traps that they advertise, unless, of course, that is what you want.

(As a final comment, on live music, you should be alert to events on the international concert calendar. For instance, there is a major festival scene in Europe each summer. In addition, you can catch individual bands as they tour major cities around the world, and as an example of this, I saw the Smashing Pumpkins, in Bangkok, on Leap Year Day 1996.

The venue for the show was perfect: the Thai/Japanese Youth Friendship Center, which is a large, acoustically-balanced high school gymnasium! I went with an expat friend of mine, his Thai girlfriend, and her sister, and we were part of a crowd some four thousand strong that included Thai alternative fans, Thai pop fans, backpackers of a dozen or more nations, expats and expats' teen kids. It was a real cultural mix.

The Pumpkins played four sets, no short in and out for them, and it was one of the best shows ever. From the first note we all went beserk: moshing, till the end body surfing, spontaneous hall-wide pogoing, and explosions of circled slam dancing. I danced until I couldn't, but our energy level from the music was so high that we kept partying, after the show, all night long.)

21. WILDLIFE OBSERVATION

There are an extraordinary number of wildlife species on the planet, and one of the great pleasures of a world trip is to observe them in their natural habitats. (This is much more satisfying than visiting a zoo.) Many people, though, miss observation opportunities because they do not visit parks, sanctuaries and other habitats that are near their travel routes. Even those people who are nature tourists often see only a fraction of what they might, and common reasons for this include:

- Not looking for wildlife at the best hours of the day, or in the right locations.
- Frightening game away by being noisy.
- Failing to spot species because of their camouflage.

The issue of appropriate expectations should also be addressed. If you visit the Serengeti Plain in East Africa during the autumn wildebeest migration, you will inevitably see thousands of these animals as well as many other species. However, observing wildlife is typically more of a hit and miss proposition. Many travelers visit parks for only one day, and then leave disappointed because they did not spot a particular species. These people need to adjust their expectations. In most cases visiting habitats will yield incremental rewards. This means that if you follow proper observation behavior, you should spot a few new species each day. If you stay for a week you will see a wide variety of the local wildlife. It is also wise to de-emphasize the importance of seeing a particular species, especially if it is endangered. To view many endangered species, you would have to visit sanctuaries that have specifically been set aside for them, and then stay long enough to ensure an observation. This might take months in some cases. If you are lucky enough to see such a species, you can then treasure the moment for the rare and valuable experience that it is, and for the significant amount of time and effort that were probably required. For example, when I was in Nepal on my world trip I would have been thrilled to see a tiger, snow leopard, clouded leopard or red panda, all of which are highly endangered. As it turned out, I did not find any of them. I was fortunate, though, to observe many other endangered species, including musk deer, Himalayan blue sheep and Indian greater one-horned rhinoceros, and for this I am satisfied. I can always return, again and again if necessary, to continue looking for the other species. Finally, one of the reasons why I became interested in watching birds, lizards and other reptiles, and butterflies and other insects, was to fill in the time between rare glimpses of wild mammals. Indeed, there are thousands of beautiful bird species, and they are often quite easy to observe.

Human beings follow routines, and wildlife do the same. Because of this, the most important skill for observing different species is to learn about their habits. Once you do this, you can position yourself where and when they will be easiest to see. Unfortunately, many species are active at night, which is of course a difficult time for visual observation. However, most of these species are also moving around in the early morning or at dusk, and it may be possible to spot them then.

There is also one rule that you can follow to increase substantially the number of species that you observe, which is simply to visit many different habitats. Every type of habitat, including rivers, lakes, wetlands, oceans, beaches, grasslands, deserts, forests and mountains, is home to endemic and migratory species. In addition, sanctuaries and other little disturbed or rarely visited habitats are usually the best places for spotting wildlife. However, some species are attracted to human settlements, such as the leopards and other wild cats that hunt around villages for stray domestic animals in many lesser developed areas of Asia. Another suggestion is to concentrate on habitats that are home to many different species. You should visit them at different times during the day and, if you can, during different seasons. I found one such location in Sri Lanka, where a large, sacred fig tree grew by the corner of an ancient, lily covered irrigation lake. (Fig trees are considered sacred because Buddha achieved enlightenment while meditating under one.) It was a magical spot, and in five visits I saw over thirty species of colorful tree and water birds, as well as crocodiles, lizards, chipmunks, a mongoose and a civet cat. The birds included golden orioles, paradise flycatchers, three types of kingfisher, bee-eaters, parrots, doves, egrets, herons and storks. It was unbelievably serene to sit by the tree for a few hours, especially at dawn, and wait to see what wildlife would walk or fly by.

As was mentioned earlier, local residents are often well-informed about where to find different species. They are also usually willing to assist you, either informally as friends or as proper safari guides. For instance, I was taken to the above spot by a friend from a nearby village. In addition, naturalist guidebooks are full of information about wildlife habitats. (I actually planned my world trip so I could visit a number of the parks that are described in Insight Guides' *Wildlife Southeast Asia*.)

Seasonal considerations include when migrations occur and when visibility is at its best. Park guidebooks usually provide information on migrations, as well as observation tips for the local habitats. Regarding visibility, in the tropics wildlife can be difficult to spot during the monsoon. Dry seasons are preferable, especially in grasslands following annual burning cycles. For example, the best months to spot

Bengal tigers in Chitwan are February and March, after local villagers make their annual harvest of elephant grass in the park and then set fire to the remainder. Visibility is good during the autumn and winter in temperate regions, when trees lose their foliage. However, some species may hibernate during these seasons. (Game species are also noticeably absent during hunting seasons.) Lastly, underwater visibility is an important issue for snorkelers and divers. There are large variations in the clarity of most seas during the course of a year. Visibility may be only a few feet when the seas are rough or when plankton populations are high, while at other times you might be able to see up to fifty yards.

A few general tips for observing wildlife are as follows:

- Wear clothing with colors that match the environment. Tans and forest greens are usually best.
- The best times for observation are at dawn and dusk. Get up early!
- Be quiet! Unfortunately, if you are in a group there will often be one or more people who forget this.
- Look for the signs of animals, including nests and burrows, tracks, territorial marks, such as claw marks on trees, and scats and kills.
- Listen for animal movements, and their calls.
- Building on this point, try imitating their calls. Indeed, some people, particularly birders, play tape recordings of the calls of the bird or other species that they would like to spot. (You can also use the game calls that are sold to hunters.)
- Look around continually, and learn to sense movements in your peripheral vision.
- Use binoculars, or a camera with a telephoto lense, to enhance your vision.

Wildlife can be observed by either of two fundamentally different methods: by finding a good location and then waiting for species to come to you; or by moving about and looking for them. For the first, many parks have observation shelters, which are called watch towers, blinds, hides or machans. A good machan has three characteristics: it is close to a location where animals are expected to gather or pass; it is inconspicuous (it should be out of sight as much as possible and, ideally, downwind from the habitat); and it provides an elevated view. A temporary machan can be made from a blanket or tarp, or loose brush. The best places for waiting for wildlife are where they eat or drink, such as waterholes and rivers, or overlooking bush or grasslands. Waterholes at the end of a dry season often have prolific animal and birdlife. A spot near a trail junction can also be rewarding. Finally, fruiting trees are excellent for watching birds and small mammals.

You should be stealthy when you go looking for game. The accepted view is to proceed slowly, but being quick does enable you to cover more ground. It is often possible to walk up on wildlife, such as when you turn the corner of a trail or come over a hillside. Wildlife will also regularly allow close approaches by people who are riding horses, camels or elephants, or who are in jeeps or vans, or canoes or other boats. Observation safaris should follow a navigational plan. Options for this include a rectangular course, or diagonal zig-zags, since either will enable you to cover a larger area. This is particularly important if you are looking for a territorial species, since if you confine your search to one individual's territory your probability of making a sighting will be low. It is better to plot a route that takes you through the territories of numerous members of the species.

If you spot an animal, but are unobserved by it, you should try to stalk it. Stay out of its vision and scent, and move towards it very slowly, crawling if necessary. You can also learn to recognize animal tracks; look for them in river banks and along wet trails and roads. (A skilled guide in Chitwan can identify the tracks of many different tigers.) You can even try to follow the tracks if they are fresh. However, if you use local guides, you may need to push them to do proper safaris, since they might try to take you only on short strolls.

You should also consider the issue of camouflage. Many species, to enhance their chances of survival, have developed appearances that blend into their environments. In order to spot such a species, you will have to recognize the slight variations that exist between it and the natural background. It will help if someone who is already skilled at this can point out a species to you for the first time. For instance, when I was trekking one of my objectives was to spot Himalayan blue sheep. I asked a Nepali man at a tea house on the Annapurna Circuit if there were any nearby, and he immediately pointed to a hillside across a river gorge. It took me several minutes to differentiate the sheep from the brush where they were grazing. After practice, though, they were so easy to spot that I could not understand how I had missed them. One other consequence of camouflage is that more people are observed by wildlife than vice versa. While I never spotted a tiger in Chitwan, I am confident that they saw me many times. Some of the tracks that we found were very fresh, and tigers are curious by nature. A tiger even walked around my tent one night at Island Jungle Lodge (IJL). I was the only guest at the time, and was staying in the second to last tent along a river bank. IJL is located in the *heart of the jungle*, which is the English translation of *chitwan*. It is real Tarzan country. One of the staff pointed to the tracks in the morning. This was a bit frightening, particularly when I remembered that I had taken a shower to cool off at 1 a.m. in a hut that was about fifty feet from my tent. I wonder if the tiger watched me walk to or from the shower. (I was up most of the next night with my camera hoping it would return.) What this story also illustrates is that with some dangerous species you may effectively have to use yourself as bait to attract them. Go diving and hope some sharks swim by, or go on a jungle trek and see what shows up, but you better have a response in mind if your plan works!

As an addendum to this chapter, one of the main reasons why I returned to India in 1994 was to achieve my unfulfilled goal of seeing a tiger in the wild. I traveled by train down the center of the country (SL class was great, a real cultural experience), and visited the following parks:

- Corbett N.P.	Uttar Pradesh
- Keoladeo Ghana N.P.	Rajasthan
- Ranthambhore N.P.	Rajasthan
- Bandhavgarh N.P.	Madhya Pradesh
- Kanha N.P.	Madhya Pradesh
- Periyar Tiger Sanctuary	Kerala

In some three weeks in these parks, excluding Keoladeo Ghana, which is a world class bird sanctuary, I took eighteen safaris, or game drives, and saw twelve tigers!

If you visit a tiger habitat, the following are a few tips for increasing your chances of seeing one:

- Visit parks at the end of the dry season (April to June in India). It is very hot then, and the tigers seek relief at the few remaining water holes.
- Morning safaris are usually best. They last longer, and the light gets better as time goes by. (Photography is easier.) While I did roughly an equal number of safaris at dawn and dusk, ten of the sightings occurred in the morning. (However, on my current trip, in November 1995, I saw four more tigers, two each in Nepal's Royal Bardia N.P. and Royal Sukla Phanta Wildlife Reserve. All of these sightings occurred in the late afternoon.)
- Jeeps are less effective than elephants. (Unfortunately, they are the only choice in many parks.) They have to stay on the tracks, and are noisy. A tiger will often sit down when it hears a jeep, and only rise after it has passed.
- No matter how long you stare into the bush, it is extremely difficult to spot a tiger without first receiving some other sign. Indeed, almost all of my sightings, including

those in Nepal, occurred after we heard the alarm call of a deer or a monkey. (Most of the time we just drove around waiting to hear a call.) We would then race in its direction, scanning the surroundings feverishly. Quite often, and usually within a few seconds, the guide would say the electrifying word: "*Tiger!*;" after which, if we were quick to follow his pointing arm and had good eyes, we would spot it too.
- As this suggests, having a good naturalist with you is essential, since they are almost always the first person to spot the animal.
- Lastly, good luck, and I hope you never experience the disheartening feeling of being in the jeep or on the elephant that *did not see the tiger*.

Of all the parks that I have visited, Bandhavgarh and Kanha offer the best chances for an observation. This is because they both send out elephants with mahouts to look for tigers. For example, if one is found at Kanha, the mahout will radio the park's visitor center, where all jeeps periodically check in. You then drive to the elephant's location, climb a ladder to board it, and walk the remaining distance to the tiger.

However, to return to the issue of observation quality, while *tiger show* sightings are great, because you can get so close, they do lack a certain atmosphere which is present when you spot one after hearing an alarm call. In the latter instance, danger is in the air.

My first tiger observation occurred in Ranthambhore, which was fitting because this was the park I was unable to visit in 1991. There are four jeep trails in the park, and on our second morning we were assigned to Trail #2. However, at a junction the driver said "*We take a risk*," and turned down Trail #3. We then proceeded to a water hole, waited for a few minutes, and saw nothing. At this point another jeep drove up behind us and, rather than get caught in jeep gridlock, we returned back the same track. After about four hundred meters we heard an alarm call, and then a few seconds later the guide said "*Tiger*," and there it was. (It was evident that the tiger had been sitting out of view when the jeeps first passed.)

The track at this spot bounded a gully, and beyond the far bank was a plain of large slabs of rock interspersed with a little loose brush and grass. It was a fully mature tigress, six to eight years old, and she was out in the open about thirty meters away walking on the rocks parallel to the gully. In the sun. It was just a fantastic observation! We followed her on the track for over half a mile as she moved away and up over a hillside. To top it off, she would turn periodically - when the driver made a call, to have a look at us. I took over fifty photos, and had a smile on my face for days.

22. PHOTOGRAPHY

You are certain to see many amazing things during your world trip. Travel is an incredible visual experience, and you will probably want to take a lot of photographs. For example, I took thousands of slides on each of my trips. Many of them came out great, but I also made a lot of mistakes. This chapter summarizes what I learned in the process. It should help you understand the basic issues of travel photography, and also guide you away from making the same types of mistakes.

Camera equipment and film

You should take the best camera equipment that you can afford, because the range of photography with a good outfit is much greater than with a simple automatic model. In addition, the most important components of your camera gear are the lenses. They give you the widest latitude in what you can photograph, and they should claim the largest portion of your budget. For instance, many shots are impossible without a lense with a long focal length, such as 200 mm or greater. A wide angle lense, of 28 mm or less, is also excellent to have, since it provides many different possibilities for photographic composition.

My current outfit, slightly upgraded after the theft in London, is as follows:

Camera body	Nikon N90, case and neck strap
Lenses	Nikkor 24 mm - f/2.8 AF D, soft case, front and rear lense caps Nikkor 105 mm - f/2 AF D, soft case and lense caps Nikkor 300 mm - f/4 AF, hard case and lense caps
Filters, etc.	Nikon 52 mm L37c UV filter Nikon 77 mm L37c UV filter Nikon 82 mm L37c UV filter Nikon 52 mm circular polarizing filter Nikon HN1 52 mm lense hood
Flash	Nikon SB25 speedlight Nikon SB17 speedlight cord

Other Lightweight tripod
Lense air brush
Lense paper
Silica gel sacs
Camera, lense and speedlight manuals

The basic features of a high quality camera body are auto (programmed) and manual exposure adjustment, a simple exposure compensation system, both auto and manual focus, a fast maximum shutter speed and a motor drive. For example, the automatic options are great when you only have a moment to get a shot. Otherwise, you have much greater control over the image if you choose the exposure settings and adjust the focus yourself. (Birds and other wildlife species may also be disturbed by the sound of automatic focusing.) Some advanced cameras also have multiple programmed modes. For instance, my N90 will pick the appropriate settings for portrait, landscape, hyperfocal, sport, silhouette, close-up and red-eye reduction (flash) situations. The best lenses have fast (wide) maximum apertures, auto and manual focusing, and excellent optical quality. The last holds for filters as well. The best flash units have a high maximum light output, adjustable flash direction, and both auto and manual controls.

I bought both my original and replacement gear from shops in New York City that cater to professional photographers. They offer wide selections and low prices, although they are unwilling to give advice on what you should buy. It is strictly "*what do you want, and how are you going to pay for it*?" Most major cities in the U.S. and around the world have stores that sell to local professionals. You can find them by checking phone directories, or by asking for references at photo studios and labs. It is also a good idea to avoid the electronic goods shops that cater to tourists. While their prices may seem low, they will not be as inexpensive as the stores for professionals and they will also have more limited selections. In any case, it is important to shop around to get the best deals. Lastly, your camera equipment should come with at least a one year warranty.

The choices for 35 mm film are slide or print, and color or black and white. Slides provide better image quality, although for simple souvenir photography print film is fine. It is also much less expensive. Many professional photographers prefer to use black and white film, because of its ability to convey atmosphere and emotion. I mainly use color slide film, though, because my favorite photography is of wildlife and color provides the most realistic species shots. Different types of film vary the spectrum reproduction, by enhancing some colors over others. I have used Fuji Velvia and Provia and Fujichrome 50D, 100D and 100 (Provia replaced 100D), Kodachrome 24, 64 and 200, Ektachrome 100 and Agfachrome 100 and 200. All are excellent films, but for my eyes I get the best images with Fuji 50D and Provia. In addition, Kodachrome is usually much more expensive than the others.

Contrary to the popular belief, you do not need to bring all of your film from home, since good quality film, especially print, is available almost everywhere. The exceptions to this are in some lesser developed countries. For example, it is difficult to find slide film in India. It is a good idea in such countries to buy film only in large cities, and from the main distributors if you can locate them. This will help ensure that the film has been stored carefully. You should avoid buying film from roadside stands and from non-air conditioned shops in hot and humid climates, and also film that is close to or past its expiration date. Finally, it is wise to stock up whenever you find a good source. This should also enable you to bargain for a quantity purchase discount.

The following are some additional tips on camera equipment and film:

- Cameras and film are fragile and sensitive. They need to be treated gently, and protected from sun, dust, heat, humidity and rain. Other care and maintenance tips include to:

  - Pack your camera equipment and film in sturdy bags or cases, and add silica gel packets to absorb moisture.
  - Use a strong and well-attached camera strap, particularly if you have a telephoto lense, and insist that other people who hold the camera use it as well.
  - Keep your lenses and filters as clean as possible. They should be brushed regularly to remove dust, and cleaned thoroughly whenever they get dirty. You should wash them, gently, with mild soap and water, and then dry them with lens tissue paper. (Do not use toilet paper or paper towels; they are made with crushed wood fibers and can scratch.)
  - Keep both unexposed and exposed film refrigerated whenever possible.
  - Never let your film be x-rayed at airports. It is almost always possible to request hand checks for your camera and bag of film. (The only places where I have been refused hand checks are Heathrow and Gatwick airports in London. The power of the English bureaucracy lives on!) It is also

advisable not to put your film in checked-in luggage, even if it is in a lead film bag. Some airports have installed special x-ray machines to detect bombs, and if your film is in a lead bag they will just turn up the power to see through it.
- Carry extra batteries, and use only the best quality available. Duracell and Kodak last the longest. You can also raid your flash unit or cassette or CD player for temporary replacements if your camera batteries run down.
- Lastly, always carry a plastic bag to protect your camera if it might rain, if you might have to jump or ford a stream, or if you will travel in a boat and might be splashed.

- Professional photographers usually carry back-up camera bodies, since having their only one fail on assignment or in a remote location such as a wildlife park would be a terrible loss. A second body can also be used to keep another lense, filter or film type or speed immediately available. Another option is to take a small automatic camera as a backup, for those occasions when you do not want to carry your entire outfit.

- Some professionals also travel with a supply of model release forms.

- I use my telephoto and wide angle lenses most often. I did not buy zoom lenses because they have smaller maximum-diameter apertures, which require more light, and because the optical quality is better on fixed focal length lenses.

- Telephoto lenses are heavy and expensive, but they are essential for wildlife photography. They are also good for sports photography and for long-distance shots of sensitive subjects, such as people from other cultures.
- Wide angle lenses are great for scenic and architectural photography, and for getting shots of groups of people. They can also be used to take photos of people who do not realize that they are in the frame.
- My last lense, the 105 mm, is excellent for portraits and for some scenic views.
- I do not have a macro lense, but they are useful for photography of interesting plants, flowers, insects and other small subjects. Good quality macro lenses can provide close-ups of subjects that are only a few inches in size.

- In the future I plan to buy a teleconverter, or a 600 mm or 800 mm lense when I can afford it, for even longer distance photography, and an electronic shutter release.

Photographic skills

Practice makes perfect, and this means taking lots of photographs. This is the only way to learn about light, the art of composition, and which images transfer well to film. The best photographers take hundreds or even thousands of photographs to get a few great shots. If your camera has a motor drive, you should use it on a regular basis. For instance, if you take half a dozen shots of a particular subject, you may be surprised at how minor differences in positioning make some of the photographs much more aesthetically pleasing. It is also fun to experiment with different film types and speeds, to determine which provide the most realistic images or interesting effects. In addition, some shots require the introduction of an outside element to provide perspective, such as a person standing next to a monument or large tropical tree, or a pencil placed by an animal track. Finally, if you have the opportunity to photograph a rare or beautiful subject, you should take many different shots of it using a range of exposure settings, from slightly under- to over-exposed. This is called *exposure bracketing*, and it should ensure that at least one of the shots will be well-exposed. It is also a good idea to take photos of such subjects on two rolls of film, as insurance against one of the rolls being bad.

It takes hard work to get the best photographs. For naturalist photographers, this means regularly leaving before sunrise to arrive at locations by dawn. The best times for photography, when natural light is clearest and subjects have the most contrast, are early morning and late afternoon. (It is a wonderful coincidence that these are also the best times to spot wildlife.) In many places, a buildup of haze, dust and pollution will wash out photography during the rest of the day. It may also be necessary to hike for hours through dense brush or up the sides of mountains to get to the best locations. In addition, skilled photographers are opportunistic. They always seem to have a camera handy to record photogenic situations, even if they are only available for a few seconds. As this suggests, you should always carry your camera, as well as its flash unit and extra film.

Good photographers understand their subjects. They know how to make people feel at ease, and how to approach wildlife without disturbing it. With human subjects, being open, friendly and talkative should help eliminate the suspicion that a camera often generates. It is better to chat for a while before asking if you can take a photo. With people from other cultures, it may be easier to get local friends to ask for you. Many people, of course, will be happy to pose. For example, in the old neighborhoods of Delhi it seemed as if everyone wanted their photo taken. Some people, though, might ask you for money. I personally would never pay for a subject's permission, since it is not a practice that I want to encourage. I would rather not get the shot. However, if someone gives me their address, I will always send them a copy. Many people around the world are too poor to own cameras, so photos that you take of them could become prized possessions.

One tip on cultural photography is to carry a Polaroid Instamatic as a backup. When you meet new people you should immediately take their photo with this camera, and give it to them as a present. This will break the ice, at which point you can pull out your SLR and portrait lense. Another option is to stand near an interesting individual and then photo something else, such as a scenic view. The person will often waive you over to take a shot of them.

Wildlife species are conceptually simple to photograph. Your images should clearly show any characteristics which define a species, particularly those that are included in its name. (A good photograph of the bird species, the Great Thick Knee, would obviously show its legs.) Good light is also critical, since direct sunlight enhances the color and contrast in the coats of mammals and the plumage of birds. On the other hand, overcast days can have a lovely softening effect. Species shots should generally fill the frame, and be in razor sharp focus. Another option is to show a species in its normal habitat, with the latter also in sharp focus. Photos showing animals in motion, with the subjects blurred or in precise focus, are other alternatives. For the latter, you can get a frozen shot by making a panning motion to follow the animal and by using a fast shutter speed. You must also get as close to the subjects as possible to get these types of images, and this can be accomplished either physically or though the benefit of a telephoto lense. A common mistake, especially with birds, is to take photographs where the primary subject fills only a small portion of the frame. Wildlife photography normally requires great patience, and the professionals who specialize in it often spend months in habitats waiting to get good shots. However, you should always be prepared to take a photo at a moment's notice when you are in a natural environment, since a member of a rare species could always come into view. If you anticipate seeing a species that may move away quickly, you should prefocus your lense for the likely distance to it. A final technique that is useful is to photograph a subject when you first see it, and then carefully stalk it, stopping every ten feet or so to take additional shots. You can continue this process until you get frame-filling shots, or the animal moves away.

Lastly, as your proficiency increases you should become more sensitive to the artistic and other compositional possibilities of your subjects. For instance, for wildlife you might look for opportunities to photograph adults that are in prime condition or with their young, animals that are reflected in water, and full-frame facial shots of expressions which reveal personality and character.

Photographic problems

The following is a review of common photographic mistakes and other types of problems.

- Inappropriate subjects. Novice photographers regularly make the mistake of taking shots of unphotogenic subjects. It is better to wait until postcard images come into view, and then take many different shots of them. (An exception to this is when you take a photograph of an unattractive subject to have a stimulus for your memory, such as a photo of your travel partner!)

- Poor composition and framing. Many people make errors in composition, since what looks good to the eye may not translate well to film. For example, photos of natural scenes, and rural or ancient cultures, should be composed to exclude anything that is modern, including power lines, signs, structures, litter and clothing. A common mistake with photos of people is to have them stand too far away from the camera, especially when they are in front of scenic views. A similar problem is for a subject to be unintentionally positioned in front of an object, such as a tree, so that on film it appears to grow out of them. Composition and planning, not to mention quick reactions, are also very important if you want to capture images of people who are exhibiting different types of emotions.

- Blurred photographs. These are caused by camera shake or because the subject moved. For the former, there are minimum shutter speeds at which lenses of different focal lengths can be hand held. (I can hold my 300 mm lense steady at a speed of 1/30 of a second, but not 1/15.) Blurred shots can be avoided by using a higher shutter speed, but this may not be feasible in poor light. Another option is to use faster film. If neither solution is available, it is better to use a faster shutter speed and get a sharp but underexposed image. You can then at least see the subject clearly, and it may be possible to improve the exposure during developing or printing. In developing this is called *pushing* the film. *Pulling* the film, or reducing an overexposure, is also possible. (Such processes can only be applied to entire rolls.)

- Out of focus photographs. This is caused by incorrect focusing of the lense, such as by trying to take a shot of a subject that is positioned in a complex background, where it is difficult to isolate the exact distance to it. It is also a challenge to get a precise focus with a telephoto lense, since lenses with long focal lengths have limited *depths of field.* (The depth of field is the front-to-back portion of the image that is in sharp focus.) In addition, achieving a precise focus is more difficult when using a wide aperture (low f-stop) with any type of lense, because of the same effect. The cure for this is to use a narrow aperture, if the light permits, and in general not to take a shot until you are certain that the subject is in focus.

- Exposure problems. It is important to recognize that camera light meters are not infallible. You need to develop a good feel for the accuracy of your camera's meter, particularly in situations where there is a lot of contrast. This includes knowing when the meter is accurate and when you need to bracket a shot including by how many exposure stops or fractions thereof. (Each change in the aperture or shutter speed is one stop.) In addition, many people try to take photographs of images that cannot be recorded well on film. A classic example of this is an image where one portion is dark and another is bright. It is virtually impossible to get a proper exposure of both in the same photograph, since if one is well-exposed the other will be significantly under- or over-exposed. If you direct your camera at the bright portion and then at the dark portion, and the light meter shows a difference of three or more stops, then you should reconsider taking the photograph. Common images where this is a problem include:

  - A scenic view, where one part is in the sun and another is in the shade.
  - Any subjects that are photographed against the sky, or a body of water, or any other bright or reflective surface.
  - Dark colored subjects that are photographed against light colored backgrounds.

The compromise that usually works best is to use an exposure setting that is appropriate for the darker portion of the frame.

- Other exposure problems. A similar problem is that it is easy to underexpose dark scenes and overexpose bright ones. If an exposure is likely to be dark, such as a shot of a subject in a recess, shadows, or under a forest canopy, you will need to let more light reach the film. As an example of this, you might shift from a 1/250th shutter speed to 1/125th, or from an f5.6 aperture to f4. On an exposure compensation system, you would use a + setting. However, if your lense does not have a wide enough aperture, or if you cannot hold it steady at the required shutter speed, you will have to use faster film, such as ISO 400, or a tripod, which will only be feasible for stationary subjects. Conversely, if an exposure is likely to be too bright, such as a shot at high noon or, again, of a reflective surface such as water or snow, then you will need to do the opposite, to let less light hit the film.

- Window reflections. If you take a photograph through a window, it is common for the film to record the window's reflection. Skylight lense filters will sometimes eliminate these reflections.

- Bright spots in the center of flash photographs, and images where the subjects have red eyes. Both of these are due to the flash burst being reflected back to the camera. They can be eliminated by increasing the distance to the subject, or by using a flash unit where you can direct the light at an angle to the subject, such as by pointing the flash up so the light bounces off the ceiling. (Some cameras and flashes also have red-eye reduction systems.)

- Frozen shutter. A camera's shutter will often fail to operate in cold temperatures. You can warm it by putting the camera inside your jacket or shirt.

- Negatives that are washed out, tinted green or that have color blotches. This may occur if your film has gone bad from exposure to heat or humidity, or as a result of poor developing.

- Scratches on the negatives. These are due to grit inside your camera or on the light proof felt backing of the film canister, or because the film was stretched too tight during developing. (Find a good lab!)

Film developing

Film should be developed as soon as possible after it is exposed. As a long-term traveler, this means you should either develop it abroad or courier it home for processing. (Prompt processing is particularly important when you are visiting hot and humid environments.) For the former, high quality developing for both print and slide film (E6 process) is available almost everywhere. You should find a professional looking lab, and then test them with one roll. (Label your exposed film to ensure that the test roll is not one with critical images.) If their processing is acceptable, you can use them for the rest of your exposed film. (Good labs can also be asked to push or pull the film, although this is sometimes more expensive.) In any case, it is wise to develop a roll periodically to ensure that you camera is still functioning properly.

If you take a lot of slides, you might consider having the negatives developed but not mounted. Even Kodachrome labs will do this if you ask. You can then buy high quality plastic slide covers, and hand mount only your best photos. Slide mounts that have anti-newton glass, such as Gepe mounts, are excellent, since they protect the negatives from fingerprints and ensure distortion free projection.

There are two options for making prints from slides. The first involves making a copy of the negative, which is called an internegative, and then using this to make the prints. Some image quality may be lost in this process. Low quality prints are made from 35 mm internegatives, although 4" by 5" and larger internegatives are often used for enlarged prints. The second process is called cibachrome. This is a direct imaging process, since an internegative is not required. The contrast and grain in a cibachrome print are superb, but the process is expensive.

Cataloging and display

It can be a massive task to catalog all of the slides from a world trip. If this is your situation, you might want to use the following procedure:

- Have your film developed but not mounted.
- Cut all of your good quality negatives with scissors or a film guillotine (available at camera stores), and discard the bad shots.
- Using tweezers, mount the negatives in plastic slide covers.
- Using a process of elimination, set aside duplicate and lower quality shots. (Having a slide viewer or light table is essential for this.)

- Label the best images, and organize them into geographic slide shows. (Labels that fit on slides can be bought in photography and office supply shops, and computer software that catalogs slides and automatically prints labels for them is also available.)
- Put the slide shows in plastic sheets (they hold twenty slides each), and store them in three-ring binders.
- Finally, note the details of your very best slides to create photographic series of similar subjects, such as travel partners, cultural subjects, wildlife species and scenic locations. Subject series can be used for separate slide shows, photo albums and framed enlargements. You might also want to include the series references on the slide labels.

23. EPILOGUE

"*It's what you want it to be.*"

- Sugar

Well, there it is: the world; our planet; our home. I have done my best to describe it as accurately as possible, and to offer advice on how you can become a traveler and take advantage of the opportunities that are now available. It is up to you to save your pennies, conquer your fears and go for it.

As for me, it has taken five years to write this book and get it printed, and I am raring to go. As I said at the start, my goal is to visit one hundred countries. I have a number of major trips planned; perhaps I will meet you on one of them.

In closing, please let me encourage you one more time. You can have an extraordinary life, and there is no obstacle that you cannot overcome. And you should start soon! You only get one life or, as Buddhists would say, you only get this life once, so take advantage of it. There is so much for you to see and do.

See you on the road!

24. APPENDIX - GLOBAL DESTINATION LIST

The appendix lists travel destinations around the world. I hope you will use it to track the places that you visit. (I do.) No one can go everywhere, of course, but an avid traveler can cover a tremendous amount of ground during his or her lifetime. You should also recognize that it is not enough to have been to a lot of countries. A *compleat* traveler keeps track of where he or she has been by many different criteria, including regions within nations, islands, mountains, forests, deserts and cities. In addition, it is worth remembering that 70% of the earth is covered with water. The first list, therefore, is of the planet's major bodies of water, which you will obviously have to cross to reach the land destinations. Many travelers also realize that there is as much to see underwater as on land, and keep track of the coral reefs and other marine environments that they visit by snorkeling and scuba diving. Lastly, some people even strive to become astronauts, and make it into space.

Atlantic Ocean and Europe

Baffin Bay
Hudson Bay
Gulf of Mexico
Caribbean Sea
Baltic Sea
Gulf of Bothnia
North Sea
Irish Sea
English Channel
Bay of Biscay
Mediterranean Sea
Tyrrhenian Sea
Adriatic Sea
Ionian Sea
Agean Sea
Sea of Crete
Sea of Marmara
Black Sea

Pacific Ocean

Gulf of California
Gulf of Alaska
Bering Sea
Sea of Okhotsk
Sea of Japan
Yellow Sea
East China Sea
South China Sea
Gulf of Siam
Philippine Sea
Sulu Sea
Celebes Sea
Molucca Sea
Java Sea
Flores Sea
Banda Sea
Timor Sea
Arafura Sea

Indian Ocean

Red Sea
Persian Gulf
Arabian Sea
Mozambique Channel
Bay of Bengal
Great Australian Bight

Arctic Ocean

Beaufort Sea
Greenland Sea
Norwegian Sea
Barents Sea
White Sea
Kara Sea
Laptev Sea
East Siberian Sea

Sea of Azov
Caspian Sea
Aral Sea
Gulf of Guinea

Gulf of Carpentaria
Coral Sea
Tasman Sea

Southern Ocean

Weddell Sea
Bellinghausen Sea
Amundsen Sea
Ross Sea

The following table lists sovereign nations and their possessions, capitals or other major cities, local times, and visa requirements for U.S. citizens. Islands, and nations that are located on islands, are in italics. Local time is shown as hours ahead of (+) or behind (-) Greenwich Mean Time. Many countries also observe Summer Time, when the local time is +1 on the figure shown. (Most of the local times are as reported in JP Morgan's *World Holiday and Time Guide*, which also lists national holidays and banking hours. It is available from JP Morgan, Corporate Communications, 60 Wall Street, New York, NY, 10260.)

The visa information is primarily based on *Foreign Entry Requirements, March 1996*. You should be aware, though, that the requirements may change, particularly for lesser developed countries. In addition, even if a foreign embassy says that you do not need a visa to enter its country, a border official could always demand one. (This has happened to many travelers at border crossings in Africa, usually as a prelude to a bribe.) At a minimum, you will need a transit visa to enter a country where a visa is noted as being required. In addition, countries that do not require visas set maximum allowable stays for visitors, and these periods are also shown. (You can sometimes get them extended, although this may require applying for visas.)

Region/Country	Capital/ Major City	Local Standard Time	Americans Need Visas *

* Visa available on arrival.

North America

Canada	Ottowa		no, 180 days
Newfoundland	St. John's	-3:30	
Newfoundland			
Novia Scotia	Halifax	-4	
Cape Breton			
New Brunswick	Fredricton	-4	
Quebec	Quebec	-5	
Anticosti, Magdalen Islands			
Ontario	Toronto	-5	
Prince Edward			
Manitoba	Winnipeg	-6	
Saskatchewan	Regina	-5	
Alberta	Edmonton	-7	
British Columbia	Vancouver	-8	
Vancouver, Queen Charlotte Islands			
Yukon	Whitehorse	-8	
Northwest Territories	Yellowknife	-6 to -8	
Ellesmere, Axel Heiberg, Ellen Rignes, Amund Rignes, Borden, Mackenzie King, Cornwall, Lougheed, Prince Patrick, Melville, Byam Martin, Cameron, Bathurst, Cornwallis, Devon, Banks, Victoria, Prince of Wales, Somerset, Baffin, King William, Prince Charles, Air Force, Salisbury, Nottingham, Coats, Mansel, Resolution, Akpatok, Belcher Islands, Akimiski			
St. Pierre and Miquelon (Fr.)		-3	no, 1 month
Mexico	Mexico City		no, 90 days
Central and western Mexico		-6	
South Baja		-7	
North Baja		-8	

United States	Washington, D.C.		
Eastern		-5	
Central		-6	
Mountain		-7	
Pacific		-8	
Alaska		-9	
Alexander Archipelago, Kodiak, St. Lawrence, St. Matthew, Nunivak, Pribilov Islands, Aleutian Islands (-10)			
Hawaii		-10	
Hawaii, Maui, Kahoolawe, Lanai, Molokai, Oahu, Kauai, Niihau, Midway Islands (-11)			

Central America

Belize	Belmopan	-6	no, 30 days
Costa Rica	San José	-6	no, 90 days
El Salvador	San Salvador	-6	yes
Guatemala	Guatemala City	-6	no, 30 days
Honduras	Tegucigalpa	-6	no
Nicaragua	Managua	-6	no, 30 days
Panama	Panama City	-5	no, 30 days

The Caribbean

Antigua and Barbuda	St. Johns	-4	no, 6 months
Bahamas	Nassau	-5	no, 8 months
Grand Bahama, Great Abaco, Andras, New Providence, Eleuthera, Cat, Long Island, Great Inagua			
Barbados	Bridgetown	-4	no, 3 months
British Virgin Islands (U.K.)		-4	no, 6 months
Anegarda, Jost van Dyke, Tortola, Virgin Gorda			
British West Indies (U.K.)		-4 or -5	no, 6 months
Anguilla, Montserrat, Turks and Caicos, Cayman Islands			
Cuba	Havana	-5	yes
Dominica	Roseau	-4	no, 6 months
Dominican Republic	Santo Domingo	-4	no, 2 months

French West Indies (Fr.)		-4	no, 3 months
Guadeloupe, Isles des Saintes, La Desirade, Marie Galante, Martinique, St. Barthelemy, St. Martin (also Neth.)			
Grenada	St. George's	-4	no, 3 months
Haiti	Port-au-Prince	-5	no
Jamaica	Kingston	-5	no, 6 months
Netherland Antilles (Neth.)		-4	no, 90 days
Saba, Statia, St. Maarten, Bonaire, Curacao, Aruba (-5)			
Puerto Rico (U.S.)	San Juan	-4	no
St. Kitts & Nevis (U.K.)	Basseterre	-4	no, 6 months
St. Lucia	Castries	-4	no, 6 months
St. Vincent & the Grenadines	Kingstown	-4	no, 6 months
Trinidad and Tobago	Port of Spain	-4	no, 3 months
U.S. Virgin Islands		-4	no
St. Croix, St. John, St. Thomas			

South America and South Atlantic Ocean

Argentina	Buenos Aires	-3	no, 3 months
Tierra del Fuego, Isla de Los Estados			
Bolivia	La Paz	-4	no, 30 days
Bouvet (Nor.)			no
Brazil	Brasilia		yes
Coastal states		-3	
Ilha Marajo, Trinidad, St. Paul Rocks, Fernando de Noronha (-2)			
Central Brazil		-4	
West Brazil		-5	
Chile	Santiago	-4	no, 3 months
Pacific Ocean islands: Sala-y-Gomez, San Felix, San Ambrosio, Juan Fernandez, Chonos Archipelago, Reina Adelaida Archipelago, Isla Santa Ines, Tierra del Fuego, Londenderry, Hoste, Navarino, Wollaston, Easter Island (-6)			
Colombia	Bogota	-5	no, 90 days
Ecuador	Quito	-5	no, 3 months
Galapagos Islands (Pacific Ocean)			
Guiana (Fr.)	Cayenne	-3	no, 3 months
Guyana	Georgetown	-3	no
Paraguay	Asuncion	-4	no, 90 days

Peru	Lima	-5	no, 90 days
Suriname	Paramaribo	-3:30	yes
United Kingdom possessions			no

Ascension Island (GMT), St. Helena (GMT), Tristan de Cunha (GMT), Gough, South Georgia, South Sandwich, South Orkneys, Falkland Islands (-4), South Shetland Islands

Uruguay	Montevideo	-3	no, 3 months
Venezuela	Caracas	-4	no, 90 days

Islas los Roques, Tortuga, Blanquilla, Margarita

Europe and North Atlantic Ocean

Albania	Tirana	+1	no, 3 months
Andorra		+1	no, 3 months
Austria	Vienna	+1	no, 3 months
Belgium	Brussels	+1	no, 90 days
Bulgaria	Sofia	+2	no, 30 days
Cyprus	Nicosia	+2	no, 3 months
Former Czechoslovakia			
Czech Republic	Prague	+1	no, 30 days
Slovak Republic	Bratislava	+1	no, 30 days
Denmark	Copenhagen	+1	no, 3 months

Fyn, Sjaelland, Lolland, Falster, Bornholm, Faroe Islands, Greenland (-3)

Finland	Helsinki	+2	no, 90 days
Åland			
France	Paris	+1	no, 3 months
Corsica			
Germany	Bonn	+1	no, 3 months
Rügen			
Greece	Athens	+2	no, 3 months

Corfu, Ionian Islands (Kerkira, Paxi, Lefkada, Kefalonia, Zakinthos), Kithira, Idra, Poros, Egina, Sporades (Skiros, Skopelos, Skiathos, Alonissos), Thassos, Samothrakia, Limnos, Lesvos, Hios, Kiklades (Kea, Andros, Tinos, Mikonos, Siros, Kithnos, Serifos, Sifnos, Paros, Naxos, Milos, Kimolos, Folegandros, Sikonos, Ios, Thira, Anafi, Amorgos), Samos, Ikaria, Patmos, Dodekanissa (Leros, Kalimnos, Kos, Astipalea, Nissiros, Tilos, Simi, Rodos, Karpathos, Kassos), Crete

Hungary	Budapest	+1	no, 90 days
Iceland	Reykjavik	GMT	no, 3 months

Ireland	Dublin	GMT	no, 90 days
Italy	Rome	+1	no, 3 months
Elba, Giglio, Ischia, Capri, Sardinia, Sicily, Panterellia			
Liechtenstein	Vaduz	+1	no, 3 months
Luxembourg		+1	no, 3 months
Malta	Valletta	+1	no, 3 months
Monaco	Monte Carlo	+1	no, 3 months
Netherlands	Amsterdam	+1	no, 90 days
Frisian Islands			
Norway	Oslo	+1	no, 3 months
Jan Mayen, Bear, Spitsbergen Islands			
Poland	Warsaw	+1	no, 90 days
Portugal	Lisbon	GMT	no, 60 days
Azores (-1)			
Romania	Bucharest	+2	yes *
San Marino		+1	no, 3 months
Spain	Madrid	+1	no, 3 months
Balearic Islands (Ibiza, Mallorca, Menorca)			
Sweden	Stockholm	+1	no, 3 months
Gotland, Öland			
Switzerland	Bern	+1	no, 3 months
Former Union of Soviet Socialist Republics			
Armenia	Yerevan	+4	yes
Azerbaijan	Baku	+4	yes
Belarus	Minsk	+3	yes
Estonia	Tallinn	+2	no, 90 days
Saaremaa, Hiiumaa			
Georgia	Tbilisi	+4	yes
Kazakhstan	Almaty	+5	yes
Kyrgyz Republic	Bishkek	+6	yes
Latvia	Riga	+3	no, 90 days
Lithuania	Vilnius	+3	no, 90 days
Moldova	Chisinau	+3	yes
Russia	Moscow		yes
West European		+3	
Central European		+4	
East European		+5	
Ostrov Kolguyev, Novaya Zemlya, Franz Josef Land			

West Siberian		+6 to +8	
Severnaya Zemlya			
Central Siberian		+9 to +10	
Novosibirskiye Islands			
East Siberian		+11 to +13	
Sakhalin, Kuril Islands			
Tajikistan	Dushanbe	+6	yes
Turkmenistan	Ashgabat	+5	yes
Ukraine	Kiev	+3	yes
Uzbekistan	Tashkent	+5	yes
United Kingdom		GMT	no, 6 months
England	London		
Isle of Wight, Channel Islands			
Northern Ireland	Belfast		
Scotland	Edinburgh		
Isle of Man, Arran, Islay, Jura, Colonsay, Mull, Iona, Tiree, Coll, Eigg, Rum, Skye, Outer Hebrides, Orkney Islands, Shetland Islands			
Wales	Cardiff		
Gibraltar		+1	no, 3 months
Bermuda		-4	no, 3 months
Vatican		+1	no
Former Yugoslavia			
Bosnia-Herzegovina	Sarajevo	+1	no
Croatia	Zagreb	+1	yes *
Macedonia		+1	yes *
Montenegro		+1	yes
Serbia	Belgrade	+1	yes
Slovenia	Ljubljana	+1	no, 90 days

Africa and West Indian Ocean

Algeria	Algiers	+1	yes
Angola	Luanda	+1	yes
Benin	Porto Novo	+1	yes
Botswana	Gaborone	+2	no
Burkina Faso	Ouagadougou	GMT	yes
Burundi	Bujumbura	+2	yes
Cameroon	Yaoundé	+1	yes

Canary Islands (Sp.)	Los Palmos	GMT	no
Gran Canaria, Tenerife, Palma, Fuerteventura, Lanzarote			
Cape Verde Islands	Praia	-1	yes
Central African Republic	Bangui	+1	yes
Chad	N'Djamena	+1	yes
Comoros Islands	Moroni	+3	yes *
Grande Comore, Anjouan, Moheli			
Mayotte (Fr.)		+3	no
Congo	Brazzaville	+1	yes
Cote d'Ivoire	Abidjan	GMT	no, 90 days
Djibouti		+3	yes
Egypt	Cairo	+2	yes
Equatorial Guinea	Malabo	+1	yes
Eritrea	Asmera	+3	yes
Ethiopia	Addis Ababa	+3	yes
Gabon	Libreville	+1	yes
Gambia	Banjul	GMT	yes
Ghana	Accra	GMT	yes
Guinea	Conakry	GMT	yes
Guinea-Bissau		GMT	yes
Kenya	Nairobi	+3	yes
Lesotho	Maseru	+2	yes
Liberia	Monrovia	GMT	yes
Libya	Tripoli	+1	yes
Madagascar	Antanarivo	+3	yes
Madeira (Port.)	Funchal	GMT	no, 60 days
Malawi	Lilongwe	+2	no, 1 year
Mali	Bamako	GMT	yes
Mauritania	Nouakchott	GMT	yes
Mauritius	Port Louis	+4	no, 6 months
Morocco	Rabat	GMT	no, 3 months
Mozambique	Maputo	+2	yes
Namibia	Windhoek	+2	no, 90 days
Niger	Niamey	+1	yes
Nigeria	Lagos	+1	yes
Reunion (Fr.)	St. Denis	+4	no
Rwanda	Kigali	+2	yes
Sao Tome and Principe		GMT	yes

Senegal	Dakar	GMT	no, 90 days
Seychelles	Victoria	+4	yes *
Amirantes			
Sierra Leone	Freetown	GMT	yes
Somalia	Mogadishu	+3	no
South Africa	Pretoria	+2	no, 90 days
Prince Edward			
Sudan	Khartoum	+2	yes
Swaziland	Mbabne	+2	no, 60 days
Tanzania	Dar es Salaam	+3	yes
Zanzibar, Pemba			
Togo	Lomé	GMT	no, 3 months
Tunisia	Tunis	+1	no, 4 months
Uganda	Kampala	+3	yes
Zaire:	Kinshasa		yes
West		+1	
East		+2	
Zambia	Lusaka	+2	yes
Zimbabwe	Harare	+2	no, 3 months

Asia and East Indian Ocean

Afghanistan	Kabul	+4:30	yes
Australian possessions			yes
Cocos (+6:30), Christmas, Mcdonald, Heard			
Bahrain	Manama	+3	yes
Bangladesh	Dhaka	+6	yes
Bhutan	Thimphu	+6	yes
Brunei	Muara	+8	no, 90 days
Burma	Rangoon	+6:30	yes
Mergui Archepelago			
Cambodia	Phnom Penh	+7	yes
China	Beijing	+8	yes
Hainan			
French possessions			no, 1 month
Amsterdam, St. Paul, Kerguelen, Crozet			
Hong Kong (U.K. until 1997, then China)		+8	no, 30 days

India	New Delhi	+5:30	yes
Lakshadweep Islands, Andaman Islands, Nicobar Islands			
Indonesia	Jakarta		no, 2 months
Sumatra		+7	
Simuele, Tuangku, Pini, Tanahmasa, Tanahbala, Nias, Siberut, Sipura, Pagai Islands, Enggano, Bangka, Belitung			
Java		+7	
Bali		+7	
Nusa Tenggara		+8	
Lombok, Sumbawa, Komodo, Sumba, Flores, Lomblen, Timor, Alor, Wetar, Moa, Damar Islands, Tanimbar Islands, Ewab Islands, Aru Islands			
Kalimantan		+8	
Anambas, Natuna Islands			
Sulawesi		+8	
Butung, Talaud Islands, Bowokan Islands, Sula Islands			
Molucca Islands (Maluku)		+9	
Buru, Ceram, Obi Islands, Batjan, Ternate, Halmahera, Morotai			
Irian Jaya		+9	
Misool, Salawati, Waigeo, Schouten Islands			
Iran	Tehran	+3:30	yes
Iraq	Baghdad	+3	yes
Israel	Tel Aviv	+2	yes *
Japan	Tokyo	+9	no, 90 days
Honshu, Hokkaido, Shikoku, Kyusu, Ryukyu Islands			
Jordan	Amman	+2	no
North Korea	Pyongyang	+9	yes
South Korea	Seoul	+9	no, 15 days
Saishu			
Kuwait	Kuwait City	+3	yes
Laos	Vientiene	+7	yes
Lebanon	Beirut	+2	yes
Macau (Port.)		+8	no, 60 days
Malaysia	Kuala Lumpur	+8	no, 3 months
Penang, Tioman, Sabah, Sarawak			
Maldives	Malé	+5	yes *

Mongolia	Ulan Bator		yes
West		+7	
Central		+8	
East		+9	
Nepal	Kathmandu	+5:45	yes *
Oman	Muscat	+4	yes
Pakistan	Islamabad	+5	yes
Palestine	Jerico	+2	
Philippines	Manila	+8	no, 21 days
Luzon, Mindoro, Samar, Panay, Leyte, Palawan, Negros, Cebu, Bohol, Mindanao, Sulu Archipelago			
Qatar	Doha	+3	yes
Saudi Arabia	Riyadh	+3	yes
Singapore		+8	no, 30 days
Sri Lanka	Colombo	+5:30	no, 90 days
Syria	Damascus	+2	yes
Taiwan	Taipei	+8	no, 14 days
Thailand	Bangkok	+7	no, 30 days
Phuket, Langkawi, Phangan, Samui, Chang, Kut			
Turkey	Ankara	+3	yes *
United Arab Emirates	Abu Dhabi	+4	yes
U.K. possessions			no
Chagos Islands			
Vietnam	Hanoi	+7	yes
Phu Quoc, Poulo Condores Islands			
Yemen	San'a	+3	yes
Socotra			

Antartica and Pacific Ocean

American Samoa (U.S.)		-11	no
Antarctica			no
Alexander, Charcot, Adelaide, Peter Island (Nor.), Roosevelt, Ross, Balleny			
Australia	Canberra		yes, 1 year
Western Australia		+8	
South Australia		+9:30	
Kangaroo			

Northern Territory		+9:30	
Bathurst, Melville, Groote Eylandt			
Queensland		+10	
Mornington, Thursday, Great Barrier Reef Islands, Fraser			
New South Wales		+10	
Victoria		+10	
Tasmania		+10	
King, Furneaux Group			
Macquerie, Lord Howe, Norfolk (+11:30)			
Cook Islands (N.Z.)		-9:30	no, 31 days
Fiji	Suva	+12	no, 3 months
French Polynesia (Fr.)			no, 1 month
Marquesas Islands (-8:30), Austral Islands (-9:30), Tahiti and the Society Islands (-10), Tuamotu Archipelago (-10), New Caledonia (+11)			
Guam and North Mariana Islands (U.S.)		+10	no
Kiribati		+12	yes
Line Islands (U.S., U.K.)			no
Marshall Islands (U.S.)	Majuro	+12	no, 30 days
Micronesia	Kolonia		no, 30 days
Nauru		+12	yes
New Zealand	Auckland	+12	no, 3 months
Kermadec, Chatham, Bounty, Stewart, Antipodes, Auckland, Campbell			
Niue (N.Z)		-11	no, 30 days
Palau	Koror		no
Papua New Guinea	Port Moresby	+10	no, 30 days
New Britain, New Ireland, Bismark Archipelago			
Solomon Islands	Honiara	+11	no, 2 months
Tonga		-11	no, 30 days
Tuvalu		+12	no
United Kingdom possessions			no
Santa Cruz, Phoenix Group, Pitcairn (-7:30), Ducie			
Vanuatu	Port Vila	+11	no, 30 days
Wake Island (U.S.)			no
Western Samoa	Apia	-11	no, 30 days